THE LETTERS OF EDWIN LUTYENS

To his wife, Lady Emily

Edwin Lutyens, one of the greatest of all British architects, was responsible among other things for the Cenotaph and the magnificent Viceroy's House in New Delhi. From 1889, when he gained his first commission, until the beginning of the Second World War he covered England with what was probably the last generation of stately homes.

Throughout his long career and many travels Lutyens wrote regularly to his wife, Lady Emily. His often wittily illustrated letters are filled with professional gossip, descriptions of the British Raj, anecdotes and fascinating comments about the buildings on which he was working and the patrons who paid him. Observant, satirical, occasionally malicious, the letters give a vivid picture of the times and of Lutyens's own character.

Clayre Percy, friend and daughter-in-law of Ursula Ridley, Lutyens's second daughter, works for the Landmark Trust. Jane Ridley (who is Clayre Percy's daughter) is a lecturer at Buckingham University, where she is a specialist on Edwardian politics.

HAMISH HAMILTON PAPERBACKS

THE LETTERS OF
EDWIN LUTYENS

to his wife Lady Emily

———⋙⋘———

EDITED BY

Clayre Percy and Jane Ridley

A HAMISH HAMILTON PAPERBACK

London

HAMISH HAMILTON LTD

Published by the Penguin Group
27 Wrights Lane, London W8 5TZ, England
Viking Penguin Inc., 40 West 23rd Street, New York, New York 10010, USA
Penguin Books Australia Ltd, Ringwood, Victoria, Australia
Penguin Books Canada Ltd, 2801 John Street, Markham, Ontario, Canada L3R 1B4
Penguin Books (NZ) Ltd, 182–190 Wairau Road, Auckland 10, New Zealand

Penguin Books Ltd, Registered Offices: Harmondsworth, Middlesex, England

First published in Great Britain 1985 by
William Collins Sons & Co Ltd

First published in this edition 1988
by Hamish Hamilton Ltd

ISBN 0-241-12476-X

Printed in Great Britain by
Cox & Wyman Ltd, Reading

· IN MEMORIAM ·

URSULA RIDLEY

CONTENTS

PORTRAITS

*For photographs and sketches of houses see
the main index.*

MAPS

INTRODUCTION

SIR EDWIN LUTYENS died on 1 January 1944. Two months later his widow, Lady Emily, wrote to her daughter Ursula Ridley: 'I get such an aching longing for Father. I am only happy reading his letters, living in the past with him, and dread coming to the end of them.' As she came to a particularly interesting letter she would head it in pencil – 'Mother and Suffrage', 'All about India', 'Mrs Besant'. Since their marriage in 1897 she and her husband had written once, sometimes twice a day whenever they were apart. There were almost five thousand letters, more than two thousand five hundred of his and two thousand of hers, which she kept in an Italian chest of drawers.

On her death in 1964 Lady Emily left her husband's letters to Ursula. Her own letters she left to her youngest daughter, Mary. Shortly before she died Lady Emily sent the entire correspondence to Ursula, who devoted the last years of her life to sorting and transcribing the letters, then housed in a daunting array of red box-files in the basement of her house in Newcastle. To this task she brought considerable accuracy, an unrivalled ability to decipher her father's handwriting and, most valuable of all, an intuitive understanding of the way his mind worked. When she died in 1967 with the work unfinished she left Lutyens's letters to her daughter-in-law, Clayre. In a sense this book represents the fulfilment of the project she originally envisaged.

To that extent, it is a work of family piety. Yet much has changed since 1967, and ours is a very different book from the one Ursula would have produced had she lived. For some years after her death the letters lived a fugitive life, divided between the old nursery at Blagdon and the garrets of the then diminutive band of Lutyens scholars. One of these was Nicholas Taylor, and it was with him – and largely on his advice – that in 1972 Clayre transported the box-files to their present resting-place in the British Architectural Library at the Royal Institute of British Architects. In 1978 the entire correspondence was meticulously catalogued by Mrs Angela Mace, a Herculean labour which has enormously facilitated the work of every student of the papers.[1]

Critical opinion has changed too since Ursula's death. In 1967 Lutyens's reputation was at its nadir. At best he was seen – if he was seen at all – as the last of the Romans: 'the twentieth-century architect of prodigious gifts who contributed nothing whatsoever to the main stream of development in twentieth-century architecture'.[2] When in 1968 it was proposed to hold a major centenary exhibition at the Royal Academy only a fraction of the necessary £12,000 could be raised and the project was dropped; in 1969 a small exhibition costing about £1,000 was held at the RIBA instead.

Though within the architectural profession interest in Lutyens steadily grew over the following decade, it was not until the late seventies that the tide turned. The concrete cracked and disillusionment seeped in; the leftish idealism of the sixties gave way to the New Right – always a favourable climate for classicism; history was no longer on the side of the modern movement, which retired, discredited, to the textbooks. Lutyens was restored once more to his rightful position as the leading British architect of the twentieth century, his revival triumphantly celebrated by the spectacular exhibition at the Hayward Gallery in 1981–82.[3]

Lutyens's revival makes the publication of his letters the more timely. The letters were used by Christopher Hussey for his Memorial *Life* (1950), a classic of architectural biography which combines an enlightened appreciation of Lutyens's work with a remarkably perceptive portrait of the man. But Hussey used the letters as building-bricks, sometimes complete, but more often misquoted or jumbled and usually undated. As Nicholas Taylor, who knows more about Lutyens than anyone else, wrote in 1969: 'The letters are a gold mine and Hussey certainly didn't exhaust it, putting it mildly. The more I read the more the *architectural* importance of the letters grew. . . . His descriptions of clients are

1. Lutyens's letters now belong to Jane Ridley, who holds the copyright. Lady Emily's letters belong to Mary Lutyens.

2. Nikolaus Pevsner, 'Building with Wit', *Architectural Review*, vol. 109 (1951), p. 217.

3. The illustrated *Catalogue* to the exhibition, compiled by Colin Amery, Margaret Richardson and Gavin Stamp (Arts Council, 1981) is a valuable addition to the literature on Lutyens.

so well written that they alone make the letters worth publishing.'

Hussey hardly used Lady Emily's letters. But when she was nearly eighty Lady Emily embarked on a literary career, and she drew on her letters for her remarkable spiritual autobiography, *Candles in the Sun* (1957). Both sides of the correspondence were used by Mary Lutyens in her memoir of her father, published in 1980, an intimate and moving account of the architect as his family knew him.

The marriage of Edwin Lutyens and Lady Emily Lytton was hardly a conventional one. They had little in common. If he, in Lord Halifax's words, was 'part schoolboy, part great artist, part mystic' – in different proportions at different times of his life – she was serious-minded, literary and religious. Where he was gregarious and gay, she was shy, antisocial and possessed of a supremely aristocratic – and sometimes acutely embarrassing – disregard for convention.

Talk did not flow between them. 'When Father, Mother and I had meals alone together there was never any attempt at conversation,' Mary Lutyens recalled of the 1920s, one of the lowest points of their marriage. 'Father would take *The Times* crossword into the dining room, throwing me an occasional anagram to decipher, while Mother read her novel all through the meal – usually a Wild Western.'[1] Yet when they were apart Lutyens could write to his wife in a way he could never talk when they were together.

He was a compulsive letter-writer. He worked incessantly and under tremendous pressure, seeing clients or designing all day and returning to his drawing-board for several hours each evening after dinner. He relaxed by playing patience or, if Lady Emily was away, by writing to her. He would dash off a barely legible scrawl on the train, returning from a client; he would write in the dining-room as he ate or in his office as he worked. 'I may be a whole day at a table with pens – of sort – and paper – of sort – near at hand and thinking much of you,' he told her. 'If I have anything I want to say I write it there and then.' Partly because he had so little formal education, partly because he read so little, his letters are remarkably unself-conscious and vivid. His thoughts run loose across the page, unhampered by the formal rules of

1. Mary Lutyens, *Edwin Lutyens*, p. 240.

syntax; often in the early letters he makes his point with a sketch.

Lady Emily's letters are far more literary. She wrote mainly in bed, in a bold, legible hand, her punctuation as accurate as a Victorian novelist's. But she was not at her best writing to her husband. Occasionally a scene lights up, and she could give succinct advice, but the over-all impression is often flat.

Our aim in editing the letters has been to include as many complete letters as possible. But we have omitted the 'Bradshaw factor' – train times and journey plans – as well as lists of unknown fellow-guests – the 'Jennifer's Diary syndrome'. Like most other parents the Lutyenses wrote and worried about their children; our decision to cut Everyday Life in the Nursery has eliminated nearly all of Lady Emily's early letters. In the last years of Lutyens's life his ailments bulk large in his letters; these passages we have cut, as well as the repetition that increases with old age. Nor in a correspondence as informal as this do we consider that these omissions deserve sign-posting. Lutyens would often start to recount an incident, digress to his train times or his health, and return to the story: to punctuate the text with ... would be to create a misleading impression.

Where necessary, we have corrected Lutyens's spelling, which on the whole is excellent. Punctuation was not his strong point; we have inserted the minimum necessary to make sense of the text, and we have standardized the !!!!!!! which are scattered liberally over the letters to ! The tops and tails which have variety and charm in the early letters we have omitted when they become stylized in the later ones. Square brackets enclose anything we have interpolated for the sake of clarity. We have standardized the dates to Lutyens's usual form – Feb.29.84. For the sake of clarity Lady Emily's letters have been set in italics.

Our greatest debt is to Mary Lutyens. Not only has she allowed us a completely free hand in selecting from her mother's letters. She has also been unstintingly generous with her time, enthusiasm and encouragement. One of the nicest things about editing the letters has been our frequent visits to her and Joe in Hyde Park Street. She read the manuscript in draft, and we are particularly grateful to her for her advice on family matters.

The manuscript was also read by Mrs Margaret Richardson of the RIBA Drawings Collection, one of the pioneers of the Lutyens revival and the author of the catalogue of Lutyens's drawings in the RIBA. She has been equally generous with her time and expertise, and her comments on architectural matters have been invaluable, as has her help with illustrations. Gavin Stamp read the Indian chapters; for his advice we are grateful. Any remaining mistakes are ours.

We have been greatly helped by the following, who have been generous with information or photographs or sometimes with both: Mrs Ralph Arnold; Mr Henry Baker; the Hon. Richard Beaumont; Mrs Alice Berkeley; the Hon. Fiona Campbell; Caroline Viscountess Chandos; Mrs Celia Clarke; Mr Anthony Drewe; Mrs John Elliott; the Hon. Mrs Faber; Mr Benedict Fenwick; Canon W. T. Hinkley; Mrs T. Holland-Martin; Mrs Christopher Hussey; Mr Anthony James; Mr Matthew Jebb; Mrs Philip Jebb; Professor Nancy Lambton; Mrs Violet Lockett; Miss MacKerrow; Dr Ellen Macnamara; Madame Mallet; Monsieur Robert Mallet; Mr Douglas Matthews; Mr Michael Maxwell; Mr Nigel Nicolson; the Duke of Northumberland; Mrs Peter Orde; Algernon and Josceline Percy; the Hon. Mrs Pollen; Mrs Marjorie Shoosmith; Mr John Saumarez Smith; Mr Peyton Skipwith; Mr John Synge.

We are much indebted to the helpful and long-suffering staff of the RIBA Library. We should also like to thank the staffs of the London Library, the County Record Offices of Devon and Northumberland; and Miss Pam Stephenson of the Alnwick Castle Estates Office.

Our idea to edit the letters was crystallized by Philip Ziegler who, when asked for his advice, offered to publish them; we should also like a 'Collins' to go to Vera Brice and Elizabeth Bowes Lyon.

Family photographs and Lutyensiana have been generously lent by Nicholas Ridley, Matthew and Anne Ridley, Susanna and Jessica Ridley, Mary Lutyens and Candia Lutyens. We should like to thank Elizabeth Rowell, Moyra, Jessica, Richard and Stephen for their help with the proofs; without Stephen this book might never have started and without Richard we might never have finished.

CHAPTER ONE

---~~~---

1896–1897

WHEN EDWIN LUTYENS WROTE his first letter to Lady Emily Lytton on 22 September 1896 he was a young architect of twenty-seven, just beginning to rise in his profession, and she was twenty-one. He had already been in practice on his own for seven years, and until then architecture had been his life.

Edwin Landseer Lutyens was the tenth of the thirteen children of Charles Lutyens and his Irish wife, Mary Gallwey. Charles Lutyens, an ex-soldier, was a painter, mainly of horses and hounds; Edwin was named after Charles's friend and mentor, Sir Edwin Landseer. By the time Lutyens was a boy, his father's artistic career was past its peak. Though they kept their London house in Onslow Square, the family was living in reduced circumstances at Thursley Cottage in Surrey. But Charles Lutyens had also been an enthusiastic rider to hounds, and at Thursley he presided over a household where Bohemian squalor mingled with sporting prowess. One of Lutyens's brothers, Frederick, was the author of that most charming and instructive of hunting stories, *Mr Spinks and His Hounds* (1896); another, John, was the human hero of Kipling's story of the polo ground, *The Maltese Cat*, while the youngest, William, for thirty-one years held the record for running the 1,000 yards.

Lutyens took no part in the sporting pursuits of the Thursley household. As a child, he was too delicate to go to school. He received little formal education, and spent much of his boyhood bicycling round the Surrey countryside, looking at houses, watching them being built and learning the builders' trades. The importance of his youthful wanderings – armed with a pane of glass on which he drew with a piece of sharpened soap – for his development as an architect needs no underlining. But his poor health had one other consequence: the most important person in his early life was his mother, a devout and gentle Evangelical, and

---

throughout his architectural career he always found women easier to deal with.

In 1885, when Lutyens was sixteen, he went to the South Kensington School of Art, now the Royal College, where he studied architecture for two years. He left without completing the course and entered the office of Ernest George, a fashionable architect, but one whose work Lutyens did not particularly respect. The office, however, was a lively one, and he met several young men who were to be his colleagues and rivals in the profession, including Herbert Baker, who was to be both. It was at this time that he became an admirer both of the vernacular Surrey houses of Norman Shaw, and of Philip Webb and the Arts and Crafts movement.

Norman Shaw's influence is most evident at Crooksbury, the house Lutyens built for Arthur Chapman, a Surrey neighbour and friend of the family. It was on the strength of this, his first significant commission, that Lutyens set up practice on his own in 1889 at the remarkably early age of nineteen. 'For five or six years,' he was later to recall, 'I went to no parties, I knew no one and worked till twelve or two in the morning. I bicycled a lot and walked a good deal but no sport and no relaxation, just work.'[1]

The Crooksbury commission was an important one. Arthur Chapman (1849–1926) was a businessman, recently retired from the Indian jute trade, a Liberal and a prominent member of the Surrey County Council. He was to become a life-long friend and, as 'Chippy', he features often in the letters. Crooksbury led to many other commissions in Surrey which, with its burgeoning population of London businessmen, was the place for the young architect of the 1890s to be. And it was in the summer of 1889, at tea with Chapman's brother-in-law, the rhododendron-grower Harry Mangles, that Lutyens met Gertrude Jekyll – the most important meeting of his early career.

Gertrude Jekyll was twenty-six years older than Lutyens, a knowledgeable member of the Arts and Crafts movement and, in 1889, about to change the face of gardening in England. She immediately saw in the young Lutyens the architect she needed to give technical expression to her artistic ideals. By 1896 their famous partnership was well established, and they had collaborated over ten gardens for houses that he had built or altered,

1. To Lady Emily, 26 January 1928.

_____

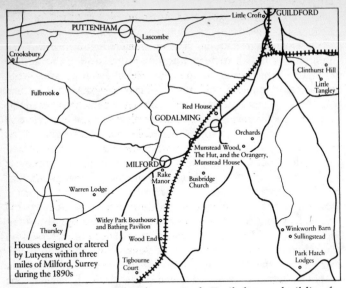

Houses designed or altered by Lutyens within three miles of Milford, Surrey during the 1890s

nearly all in Surrey. When he met Lady Emily he was building for Miss Jekyll what was to be the most successful and important house of his early career – Munstead Wood, Godalming. All his early houses were built in the West Surrey picturesque manner but, influenced by Miss Jekyll, this had a new simplicity about it. As one critic has put it, 'the house seems to grow out of the ground in the natural way that one finds only in the very best Arts and Crafts buildings'.[1] Munstead Wood was an immediate success, and its architect found himself more in demand than ever before. In 1897 he completed twenty-five commissions, which was as much as he had built in the previous six years.

1. Roderick Gradidge, *Edwin Lutyens* (1981), p. 27.

9

Lady Emily was the youngest daughter of the first Earl of Lytton, who had combined a diplomatic career with writing poetry under the pseudonym of Owen Meredith. He went on to be Viceroy of India (1876–80) and Ambassador in Paris (1887–91). Lady Emily was brought up at Knebworth House, the Gothic castle created out of an Elizabethan mansion by her grandfather, the novelist Bulwer Lytton, a leading member of the Young England movement and a friend of the young Disraeli. She remembered the Knebworth of her childhood as haunted by the 'sham medievalism, the romance, the rather maudlin sentimentality' that was the 'spirit of Bulwer Lytton'.[1] From both her father and her grandfather she inherited what she described as the Lytton temperament: a tendency to 'moods of black melancholy for no apparent reason'.[2] She was also subject to migraines.

Lord Lytton died in 1891 and her mother became a Lady of the Bedchamber to Queen Victoria. Knebworth was let, and the family lived nearby in Hertfordshire at The Danes. They were not well off, but they were still part of the great world. The eldest daughter, Betty, to whom Lady Emily was devoted, had married Gerald Balfour, younger brother of Arthur Balfour. Betty Balfour was both beautiful and amusing, and she fitted naturally into the exclusive and intelligent world of the Souls, the social clique that revolved round Arthur Balfour – a world to which she introduced her youngest sister, as it was she, rather than the retiring Lady Lytton, who brought Lady Emily out. Lady Constance Lytton, the other sister, was to become a famous suffragette; there were also two younger brothers, Victor, by now Lord Lytton, and Neville.

Intensely religious, Lady Emily was an unconventional young woman. Though she rebelled against the social life of her contemporaries, and despised the young men she met there, she found her sister Betty's milieu equally distasteful. As a child, she had become the passionate admirer of the Reverend Whitwell Elwin, a literary friend of her father's and the rector of Booton in Norfolk.[3] From the age of thirteen she wrote to him nearly every day. When she was seventy-nine Lady Emily published these letters under the title of *A Blessed Girl*. They give an amusing and

1. Lady Emily Lutyens, *A Blessed Girl* (1953), p. 18.
2. ibid., p. 8.
3. Elwin (1816–1900) succeeded Lockhart as editor of the *Quarterly Review*, 1853–60. He was a friend of Dickens, Thackeray and Bulwer Lytton.

critical picture of her family and of the Souls, as well as an extraordinarily frank account of her inner life. In them she describes another friend of her father's, Wilfrid Blunt, traveller, writer and womanizer. When she was eighteen she wrote to His Rev, as she called Elwin:

> You have guessed rightly the reason Blunt fascinates me. He is the handsomest man I have ever met, and I think the most physically attractive. As I feel it is almost impossible to realize that the way in which he cares for me is a way of which I should be ashamed instead of pleased, I still feel that his affection for me draws me to him.

She continued to be attracted by Blunt, and only broke with him two years later, when she was the object of one of his corridor-creeping expeditions. His only daughter, Judith, remained her greatest friend, and she appears often in the letters.

In September 1896 Lady Emily was staying with Barbara Webb at Milford House in Surrey and Lutyens came over from Thursley on his bicycle. Barbara Webb was one of their few mutual friends. She was the sister of Sir Alfred Lyall, who was Lord Lytton's Foreign Secretary in India and a minor poet. It was while staying with her brother in Simla that she became a friend of the Lytton family. Later she married Robert (Bob) Webb, the squire of Milford, and became a neighbour of the Lutyenses. She befriended Edwin Lutyens as a boy, encouraged him in his work – it was she who introduced him to Arthur Chapman – and gave him the confidence, and perhaps the social polish, that he lacked. He was deeply fond of her, and his symbol for her was a lamb with a halo. By this autumn she was fatally ill of cancer.

Earlier in the summer Lutyens had seen Lady Emily at a party in London and fallen in love with her. He used to tell her that she had looked so miserable that he had decided there and then to make her happy. He had engineered his invitation to Milford to see her, and the first letter he wrote to her on his return to London on 22 September was almost a love letter. On the same day Lady Emily wrote to Elwin about their exploits the day before:

> In the morning Mr Lutyens took me to call on Miss Jekyll, who lives about four miles from here. She is the most enchanting person and lives in the most fascinating

cottage[1] you ever saw. Mr Lutyens calls her Bumps, and it is a very good name. She lives in a little cottage, with a small kitchen and parlour, and a big room which is her workshop. The big room is full of drawers and cupboards and everything is huddled together in the tidiest manner and yet all untidy. There is a huge old-fashioned fireplace, with chimney-corner seats and big blazing logs.

Well, when the rain came down yesterday we suddenly thought we would go and have a surprise dinner with Bumps. We spent the afternoon buying mutton chops, eggs, sponge cake, macaroons, almonds, and bulls'-eyes, and turned up about 6. Getting out of the carriage I of course dropped all the eggs and smashed them! We reeled into the house shrieking with laughter. Bumps has about six cats, three quite kittens, and they romped about the room.

Bumps bore the shock splendidly and was delighted to see us. We set to work to cook the chops and peel the almonds and make tipsy cake, and then we sat down to the best dinner I ever ate. After dinner we sat in the big ingle-nook and drank a variety of intoxicating liquors, brewed at home by Bumps, ending up with hot tumblers of elderberry wine, the most delicious stuff you ever drank. It was altogether the most heavenly evening you can imagine.

Mr Lutyens has gone this morning but returns on Thursday.

Not surprisingly Lady Emily was soon in love with this young man who made life such fun.

Not surprisingly, either, Lady Lytton forbade the marriage. They neither of them had any capital, and the obscure and flippant architect was not at all the kind of young man Lady Lytton expected her daughter to marry. The love letters come to an abrupt halt in October 1896.

Influenced perhaps by a persuasive letter from Betty Balfour, Lady Lytton soon relented. There were strings attached, however. The couple were not to marry until Lutyens had fulfilled

1. This was The Hut, the garden cottage at Munstead built by Lutyens for Gertrude Jekyll in 1894, for her to live in while he was building Munstead Wood.

the financial conditions suggested by the Lytton family: a life insurance out of income of £10,000. Though the annual premium
was to be a standing – and perhaps unreasonable – grievance with
Lutyens throughout his marriage, he assented readily enough at
the time. In December he placed his financial position before
Lord Loch, Lady Emily's uncle and the family counsellor on
money matters, and it was on the strength of this interview that
Lady Lytton gave her consent to the marriage. From the end of
January 1897 Lutyens and Lady Emily write as an engaged
couple.

Like most engaged couples in the 1890s, Lutyens and Lady
Emily knew each other very little, and their love letters – they
often wrote twice daily – abound with conventional sentiment,
much of which we have omitted. But Lutyens was never one to be
bound by convention, and he varied the theme with drawings –
sometimes witty, sometimes whimsical – and by fantasizing
about their future life together. It is in one of his first letters that
he introduces the little white house of their dreams – a dream that
was to recur throughout their marriage. But reality obtrudes in
the shape of another recurring theme: money. Though he loved

the little white house as a romantic idea, and he was a very romantic young man, as an architect it bored him – or, rather, he knew that what he would be able to afford would bore him, and with Lutyens, as Lady Emily was to discover to her cost, the artist usually won. Indeed, it was during their engagement that Lady Emily received the first of many letters giving a balance sheet of home and office expenditure and a forecast of the income he hoped to receive.

Closely related to the dream of the little white house was Lutyens's fantasy of domestic life. Lutyens's domestic ideal was a house run by Gertrude Jekyll on the lines of Munstead Wood – a vision of blue linen, log fires and pot-pourri; but this was not a fantasy that Lady Emily could share. As her daughter Ursula remarked many years later in a letter to her mother: 'Brought up only for the Social Round, people, talk etc. you were quite unable to adjust yourself to the Bumps attitude that Father had preconceived for you.' For Lady Emily, housekeeping was a joke or a worry, not an art in itself.

Nor could Lady Emily share Lutyens's point of view about relations with his clients. During the summer of 1897 he was building for Princess Louise, a daughter of Queen Victoria. Lutyens's familiar, jokey technique with the Princess went against the Lytton family's advice and also against Lady Emily's inclination. But Lutyens knew best how to get his own way and, however much he asked for advice, he had no intention of changing his style. Lady Emily never entirely came to terms with Lutyens's technique but, rather than complain, she gradually opted out.

Towards the end of their engagement, in July 1897, Lutyens describes 29 Bloomsbury Square, the house that was to be their home until 1912 and his office until 1910.

On 4 August 1897 they were married at St Mary's Church, in the park of Knebworth House.

6 Gray's Inn Square
[Lutyens's office]

Sept. 22.96.

My dear Lady Emily   About plots.
        Since I left my Angelina [his bicycle] at Milford I will have to fetch her the first thing Thursday morning and then go to Puttenham.[1] Would this amuse you? I am awfully low and désoeuvré after yesterday's gorgee at Bumpstead and Thursday seems years ahead. Colonel Spencer will keep me an hour or so. What will you do then? It is too cold for a book which I would love to carry for you, however large. We could then go on to Crooksbury but I'll think of something better. Friday Miss Lawless[2] has collared me, but I am writing now to say it is impossible – impossible is an impossible word, anyhow it does and I forgot the tea at Bumpstead. Whatever happens you must not be bored.

I feel awfully guilty at playing truant to work. I have never done it before, so do be kind to me and make me feel it to be all right.

The cartoon for the week is doubtless the stern spirit of Architecture swearing at me for going – whither I would follow.

    1. Lascombe, Puttenham, altered by Lutyens for Colonel Spencer.
    2. The Hon. Emily Lawless, daughter of the 3rd Baron Cloncurry, for whom Lutyens was building at Burrow's Cross, Shere.

We will go house breaking Thursday night somewhere and Friday and Saturday we will dine all three with Bumps, Sunday house breaking again at night to Warren Lodge[1] and then Monday (for me) it will be heart breaking.

    Y s v. sincerely
    Ned Lutyens

6 Gray's Inn Square   Sept.29.96.[2]

My dear Lady Emily
    The little ewee bible found me this morning hard at work, I send it to you, tho' it seems so small a thing to give where I would give so much. . . .
    The casket[3] is rapidly gaining shape in my mind and on paper and will soon be put on the stocks. I hope it will be ready to go to its owner by Dec.26.96 [Lady Emily's birthday].

Here is a very rough sketch and the colour has made the ink run. Anyhow it gives a suggestion as to how it will come – outside. The upper part of green leather with a polished surface tooled with gold in many quaint and cunning devices, with gilt handles, hinges, lock plates, etc. Standing on and secretly attached to a stand of hardwood painted in divers colours on a white ground, with birds and flowers, and emblems galore.

Inside will be divided into spaces 4. Viz to the right will be lodging for Marcus [a little brass pipe-stopper], next to a division for the Bible. In the centre there will be a space for two trays giving three compartments. The top shelf will contain an anchor, the second a heart and the bottom, under the trays, will contain a

    1. Which Lutyens was building for Bob Webb.
    2. The manuscript of this letter cannot be traced. This version is taken from Ursula Ridley's transcript.
    3. Now owned by Nicholas Ridley.

book bound in white vellum about 2 inches square and strapped with vellum and sealed and this book is not to be opened nor the seal broken (not even Röntgen Rayed), nor the contents ascertained until I am man sufficient for the revelation.[1]

The book shall have on it a ⊬ tooled by Roger de Coverley who does my book binding, the third emblem, and the contents illuminated. Will you keep this faith? The fourth space will receive a roll of plans for a house such as we talked of and like to where we sat, drinking the elder vintage.

You nearly lost your casket today! I got pitched softly out of a cab and rolled amongst the busses. Glad I was there was no mud.

The Batterseas[2] have put me off for a week. So I will be able to make up time and regain the good graces of Bumps, at least I hope.

I saw in today's paper an epitaph which amused me, listen —

> Beneath these monumental stones
> Lies the body of Mary Jones
>   NB
> Her name was Smith, it wasn't Jones
> But Jones was put to rhyme with stones

Yours truly
Ned Lutyens

In train from Paddington   Oct.17.96.

My dear Lady Emily
        It is with your little pencil that I write. I felt wretched in the train, leaving you this morning and now how I regret — Bumps or no Bumps — that I did not have the courage to play truant to my work and stay by you — but then I should have broken away and you might have hated me.

1. It contains a long, sentimental and barely legible poem by Lutyens called 'The Mists of Lore'.
2. Lord and Lady Battersea for whom Lutyens was building The Pleasaunce, Overstrand, Norfolk, one of his most inventive houses. Cyril Flower (1843–1907), a Liberal MP, was created Lord Battersea of Overstrand in 1882; his wife was a daughter of Sir Anthony Rothschild.

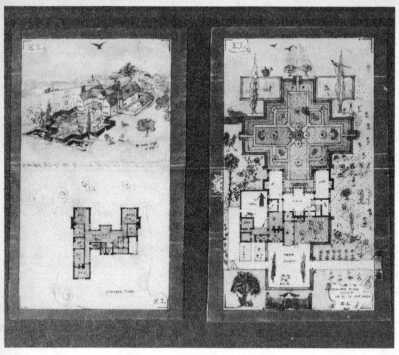

Designs for the little white house of their dreams from the casket.

I would have told you how I loved you.

Would you have laughed? Except my love I have nothing to offer you. I am poor, unknown, and little altogether.

My life's work would be yours and I shall now work the more earnestly so that I may, in time, become more worthy of your dear self. All that I have is at your feet. I love you ever so. I dare not ask anything of you. The little hope I have in me is so large a stake to lose, that the very thought of it makes me feel ill and sick.

One word from you would turn my world to one great sphere of happiness and I would become a man. Give me some chance to prove it.

Before I realised your name I loved you and being with you at Milford House has only made it grow the more, so that my whole horizon is filled with and by you.

I am in a coupé at the end of the train, the receding landscape through the windows draws, with quick perspective, my very hope even as I write.

Everyone must love you so that I can only be one amongst many others. I could write miles to you but I dare not persecute you and after all I cannot say more than that I love you, I love you.

Yours

Ned Lutyens

The Danes   *Oct.19.96.*

Dear Mr Lutyens

 Your letter touched me very much. Why did you think I should laugh? At present I can only say thank you for what you say to me. My mind is too uncertain for me to say more one way or another, and I can only ask you to wait and give me time to think it over. But whatever I settle I hope that you will believe that my interest in you and your work is very real and deep. Bumps is quite right in what she says. I do not want to be a frivolous influence in your life, but the reverse, and your work is always what will interest me most. No one will be more pleased than I am to hear that you are getting on and making a name for yourself, as I am quite sure you will in time.

 Does my letter sound horrid? I hope not, but it would not be fair if I said more, when I know so little at present what I feel.

 We saw Bumps yesterday who was charming to me. I do love her.

 When we come back from Paris perhaps you will come to The Danes for a day or two and we will talk about it.

Yrs very sincerely

Emily Lytton

p.s. Thank you for the little pack of cards, strange that Judith [Blunt] should have sent me a pack of cards by the same post. A wicked post for Sunday morning.

6 Gray's Inn Square   Oct. 19. 96.

Dear Lady Emily
        I felt so unworthy in all respects that laughter would have
brought me no surprise. It is no frivolous influence that you have
on me. Your influence is great and I know full well, how good. If I
frivol when with you, it is with the happiness of being with and
near you.

        That you should be kind is all I could expect from what I know
to be you, only I have so little to offer you – a small white house
and my poor life. I always see you in that wee white house, with a
red cabinet. It is not size that helps in life – so long as all one
would have is there.

        A band outside is playing the Washington Post. It makes me
ache.

The Danes   *Oct. 23. 96.*

Dear Mr Lutyens
        *I have been thinking a great deal about your letter, and
have told my mother about it, and I feel that I ought to tell you at
once that it is hopeless for you to think of me any more. You
probably do not know that I have no money of my own, and you
tell me that you have nothing but your love to offer. Under these
circumstances you will feel yourself that it is hopeless to consider
the matter any further. If I saw any hope I would give it you, but
there is none. Mother says that she would rather we did not meet,
or write or see each other again.*

        *I shall hear of you sometimes from Mrs Webb, great things I
hope and believe. She will help you I know.*

        *Will you send me the casket still? I should like to have it, only
perhaps it would be better not. Do as you think best.*

        *I should like to hear from you just once again to know that you
understand what I have said so badly, and that you will take
comfort and courage, and go forth like a knight of old (as you
said) and conquer a name and fortune for yourself. I ask it of you,
tho' perhaps I have no right.*

———

*Goodbye, and may God bless you always. It is the prayer of
Yours? (I cannot write sincerely)*
Emily Lytton

*For the inscription [on the casket] I do not know. I read these
lines yesterday in a poem of my father's: 'Man cannot make, but
may ennoble fate by nobly bearing it.' Would they do, do you
think? If not you must think of something better. [Lutyens added
'Yet as Faith wills/So Fate fulfils'.]*

16 Onslow Square   Jan.28.97.

My own darling Em
        To think that I may after all these months write and tell
you how well I love you seems too wonderful! I can find no
words, they all seem such little inexpressive things to tell you
what I feel for you.

The Danes   *Jan.29.97.*

*Oh Ned my darling! It is too wonderful to be true and I feel like a
person in a dream. I am so afraid of waking and finding there is
nothing.*

6 Gray's Inn Square   Jan.29.97.

When my beloved E gets this I shall soon be with her.
    Mr and Mrs Cook have just gone and I wait the coming of
Archibald Grove[1] and betwixt their coming and going I just write
to my E.
    I have done such a lot of work today more than I have done for
days past. This is all your doing it is gorgeous. Cook is building a

1. Archibald Grove (d. 1920), for whom Lutyens built Berrydown, Hampshire, was a businessman with interests in Rhodesia and a Liberal MP. He and
his wife were among the few clients to become friends of both Lutyens and Lady
Emily. 'He is said to have been a very small enthusiastic man, with a very tall
wife and stepdaughter, whom it was diverting to see him energetically chivying
around, and he had a passionate admiration for artists' (Christopher Hussey,
The Life of Sir Edwin Lutyens (1950), p. 151).

house [Sullingstead] at Hascombe near Godalming and Grove at Overton in Hants.

This is Cook's

I can't draw you a little picture now, but I will make for yourself, if you like, little pics of all I'm doing.

Jan.30th! 16 or 17 hours more and then. . . . I can think of nothing else, even when hardest at work I feel thrilled and then I realise why.

I have no great city to offer you to reign over, but with such little as I have I worship you and pay homage to my queen. God save her! Oh what a lot we will have to talk about! beginning right at the beginning when I first met you, and on on on into a beautiful blue distance of happy times to come. Oh Emy it's splendid. I may call you by your name mayn't I?

Oh Em you will won't you? Then I shall become strong and

magnificent and defy all troubles and with, perhaps, some modern grace, have the valour of that knight of old.

Here is Grove, I keep him waiting whilst I write.

Your ever loving NED, and the greatest of these is E.

6 Gray's Inn Square   Feb.5.97.

My own belovable darling Em
        No news, a batch of congratulatory letters.

Gerald Streatfield has just been here and I have arranged to meet him on the site at Elstead[1] [Surrey].

I have given my men a warm half hour here. They ask such stupid questions. I was *not* cross! only very dictatorial and impressive using Bumpsicaical language. They never realise that a working drawing is merely a letter to a builder telling him precisely what is required of him and not a picture wherewith to charm an idiotic client.

Oh my darling I love you and the joy of being able to write instead of the dull ache of waiting and wondering.

To Brighton   Feb.5.97.

My own and ever precious darling
        I wrote to Lord Loch[2] before starting. I said that I wanted to save money so as to start comfortably and that I had told you all about it. That he knew my exact position and that I would do what ever he told me, that I wanted to see some friends first before

---

1. Fulbrook House was the result. The correspondence about the house between Lutyens and Mrs Streatfield (for whose father, Richard Combe, Norman Shaw built Pierrepont) still survives. Lutyens went into great detail, even providing an owl. According to Hussey, writing in 1950, the design of Fulbrook, 'undertaken in the first flush of his excitement following his betrothal, is the worst he ever made' (*Lutyens*, p. 72). Twelve years later Ian Nairn described the west front as 'a superb composition in the Norman Shaw style but without Shaw's long-windedness' (*Surrey* (1962), p. 213).

2. Henry Brougham Loch (1827–1900), High Commissioner for South Africa 1889–95, created Baron Loch 1895. He married Elizabeth Villiers, twin sister of Lady Lytton, in 1862. Both twins lived to celebrate their ninety-fifth birthday.

calling on him, also I hoped his negotiations for the place in Suffolk would be successful so that I might have an opportunity of proving by my work my gratitude for his and Lady Loch's great kindness to me. Was this right and proper? and will it please as I wish it to?

I enclose a note from Mrs W. Flower, it amuses me and she is such a dear clever woman and with real taste, most forbidding in manner with little black eyes without whites or pupils. I answered her so prettily and hoped I might some day bring 'my Emily' to see her. Her house is quite beautiful and her husband a brute to her. Will you come?

I wish all the women in the world could be brought before me, that I might 'choose' you before all. An idea quite absurd. Oh Emy but it is wonderful of you that you should choose me, you have such a large choice, and I am so architectino.

No letter from Princess Louise.[1] I s'pose she waits to see me, or is she in a Plantagenet rage?

Do tell me darling all Bumps says. D'you know Bumps is also known by these names Oozal
                                   Woozal
in austere moments Miss Jekyll. If you get this in time come out with Woozal. She will laugh. The 'Crassness of the Woozal' means when she is more than ordinarily gug.

Bless Oh God my Emily and God make me worthy of her dear self a husband worthy of so sweet a wife. Darling darling darling, Your beloving

Ned

---

1. Princess Louise (1848–1939), fourth daughter of Queen Victoria. In 1871 she married the Marquess of Lorne, who succeeded as 9th Duke of Argyll in 1900. A talented sculptress, her works include the statue of Queen Victoria outside Kensington Palace. She and her husband owned a house in Surrey and it was through Gertrude Jekyll that Lutyens knew her. Lutyens designed the Ferry Inn, Rosneath, Dunbartonshire, for her in 1896–7.

Feb.8.97.

This is what I saw and what I would go through
1,000,000 times to win the best and most darling
little wife.

6 Gray's Inn Square   Feb.11.97.

My own Emy
       My darling, I feel so happy just to have
seen you today, although it was all P s and Q s yet
it was with you, and expectedly delicious and far
more so than expected!
       What a bore Lady Frances[1] is, I hope she won't
blast me with the Princess. I know Princess Louise
dislikes her yet the whole thing is rather like an
European question and allies are chucked at crucial crises. I feel Lady F.B. is so small that she is
quite capable to be jealous of a young architect in
the family! But my conjectures on people are
often if not always wrong where I am concerned. I
have only seen her once and had a terror of her.

Lutyens with Lord Loch
and Gerald Balfour.[2]

       I was shy last night, but that was better than flippant bounce
warn't it? I shan't dine out next week at all at all except when my
own comes to town!
       I wonder what W. Robinson[3] will say. I wish he would give us

    1. Lady Frances Balfour (1858–1931), daughter of the 8th Duke of Argyll,
and hence a sister-in-law of Princess Louise. In 1879 she married Eustace
Balfour (1854–1911), architect and brother of Gerald.
    2. Gerald Balfour (1853–1945), second brother of Arthur Balfour, MP for
Leeds 1885–1906, Irish Chief Secretary 1895–1900, President of the Board of
Trade 1900–05. Married Lady Emily's sister Lady Betty Lytton in 1887.
Famous for his elongated good looks, he took a first in classics at Cambridge
and subsequently became something of an intellectual tyrant. Lutyens gave a
telling description of him in 1908: 'He (Gerald) said "They say that she is afraid
of me." I said we were all that. If Pamela [Lytton] said what a lovely blue the sky
was, he would, in a few terse words, prove how, under the circumstances it was
impossible for the sky to be blue at all' (to Lady Emily, 12 September 1908).
    3. William Robinson (1838–1935), editor of *The Garden* 1871–99, author
of several books on gardening including the classic *The English Flower Garden*
(1883), and friend and colleague of Gertrude Jekyll. He was 'the leader of the
revolt against "bedding-out" and the excesses of the formalists' (Francis Jekyll,
Gertrude Jekyll: A Memoir (1934), p. 102).

£1000 a year and then save all we can make! He told me he lost £1200 a year farming and that he was going to stop it, so that if he gave us £1000 he would still save £200. This is a grand scheme, neat and ingenious eh? darling. If we had money we would not have half the fun and excitement we will have, but then if we had we could get married at Easter say and never be separated now for a day at all. Would that tire and bore you?

I am as happy oh so happy as a sand boy. I don't quite know what a sand boy is and probably happiness is our only common territory, the most prized in all the world. Fancy Emy when we are settled and go demurely to church.

I asked Robinson to our wedding and he was delighted. Don't smoke before him until we have got out of him everything we can get! Oh what a little villain I am.

Now I must *work*.

I enclose a poem received from Oozal that is called Bumps this morning:

THE LAMENT OF THE NEGLECTED

The Architect's wanted galore, galore,
The work's at a standstill for evermore;
The brick layers playing – they've nothing to do,
The carpenters smoking – they're idle too.
The plumbers carousing till all is blue.
　'Oh Plazzoh[1] go hang, old Bumps is a bore
　For Nedi's gone courting galore, galore!'

Bumps Poet Galoreate

Rather good isn't it?

6 Gray's Inn Square　　　　　　　　　　　　　　Feb.12.97.

My own, the best beloved wife to be

Saw Uncle Loch this morning who was all that was kind, reasonable and nice. Aunt Loch is very keen that I should do the South Kensington Museum. That would be a JOB! Uncle Loch thinks BLOOMSBURY by far the wisest plan.[2] Bravo Loch.

1. Lutyens's and Gertrude Jekyll's name for Munstead Wood which he was building for her in 1896–97.
2. They were house hunting.

Shall I design a dining table? No not green, do you think? It would be too ARTY. And then the plain wood would look so nice peering up through the blue table cloth. For I vote if E approves to have one little blue cloth for each person and not a great sheet of superfine damask. We shall have say two dozen of them kept in a press in the dining room and if anyone unexpected comes in to feed wi' us then Josef[1] vill go to de press and get himself anoder liddle cloth, salt cellar, knife (green handled), spoon and fork etc, *tout complêt*! Salt cellars in some nice Delft ware, coloured, and a brass pair of candles to each body.

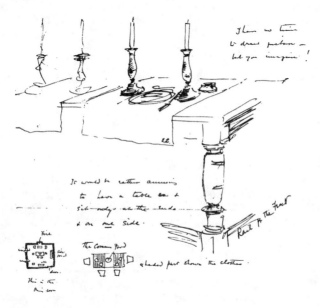

Blue cloths, oak table, white china and brass candles. Coloured Delft ware and green handled knives would make a most pretty and dear effect. Then will we put coloured gourds and heaps of coloured fruits for desserts on occasions of state, that is when another couple are tolerated by we.

The drawing room which we should call Parlour will be just a simple room with what you want in it for use and no more, and

1. Miss Jekyll's manservant at Munstead was a German Swiss.

everything to be as pretty as possible and so in some small way be worthy of my own, darling darling E. Oh Emy I love you so

Your very own
Ned

6 Gray's Inn Square   Evensong. Feb.15.97.

Oh I say Emy, a confession! A whole host of jewellers' circulars and one all about bridal bouquets! Then there was a parcel addressed to my Emy and as Emy *is* my own I looked on the parcel as mine too. So I (really thinking it was some advert) opened it and found it was a naughty silver toast rack from 'Carry' with love to Lady Emily. Who is Carry? Not a cousin – she lives at Leominster, some lodge at some park. It won't do at all well – not at all at all – on a little blue cloth. Oh Emy our troubles *are* beginning. You will stick to me darling, won't you?

The Danes   *Feb.16.97.*

The naughty toast rack is from my old nurse and it is very touching that she should have sent me anything as she is dreadfully poor. So just soften your little hard heart and don't think any more of the naughty thing which shall disappear. So long as we don't have naughty things all over our house, just because they were presents, we can put up with them, and scrape up admiration and gratitude which we don't feel.

Dearest darling, of course open all my parcels. All my letters you can read too, except when they concern other people – and then it is not fair that you should read what is not meant for you to know. Judith's[1] letters I shall keep for myself because affairs and feelings are all mixed up with what she writes about me, and I think she would rather I did not show them. You will understand this darling, and not think I have any secrets to keep from you.

There can be no real love where there is not perfect trust, and you must always trust me as I trust you.

1. Judith Blunt (1873–1957). According to Elizabeth Longford 'there is reason to believe that Judith's love for Emily equalled or excelled anything that she was to feel for a man' (*A Pilgrimage of Passion* (1979), p. 319).

I hear you laughing at me and thinking flippant thoughts – but it is quite serious – as serious as my love for you – and you would not laugh at that!

I have so much ambition for you. In that miserable time when I told you there was no hope I was wretched at losing you because I loved you so – and I wanted your love more than anything in the world. But my pride suffered too – because I knew that some day you could be a great and wonderful man, whom everyone would kneel to, and admire and praise. And then I thought you would have found someone else to love, and would have forgotten me, and another woman would have the right I longed for to be proud in your greatness and success.

6 Gray's Inn Square   Feb. 16.97.

Oh Emy don't say I have a hard heart! and don't hide the toast rack *please*. I am most awfully inquisitive – a fault you must teach me to be rid of. One of many you will find.

If I could not trust the one and only woman I have loved I should *know* I was utterly unfit to be more to you than a stranger in a far land, whether the letter is from Judith or from any man, woman or child. I will probably, I fear, ask to see it – but tell me *NO* – and I should fight as for life rather than any eyes should see what you hold sacred.

Darling I am not flippant. I appear to be, it is such easy work – flippancy. But Emily my darling (I *love* your scold) believe me that in my great love for you comes all trust in you, faith in you, amounting to a grand religion – the greatest I have ever met with – the steps to the throne of a very God.

THE WORLD.

29

If I fail in this world's greatness and do not win for my darling the world, my Emy will still have a warm corner in her pearl of hearts for me?

And God grant that I may bring a crowned grail to my best beloved Emy.

Your dear faith in me touches me so deeply God grant me no failure

6 Gray's Inn Square   Feb.16.97.

My darling MY darling most precious of things is Emy to me

This morning, darling, I had a note from Princess Louise asking me to go to her at Kensington – she was very kind and pleasant and wants to know *you* and she wants me to arrange some mantelpiece at Kensington whilst she is away. You must come with me darling. Lorne [her husband] may or may not be there. I saw him, he was very kind and pleasant, Princess full of bounce and fun and I gave her Robinson's book and I have written to Robinson rubbing his waistcoat just the right way and bombarding him with HRH and Nedi will go up I with toady Robinson.

Princess said lord what a lot of cousins you will have and advised me to do what she always does and keep clear of 'em (her relations she meant). Whereon I smiled and said nothing thinking of Aunt T's[1] advice.

And now, with God's help to work.

Your own worshipping
Ned

Preliminary sketch for the Ferry Inn, Rosneath

In train from Glasgow to Craigendoran[2]   March 2.97.

My own beloved

I have been doing budgetary estimates to relieve my ache for you: for this half year to September I must gather together some £1100. I feel sure of it. Of this £450 would have to go to office expenses, insurance and me! (what a bore I am). This will leave £650 to start on at least.

Say then we don't spend more than £300 to £350 on furniture to begin with could we start with £300 to £350 in the bank? Would it be wise to ask Aunt T? If she thought it was absurd it would be awful. I make no allowance for wedding presents – say £100 each – viz. £200 towards furnishing. But say we got 200 presented and 300 of mine would 500 do what we want? I fear me no. Budgets have a way of diminishing themselves somehow and

1. Theresa, Mrs Charles Earle, eldest sister of Lady Lytton. 'Without any of the beauty of her twin sisters, or their grace (she was short and stout), she had far more intelligence, humour and liveliness' (Mary Lutyens, *Lutyens*, p. 66). Author of *Pot-Pourri from a Surrey Garden* (1897).

2. On his way to Rosneath where he was altering the house and the Ferry Inn for Princess Louise.

this is why I feel nervous. . . . My income is not like a settled one with dividends every quarter gently falling into my lap.

I like this Clydeside railway, with the shipping and ship yards, snow capped hills and the murmur of a not far sea, with liners slowly steaming home, bringing joyous Neds to loving Emys! How I wish I was going t'other way about! I must put on full sail and so bring my own Emy to my own port.

It always tickles me why? when a railway station chances to be comparatively within the district of an ancient fortress, do the railway companies affect an absurd castellated form for their railway buildings.

Oh I sent Betty five Randolph Caldecott[1] books. I don't know if they are of any value as being original editions, I should think not, but they are difficult, I believe, to get. So if Betty wonders where they came from, say so, with my love. This is coals of fire on her head for her neglect of me on Saturday. I shall cultivate eyebrows so as to attract her!

Ever your ever and ever beloving
Husband! 2B

---

1. Caldecott (1846–86), the illustrator of nursery rhymes, was a frequent visitor to Thursley in Lutyens's childhood. 'Lutyens used to say that Caldecott's drawings first turned his eyes to architecture' (Hussey, *Lutyens*, p. 9).

Rosneath   March 2.97.

Look ye here

There are all sorts of impossible points about the above bed
which must be worked out. Red gold posts, blue curtains, red
ceiling, shelf for candles and the casket! wish I had paints here
and a decent pen.

It would be jolly to keep all washing apparatus in a separate room
and make the Bedroom itself jolly without cluttering it up with
paraphernalia.

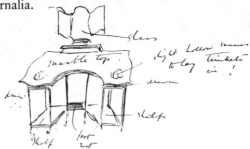

You *shall* have the dearest little glass in the world and a three
sided one too.[1]

1. The bed and the dressing-table were both made. Nicholas Ridley now has
the dressing-table.

But one really wants the house first and I don't want to rent a house and not use it! A year's rent would go a good way in furnishing.

The drawing room, more, rather, parlour is what puzzles me. A good fireplace is essential in all rooms, arm chairs and sofas etc. covered with jolly stuffs, then your cabinet which is now in my office and a good writing table for my darling and a long range of low bookcases. What about a piano? This I shall design when the time comes, small square and refined and the colour inside gorgeous. I shall try to get Guthrie[2] of the Glasgow School to paint – whisper – I almost prefer his painting in this sort of decoration to E. Burne-Jones.

I shrink in terror lest they want to give us pictures – people in general! I don't want a full length portrait of Emy! nor does she want one of me so bourgeois too!

 The pictures we shall have if any will be small, Italian in feeling, gorgeous in colour and in exquisite frames, Madonnas and Saint Georges to inspire our respective selves.

Flowers yes, but few and then arranged very simply. Japanese methods I love but they must not rush at one shouting vive Japonaise! Remember Holland! de Hoogue's interiors. Does all this alarm you darling? mind you say what you want.

When you go back to The Danes shall I bring drawing boards etc. and spend Saturday and Sunday designing our furniture with you? Would it bore you?

Poor Gerald Balfour, I have an immense admiration for him and love him if only for Betty's sake! so don't let little gibes hurt. It is really jealousy on my part that Betty should own a beautiful face which is a thing you can never own yourself – I own yours and mean to keep it, so close, darling.

Yours always and for ever

Ned

March 3. I am off gold bed!

The Danes   *March 12.97.*

I did sort of estimates yesterday for linen and kitchen things. Thought about £55 would do us in pots and pans, sheets, towels, dusters, napkins, etc. But I know nothing of quantity required or prices so it may be all wrong.

I shall wear a large apron and have a bunch of keys dangling from my waist. This will look businesslike for the morning. In the afternoon I shall change and be very smart and pay calls till dinner time. Then I shall again become a housekeeper in an apron and perhaps read a chapter of Good Works *or* Sunday at Home *– while you work beside me. Other evenings we will go out to dinner and be frivolous. Only Sunday evening when we are at home we will both have a holiday and just enjoy ourselves!*

6 Gray's Inn Square   March 30.97.

My own precious darling
        I came back from that train. Oh it was a brute! that puffed defiantly with you inside and me very much out. Did you have a comfy journey, no colds? nothing caught? and Saturday shall come and that early.
O! O!! O!!! O!!!! OV OV! OV!!
    I sent off drawings to Bumps. Great good. Cheers.
    A long letter from the Busbridge parson[1] telling me to go on. More work. You looked so well today which means you will just bust with strength and health soon and Nedi shall work and *we* shall just bust with wealth and some day astonish your mother who will call, God bless her, and find the door opened so! Please observe the size of the door knob, and should Conny want to clean it[2] say NO think of Ned's feelings.

1. Lutyens was altering Busbridge Church, Surrey.
2. Lady Constance (Con) Lytton (1869–1923), unmarried sister of Lady Emily. In *Prisons and Prisoners* (1914), her account of her experiences as a suffragette, she wrote: 'Washing . . . and making the crumpled and uncomfortable things smooth, was my hobby' (p. 43). According to her niece, Mary Lutyens, she polished all her copper coins and her birthday treat was to clean the lavatory.

Oh for the wings of a dove to fly to mine own little love. Poem. Really without chaff, that's all I want.

And Emy, we shall be one, as are two rivers when they join. We are running oh so closely now, but stern fortress walls of Château chaperone do separate us but a few more bends and then over a weir of happiness we splash each to the other into one broad stream of great contentment. Darling is that true for Emy? really true? and then we'll glide slowly as only a large deep river can move, by flowery banks and soughing willows down to that great expanse of ocean of which we have no measurement and men from laziness call heaven.

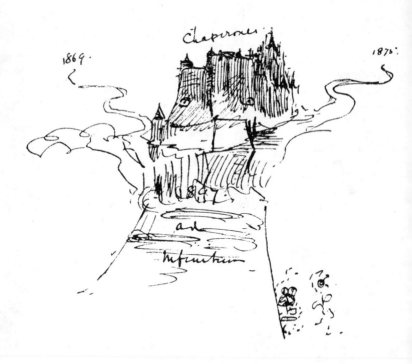

In train returning from Peterborough   April 9. 97.

My own darling

Arrived. Bishop[1] and his lady kind, all well. Went over the Cathedral with the B. HRH was to have come down today but didn't.

I have a great mind to come to Liverpool Street tomorrow! with a beard and large moustachios and see as a stranger what you are like. Would I fall in love with you? and *you* me!?

129 days to Août 16! Then Emy darling you shall come to me. The duties of the day shall be heralded by the striking hour and we shall rise – but how difficult! Breakfast, simply and prettily placed upon an oak table. Breads and fruits and flowers one or two, crisp curling bacon in its casserole, on occasions of great state a sausage! hams, and eggs to boil at our own pleasure and tempting toast upon a bright iron grid before the fire – of wood! The smell of popery – pot-pourri – by Bumps and the blue cloth with lavender's fresh presence there. So we shall eat and read the other's letters each to the other. Then to my work I shall have to go. The cloths shall to their press retire and the table left bare with the one small glass pot of flowers and all be left in neat rectangular arrangement.

Emy to her accounts shall go and write in her nutbrown ledgers the moneys of the day. Peerless mistress, with apron and a bunch of keys that chime of home and honey in the store and to the kitchen, where the pots and range glisten in the light, where the cheery cook turns mountains into molehills and frugal fare into a feast. The bread pan with his father oven (curious genealogy) open and shut in busy intercourse. The larder is restocked from Smithfield Mart and the washed bins are filled with clean vegetables from Covent Garden. The day begins to hum.

It shall be sunny always for Emy's smile is my loved sun. Lunch. A simple meal to which I shall return, perhaps a friend, cold meats, a salad, quaintly dressed in coloured bowl and refreshing coffee brewed by host and hostess – Mocha freshly ground, cream and golden candy placed upon its own green linen cloth. Exchange of news and then away I go to work and Emy to her duties social. The evening shall draw in, bringing with it the

1. Edward Glyn, Bishop of Peterborough, married Lady Mary Campbell, a sister-in-law of Princes Louise. Lutyens was making a small alteration to the Palace.

---

dinner hour. Tea in or out not in the drawing room but in the dining room a kettle on the hob, crumpets and buttered cakes and frothy cream on gala days. But dinner, four softly burning candles, two more for every guest. Food matters not! except it is served with quiet grace with all hospitable intent. Then darling the loving quiet evening that shall ever draw our hearts the closer, the white fire lit room, the bared table except for what we have in use, two chairs quite close so love may speak in whispers. Hope's aims and failings and high ambition's way shall be the drift of what we talk of.

Ever your loving and devoted husband

Ned

6 Gray's Inn Square   April 9.97.

I ought to design and get things made *now* only I have so much other work to do! but I shall manage. The bed I think of from time to time.

Side convenience, oh? More furniture to fill room I say. Will we want one on each side? O Emy! Personally I don't think convenience is as healthy as under! The one is bottled up and near your head, the other away and on the floor where there are always draughts etc., but there is no reason why I shouldn't design one.[1]

[The Pleasaunce] Overstrand gate piers. Go, do, and see if they are doing them, down the road that leads to the entrance.[2] Lord Battersea is there I believe. Tell me all you hear and pump your landlady about the house. It's always amusing.

Ever your own devoted and loving

Ned

I must tell you, *Daily Mail* says today that it is G. Balfour's birthday who has not (!) the forehead of Lord Salisbury,[3] married to Betty who has her father's brain and her mother's charm of manner. Her sister Conny is going to marry in the summer Mr Lutyens the architect! Poor Conny do cheer her up and say I am not responsible for the report.

1. They never had pot cupboards.
2. Lady Emily was staying in a lodging house in Cromer, the Lyttons' holiday house of her childhood.
3. The 3rd Marquess (1830–1903), Gerald Balfour's uncle.

In train to Kingscote for Gravetye[1]   April 10.97.

My own darling

Here am I. Robinson is there, black frock coat, brown billy cock hat and all! A fat Jew is making at the moment investigations in his right nostril with a black fore finger.

Just caught the train.

Your darling little note this morning. I like the night ones best they are longer! I try so hard not to read them until I am in bed and comfy, it is so difficult. I open, read a bit, off goes my shirt, another bit read then a plunge into bed, a nestle and nestle to get proper bearings and then read read read, gloat over every word you say. Blow out candle, thank God and to sleep at once!

In the morning I try to rise before reading your letter, this I fail to do entirely, push off the clothes, then I fall – I open the letter! back come the clothes and a nice warm carousel over my darling wife-to-be's blessed letter. There!

Robinson always bores me. Will he give me £1000? NO certainly not!

I long just to kiss you.

Gravetye   Sunday even. April 11.97.

My own belovedest darling

Been out for a long walk, W.R. went on, I left him, he bores so. How he wastes time. He starts for a walk, never says where he is going and then stops here and there and goes off at tangents, his conversation is wayward and contradicts himself every two minutes, until one feels inclined to explode! Ow how I long for the Emy that I worship. Robinson picks one's brains, he takes one to an old building and asks questions then gives them on to his builder, who carries out my ideas. All wrong. So I just rounded on W.R.! He took it quite nicely! and all as a matter of course! It is so funny! People are extraordinary!

How I wish this was a Sunday in our little home. We must have in our dining room a press for linen. What do you think? A press where you squeeze the cloths between meals. They are never used

1. Gravetye Manor, East Grinstead, William Robinson's house which Lutyens was planning to alter.

now, I wonder why, the cloths are so big? or why. Mrs Bush, W.R.'s housekeeper I have just asked, says 'Oh they're all right'.

Here comes W.R. I'll write more later.

W.R. is dressing for dinner. I refuse to as I am cross! and only want to think of you and write to you. What shall we cover our chairs with? in parlour room. Some nice simple cloth I think and not attempt drawing room. Or what would my own love like?

I must find a dear little old chandelier for the dining room with five or six candles on it. I remember seeing a delicious old one in Rug Church in Wales, all made of wood and painted green.[1] Shall we design one? Oh how I want to see our house first. We must really get one as soon as possible.

I wish we could get one of those two old houses in Gray's Inn looking into the gardens. I wonder if by chance a house is to let belonging to St Paul's Cathedral. There are some delightful houses there and the very shadow of St Paul's would be lovely.

I hope we find a good creature for cook who won't bother and rob us and be economical and have nice ways too. Clean and brisk, making no difficulties and loving my Emy! No tantrums and no leaving us in lurches, abstract, which I believe are places not unlike ditches in the concrete world. Muddy often and difficult to get out of without effort. More so with grace.

Gravetye Manor   April 11.97.

It is such a lovely day and I have been in all the morning writing letters.

Robinson bores me he is so crass and idiotic and anything he does is wrong. He is to deal with exactly like a jibbing horse and it does tire me getting him along. He is very anxious to marry (well

1. Seen when on a walking tour with Herbert Baker in 1890.

from what I gathered last night in the moonlight, such a lovely night and how I longed you were there), to marry Conny! Darling Conny. It is delicious the idea of brilliant Conny marrying such a foozle headed old bore.

A dear white owl lives in the house and I saw him start a-hunting yesterday evening as the moon came up and the stars began to twitter. He wouldn't hurry himself a bit, so calm. But he has a temper, for yesterday he was sitting at his hall door when some starlings spied him and flew round him and teased him, one went a trifle too near, grab with one claw and with the other he pulled the starling's head off! and threw it away! and sat there quite calm and serene and wasn't bullied no more dear thing!

Gray's Inn Square   April 12.97.

My own beloved darling wife 2B
          The Princess said Lady Frances was dreadfully hurt so she had to ask Eustace and F.B. to lunch to make up. They seem to have scoffed at me! and the Princess stuck up for me. Princess warned me to be very careful. They say I can only build cottage things and I am not to make Peterborough look cottage. How can I make a few servants' rooms and a coal hole etc. look like a palace?! She says they are all sure to be at me! and the Duke of Argyll[1] will go with his nose in the air to the House of Lords and do me a lot of harm! It makes me a bit angry – it is so unfair! Are they jealous? Is that possible?

1. The 8th Duke (1823–1900), Princess Louise's father-in-law and Lady Frances Balfour's father.

Marlborough House, Cromer   April 14.97.

*About Peterborough sweet darling it is a great and awful bother.
I have no doubt at all that Frances is fearfully jealous of you and
much hurt at the Bishop in employing you. Eustace is too kind to
have nasty feelings. Frances is not worth considering, she is half
mad and abuses everyone without exception. I think the Bishop
was frightened of her and therefore doubtful about you and
generally tactless. I think you made a mistake in your letters to
him in this way. You should have made him feel that it was
entirely in his interest to have you and a matter, at any rate, which
he must decide upon, as of course you had far too much work for
it to make any difference to you. Instead of that you took the
humble line and made him feel he was bestowing a favour on
you. This naturally adds to his qualms about your competency
for the work.*

*It may be quite true that you build in a cottage way because
you have chiefly built cottages. You know quite well that if you
built a Palace you would not make it look like a cottage so why
mind what Frances thinks?*

*Where you can be very careful is in your manners and that is
where criticism will most affect you. The great thing you try for is
to conciliate men, horrid creatures, and you will only do this by
being absolutely business like and practical.*

*Betty says that when Eustace goes to see the Duke of West-
minster as an architect, he is never even offered a chair or expects
it. And that is what men expect of you – to draw the line
absolutely and distinctly between business and friendliness. With
women it is different because they are not naturally businesslike
and they like mixing business up with other things. But men
resent this.*

Munstead Wood, Godalming   April 15.97.

My own most precious priceless darling
        After writing to you I saw Bumps's builders and did all
those things necessary for my salvation – in Bumps's eyes.

I then took Angelina by the handles much as you take a bull by
its horns and sped away to Godalming. Called at the Post Office
for letters, found four, two from Emy! one from Betty, a dear one,

she is kind to me, and one from North, my man at the office. He writes and asks for a holiday as he is to be married on the 28th! He gets £2 a week from me and is aged 25 years. I wrote so nicely to him and hoped he looked forward with as much happiness in his new life as I did and gave him a cheque for £2.2s as a small present. I feel as though it was your earnings I have spent, do you mind?

Bumps sends you her best love. She is so nice and just creams with affection, nonsense games and comfy all round. I read her your darling lecture on business relations. She thought you so wise, and was so astonished, I think you went up and I with you leaps and bounds I know, in Bumps's sterner fibres! And dear old Bumps is so kind and if she is let into our lives it does warm her dear old soul up and I know she *loves* us *both* just as her own special sort of human pussies. By the bye sixteen new kittens all dead except one. This one is appropriated by two mothers who take turns at feeding it. The result it looks like a bran new bicycle with its tyres too tight!

Betty spells Bumps Bumbs, splendid!

> And the Beauteous Bumbs in Bumbazine
> Read the May month magazine
> The rest of my tale is to be seen etc. etc.

haven't time to finish lyric.

I now have a great disappointment to tell you of. I am low about it. That splendid house in Gray's Inn was to be let and now has gone! I don't know the rent at all, but I can hardly speak of it! The only points that console me are these, it looks entirely to the north, which is a miserable cold aspect and a really serious consideration no matter how nice the house itself may have been. A dull sunless house is cruel to live in. Then the rent might have been too much and the cost of doing up prohibitive.

Then I came back here and had a cat hunt armed with a bag of sand to throw at a marauding stranger, most exciting but scored no hits and got very hot. Had dinner talked to Woozal all about Emy and how I loved her and Bumps thinks me so lucky and I agreed so heartily with her, and we just purred and I gave her a good hug (because she loved Emy most unbusinesslike).

Bumps is going to talk wedding presents with me tomorrow. You know Bumps lent me to start with £100, God bless her for it, and since then I have done work for about £4,000 or more, so that in the ordinary business course (when you don't *hug* clients!) she would owe me £100.[1] Of course this would be absurd and however poor I was I would hate to spoil Her Gift! of £100 and my service to the best friend a man could ever have found.

Stoke College, Suffolk[2]   Easter Sunday. April 18.97.

Wilfrid Blunt, I have an instinct means to be unpleasant, he is conceited enough to think that when he shows himself to you you will forget me! and he will be vicious, darling. I have no fear except he will be rude to my loved and honoured Emy. When he is in London you are not to go anywhere by yourself. He is quite capable of kidnapping you!

Poor dear Judith.

Oh Emy if you threw me over I should just wither and die. Write and tell me I need not fear to lose you.

Cromer   *April 19.97.*

Don't be afraid of H.F.[3] He cannot hurt me, he has no power. He is conceited enough for anything and if he had the opportunity he would try to make me love him still. I would not be alone with him, not that I fear him, but because of what he is. I should wish never to see him or speak to him again. But I shall always be a sore subject between him and Judith. But now my darling stands between me and all that past horror, and for the future I have no fears of any kind.

Stoke College   April 19.97.

My own darling

       Your boy went to church on Sunday and stayed to Communion. A dear old church rather spoilt, with beautiful silver plate. Flagon, paten and chalice all good.

---

1. Lutyens charged a commission of 5%.
2. Lutyens was altering Stoke College for Lord Loch.
3. Head of the Family. Initials used by Judith when referring to her father.

A lovely little 14th century pulpit, so narrow that one wonders
how the parson who is a beurre
pear shaped man can get up. He
can't breathe when he is once in –
I'm sure, and such a funny parson, an old old man who has
no voice at all at 11 o'c. and by

1.30 roars like a Bashan Bull, it waxes louder and louder as
the service drags its picturesque and rural length. When he was
young he was a 'new' curate and altered one or two of the prayers
and got the grammar wrong. He is now an old parson with the
old ways and the grammar is still wrong. He reads so funnily and
makes different voices for the different peoples speaking. When
God speaks to the Israelites about the Passover it is in a basso
profundo and the people, mortals, who ask questions are made to
speak in high falsettos.

God bless and keep you for ever your Ned's

6 Gray's Inn Square   May 5.97.

Tell me exactly what you think and advise about the Princess and
how much and where I do wrong, and have people said I run after
her?

When I knew her first Bumps rose in her thousands and gave
her such a lecture about wasting my time and she always asks if I
can do a thing and is so grateful and says such pretty things – and
then it gives me a certain valoir with the Guildford Town People,
which is all good for work and you gain the respect of Local
Authorities who on hot days look like this, yet essential for
interest where public buildings are to be built.

The Danes   *May 5.97.*

*Mother says you must be very careful about Princess Louise and
she is afraid you will get too intimate and that Louise will turn
and rend you. Mother seems alarmed lest you should find her too
fascinating! Of this I have no fear.*

———

6 Gray's Inn Square   May 6.97.

Princess has sent cheque for £43.3.9 so put it down. She always pays by return of post.

6 Gray's Inn Square   May 10.97.

So glad I had my bike! I charged to Paddington got there at 5 to 11 – no Princess! Posted letters got tickets and one minute before 11 H R H arrived. Jumped into train how we laughed. I forget what at. Passed the Queen's train.

She was without Lady so we hid when a Queen's messenger was seen, too funny! and at Uxbridge Lady Curzon appeared at the station when we made panic like Greeks from Larissa[1] much to the astonishment of a cabby into whose cab we were getting.

Have no time for any but impressionist pics.

We got some lunch in a shop, buns and ginger beer. 6½d for 2 lunches, not bad, considering the Co. too! Got back to Kensington Palace 3 o'c. where we had a regular lunch. Col. Collins looked rather stuffy being kept so late.

Lord Lorne came in as we were going through Rosneath Castle plans, most awkward! anyhow no help for it.

O My!

I was tickled. But my darling I want you Oh so.

---

1. Larissa, Thessaly, was the headquarters of Ali Pasha in the Greek War of Independence and featured in the Graeco-Turkish War of 1897.

The Danes   *May 11.97.*

Princess yesterday sounds most amusing. What fun you have! I shall certainly go choosing houses with beautiful princes!

6 Gray's Inn Square   May 27.97.

My own Emy
        I'm in the train steaming to Bumpstead. Bumps writes to say,
'Something most amusing, highly flattering to Nedi and rather mysterious, want to see you about it as soon as possible, Friday or Saturday this week if possible. The mystery is quite galorious.'

Oh love what can it mean?! Well I can't go tomorrow and Saturday is full, *so full* darling. I did such a lot this morning after I left you. I am in splendid *form* and Oh so happy, my darling. So here I am en route for Bumps I shall arrive about five and shall dine there and leave Friday quite clear for work.

What can it mean? Someone wants to give me an enormous job! Some rich body wants to adopt us and give us £40,000 a year. The Duke of Westminster wants to give me some appointment? G. Balfour?? Princess Louise wants to know if I would rebuild Windsor and should she give my name to her Mamma? What can it be love?

I shall write and tell you tonight. Oh how disappointed I shall be! and I know I haven't guessed anything. Is it to do with Africa's Cathedral? Or is it a big church in England? Shall it enable us to marry in July? or June?

I saw three builder people at Gray's Inn. When I get excited and rather hurried I do the best work, isn't that funny?

May 27.97.

Please to read this after the other letter written today.

My own sweet love
        So amusing and exciting all my guesses quite quite wrong – (of course).
        In Godalming High Street I met Bumps herself, so she drove me

up. She would not tell me the mystery and said she must tell it quietly. Half way to Munstead we met the Webbs's carriage, who said (Slow spoke) that Mr Webb was at Munstead. We got to Munstead Wood where I saw in the garden a tall, strange woman dressed in white. I looked and wondered who it was, when suddenly an idea struck me and I put my hands to my mouth and hollared 'Conny', for sure it was dear, elegant and beautiful Con, so I had the joy of presenting her to Bumps and showing them both off. How I longed for my sweet love to be there too. Then after we went round the house and garden Bob found us and we had tea, then after they went back to Milford we went round Plazzoh and I did with Tom such an arrear of business!

After all was over Bumps said 'Now shall I tell you the Mystery?' and I said yes, and we sat cheek by jowl on the Cenotaph[1] to Sigismunda (the seat under the birch tree, so called on account of its monumental simplicity – do you remember?). 'Well' said Bumps 'Do you remember some time back I told you of Mr and Mrs Chance coming here with their architect Mr Ricardo?' Yes says I. (Ricardo is a very clever architect about 45 years old and well on in his profession a great friend of the Chances people of great taste etc.)[2]

Well says Bumps. They came and were fearfully impressed with Plazzoh as was Ricardo and they all said all sorts of pretty complimentary things. Well, they have been several times since and last time they came they told Bumps how unhappy they were. Ricardo was a very old friend of theirs and they liked his work but they liked Nedi's better! and they wanted a Nedi house, what could they do? So Woozal said they could not possibly chuck Ricardo and that Nedi would not oust Ricardo on any account, and they became all the more strenuous to get hold of Emy's Ned. Oh Bumps has such a long story to tell, and to make it short, the Chances have chucked Ricardo and I am to do the work – and I meet them on Wednesday on the site![3]

1. The name was to reappear with the Whitehall Memorial.
2. Halsey Ricardo (1854–1928), who played a leading part in the Arts and Crafts movement; he was spectacularly good-looking and had private means.
3. This was Orchards, Godalming, built for William, later Sir William Chance, 2nd Bart (1853–1935). The owner of a glass works, Chance was also the author of several works on Poor Law reform; his wife was a sculptress. Orchards is described by Hussey as 'a symphony of local materials conducted by an artist, for artists' (*Lutyens*, p. 86). The garden at Orchards is one of the best Lutyens – Jekyll collaborations.

Isn't that a success for my darling! Oh love I love to tell you these pleasant things, but I am sorry for Ricardo, aren't you? Fancy just if R. had got one of my friends' jobs. How you would have to halve my sorrow and comfort me.

Bumps played so nicely with the Chances and after several visits and letters undertook to overcome my scruples. Needless to say my scruples are overcome and I am to be installed Architect.

Isn't it a chance? I know I shall for ever be talking of good chances to Mrs Chance.

Bumps was quite delicious, sends you her 'sweet love', thinks me so lucky, whereupon I danced with her.

Chance won't hasten our wedding, but it will be all the better to butter our bread with and they will tell all their friends and so another rippled ring will be made by my splash in the surface of the world.

The Danes   *May 28.97.*

I feel I must rush off to Bumps and dance with her and hug her it is all so glorious and exciting.

In train, Milford Station to Clapham Junction   June 2.97.

I saw Bob Webb and dined alone. I did not see Barbara, and I am so low. From the lawn I saw the pages of a book she was looking at turn page by page, nothing else – not even the top of her head. Oh how I wanted to see her dear bright smile and excite her brilliant laugh. After dinner I wrote her a letter but my heart was not in it and I could neither write nor draw and the quill would not be but querulous.

In train Glasgow to Rosneath   June 17.97.

Such fun, after I wrote to you I went and called on James Guthrie[1] a glass painter and decorator, 'the Collie of Glasgow'. He took

1. Of Guthrie & Wells, well-established firm of furnishers and decorators in Glasgow.

me to a Miss Somebody's who is really a Mrs Somebody else.[1] She has started a large Restaurant, all very elaborately simple on very new school High Art Lines. The result gorgeous! and a wee bit vulgar! She has nothing but green handled knives and all is curiously painted and coloured. Most delicious blue willow pattern sets of china ware she has and as a great favour she is going to make me up a basket. Then she gave me two beautiful clay pipes, quite a joy – Oh Emy I wanted you to be amused along with me – all plain white and a good thick stem, beautiful large cups, all sorts just the sort for breakfast. Some of the knives are purple and are put as spots of colour! It is all quite good, all just a little outré, a thing we must avoid and shall too.

I saw at Guthrie's a delicious sofa just the thing for my Emy's comfort and setting.

6 Gray's Inn Square   July 14.97.

My own precious and most beloved darling

Now darling if I were a Duke I should love to take my Emy to live in 29 Bloomsbury Square. The house is beautiful – large, airy rooms, beautiful mantelpieces and staircase. You enter a square hall and a beautiful staircase is beyond, three rooms which the great Norman Shaw used as his offices![2] during his busiest period! Such lovely doorways and cornices everywhere. Kitchens splendid, all in working order and so good and simple. Aspect east and west, good. Garden at back. Upstairs drawing room, large back room, a large dining room, the third small room is a sort of pantry with a lift from the kitchen. This would work.

Above, three bedrooms and a bathroom and above four bedrooms all good and pretty, good shapes.

Now about rent. The ground rent is £60 a year for a 16 year lease. A Mr Heaton[3] has spent £2000 on it. He asks £250 which I

1. Miss Cranston, one of the best-known figures in Glasgow, originator of the Glasgow tea-rooms and patron of artists of the Glasgow School, married Major J. Cochrane in 1892. The restaurant, 91 Buchanan Street, had just opened; it was decorated and the furniture was made by George Walton. Charles Rennie Mackintosh painted the exotic murals, a different colour for each floor.

2. Richard Norman Shaw (1831–1912), leading country house architect. Lutyens revered him and had wanted to get into his office.

3. Aldham Heaton decorated for Norman Shaw and founded the stained-glass and decorating firm of Heaton, Butler & Bayne.

said I could not afford, but he said he would like to help you and me to have his home and would take £200 perhaps less! Darling, is £200 too much including office?

Three servants could work it Mr H. says. You see we need not spend a penny on repairs and gradually convert to white as we grow richer. Ask Betty about it and see what she says. Such a beautiful staircase, with a delicious wooden gallery upstairs overlooking it. It is like a country house, like Milford House but the architecture is good, so good, instead of being half and half.

House	£200
Taxes	£ 60
Assurance	£190
Living	£500
Clerks	£400
Odds and ends	£100

£1450   This means £29,000 worth of work in a year which I ought to get.

24 Addison Road [Gerald Balfour's house]   July 15.97.

I am so excited about Bloomsbury Square, have consulted Bets, Gerald and Con who all say go in for it without a doubt – and blow the £200.

6 Gray's Inn Square   July 14.97.

Oh beloved Emy
  So absurd to write to you again but I have had dinner and I must say grace to my own love after meals.

I am so full of 29 Bloomsbury Square, the house is so delicious. It does for an office so well, first because the first architect of our day used them and then the charm of the house is in its plan. Although it looks grim and square outside, inside it is a paradise. The outer hall gives access to the offices all with their own WCs etc. and then from this dear square hall you go into the bigger hall with the big staircase and there is hardly a dark corner anywhere and all is fair square and spacious with any amount of cupboards and housewife's delights. Fancy my having a house wife! Oh Ems! Joy.

Oh Emy love will Saturday ever come, what fun if on Saturday we can say we have got a house. I do wish you had come in today.

Mr Heaton is an old man, made a fortune decorating (for Norman Shaw principally), 2nd class so called is he. He has had a stroke and has one arm bound up. He discourses on art and truth of beauty whilst his upper teeth insecurely fixed clap applause, most bewitching and engrossing to observe. Mrs Heaton, with gout in her knee, is fat, iron grey and oh so motherly. God made her – not a 'soul' – very frightened _____ of your coming is she!

Oh love my own how I want  [Barbara Webb][1] to be here so that I could tell her and how her darling laugh would thrill me. I used to tell her long stories how she would come to a valley full of daisies, framing a merry rippling river, rolling in happiness to the sea and that the Baa Lamb would be so happy and all should be sunny and beautiful trees should throw soft shadows over her, as blessings, when she paused her gambols, midst the daisied meadows. Then when she was ill I drew pictures of the Baa Lamb in amidst the daisies and over was the hand of God to bless and his wing to give protection. Now it seems all to come true somehow. The hand of God is still there, but the wing has folded round her and hid her from our sight.

Oh Emy don't think me cracked, but it is so much easier to write as a child as I used to write to Mrs Webb than as something of this world 28 years old! and she said she loved it. To write as a man requires more words than English gives, so by lowering the ... well I don't quite know – lowering the key to fit my weakly voice.

Oh Emy my own loved one, when the time comes for us to part, silence, just silence will be my medium of expression. I so often think if I had but words at my command to speak my thoughts I should never be thought to be flippant and quite shallow.

Barbara has blest us, so God bless you my own own darling.
Thank God I am your Ned

1. She had died the previous week.

CHAPTER TWO

1897–1902

THE HONEYMOON WAS SPENT mostly in Holland. It was not a success and there was a family story of the newly married couple sitting back to back on the beach in basket chairs, he looking at the land and she at the sea, which he hated and she loved. Lady Emily never forgot the physical misery of their honeymoon, but when the letters re-start in the autumn of 1897 there is barely a shadow on them. The letters, rather than memories recalled at a later, unhappy stage of their marriage, are probably the best barometer of their feelings for each other at this time.

Soon after their return they moved into 29 Bloomsbury Square. Barbara was born there in August 1898 and Robert in 1901. By that date the main rooms were as their second daughter, Ursula, described them: 'the drawing room was painted black with white ceiling and woodwork and yellow curtains and the dining room had Venetian red walls'. She also remembered Delft salt cellars and green ivory handled knives. This style of decoration probably owed something to the contemporary Glasgow School, and it was a recipe that Lutyens was later to use in many of his interiors.

Lutyens's office occupied the entire ground floor. At Gray's Inn Square he had only employed one assistant, Barlow, a simple, pious character, who moved with him to Bloomsbury Square. In 1898 Lutyens took on Dalton as office secretary, and in the same year E. Baynes Badcock joined him in an awkward partnership. Both of these arrangements ended badly. Dalton, an excellent secretary, bolted with the cash box and a Bloomsbury Square housemaid, and in 1901 Badcock broke off his partnership amidst mutual ill-feeling.

The office was separated from home upstairs by a strict barrier and office life does not impinge on the letters unless there is a crisis, as there was when Badcock left. Lady Emily was in many ways more practical than her husband, and Lutyens was always grateful for her advice. 'Your dear breezy matter of factness does *so* enormously help,' he says in a letter of August 1901.

As well as Barlow and a secretary, there were four or five young men in the office who were either paid assistants or articled pupils. Lutyens never discussed design with them; he would correct their drawings talking unintelligibly as he drew, or at night after they had gone home. Indeed, so autocratic was his attitude at this time that it triggered a minor revolt and two young men walked out. With experience his attitude changed and Hussey describes a very different office with the atmosphere of the studio in George du Maurier's *Trilby*, full of jokes, enthusiasm, hard work and idealism.

It is doubtful whether Lutyens would have enjoyed the companionship of a wife who talked architecture with him, but with Lady Emily there was no chance of it. Hers was an intellectual not a visual intelligence. Hussey tells a sad little tale – told to him presumably by Lady Emily herself – of how she collected together the loose photographs she found in his room, stuck them into an album and presented them to him entitled 'The Works of Edwin Landseer Lutyens' – only to find, to their mutual embarrassment, that they were not 'his work at all but odds and ends, advertisements and "awful warnings" '.[1]

Lady Emily hated London, and she escaped from it as often as she could. She often stayed with her mother at The Danes, and from 1901 onwards she spent two months of every summer at the seaside, usually in lodgings on the Norfolk coast. When she was there she wrote once or sometimes twice a day, but the letters rarely rise above the monotony of sand and baby ailments. They are a disappointing sequel to the lively letters she wrote to Elwin.

Lutyens's practice expanded rapidly after 1897. Through Colonel Jekyll, Gertrude's brother, who was on the committee for the Paris Exhibition of 1900, Lutyens gained the commission to build the British Pavilion. The building – a copy of a seventeenth-century manor house – gave him little scope, but from a prestige point of view it was important. After his marriage, Lutyens began to break out of the world of Surrey neighbours and businessmen, and to build for a wider range of clients. As his letters show, his

1. Hussey, *Lutyens*, p. 145.

practice after 1897 was dominated by two new types of client: Souls and plutocrats.

Lutyens's spectacular success was often attributed by envious colleagues to his having married a wife with a 'handle'. The truth was more complicated. Lady Emily refused point blank to play the part of the ambitious wife and scheming hostess. But, as she herself wrote after Lutyens's death, his marriage 'gave *him* confidence in a *social* way and gave the social world confidence in his abilities'. This confidence manifested itself in the commissions that he now received from members of the Souls, such as Gerald Balfour, Alfred Lyttelton and Lady Horner.

An aristocratic governing group in mild revolt against conventional society, the Souls stood, above all, for the rejection of the territorial principle. Instead of hunting and shooting, they played tennis and golf; where conventional society was aggressively philistine, they played intellectual paper games and talked about their souls. With houses like Fisher's Hill (1900) for Gerald Balfour or Grey Walls (1901) for Alfred Lyttelton, Lutyens provided the architectural setting for this style of life: imaginative homes in the country rather than conventional country houses.

At the opposite end of the spectrum was the second new type of client, the plutocrat. The florid opulence that surrounded such clients as Lord Hillingdon or Willie James, a friend of the Prince of Wales, could hardly have been further removed from the world of the Souls. But there was one thing the two had in common, and that was their rejection of traditional country life. For the Hillingdons or the Jameses a country house was not the nerve-centre of a great estate, but rather a luxurious setting for the new fashion of weekend parties – for 'eating too many big meals, meeting too many rich Jews and shooting too many fat pheasants'.

Lutyens owed his popularity with the plutocrats to the fact that he had become a fashionable young architect – a fact of which he himself was jokingly aware. For this he had one man in particular to thank: Edward Hudson, the founder of *Country Life*. Lutyens met Hudson in 1899 through Miss Jekyll, and in 1900 Crooksbury appeared in the first of many illustrated articles on Lutyens's work in *Country Life*. As well as puffing Lutyens's houses and

introducing him to prospective clients, Hudson was himself a discriminating patron and a friend. It was for him that Lutyens built Deanery Garden (1899–1902), Lindisfarne Castle (1902), the *Country Life* building (1904), and Plumpton Place (1927), all among his most successful houses.

In train for Cromer
[to Overstrand for the Batterseas]   Sept.25.97.

Past Ipswich and no stop yet. Do we stop at Norwich? I wonder. I believe this goes bang to Cromer and I seem the only soul inside the train except the guard. I have no fellow travellers to describe. Nought but the buttons on the cushions to see me and they gaze, gaze, gaze blankly at me with never a wink. There are 340 in all. A lavatory for change of scene alone beguiles me, a change of air no doubt, but not for the good I trow.

I have written two letters besides this to you.

The panels above the cushioned-stare-buttoning backs are adorned with photographs, photographs of Sandringham – God help the Prince of Wales – and a looking glass wherein I may see that which my darling love loves best and search for pimples and such small human failings. Cows, sheep, fields, trees, villages pass in quick succession. I should say the train passes and I, your husband, am tossed about like a pea on a drum, an expression I never quite understand or where it was derived.

Miss Cranston's, 91 Buchanan Street, Glasgow   June 1.98.

Angel Wee Wifie

Am here in Glasgie, all well, good night, good journey. Arrived about 8 o'clock, came here to these queer, funny rooms and had a most excellent breakfast – tea, butter, jam, toasts, baps and buns – 2 sausages, 2 eggs – speak it not in Gath – all for 1/1d! so clean. Most beautiful peonies on the breakfast table and the china the same as ours – in fact this is where, through the courtesy of Miss Cranston, I got those breakfast things.

Miss C. is now Mrs Cochrane, a dark, busy, fat, wee body with black sparky luminous eyes, wears a bonnet garnished with roses, and has made a fortune by supplying cheap clean foods in surroundings prompted by the New Art Glasgow School.

Green, golds, blues, white rooms with black furniture, black rooms with white furniture, where Whistler is worshipped and Degas tolerated, Rodin extolled for his sic impertinence and admired for the love of oddity, sometimes called originality.

I sit in the billiard room to write this and I look around to catch, if possible, from what source the motive of this room be drawn. It's all clever and original and not till I noted the billiard marker did a clue seize upon me – tombs of the Pharaohs – and shadow of the pyramids (in using 'pyramids' I do not mean a play upon billiards) the pilon and the sphinx. That's all good – but the late seen Hatfield is a scent rather than a reality mixed with an undercurrent of Arras Abbeville, which last I can but imagine never having seen. So am I much amused and greatly entertained. The food! etc. at a third the cost and three times better than the ordinary hotel, and the surroundings full of space for fancy and amusement. There is tradition of every country and I believe planet! of the universe – yet 'tis all one. From Japan, through Italy, to Spitzbergen. You start at Japan and take a hold of Whistler for your guide. Egypt is certainly touched, and methinks the Red Sea was just a trifle dry which makes it awkward. Greece was the next call, from whence a visit to the Turk was paid – before the war I hear! Italy, France, Spain and the Algerian coast. Crossed to America for the inventor's ceaseless spasms of discoveries. Then to old England – across to the Low Countries, then a tack across the German Ocean to the Hebrides with a guide book to Holyrood in hand – and then: I must leave the expedition. It is reported the North Pole was reached, but anyhow much and many got lost and methinks me little should ever they return. Now can you realise Miss Cranston's, 91 Buchanan Street, Glasgow?

The bruise on my head has formed an offensive (particularly offensive I think) and defensive – defensive in that you can't touch one without the other – to begin again and bother parenthesis – an offensive and defensive alliance with a pimple. Stay the anguish of your pity. I have written you, sweet darling, a letter full of frivolous nothinks and reveal a mind more frivolous than thoughtful, yet under it all is a great big pumpkin of welling love for my own and best little wife.

Varengeville[1]   Aug.1.98.

Such a day of it yesterday. Seven French builders, the different trades. Oh such a talking – such tremendous demonstrations and the excitement at times beyond all description. From 9 a.m. till 7 p.m. did this war (or Wagnerian Opera) of tongues cleave the air. You would have laughed. Whenever excitement reached its highest we all went on our knees and drew pictures on the floor, regardless that our pencils were mere dumb stumps from much wear. Oh Emy it is so lovely here, so quiet and delicious, gloriously fine, yet quite cool and pleasant and the smells are all so good. You will come here some day. I must soon be off again to these builders.

Booton Rectory[2]   *Sept.1.98.*

Of course, love, ask Badcock or anyone to stay with you. Anything is better than thinking of you all alone. Only remember the cook is alone, do not give her too much to do. I also feel rather sick at the thought of Badcock and his Missus occupying our bed,

---

1. Lutyens was altering and enlarging *Le Bois des Moutiers* at Varengeville on the sea near Dieppe for M. Guillaume Mallet, a Huguenot banker. 'In the design . . . whether deriving from Paris or Glasgow, occurs one of the rare instances in his work of the influence of *nouveau art* modernism . . . the Varengeville house is another instance of that hesitation in his development which, if pursued, might have transformed the course of English architecture in the Edwardian decade' (Hussey, *Lutyens*, p. 85). Yet *art nouveau* is by no means the only theme at *Le Bois des Moutiers*, which combines local Norman features with a music room which owes as much to the early Renaissance as it does to Glasgow. The Mallets were anglophiles of discerning taste – they bought Burne-Jones paintings and Mackintosh furniture – and they were to play a continuing part in the lives of Lutyens and Lady Emily.

2. Lady Emily was staying with the Rev. Whitwell Elwin for Barbara's christening in Booton church.

Le Bois des Moutiers
'One of the rare instances in his work of the influence of *nouveau art modernism*.'

---

as I suppose they would. Fancy an infant Badcock begotten perhaps where Barbara was born! Ugh! I do enjoy the country and feel to get so well and strong in the good air and it is also very nice for my lazy mind to have no household worries or thoughts or cares, but after two months holiday I shall come back with fat red cheeks all prepared to enjoy my housekeeping.

29 Bloomsbury Square   Sept.1.98.

Just had dinner. Most excellentissimo beefsteako puddingho. Had a good hard day's work and will go on after this, but Oh how I miss you and the house is so silent and blank and growls at me because you are from it. Darling how is our little Barbara? Oh I do want to wake her with a kiss.

Badcock and Mrs B. stay the night, Brotherstone [the cook] don't mind. I shall give them the nursery not the sacred bed, fancy Badcock in our bed!

Debrett Peerage proof came today so I added our address and has issue Barbara b. 1898. An 'issue' to describe our Barbara!

29 Bloomsbury Square   Sept.15.98.

Angel Wife

Such a joy to get your letter and such blank feeling after it is read and the paper once again becomes a dead thing without all that bounce of life it has in the first reading.

I am sorry Barbara is constipated. How do you know? Give her something Oh so mild and sweet, if not she will welcome me in spots!

Do describe visitors and scenes at Booton. If you drove out to Overstrand you might see Barlow there measuring.[1] He went yesterday. It's an opportunity not to be missed. He binds himself

---

1. Overstrand Hall, which Lutyens was to build for Lord Hillingdon.

in straps and carries an ink bottle in his button hole, gaiters and an invariable demeanour, very solemn.

I must go to work – Dalton and the office wait.

Your devoted husband, Ned.

29 Bloomsbury Square   Sept.15.98.

I am so so happy for your holiday and want your life to be all happiness and holiday. I don't think I made more than a 'silly' impression at Booton such as the Great Barbara [Webb] would have reviled me for. No matter and what does it?

Sketches of Fountain (*left*)
Barlow (*right*)

Booton   *Sept.17.98.*

Nonsense! silly impression indeed! Oh love how foolish you are. You did nothing here that the beloved Barbara would have disapproved. I am sure you made a very good impression on Amy and Fountain[1] and that they took much to you. As for his Rev he took to you far more than I had ever dared expect. He never likes any man – very like Wilfrid Blunt in this respect – any description of petticoat rather than the best pair of trousers. Sometimes – as with Gerald [Balfour] – he is too frightened of him to show dislike. So you may feel quite happy.

In train to Paris   Sept.27.98.

Angellest of wives
    Just started.
    The Emproaress Eugenie is in this train. I guess she'll be put on

1. Fountain Elwin, the Rev. Whitwell Elwin's grandson who had chronic asthma and lived mostly at Booton, in an Italianate house he built for himself. Amy was his wife.

———

the throne and I shall become her first minister.

You ask why? Because there is never any rhyme or reason in affaire Française, so there is nothing beyond our imagination which may not happen.

If I wire to you 'come best Gown' it means I have assumed some power in France and I want you to hold a salon and we shall entertain largely. . . . Remember. Dreyfus *is* guilty and that *Fashoda* is a small place on the shore of the *Red Sea* in Abyssinia.

By this nonsense you see I have no news. Don't you?

Only that I do so love and adore you and worship you. All together.

So sad about soreness and I feel so brutal, yet I knew at the time I would be no better and just as begging, and impassioned of my most precious beastie. The deep set reverence, darling, that I had for you at first is still a *very living force* and I hated to think of coming near you (as I do now! away from you) – it seems so cruel, only my angel when with you I can't help it. And oh I love you altogether, oh darling wife so well so tremendously – and even through it all – away from you – I want you! I can't do else. So all that I can do is to give myself entirely to you, at your feet and at your service humbly and you must hold me and chide me and guide me and teach me to obey your wishes for love I am yours even as you wish and I am yours so willingly, and it makes me so happy, after, to think I can not do something I want, for your sweet sake.

We are just one body Emy and Ned, and the health of neither is right unless both are well. D'you see?

Hôtel du Jardin, 206 rue de Rivoli, Paris   Sept.28.98.

My own Angel Wife

After *déjeuner* I went to see Madame Mallet.[1] Some French ladies came in. I can't do the gabble gabble of Society one wee bit.

There is a strike on in Paris and the streets round about the Exhibition *chantiers* are every 100 yards garrisoned by a brace of

1. Madame Etienne Mallet, sister-in-law of Lutyens's client.

horse soldiers. I can't make horse and soldier man fit, but they look a fierce and silly and irresponsible lot.

French ladies are either dowdy or outré – there is no nice black coloured tailor made people – I don't mean stick up collars and blazing tweeds. Oh! do give Barbara a little dark frock. Black foulard in a frame *crêpignéd* with satin ribbons horizontal. The hat black trimmed with Dutch dolls! and for winter a black moireen trimmed with sable, sable boots!

The Danes   *Sept.30.98.*

Your two dear letters this morning. I showed pictures of soldiery on horseback, and Neville[1] said, 'I do think Ned has a genius for drawing. I should think he did things quicker than anyone in the world,' and it was all said in a tone of genuine admiration.

29 Bloomsbury Square   Sept.30.98.

Back cheers! . . . but Oh I have a lot to do. It seems sometimes, especially when Emy is away, like wading through lead shot.

1. Her brother, Neville Lytton, who became a painter.

I feel like a time table 5 a.m. to 12 p.m. and all the morning
trains late by an hour and as the day has a limited number of
hours s'welp the last train at night. D'you follow?

French builders are too funny and all most amusing. Rather
anxious though, somehow. Madame Etienne Mallet charming.

Made a French joke with IMMENSE success with the French
mason. He wanted to do something in stone which belonged to a
wood construction, so I said in indignation it was pour bois! and
added 'Mais pas pour boire!' Great fits and I *was* pleased. M.
Riche, the entrepreneur and bricklayer, is intelligent and a good
sort of keen energetic man – very fond of practical demonstrations and drawing of pictures upon the floor – a game at which I
excel too. So we have the most wonderful of conversational
declamations on the walls and floors in white chalk. M. Riche
asked me my age and thought I was well advanced for it.

Oh Emy I so long for tomorrow evening when we shall again be
together. I want to see you and our Barbara. Even Sleath[1] has a
nice homey feel about her. Oh for the winter when Bloomsbury
Square is once more herself again.

29 Bloomsbury Square   Oct.12.98.

Any news of Neville?[2] I can't see how it can come off. Fancy
Barbara marrying someone now who won't be born for seven
years!

The Danes   Oct.12.98.

*Dear Neville, I am glad he is happy. He doesn't seem to realise,
when he says both have suffered from the same cause, that his
suffering was for love of Judith and her suffering for love of
someone else.*[3]

---

1. Alice Louisa Sleath (1873–1938), Nannie to the Lutyens family, who
stayed with them till she died.
2. About his engagement to Judith Blunt.
3. Judith had been in love with Neville's elder brother, Victor. She married
Neville in February 1899. He was nineteen.

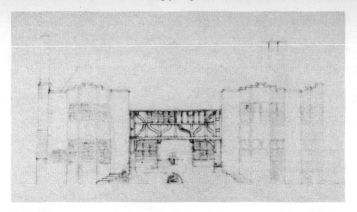

Sketch for Overstrand Hall

In train, Cromer to London   Oct.13.98.

Angellest of wives
        Saw Lord and Lady Battersea – both kind. Lord B. wants
to alter more and is in a spoiling mood.[1] The Curzons were there
but I weren't introduced. Lord Hillingdon[2] seems pleased and the
house will be good and a jolly one to do. I don't think Lord
Battersea quite likes the idea of a beautiful neighbour. Lord B.
thinks Hillingdon don't like him and vice versa, so I carry
imaginary remarks back and fro which softens them and they will
embrace on Sunday. It's rather a nice game to play.
        Last night at dinner Lord H. who has made a famous collection
of books said that his favourite book was one which I wouldn't

    1. Soon after The Pleasaunce was completed Raymond Asquith was staying
there and wrote on 2 August 1898: 'I expected to find a handsome athletic
comfortable amusing weekend party of the ordinary kind: nothing of the sort:
[Lord Battersea] suffers terribly from his wife, who is full of philanthropy and
temperance and all that sort of nonsense and he has been deputed to arrange a
cricket match between the serfs of the Overstrand estate and the tenants of his
Battersea shops: and here they are eating and drinking and exhaling a poiso-
nous atmosphere of retail religion through one of the most beautiful houses in
Norfolkshire' (*Raymond Asquith Life and Letters*, ed. John Jolliffe (1980), p.
42).
    2. The 2nd Lord Hillingdon (1855–1919) was a partner in the family firm of
Glyn Mills Ltd, and had been a Liberal MP. Lutyens built Overstrand Hall for
him.

know – it was called *Dame Wiggins of Lea*.[1] I jumped and cheered. He has an original, a coloured edition. He knows his Struwelpeter by heart and is awfully keen to get the three bears[2] as Elwin has – rather nice of him.

I interviewed Bartholomew the cook and the picture he made me of his requirements was so nice. He is an enormous man with bald curly greasy hair and a bland smiling face with obsequious manners. (His son is a butler to the Queen.) He is so fat he will soon have to give up as his legs are too weak for his superabundant carcass. I suggested a chair on wheels.

Then I interviewed Mrs Stokes the housekeeper – a nervous old lady harassed with the cares of five houses! and not at all a picture book housekeeper and was much more afeared of me than I was of her. Then Brooks the butler, who is exactly like the monkey in Brooks's soap advertisements. He, as well as Bartholomew, wants a room to himself. I think Lord H. will do lots of building. He talks of building at Hillingdon [Uxbridge] and wants me to go down and see, it's an enormous house. But he won't do two things at a time. Such a lovely day it's been, very foggy near London now.

Oh how I long for you to be home and settled at Bloomsbury. Angel darling I love you so.

1. *Dame Wiggins of Lea* (1823) was supposed to be by Agnes Strickland. It was reprinted with additional woodcuts by Kate Greenaway.
2. Probably one of *Aunt Louisa's Toy Books* (1872–85) illustrated by Walter Crane.

29 Bloomsbury Square   Jan.3.99.

Angellest of Wife

I hear there is an awful gale in the Channel and the boat went down last night – the Dieppe boat! This is an exaggeration doubtless, but I feel very brave and stalwart facing real elements.

I shall take patience cards with me to pass time. I write on this paper and think of Conny and I think of our Lady Mother when I play patience. So dear of her to say I am good tempered and nice. Were you all cross at Christmas?[1] *'Be* cross if you're happy in the being of it' sounds like a Conny smooth, and when Conny strokes peoples must purr and cringle.

No news no news at all. So sleepy this morning. I was very naughty and had a fire in my room last night.

Wouldn't Barbara make a darling angel Pope. Pope Barbara. Or at least a Bishop. Whether she be Pope Bishop or Queen she holds my heart in complete subjection and I long for her Presence which means *you* too.

Pasture Wood, Dorking[2]   Feb.10.99.

Angel wee wifie,

No letter from my Emy! and it's lonesome without you.

All very satisfac here, and have done all there is to be done and now sit and write to the best wee woman in the world.

1. They had spent Christmas at The Danes, but Lutyens had returned to London immediately after.
2. Lutyens was staying with Frederick Mirrielees (d. 1914) for whom he built Goddards near Abinger, a House of Rest for ladies of reduced means. Mrs Mirrielees was the daughter of the shipowner, Sir Donald Currie.

There is a Bullfinch in this room which pipes the same song as Mrs Webb's Bully used to pipe, and stops on the same bar to repeat the opening over and over again.

The coachman's wife was buried yesterday here, and Celia the little girl of the house asked what was the 'neat box covered with cloth for?' that she saw. I watch the little girl and try to realise how much more delicious our Barbara will be when seven.

Fancy Barby ours has never heard of death or anything, so for all she knows Mother will come and give her soft human warm bottles every three or four hours for ever and ever in a world without end.

Whoo who who w whooo whooo w whooo we so goes bully.

Such a lovely day it is a fresh warm wind and sun, and a smell of spring all about the place.

The Mirrielees hope you and Barbara will come here. They are a good sort of a small sort, but any amount of horses and a delicious country and numberless animals of all sorts, rats, doves, squirrels, Esquimaux (sic)? birds from Africa, dogs, hounds, puppies.

A new house, architect Flockhart[1] by name, ornée, rather, comfortable, bad service rather. I mean you go to dress and find your bag [not] unpacked and in the morning the maid knocks timidly at one's door leaving cans and boots outside in timid propriety. Such a bore!

Mrs M. is a daughter of Sir D. Currie and will eventually come in to a £1,000,000 of money so they say, so it's, say I, worth business while to 'cultivate'. This sounds beastly and is, specially as they are really wondrous kind and easy to get on with.

No news and then only the old news – never too old I hope darling – of how I love and adore you.

The Danes   *April 11.99.*

Had a delicious talk with Betty last night until nearly 1 o'clock.
She says the D D Lytteltons[2] are bent on building a house – that

1. William Flockhart (*c*1850–1913). His practice was mainly in London's West End.

2. Alfred Lyttelton (1857–1913) married as his second wife Edith Balfour, always known as D D. Lady Emily described her in 1892 as 'one of the most fascinating people I have ever seen' (*A Blessed Girl*, p. 183). A first-class

they have made an offer for a piece of land in Scotland near Whittingehame [A. J. Balfour's house]. I think it was North Berwick. D D told her they wanted to employ you. She said she had consulted Aunt T who said she thought the mixture of you and D D ought to make an absolutely perfect house. Betty said that of course she could not urge them to have you as she had two brothers-in-law and it was Eustace [Balfour]'s country and she naturally felt she ought to give her vote for him. To this D D replied that she might make herself quite happy as nothing would induce her to employ Eustace and Alfred felt the same. So then Betty said of course they must have you. Alfred has seen your work in Surrey and greatly admires it and raves of Bumps's house. D D said there were points she would insist on – as for instance she would have big windows, plenty that opened and that she could get out of. She could not bear a dark room and she thought your little windows did not give enough light. So if you get the job you will have to remember this. They want stone and, Betty says, to suit the country they want something solid looking and as if it would withstand a siege. This of course your houses do particularly.

Betty says one should tremble for the fire of criticism that would be passed on it – from Frances [Balfour] and co. But I said that as it was quite certain she would not like your work whatever it was, it was not much use paying any attention to her remarks.

Won't it be fun if you do get it? and I think D D would be delightful to work for and that they would get to know you in the best way through your work. Of course you will have a little to mind your P's and Q's and be very careful – first, to be very business-like and exact about money, and try not to let them in for more than they want to spend. Their approval might be a very good thing for you and their blame do you a good deal of harm, and your reputation is rather that of being extravagant and not exact about money. This you must try in every way to contradict by being extra careful. Then you must be on your best behaviour and not smoke your pipe in D D's face, or sit in her pocket, or offend Alfred Lyttelton in these small ways, he being very much

cricketer – W. G. Grace called his play 'the champagne of cricket' – and a Unionist MP (1895–1913), Lyttelton was an intimate friend of Arthur Balfour; through his first wife, Laura Tennant (d. 1886), he was closely involved with the Souls. The house was Grey Walls, Gullane, East Lothian, which Lutyens built for them in 1901.

the business-like man with a thorough school education. It will
be a splendid opportunity of making a good impression on the
Balfour family. I hope it may come off.

29 Bloomsbury Square   April 11.99.

Just one wee line to say have got yours tonight. Bless you. So
exciting and your scold falls on such nice moist growing ground.
Have written to Bets. Keep all my 'no news' till tomorrow.

I am sitting in the dining room, as my blinds are yet at the wash,
and I don't like to be gazed in upon by every passer by.

Mrs Lyttelton can't have a fortress and large windows too.

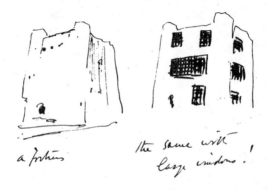

a fortress   the same with large windows!

This perhaps begs the question. Criticism don't hurt if people
don't lie.

I shall take such care of my P's and Q's and give them all to my
sweetest little wifie for safe keeping.

Darling wee Barbara how I love her. She seems to be getting
away from me, now she is so grown up.

Do you remember the pictures, love, I drew of us bound round
with bonds of love? Look now and see how tight they're pulled.

The Danes   *July 1.99.*

I got to King's Cross and found [Lutyens's] mother and father already seated in a carriage absorbed in Drefoo [Dreyfus] as mother calls him. Both looked so smart. Father had a beautiful white waistcoat and his best grey suit. Mother told me he had been pipe claying his suit and inking his hat to make both look their best! Rather nice. He looked splendid with his curls clustering round his head.

Pasture Wood   July 20.99.

My sweetest, most beautiful wife

So jolly hot and galorious I'm sticky all over so that I'm cumbered with it. A change of pen. No news, all well.

There is a dolls' party going on and Mrs Mirrielees has just been severely reprimanded for calling her daughter darling, 'You're a visitor, and visitors don't call you darling'. And oh how hot the dolls look, with remorseless eyes all wide and blank and clothes all stuff, buttons and wrinkles.

I had hoped the Ms would have driven me to Munstead but nine horses are ill with inflammation of the lungs, two at the point of death. They are being fed on beef tea and butter and port wine! Those that are better are having ale. I didn't know a horse would eat butter and beef tea.

You try and make a horse sit on a chair!?
I must go. Ever your very own, ever loving Nedi.

Booton Rectory   *Aug.4.99.*

They like your chapel. Fountain says it is very Dutch and he says it is the best ventilated church he has ever seen. I am longing to see it.

Munstead Wood   Aug.7.99.

It is no use looking at the Overstrand Chapel,[1] it cost 2½d and is not Dutch or anything at all just a brick wall and a skylight and a door and a stove. The inside spoilt – as its one salvation was simplicity – by a d—d moulding and horrid E. light fittings. So long as they can make a noise in it, no one else cares for aught else.

1. Commissioned by Lord Battersea.

Munstead Wood   Aug.6.99.

My own angel wife

Oh! I am not naughty – I did write to you, it is the postman that is naughty I am so sorry. Delicious letter at Rake[1] and two here, one this morning.

Yesterday I went to Thursley! and honoured my Father and my Mother that our days may be long in the land we have not yet got. Saw Father, Mother and Aileen [Lutyens] (Bob Webb en route at the Hammer Ponds). Father looking magnificent and quite recovered, full of admiration and delight at Conny's letter, her wisdom, 'wonderful wonderful', and it was a good letter, said just what she thought! and fitted in to Father's point of view and he lives happy ever after.

Then I went on and saw Col. and Mrs Jekyll and had tea there.[2] Col. quite delicious, roared with laughter at the idea of stuffing a minnow for the 10lb dolls' house trout, and was sympathetic about Paris Pavilion and altogether nice. Borwick[3] is there now, the Muir Mackenzies[4] and old Braby Brabazon,[5] a Sussex squire looks like a very thin Prussian Colonel and paints delicious impressionist watercolours in Venice. Loves young men and fathers them and I believe does them all sorts of good and kindnesses. I dine there tonight. I think I shall like Borwick, he raves of 'Plazzoh'.

Slept well rather too heavily – after beer! but Oh I wants Emy so and the Barbara.

Mrs Irving said, what she did admire us for was not minding parting from one another, and I said, but I *did*, I minded very

1. Lutyens was adding a new kitchen wing to Rake Manor, Milford, Surrey, for Mrs Cavan Irving.
2. Colonel, later Sir Herbert Jekyll (1845–1932), Gertrude Jekyll's brother, who was Assistant Secretary to the Board of Trade, 1901–11, lived at Munstead House. His wife, 'Aggie', was a sister of Lady Horner; their father was William Graham of Edinburgh, a friend and patron of the Pre-Raphaelites. The author of *Kitchen Essays* (1922), she became involved in public work and was made a dame. Munstead House was the Jekyll family home.
3. Leonard Borwick (1858–1925) was a concert pianist.
4. Lutyens built Red House, Effingham, Surrey, for Miss Susan Muir Mackenzie in 1892.
5. Hercules Brabazon Brabazon (1821–1906), a friend of Gertrude Jekyll. Ruskin told Herbert Jekyll: 'Brabazon is the only person since Turner at whose feet I can sit and worship and learn about colour' (Betty Massingham, *Miss Jekyll* (1966), p. 50).

much – she thought it so wise and said the Eyres[1] wouldn't let each other out of each other's sight and got on each other's nerves.

(So nice turning over) [the paper is four times normal size]

Bumps says that all the best she has written about flower borders is in a chapter called Flower Garden and Pergola in *Wood and Garden.*[2]

Tell Mr Elwin that it is as easy to rail against architects as it is to rail against parsons, solicitors, doctors, barristers. The layman always approaches a subject from a different point of view than what the professional does. The layman talks of it only, the professional has to be up and doing – against the layman and other natural difficulties.

Dictatorial Bumps says I am to tell you that Nedi is a great dear (something awful coming) but that I am kept occupied the whole time he is here in shutting the doors that he leaves open. *I* call this rude.

Bumps has made a lot of delicious photos for her new book.[2]

A tortoise has appeared on the lawn and has caused a flutter in the Woozal pit and gives ponder to the heart of cats. Swiss Albert announced it as a tortoise shell on the lawn, which rejoiced Bumps mi carême thinking he meant yet another pussy.

Bumps thinks this is rather cruel to make SO much of her innocent rotundities

No more news I have only done half the paper. It is raining for which many thanks are offered up. Col. Jekyll

1. John Eyre (d. 1927), watercolourist and book illustrator. Lutyens made a small alteration to his cottage at Cranleigh, Surrey, in 1900.

2. *Wood and Garden* published in 1899 and illustrated with photographs by the author.

told rather a nice story of India where some natives were found offering a sacrifice of goats and bullocks to some new god, a great god, but they would not for long give the name of this great god, but after due persuasion they confessed that it was no less than the 'Judicial Committee of the Privy Council'. Also a native who wrote to a Governor General addressing him as 'Honoured Enormity'.

Ever and ever your own ever loving Husband
Nedi

The Hall, Munstead Wood

Oh! Oh! Oh!
Such fun, joy. Bumps proposes (and God is ever disposing) to go to Thornham Sept. 2–16 and says Emy Barbie and Nedi may have Plazzoh for ten days out of that time!
This would be glorious, and oh such fun! and we shall have a honeymoon in Plazzoh in Plazzoh in Plazzoh. This will be joy.
[They did go.]

29 Bloomsbury Square   Aug.8.99.

Darling Ems

Oh I do want to be with you I feel so lone and missedful five days without Emymine and coming back I find all up and no Emy nor nothing. I am in the drawing room for tea and it's all drêpe de chine that is to say everything is drêped and swathed in white absenteeism up to its chin, even Nedi.

I feel eclipsed and all sunless without my own wife and it's too miserable for words.

I wants you Ems

Yes I *do...* . . . .

I *doo...* . . . ...

I enclose you a picture of you, a draught of a picture, of the size and style for the dolls' house, please note the 18th cent. pose, the 18th cent. proportions and hands shoulders etc. sort of thing.

I wonder what time you wrote yesterday as to whether there will be another letter today or shall I have to wait wait WAIT till tomorrow.

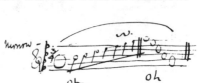

The above is the music for occasion, very flat and all O in key of E minor time very slow.

I am your own own ever own
                                    Nedi

Calcot Park, Reading   Aug.26.99.

My own sweet love wife

    Arrived here safe. A smart brougham with inflated rubber
tyres met me at the station and I drove out here about 3 miles
from Reading. A. Mills[1] has a voice exactly like Lord Hillingdon's – all families have one voice – but 'tis curious and makes
one feel one knows a man. Very kind, pleasant and easy to do with.

    We go over to Mapledurham[2] tomorrow – morning – and
lunch at the Roebuck nearby and go there again in the afternoon.
Mapledurham is about two miles from here.

    This house is so like Milford [Barbara Webb's] House as to be
creepy. It is bigger, more rooms and different but yet the feeling is
ghostly like Milford. In the front where be the high road at
Milford here be a quad of stable buildings, so that from the hall
door you see your carriage washed and your horses brought out.

    There are deer in the park which give it a Cockney appearance.
The decorations of the rooms are vile and altogether bad, done by
the owners and not Mills himself. He wants me to build new
offices and alter one or two things about the house and spend
about £4000. Blount the owner of Mapledurham is going to
build stables for him, but with this I have nothing to do.

    No one is here, but his boy of 13, I have not seen, and a tutor
who appeared at dinner to disappear directly after.

29 Bloomsbury Square   Aug.27.99.

My sweetest most beautiful wife

    I must tell you of my day yesterday, and all about it, Mills,
and everything. But there is so much to tell and so little to relate,
and in writing points are so difficult to make, letters should be in
bordereau style.

    Breakfasted at 9. Mills came late, 9.45. A nice spoilt son 13
years old and a dry young consequential quiet tutor. Gorgeous
breakfast – pies, hams, grouse, beefs, muttons, kidneys, eggs,
fish, bacon, coffee, tea, but all wasted on me. Scented tea and big
cups woke me to life, and a darling letter from Emy, but rather

    1. The Hon. Algernon Mills (1856–1922), 2nd son of 1st Baron Hillingdon.
    2. One of the largest Elizabethan houses in the country, belonging to the
Blount family. Mr Mills wanted to take it.

---

sad, put strength in my bowels. We sat on the lawn and talked buildings and things, Mills and I, till 11.15. Then we started on bikes – he mounted me on a superfine green Elswick. I told you of Mills and of Calcot Park.

He is a quiet easy man, shrewd about money but not quite so careful as Lord Hillingdon. He is rather sad, not from ever present grief but he has got into the way of it. [His wife had died in 1895.] And Oh! it must be lonely in that big house all alone with a boy absolutely useless for sympathetic purposes – a boy unreasoning, skittish, can't sit still, and making a continuous flow of questions and being very tall for his years you expect more sense than his age would warrant, and this, I think, gets on his father's nerves for it is for ever don't do this or that, and you look up to frustrate the father shaking his head, frowning, and general maniflexions upon his son's conduct.

We biked about two miles and then ferried across the river and a quarter of a mile's walk brought us to the old Mapledurham[1] house and it is a good'un. Quiet, big, impressive, and though treated with carelessness and with a happy go lucky policy, it yet preserves its character of simple sublimity! It is of red brick with patterns over it in grey and a tiled roof. It is under one big roof with low projecting wings at each corner making a shape like this

an H or some call it a double E – a form dear to the Elizabethan archaeologist but by my halidom I trow the architect never thought of it. On the south end is a dear old Henry VII building – a cottage and the stables. These stables we propose to pull down and build new offices and incorporate the old Henry VII building. It all comes at XYZ in sketch. An E is a natural and pleasant disposition for a house, and no doubt a flatterer of the day did not lose the opportunity of pointing it out to Elizabeth. The truth *is*

1. Margaret Richardson has suggested that the design for Little Thakeham (1902), which 'evokes an Elizabethan manor house', may have been inspired by Lutyens's visit to Mapledurham (*Catalogue 1981*, p. 106). Nothing came of Mills's plans to build there.

that it were prophesied the gloriousness of *my Emy* to come – the love of her and perfectness so the many followers of this prophet built their houses for the sake of darling Emy– not for a rank old Spinster Queen, but for a *real* one in the shape called E – and for proof, why my Emy is the proof of it! and no man shall dare deny.

A Frenchman, spruce and very French, has taken it till March. Has a housekeeper and three servants (Mills says you can't work the house under ten servants) and a sister! (sic). We are all much exercised as to how they will manage – specially in the winter when the place is freezing cold and draughty. Mills proposes to build a kitchen, scullery, larders, still room, housekeeper's room, servants' hall, 2 staircases, 6 maids' rooms, and 7 men servants' rooms, 2 baths and 2 WCs making the old kitchen into a dining room, a pantry and a safe room, a linen closet and a store room, also a brushing room. Mr Blount, the owner, is to build new stables for him – so. He won't get possession of the house till March, unless the Frenchman gets sick of it; and the stables can't be pulled down till the new ones are built. The house itself can't be touched until the new offices are built. It sounds hopeless, but the saving clause is that Mills himself is not there for scarce six months in the twelve.

Blount seems very careless and casual and can never make up his mind. He has a brother who Mills says is hopeless and if he has anything to do with it Mills won't take the house. No one knows except the brothers who the heir is – it is a male entail – and the owner has only a daughter and the brother no children at all. It's a very old family. Mills says if he could buy it he would spend £60,000 on it! If he builds he will build in Dorsetshire and get an old place to start on. I hope he does.

I have a large sore place on my chin. The head of a wax match blew off – *bang* – and burnt a hole in me. The noise and the flame and the pang of burning frightened me dreadful. This took place Friday night. No fear the patient has done wonderful well.

Oh to see your dear face again and to hug you darling. I love you Oh so well and truly.

Ever your own very own *husband* Nedi.

Blounts are Romans. There is a chapel and a resident priest. We lunched at the Roebuck and then Mills punted me down the river after lunch – a poor one – saw the house again. We went for a walk and home by 5.30 – so was the day spent.

———

In train Cromer to London   Sept.19.99.

Angellest wee wifie

On the way home. Hillingdons very kind and Lord H. gives me all I want. Lady H. wants to rebuild Overstrand Church and I hope she may! After lunch I met Lady Lewis. Sir George has offered for land at Overstrand and I am to build them a small house, isn't this good?[1] Met the ever present Lord Suffield,[2] who begins to like the colour of the house – isn't this amusing?

I had a telegram from Vic at Cromer asking if I could put him up Wednesday, of course says I and I shall be very glad to see him.

Lady Hillingdon is a funny person. She said at lunch – talking about when the house would be finished – 'at all events if the house is not finished we shall have you'. This was greeted with a roar of laughter – and she tried to explain it away but couldn't, and then said 'to explain the plans'. What do you think she meant?! Her remarks are always inane and helpless – always kind. She seems to live in a dream – sat upon – but never loses her even temper, nor does she seem to mind it very much. I like Lord H. awfully. Although he bullies her I don't think he means it unkindly and her apathy is rather riling. He is clever – *quite*, most amusing, a pleasant modest and keen insight into matters of art and men, practical, economical and not unduly mean. He likes all I like and looks at many things from the same point of view. His enormous wealth makes of course the same width gap between us as there is between our fortunes. I wonder if Lady H. has any influence and if so what? She had a very pretty gown on last night – lace over blue (how you are laughing) and the lace was in bows on her shoulders and rather full about the paps, can't draw in the train

There were many néed Harbords, very much dressed in tailor made ballooned coats, full in the hips and even below

1. Sir George Lewis (1833–1911), the great Edwardian solicitor. Oscar Wilde said of him: 'George Lewis? Brilliant. Formidable. Concerned in every great case in England. Oh – he knows all about us, and he forgives us all.' Lewis used a different architect.

2. Lord Suffield (1830–1914), was Lady Hillingdon's father. The family name is Harbord.

them, sailor hats of sort, sporting gloves, sticks, and spatted boots – excuse disjointed picture. No room for the head so I

had to put it off. Lady H. had a blue canvas gown, an awful blue and yesterday she wore a black and white check. Lord H. very pleased that Sir G. Lewis is going to build as he told him (Lord H.) he was a fool to build when he began.

An old stopped tooth has been aching for the last week or 10 days and I think it may become a gum boil. I have evidently caught a cold in it. It is not bad but it is a bore. It comes on about five to six first thing in the morning and the last at night and I do *hate* the idea of a dentist.

I do so look forward to your letters when I get home. Give my fondest love to all at Thursley the Father and Mother and Oh Emy such a big lump of loving adoration to my own sweet lovable wife.

The Cottage, Thursley   *Sept.20.99.*

Such a delicious long letter from you this morning and I am glad about Sir G. Lewis and new job. It is all good and I do rejoice for my darling's sake and our Barby.

Am so glad Vic puts up with you today. Give him a fire and all he wants. It is quite bitterly cold here. I could not sleep for cold last night. Howling north wind. Father was too funny last night at dinner. There were some chip potatoes, rather hard which he could not eat, and when they were mixed up with bread sauce, tomato and gravy, Father said: 'Oh I can't eat these. I am going to soak them in my tea to soften them.' Consternation of the family. Margy[1] and I nearly got hysterics. At tea time there was no knife to cut the cake and he would insist on doing it with his tea spoon! He was reading the paper in the evening and suggested to your

1. Margaret, Lutyens's youngest and least favourite sister. She married late in life and Lutyens remarked: 'I thought I'd come to your funeral but never to your wedding.'

*mother she should take it to bed and read it in the morning. 'Oh
no' said mother, 'I always read my Bible in bed.' 'Well, this is just
the same as the Bible.' 'My dear Charles, what do you mean?' 'I
tell you, Mary, if you look at it in the right way it is a kind of
Bible. Oh my, it is a strange story.'*

*Yesterday to Milford House and saw Bob [Webb] for a mo-
ment. Bob most characteristically proceeded to put me tidy and
turn down my collar.*

29 Bloomsbury Square   Sept.20.99.
                                                                    even

Angellest wifie, my darling

Am awfully busy. Hudson wants some drawings by Friday at 9.00 and tomorrow is so full. I am glad Vic had to go out.

Your delicious and amusing letter, but oh how the pigginess of
Cottage life palls upon me. I am *so* sorry Bob should have found
fault with your collar! You must be ever *so particular* when
coming out of the Lutyens nest, or else you'll get tarred with their
untidy brush.

I thanked Vic for his present. It is rumoured Judith is in an
interesting way, I am so glad.

Oh! those chip potatoes. If it had happened before I knew my
darling loved me (when nothing outside hurts us) I should have
died.

I should strike at going about and seeing 1st people who won't
build, 2nd people who bore you, 3rd people you don't want to
know. How badly they always manage things in muddled Thursley.

Oh Emy I do want you here comfy and alone.

The Cottage, Thursley   *Sept.22.99.*

*I was not a bit untidy when I saw Bob — very smart on the
contrary — only one side of my collar was turned up, and he loves
to put things right.*

29 Bloomsbury Square   Sept.21.99.

My own Angel wee wife

Been so hard at work all day and *so* cross and rowed
Badcock who has gone off in a huff, so I just sit down and write
Emy mine and find peace. The only thing that keeps me alive is the
day after tomorrow! Today got up and had a cold bath and poor
Vic had one too! Jane says she lit the fire early – no matter! We
breakfasted and then Vic went out. Various people came and had
a big morning at Paris work. At 12.30 I went off to see A. Mills,
he said the plans were just what he wanted, but Blount, the
owner, seems shy of having his house added to (and I rather do
sympathise). The bother is that he plays fast and loose with poor
Mills, which is not fair.

Then I started home and just outside the Mansion House in a
coupé I saw a face I knew – it was – *yes* it was Judith! She didn't
see me, and then I let them go. I looked round and seeing the
coupé in a block, I rushed up and popped my head into the
window and said hullo! They was rather astonished – and Neville
gathered his wits first and said, Why! it's Ned get in, so I just
scrambled in and drove with them to Liverpool Street. Judith was
looking splendidly well, but Neville looked rather white and
seedy, though I told him that he *did* look well.

I got back here about 1.30 and lunched with Badcock. Several
people came after lunch and then I went on working. Vic came to
tea at 4 and went off ½ after four. I gave him 2 eggs with his tea au
casserole and he said our bread and butter was the best he ever
had.

Oh! I want to wrap you round as an apple does its core and just
hide you to myself and keep you always.

Your own own loving and adoring
Ned

29 Bloomsbury Square   Dec.28.99.

I caught the train so comfortably, having about seven minutes to
wait. Vic and Nevs cheered my way with songs and various
mimicries.[1] I caught a glimpse of Hatfield, it is so quiet and

1. Victor and Neville were on their way to Hatfield to stay with the
Salisburys.

impressive and altogether comforting to one's nerves. It was very bad to leave you darling, Barbie and all, and go to this drear house of work and toil.

I was rather sorry for Neville and I do admire his vegetarianism. Vegetarianism I have good reason to and do hate, but his high spirits over it are most exhilarating and his persistent courage in the face of the worst of critics – a family. To go to Hatfield with your pockets full of bread and cheese lest you get not enough is heroic, and to produce them is . . . words fail. I have used up heroic and have nothing left but 'marvel'.

The next two years are of fearful importance to Neville to make or to mar.

Milford House   Feb. 3.1900.

At Clapham Gerald [Balfour] got in. We talked houses, war, war, houses. He was really nice and ever so tame and awfully kind and I think appreciated my coming. Betty joined at Guildford. At Milford Bob [Webb] joined us. I felt a regular snowball collecting as I went. At Witley we all got out. No fly and very deep snow. We walked to Tigbourne[1] and I got a two horse brougham in a quarter of an hour. Gerald was very appreciative and nice and Betty ventured up a ladder, and I told her how well you did it! and told her how thoroughly at home was my Emy on a scaffold. We then drove on to Milford, here, where we had a regular Milford excellentissimo meal. Bob, ever so funny, talking seriously about 'small holdings' and by the way pointing out the workhouses, schools, lunatic asylums, and other local interests. After lunch at three we had another two horse brougham and drove, first Gerald and I driving, Betty and Bob walking, to Bumpstead [Munstead Wood] and walked up through the garden and found Bumps in! She had lumbago. Gerald thought the house, he said, fascinating, and was quite tame and kind. We then walked up the lane and saw the site next to Bumps's and then drove on, the carriage meeting us at Colonel Jekyll's gate, to Winkworth Farm.[2] We found the door open and no one in the house and we

1. Tigbourne Court, near Witley which, with its striking façade, 'summarizes all that was so sophisticated and original in [Lutyens's] early work' (Daniel O'Neill, *Lutyens: Country Houses* (1980), p. 71).
2. Where Lutyens had remodelled a barn in 1895.

went all over it. Gerald was much amused and Betty quite enchanted with the rambling romance and oddness of the place. We then drove back to·Godalming where G. and B. caught the train for London. They dine with the [Joseph] Chamberlains tonight. I do wish they could have stayed.

I do wish you had been here darling but Oh! the misery and dreariness of the weather. The procession through the snow. First Bob, in huge waders, Gerald Geraldie and very neat, spats and rug and long grey coat. Nedi buttoned and unbuttoned, pipe, hair all over the shop, Betty radiant and full of pluck, energy and spirits, delighting in everything Bob said, seriously or not so. Post just going.

The Danes   *April 8.1900*

I hated leaving you in the night and having no proper good-bye, but I know you did not really mind my going and had you seen poor Judith you would have been so glad to let me be of any use. It was awful to see, much worse than I go through myself. She was too pathetic, and her appealing eyes and her cries were so like an animal. She said to me I never never shall forget your goodness and I feel that it has made the whole difference to our relations. I could not have let her suffer alone when I was the only one who could go to her.

I pined to get back to my baby after seeing the other[1] and I long to go through it all again and have a bundle in my arms at the end.

Rake Manor, Milford   *Aug.25.1900*

My own love
        We had such a delicious afternoon with Bumps. Barby and I drove over in the brougham and found Bumps writing in the workshop. She was very dear to us, but Barby rude and refused to kiss her. She said she was very busy and I said I would go off to the Chances' house [Orchards] and return to her, 'I should like to come too,' she said. 'Do', say I. She hesitated some time between pleasure and duty and finally yielded! Wasn't that a

1. Anthony, who became the 4th Earl of Lytton.

---

*triumph? We drove in the brougham, Bumps thoroughly en-
joying the luxurious india rubber tyres and saying there were
some compensations for being rich! She was most delicious and
amusing. Mrs Chance was resting but Mr C. came out in very
gardening attire. He very kindly showed me round the house
while Bumps did the garden. I think it all quite charming, dining
room lovely and staircase and landing delicious. I raved freely of
its beauties and Mr Chance said, 'It seems funny for you to be
admiring your husband's work', and I then felt shy. He went on
to say how everyone liked and admired the house and how very
clever you were. Then we joined Bumps in the garden which is
also lovely. Drove back to tea which Bumps and I had together
and a delicious chat. She mooted a plan which has set me terribly
dreaming – though I know it is impossible. She says the Trehernes
are leaving Warren Lodge, 'And oh! I wish you and Ned could
take it. I am sure Bob would rather have you there than anybody,
and it would be nice. Couldn't you put out feelers to Ned, he must
be getting on so well now, and if all went well next year wouldn't
it be possible?' She kept returning to it and I thought it was so
delicious of her to want us so. I see myself cooking and gardening,
and no more visits to Lockers,[1] but our own country home! Oh!
Nedi what fun we could have if we were only richer. If we were
only out of debt and the house had not to be done up.*

Now I am just off to Thursley.

Your own Emy that worships you Nedi darling.

The Danes   *Oct.28.1900*

*Try and be a little tender and thoughtful for me – especially if you
would think and remember that smoke makes me feel so awfully
sick. I don't mean I don't want you to smoke in the room, only try
not to smoke in my face – or in cabs or in small places. I know you
would never do it if you knew how I hated it. You see you have a
share in my sufferings, so you must help me to bear them too. [She
was pregnant with Robert.]*

---

1. Mrs Frederick Locker-Lampson, a family friend of the Lyttons, lived at
Cromer, where Lady Emily often stayed.

---

29 Bloomsbury Square   March 27.01

I have been very busy and working hard. Badcock comes at 11 and leaves at 4.30 so I wrote and scolded him well. He has written to say he will not come again except to collect his few things and to come and bring Mr Collins, his solicitor with him to settle up things. This is just like him to leave one in the lurch. Anyhow I must just brace myself up and face it.

He says he neglects work because I don't introduce him. If I introduce him he is familiar and behaves, well, like a cad.

Look at the jobs, those with a cross he has given a belated assistance in, those not marked I have had to do everything.

Sonning	I alone	[Deanery Garden for Edward Hudson]
Fisher's Hill	+	[for Gerald Balfour]
Woolverstone	+	[St. Peter's Home for Lord Berners]
Rake		[for Mrs. Cavan Irving]
Tigbourne [Court]	+ awful mess	[for Edgar Horne]
Varangeville	+ late	[for Guillaume Mallet]
Paris	I alone	[English Pavilion]
[Great] College Street	+ mess	[for Lytteltons]
Lyttelton	I alone	[Grey Walls]
Rossall	„ „	[New Town, did not materialise]
Hillingdon		[Overstrand Hall]
Mirrielees		[Goddards]
Watson	E.B.B. mess	
Abbotswood		[for Mark Fenwick]
Marshcourt		[for Herbert Johnson]
Hoare	+	[Cottages at Basing]

He won't apply himself to anything but talk.

I shall speak privately to Hudson about it and get his advice.

Darling I do so love you and it is such a relief to have you to write and to confide in.

Sketch for Deanery Garden

The Danes   *March 28.01*

Your letter is so exciting I don't know what to do. I so long to talk to you, but I do beseech you by my love for you and everything that has power over you don't lose this opportunity of getting rid of Badcock. He is not nearly conscientious enough or hard working or business-like in any way. He is a chattering conceited cad, to put it mildly! The correspondence between you, you will find in a long envelope, addressed to you in B.'s handwriting, in a wooden box full of letters and papers in the spare room.

29 Bloomsbury Square   April 12.01.

A large tombstone has been made for E.B.B. in the office

In memory of E.B.B.
for 3 years sleeping partner at 29 B.S.
Died of talking and from doing no work etc. sort of thing.
I only got a glimpse of it.

Meldon, Morpeth, Northumberland   April 23.01.

Arrived here about 6.30 last night and found them playing croquet. Mark Fenwick,[1] Mrs Fenwick, Captain H. Fenwick and his wife, children – one of Captain's and four of Mark F.'s, make the party. Mark Fenwick client, you know about. Molly his wife quite delightful. Captain Fenwick who knew [brother] John in India ugly but nice good face, very tall, lovely hands and very thin, awfully well made and energetic – lots of money in coal – is building with a Slough (of despond) architect. Mrs Captain, American, beautifully and rather over dressed, by way of being v. literary – French – German – Italian – artiste, loves Carlyle and other erudite authors, affected in conversation, by way of brilliance is apt to degenerate to either puns or rudeness. Quite kind, affects to hate to get up early and very precious of her really good pink and white complexion under a mass of red hair.

Mrs Mark Fenwick is delightful, quite simple, straightforward, absolutely unaffected, not clever, but not expected to be, but very kind and an excellent hostess. Peggy, eldest daughter,[2] hobbledehoy age, but animal and country loving and unaffected and altogether good sort, shy but not too shy or uncomfortably so at all.

This morning we made an early start by omnibus – seven of us – and went to Chesters. Chesters is where Mrs M. Fenwick's mother, Mrs Clayton[3] lives. A big, very big, Norman Shaw house. It was lovely and lovable in great and many respects, but there are mistakes which I could not help thinking I should have avoided. An enormous house and all details left go lucky beyond a point. Yet the planning of it all is a masterpiece[4] and the big library is quite delicious.

1. Mark Fenwick (1860–1945), distinguished gardener and friend of Gertrude Jekyll, worked as a young man in the family bank, Lambton & Fenwick, in Newcastle. Lutyens was altering Abbotswood for him in the Cotswolds. They had taken Meldon from the Cookson family. He married Molly Clayton (1863–1924).

2. Later Mrs Vere Chaplin.

3. Widow of Nathaniel Clayton, MP for Hexham, who had died in 1895. Augustus Hare described the Claytons, when he stayed with them in 1862, as being 'like merchant princes in Newcastle so enormous is their wealth'.

4. Chesters (1891) has a butterfly plan like Papillon Hall, built by Lutyens in 1904.

Mrs Clayton you would love. Unfortunately I did not see near enough of her. Black hair and a mousy face – with a big light in the forehead. The black hair very smooth – with lovely streaks of grey in it and deliciously robed – simple in black – a diamond here and there in ears – and a brooch of evidently rich and goodly value – £100,000 a year! rather like a very well brushed and slim Bumps.

We came back here by 6 o'clock and had tea – unwanted and dinner-spiriting after the Chesters lunch. After tea I went and caught a trout or two – little things. Tomorrow I shall fish au grand sérieux and catch 5.30 train to Edinburgh. I write this as they are playing bridge. They say here coal is going to be 5/- a ton! very cheap – they ought to know.

29 Bloomsbury Square   July 31.01.

Badcock is building for Princess Louise in Cowes![2] I am sick about it. I wish I could get someone to have a go at him, he seems to have scored off everyone and Princess Louise leaving me will do me a good deal of harm.

I do so love your letters and with you away worries loom so large.

I must get on with my work, do better, and get, if I only can, a better class of work, not so many little things and all one's ingenuity has to go in saving tuppences and not in doing best work. So you see I am rather depressed and upset by Badcock and

1. Drawings from a letter to Lady Lytton, 2 August 1901.
2. Badcock's sister Mary had married William Probert, who was equerry to Princess Louise from 1902 to 1913. His wife Ethel, daughter of H. R. H. Davies RA, was a woman of considerable artistic talent; she was a friend of Princess Louise, to whom she also acted as unofficial lady-in-waiting.

all this season I have seen no one hardly and not dined out or made new friends etc. or influences.

Do make a plan to upset E.B.B. with Louise! It requires diplomacy.

2 Marine Villas, Paignton [Devon]   Aug.1.01.

About Badcock I don't feel a bit depressed for this reason. I am quite certain Princess Louise only took you up because you were a nice young man to flirt with and a cheap and unknown architect, whom she could make use of and bully. Since our marriage she has lost all interest in you as a young man and since your reputation has so increased, she feels she can't do as she likes. Badcock is still a nobody and she can get things out of him she can't from you. If however you want to put a spoke in his wheel I should get Bumps to say something to Louise about Badcock when next she sees her.

About your work love, of course you only see how little *you do, and it is for others to see how much. I am* sure *that bigger work will come in time, and you are very young to have got on so well, but there love I know it is useless to tell you this as the depressed moods must come and one just has to work oneself out of them.*

Guildford Station   Aug. 5.01.

I am very anxious Mirrielees should add to Goddards! It is such a happy pleasant form of charity for a rich man to indulge and suits me exactly! At Chichester there is a building called St Mary's Hospital – an Almshouse. It is an old church adapted some centuries back to an almshouse purpose. The aisles are filled in with rooms for the brothers and the sisters – on opposite sides. The nave remains as a common hall, the chancel screened off in the old way and usual way, is the chapel. Can you imagine a more delightful scheme for a home of rest? and this is what I want him to do. He laughs nicely, but likes the idea. I think he is rather frightened of 'the church' and what parsons would say – ! which reason is silly. There would have to be possibly a big kitchen big enough to have kitchen, pantries, scullery etc. all in one room as the monks all do their own work. Would you ever care to stay in a place like that – with Nannie and Louisa and we making our own beds and nurses to cook for us? It might be *so* happy – and a feeling of luxurious peace that a well built building can alone bring.

I am going to send him sketches.[1]

Just got into the train.

My own love, I have been wondering whether if if if I could or might run down to Paignton whether there would be room for me at 2 Marine Villas. I fear not, but I just was wondering, if one day you came in from the beach and found me sitting there whether it would be necessary to turn me out for the night? I was only just wondering and would like to know, not that there is any possibility of it but it would be nice to know.

Forever your very own body and soul husband

Nedi

2 *Marine Villas*   *Aug.6.01.*

About coming here, the very thought of seeing you makes me throb and quiver with joy and yet I don't want you to come all this way and the journey costs so much and I don't quite know if there would be room. The room I am in is about the size of my cupboard at home. [He did come.]

29 Bloomsbury Square   Aug.13.01.

My own angel Birdie

No news, except a long letter from Lady Ilchester upsetting all my plans and I must begin *de nouveau* – she is an ass. This is *very* depressing. I have written her a letter! Oh Emy it is awful being without you. If I didn't want money so much I should chuck the Ilchesters altogether. There is Lord I., Lady I. and a clerk of works. . . .of course if the c. of w. is quoted I shall resign the job[2] at once.

I shall stop now. I must do some work but have little heart to. It is impossible to do anything worth while for 2d. Fancy if a painter

1. The idea was not accepted.
2. New wing at Redlynch House, Somerset, where the Earl of Ilchester owned 16,000 acres. It was executed.

had only one tube of paint to paint a picture it taking more than a tube to cover the canvas . . . all this makes work almost impossible to tackle and certainly no pleasure in it, and I have all the letters to write too as Dalton is away.

Ever your very loving husband
Nedi who loves you so

29 Bloomsbury Square   Sept.8.01.

I have an appointment to go over the Savoy on Monday 16 and have been asked to make sketches for the job. This gives me all possible chance of getting the job and it remains with me and my power to get or lose it.

Lee Hill the manager is a man of about 45, very young looking very healthy and English all over, blonde, jeune et not at all timide, simple and outspoken but by no means brusque he has a distant manner, more felt than seen – of the hotel manager: superior shop walker. He is a frank clean sort of man, copious straight hair brushed back, leaving a deep set parting to the centre leftwards and soft looking red cheeks from sunburn and a complexion clear as a bell and not what one would expect of a man managing the Savoy, Claridge's and the Berkeley[1] hotels! Devoted to authors of the R. L. Stevenson type – Barrie etc. Very interested in Dr Haig and a certain champion tennis player to whom he wrote so as to discuss food and health questions. Very keen too is he on shooting, fishing and spends time at the Zoo and seems to know animals as individuals and loves them all. A firm mouth covered by well grown but compact moustachios. Long and thin – energetic and withal wears a turn down collar. Do you see the man with whom I may have much to do, many details to fight over with.

Sonning is coming on all right I think.

1. Lutyens altered the Berkeley in 1902 and redecorated the grill room in 1913; as a result he 'was allowed to take his family there free on festive occasions' (Mary Lutyens, *Lutyens*, p. 159).

The Danes   *Sept.11.01.*

Mother and Con went to little Anne's[1] christening yesterday, which seems to have been comic. The priest gabbled fearfully and was attended by a female acolyte, some relation of Lady Anne Blunt's[2] who suffers from tubercles of the brain and goes about on a stretcher. There were only servants present. Instead of tea, for which Mother longed, there were ices of which Lady Anne ate a large number. Judith was still in bed with a dead flower in her hair. She says she is sorry to have brought a girl into the world.

In train, Edinburgh to Beauly   Sept.12.01.

Mrs Lyttelton said that Pamela Plowden[3] is very much smitten with Vic and hopes Vic won't be caught by her. She thinks she is an intriguing little thing etc. and not truth loving. She said she would not say a word to Vic in case it might happen and then he would be lost to her. . . . She don't think P.P. near good enough for him, nor do I, but she is enormously attractive . . . to men.

Beaufort Castle,[4] Beauly, Inverness-shire   Sept.12.01.

Have just arrived. They dine at 7.30 to save servants, sounds absurd. There are nine in the house. Mr Phipps[4] has American

1. Judith and Neville's elder daughter.
2. Judith's mother (1837–1917), converted to Catholicism in 1880, was Lord Byron's granddaughter and Baroness in her own right. With Wilfrid she founded the Crabbet Arabian Stud. Their difficult marriage is described in Elizabeth Longford's *Pilgrimage of Passion*.
3. Daughter of Sir Trevor Plowden. In 1898 Raymond Asquith wrote: 'There is quite a jolly little girl staying here now – one Pamela Plowden: it is her first season and Margot is bringing her out . . . very pretty and young and too clever to be offensively ingenuous; but I shan't marry her' (*Raymond Asquith*, p. 38). A famous beauty, Winston Churchill wanted to marry her – they always lunched together on his birthday – and she became a lifelong friend of Lutyens's.
4. The seat of Lord Lovat built by Wardrup in 1880, H.H. Asquith described it as 'a most unlovely specimen of the modern Scottish baronial style' (Michael and Eleanor Brock ed., *H. H. Asquith, Letters to Venetia Stanley* (1982), p. 23). It was altered by Lutyens for Mr and Mrs Phipps, who had taken the castle while Lord Lovat was in South Africa with the Lovat Scouts. Mr Phipps was the father of Paul Phipps, who was in Lutyens's office – who in turn was the father of Joyce Grenfell.

boots. It seems a big house in what they call the Scotch Baronial style. Architectural anachronisms at every corner. The house is in decorations unfinished and has a barrack like feeling and none of the charm of emptiness.

29 Bloomsbury Square   Sept.16.01.

Came up [from The Danes] with Aunt T who was very affectionate, very intimate, most interesting in consequence and *full of admiration for my own true love* and thinks though that she should make every effort to develop herself before family duties become too big, to go amongst people and to force herself to make conversation at dinner, etc. etc. She thought our marriage was turning out so happily and so successfully, etc. and such splendid children. Full, she was, of sexual intercourse, etc. My own dear love is to me perfect and she must do what she likes and thinks right – (subject to clauses hereinafter to be laid down). . . .

The Danes   *Sept.17.01.*

Pamela has been asked to Gisborne to meet Vic and hear him speak. Everyone seems anxious to bring them together. Mother is I think anxious, but philosophical. She would not wish it, but if it is to be she will make the best of it. She seems, like me, to be haunted by a dread of anything happening to Vic, and Nev and R.C. heir getting Knebworth, and I think any *marriage that would produce a son would bring her joy. Pamela would I think be a nice daughter-in-law to Mother, but* not *a desirable wife.* [They married in 1902.]

The Danes   *Sept.20.01.*

I have thought of a lucrative occupation – I am going to get a rich old bachelor to give me the arranging and cataloguing of his library! I can devote two hours a day to my work and shall improve my mind by skimming the books as I arrange them. I may fascinate the old gentleman and get his money! Neville is going to arrange the job for me through Mr Cockerell.[1] Will you approve?

1. Sydney Cockerell (1867–1962), bibliophile and calligrapher, was secretary to Wilfrid Blunt from 1898.

29 Bloomsbury Square   Sept.21.01.

Certainly *NOT* are you to think of undertaking any job and I
hope sincerely that Neville did not take you seriously least of all
through Cockerell. This has depressed me more than anything
else!

I am so awfully busy darling that I must wait till tomorrow to
say how I love you, my pet.

Gosford, Longniddry, Scotland[1]   Jan.2.02.

A good journey up to Edinburgh and then to Grey Walls, getting
on slowly. The Lytteltons *love* the grey tiles – ain't that comforting? Lady Wemyss likes it too, Lord Wemyss has not been over.
Gosford has great qualities and good in conception but oh so
many technical mistakes – in the grand classic is like music on a
big scale, if the drum beat loud and the people shout God save the
King all flat is a bit of a nuisance and stupid too.

Lord W. is a dear old man but getting so pathetically old.[2] His
frailty (not in Queen Victoria's sense) is so apparent through his
geniality.

Just got a telewire from Hudson saying he has got Lindïsfarne
Castle – will I go and look at it as I am up here so I had better. It
will be amusing.

The party here is Lord W., Lady W., she seems to be acting a
part of stately reserve, very pleasant therewithal, Alfred and Mrs
Lyttelton. The big hall was lighted up for me and oh it looked so
thin but don't say this. I feel I could have done *so* much better. . . .

29 Bloomsbury Square   March 15.02.

Let me know how long does Bumps intend to stay? I don't want
to lose an ounce of her bulb!

I arrived yesterday, met at the station by neat brougham. The
house, West Dean Park, fairly close by, is a church warden

---

1. The seat of the Earl of Wemyss, Gosford had been extensively added to by
William Young in 1890.
2. He died in 1914 at the age of ninety-six.

pseudo Gothic erection – big, all built of knapped flints and curiously worked. Added to by Ernest George so bad I think, and added to again by Mr James[1] and the estate, practical but worse – well, as bad. Very smart and luxurious and lots of beautiful things, and a ping pong table, etc. etc. No untoward evidences of Royal favours, by way of photos.

I arrived about seven. Shown into her sitting room – of course I saw Mr James first and was astounded to find him so much younger than I expected and so much more gentlemanlike. Mrs James is expecting and lay on a sofa. Mr James very neat, small, thin, young, turning towards, but gently, to middle age. Very quiet, reserved, collected, an occasional spark of human feeling shown by a twinkle. Improving on acquaintance and for a very rich man, sitting in Hoheit's [Royalty's] lap, delightful.

Mrs James. 1st impression. Round about barmaid, quizzy, cynical and conceited. 2nd impression. *Very* short sighted, strong pince nez, hair done in *horrid* Batten way not suited to a round cheruby face. Nose tipped and very tilted, lovely hands, gay, thoughtless, extravagant as she has rights to be, beautifully dressed, lovely rings. Makes all the noises, squeaks that only a

lots of clothes

1. William James (1854–1912) had inherited a large American fortune; he bought West Dean (W. Sussex) in 1891 for £200,000. A Wyatt house, it was remodelled by Ernest George – in whose office Lutyens had been a pupil. Willie James was a friend of Edward VII; his wife, a daughter of Sir Charles Forbes, 4th Bart, was one of the King's favourites.

little woman may or dare make. Burdened with nearing mothera-
tion, but brave and with periods of gay energy. Works a stocking
machine, makes a sock, heel toe etc. in half an hour. Her tastes
French. *If* her sincerity was convincing I should be prepared to
like her much.

But I *do* think a woman's figure enceinte is becoming either
Pamela

or
Mrs
James

types

    Three little girls, 8, 6, 3, evidently fruitless endeavours towards
a son.[1] Dear darling things and all devoted to parents and parents
to they. I arrived during the children's hour. They after dinner
played bridge. Mr J. delightful but quite insincere, keenly alive to
all the oddities of others.

    This morning we motor carred to the site[2] four miles and then a
mile and a half walk. Site quite lovely, wild, beech, heather, gorse,
thorn, grass, down, with views across hills and Chichester to the
Channel. They want a small house for Mrs J. and children to go to
in hot weather etc. when West Dean becomes relaxing. W.D. is
very low down in a valley. They liked my ideas and then asked me
about a summer house in the garden for Goodwood parties. This
will be fun and I shall be happy, I think, in the doing of it all, a
house about the size of Homewood,[3] but there will be additions
of cloisters etc. and a more generous layout to a glorious south
view.

    James walked with me to the station and here I am.

    I should rather like Barbie to know the James children. The one
3 years old has bright red hair and so funny full of picture
drawing and talk. The middle one talkative with great manual
gestures. The eldest one of 7 or 8 very quiet shy and self-possessed
old maidish too. The most obedient children too.

Barbie

    1. She did have a son, Edward.
    2. Where Lutyens built Monkton House.
    3. Lutyens built Homewood, Hertfordshire for his mother-in-law, Lady
Lytton, in 1900.

Buckhurst,[1] Sussex   Aug.9.02.

I am here and it is just dinner time. I don't know where to begin, but now is as good a time as another.

I don't think Mrs Benson likes St Peter's[2] – at least the south front. She is one of those people who don't understand a blank wall and sees in it no difference from a mere factory wall. Nor does she understand the absence of bay windows and porches, etc. But that is her fault not mine. She did not say anything to me about it though and never mentioned St Peter's at all.

Friday I was awfully busy. I worked in the big office all day and kept them all at it until Nicholson[3] came to dinner – which was very good for me but rather disturbing. He was very amusing and nice, wrote and asked Neville to come and meet him but he wired to say it was impossible. He stayed until 11 and then I took him to see Newgate![4] He had never seen it. Nicholson is going to illustrate the Oxford Colleges and I wanted him to do Newgate before it goes. It would be so splendid for his wood block cutting methods – the stone upon stone – its grim severity and grace withal.

Got to bed about 2 o'c. finishing James's drawings and getting them off.

At about 11 I sallied forth [to watch the Coronation of Edward VII] with top hat and tail coat and got a hansom and drove down Oxford Street and Park Lane – practically no crowd, at least no difficulty to get to one's destination. I got there about 11.45, at Mrs Beaumont's[5] I mean. Guns were fired at 4 o'clock in the morning which woke the whole of London and were going off intermittently all through the day. I met to speak to, Mr Beaumont, gruffy and difficult of soul, Lady Malmesbury and her

---

1. Built by Repton in the 1830s. R. H. Benson, the banker, had taken Buckhurst from Earl De La Warr. Lutyens was altering the house and designing gardens.

2. St Peter's Home, Woolverstone, Suffolk, built by Lutyens for C. H. Berners in 1901.

3. William Nicholson (1872–1949), the painter, one of Lutyens's few great friends outside his work.

4. Newgate Prison, built in 1775–85 by George Dance, was demolished in 1902.

5. Second wife of Wentworth Beaumont, later Viscount Allendale. Their house was 144 Piccadilly.

Sir John.[1] She as vulgar and as assertive as ever, he a regular idiot soldier of distinction in full war paint, orders and medals, but nice, stroking her hand on every occasion and even getting the point of his cocked hat into her eye. Augustus Hare[2] with whom I made agreeable conversation on matters of artistic citizenship.

He has bought the Queen Anne statue [by Francis Bird] that stood before St Paul's and erected the fat lady and her four attendants in his apparently small garden. When you realise she would not go under any tunnel and had to go on 3 trucks lying on her tum tummy you can imagine what it means.

Mrs Beaumont was very talkative and I thought schoolgirlie silly. Very keen that I should induce Mr B. to let her build with me a house – rather nice of her.[3] She, Mrs B. had been staying at Munstead [House] and had evidently had a dose of me! and realises for the first time that I am an architect.

It was a long weary wait and I got hungry and hungrier and feared I should miss my train. The King did not come by until 2.30 instead of 1.30 as expected. The crowd was very quiet and there was a flat feeling of depression – waiting for rain which luckily did not come until Majesty arrived home. And oh Emy 'twas pathetic the sight of it.

Then the procession started to arrive – the guns booming. The Prince and Princess of Wales and escort. Household escort. King. Queen. Household, Colonials, Indians, troops of sorts. No other royal carriages on return journey. Kitchener and Roberts received great ovations to which Roberts saluted and which Kitchener ignored.

The King and Queen with a Filigree looking crown on, well on to the middle of his head – looking dead white and, I thought, very old. The Queen difficult to see being on the far side from me.

1. Susan Hamilton, widow of the 3rd Earl of Malmesbury, married Major-General Sir John Ardagh in 1895.

2. Augustus Hare (1834–1903), author.

3. Though this came to nothing, Lutyens altered 32 Queen Anne's Gate for her in 1907.

All in a real fairy story gilt coach looking absurdly large and ginger bready swaying like a ship at sea.

I cannot help feeling the cheap mockery of the great spirits that moved the men of old to pageantry now but a husk that shelters little aught but sheer vulgarity. But it moved dissolute majesty – dissolving in age so near its dissolution. (Others said how well he looked.) His bow so lame and overpowered by a crown whose shape I could not read. It was a complex muddle of material and might have been feathers!

Some said how handsome he looked and how the crown gave the size to the head demanded by his powerful jaw!

So slowly rocked the gilded coach past out of view. The little knot of colonials on their dowdy bay ponies – in khaki 'mongst the Household Brigade Bands – choked me as much as anything. There was a feeling of simple reality about them that all else seemed to want.

'Twas 3 before 'twas over, and then lunch.

I saw lots of Peers and Peeresses in coronets galore which tickled me. And I like the way the coronets sat on their heads – full, round and fairly – not small things perched all on the top, sitting like a man's straw hat.

 I imagined they would wear them so –

A porter got my bag and I got the train quite comfy and here I am. Top hat and tail coat very uncomfortable.

CHAPTER THREE

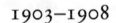

1903–1908

BY 1903, THE YEAR Hussey called his *annus mirabilis*, Lutyens had emerged as the leading English country house architect, and he was increasingly in demand. But the next five years were to see not just the growth of Lutyens's practice, but also a change in his style. Before 1903 most of his houses can be described as romantic vernacular. Between 1903 and 1908 he moved away from this early style towards a new classicism.

Lutyens's turn to classicism has divided his critics. For commentators such as A. S. G. Butler, the disciples of Geoffrey Scott and *The Architecture of Humanism* (1914), Lutyens was quintessentially the heir to the Renaissance. Writing in 1950, Butler dismissed romantic vernacular as a 'kind of infection' to which late-nineteenth-century architects were prone; fortunately in Lutyens's case the 'fever' was a 'transient' one, deserving only the briefest of treatment in the Memorial Volumes.[1] In the 1960s and 1970s the pendulum swung the other way. With the revival of interest in the Arts and Crafts movement – which was, after all, the precursor of the Modern Movement – Lutyens's early vernacular houses came into their own and, taking their cue from Pevsner, critics talked of his 'fatal' reversion to the cul-de-sac of classical revivalism.[2]

Yet in Lutyens's case the dichotomy between romantic and classical was by no means so sharp as these conflicting views suggest. Despite his increasing fascination with the 'grammar' of classicism, Lutyens remained a romantic at heart, and his best classical work is informed by a romantic ability to project his imagination into the life of his buildings. From vernacular architecture too Lutyens derived that skill in the handling of

1. *The Architecture of Sir Edwin Lutyens* (1950), vol. i, p. 19.
2. Pevsner, *An Outline of European Architecture* (Penguin edn, 1953), pp. 266–8; Nairn and Pevsner, *Surrey* (1962), pp. 65–6, 322.

materials that was to distinguish so much of his later work.

Nor was the shift an abrupt one; 1903–8 were years of transition, when Lutyens experimented with a wide variety of styles, combining classicism with Tudor, Jacobean and English Georgian. This was not mere historicism or pastiche. On the contrary, the excitement of these houses derives from Lutyens's extraordinary ability to distill the essence of a style, and thus to reconcile the tensions implicit in the juxtaposition of two conflicting aesthetics, the classical and the romantic.

Not all the houses designed during these years conform to this pattern. Two of the most successful commissions he executed were entirely romantic in spirit: Lindisfarne (1903) and Lambay (1905–12). Both were castles on small islands – Lindisfarne on Holy Island, off the Northumbrian coast, Lambay off the Irish coast near Dublin – and both played an important part in his private life. Lindisfarne was for Edward Hudson, and Lady Emily spent the summer of 1906 there with the children. Lambay was bought as a refuge by Cecil Baring, the banker, later Lord Revelstoke. He had run away with the wife of his New York partner, a charming American, and they were not at first received in London society. At Lambay they lived a life of Arcadian simplicity; Cecil Baring even taught his wife Greek so that they could read Homer and Theocritus together.

Yet there was something new about the romanticism of Lindisfarne and Lambay. In neither case did Lutyens attempt to reproduce the historical styles of the original castles. At Lindisfarne he made use of the existing horizontals of the batteries, and his little castle seems to be part of the rock, a stark, solid mass, 'like some great decayed tooth thrusting out of the mud on the Northumberland coast'.[1] At Lambay Lutyens reached what Hussey has described as 'the climax of his romantic architecture as well as foreshadowing his more abstract conceptions in the future'.[2] With these island castles Lutyens anticipated a new romantic aesthetic, looking forward to the abstract rather than back to the vernacular.

At the opposite pole was the pure classicism of this period. It was in about 1903 that Lutyens conceived an enthusiasm for the 'high game' of Palladio and Wren – a game that called for 'hard labour, hard thinking, over every line in all three dimensions and

1. Gradidge, *Lutyens*, p. 40.
2. Hussey, *Lutyens*, p. 114.

in every joint'[1]. He went some way towards realizing this ideal at Heathcote (1906), a remarkable interpretation of a Palladian villa, but, as he bemoaned, the High Game called for something on a grander scale than the country houses that were his stamping-ground.

His chance of bigger work came with the competition for the new London County Hall building on the south bank of the Thames in 1907. Ninety-nine architects sent in designs and he was one of the eight who were invited to submit detailed plans for the final competition. Lutyens was the only architect who looked at the important site with the other historic riverside buildings in mind, and his design, which was a sensitive one, recalls the work of Inigo Jones at Greenwich. The work involved was colossal, and it was a bitter disappointment when Ralph Knott, who was not even one of the selected eight, was announced the winner.

Meanwhile in Lady Emily's letters the nursery predominates. Nannie Sleath becomes a central figure. The day she first came to the family was celebrated like a birthday; when she came back from her holiday in April 1906 Lady Emily wrote from Homewood, where she was staying with her mother: 'Now I can tell you about Nannie's return. We spent the afternoon making a triumphal arch in the wood with green wreaths and cowslips and Welcome Hurrah in printed letters.' Ursula, her father's favourite, was born three years after Robert in 1904, Elisabeth in 1906 and Mary in 1908.

Years later, in May 1944, Lady Emily was rereading these letters, and she wrote to Ursula, by then Lady Ridley: 'I have just got to Betty's birth and the summer at Holy Island. Such a strange world to go back to. Father's feeling so frustrated because no big work came his way, constant worry about money, I always feeling ill and tired with babies coming or nursing, both of us fretting over separations that were quite unnecessary. It is like reading a novel having looked at the end.' The seaside holidays, so unnecessary in retrospect, were never questioned in Lady Emily's letters. At that date it was unthinkable for someone of her social background to remain in London during August.

From 1903 onwards the tedium of these holidays was broken by Mrs Webbe, or Aunt Pussey as she was called by the children. The wife of A. J. Webbe the cricketer, she was a great talker and an enthusiast for women's rights, which she and Lady Emily

1. Letter to Herbert Baker, 15 February 1903, ibid., p. 122.

would endlessly discuss. Lutyens could not abide her. Ursula Ridley remembered being told 'how she used to go to the Lock Hospital and read aloud fairy stories to the prostitutes suffering from VD' – an activity in which she was later joined by Lady Emily. After 1906, when his wife died, Arthur Chapman joined the party. He stayed either in the boarding house or in a hotel nearby and played golf. He was lonely and enjoyed family life and was no doubt in love with Lady Emily in a quiet way. She enjoyed his companionship. In August 1907 she wrote to Lutyens: 'I wish we could ever have fun together. I miss Chip Chap so, which makes me realise what a great pleasure in life is doing things in company and having interests in common.'

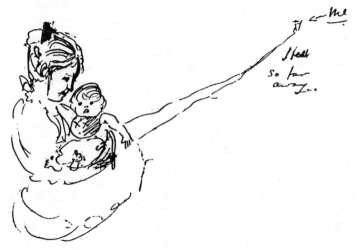

In train to Holy Island   Aug.24.03.

May,[1] the architect, called the other day and wanted to know if I had built anything in the nearer parts of Kent and Sussex as he was going on a walking tour with his second son who is to be an architect and he wanted to show him my work. He hoped I wouldn't mind. I told him I looked upon it as a subtle form of flattery – and he hoped I would. It is rather nice to have professional admirers. He wants to take me to the Art Workers' Guild to introduce me. That too is flattering. I haven't been there

1. E. J. May, best-known for his Arts and Crafts houses in the home counties.

for ten or eleven years, and then no one knew me and those few that did patronised or snubbed me.

I met Reginald Blomfield[1] at Waterloo Thursday and talked a little, and we agreed how terrible was Aston Webb's[2] work. He laughed at my idea of cutting a statue of W. Robinson in yew! as a monument to all he has done for gardening.

May laughed at my joke calling the A.A. [Architectural Association] the I.I.

Are my stupid jokes depressing you? It is like holding you at arms length that I may draw you back closer to me.

Little did I think when I first saw you at Blumey's[3] all that great store of happiness you held for me, though I knew by some strange instinct, and the knowledge of it flashed upon me on first sight of you, that there was a face I could always find happiness with and that must be eight or nine years ago, was it that I read in your dear face your absolute unselfishness, your great moral courage? darling? Those very qualities I most have need of. It was no body need you appealed to then, but how soon that followed!

Those days at Milford recalling to mind the green stain following the contours of that beloved nose and cheek![4] Do you remember? That letter that turned the ill cleaned Onslow Square into a heaven of burnished gold, in which you said you might have loved me well – which meant you did.

In train, London to Felixstowe   Sept.9.03.

I have been so busy and rushed, Thomas[5] being away too. I have lots to tell you of a mild kind. Yesterday I went to Buckhurst and

---

1. Sir Reginald Blomfield (1856–1942) was President of the RIBA 1912–14. Elisabeth Lutyens quoted her father as saying to him: '"You are a werry nice man but a werry, werry bad architect." (He could never pronounce his Vs.)' (*A Goldfish Bowl* (1973), p. 44.)

2. Sir Aston Webb (1849–1930) was at that time President of the RIBA. He was generally disparaged by the more progressive architects: in 1901 he had won the competition for the Victoria Memorial, for which Lutyens had made a design.

3. Jacques Blumenthal and his wife were friends of Barbara Webb's and Gertrude Jekyll's. It was at a musical evening in their house that Lutyens first met Lady Emily in 1896.

4. She was wearing a green straw hat and the dye had run down her nose.

5. A. J. Thomas joined Lutyens as his office manager in 1902 and remained with him until 1935.

stayed the night. They are quite pleased with the garden so far. He is 'fascinated' by the circular stairways and niches.

Went down to the Groves and found them all camping out. Mrs G. cooked the most excellent delicious ragout of veal, beans broad and French, bacon, potatoes quite excellent in casserole and French tasting, an excellent Irish stew, an excellent macaroni all on a little oil stove about 1′6″ square in a tent she had to crawl in and out of.

The site is quite quite good.[1]

Bob Webb and Mrs Grove

29 Bloomsbury Square   Sept. 16.03.

I am in the train on my way back to London from the Hoo.[2] The Hoo is a great success – all windows! You must see it, and I am treated with great deference as architect and all my jokes are much appreciated! so I am cheered. After arriving we went onto the Downs and flew a box kite. I got out a mile of string! It cleared my headache. Today is lovely, warm and sunny. Directly I get to London I must go off to Petersham Terrace[3] but I have wired for someone to meet me at Victoria with letters, which will include yours!

1. For Pollard's Wood, Chalfont St Giles, Buckinghamshire, a Georgian-style house with green shutters, that Lutyens designed, but never built, for Archibald Grove, who had found Berrydown unsatisfactory. Forbes, of Forbes & Tait, was employed instead.

2. The Hoo, near Eastbourne, altered for Alexander Wedderburn, KC (1854–1931), best-known as editor, with Sir E. T. Cook, of the Library Edition of the works of Ruskin in 38 vols, 1903–9.

3. No. 7, which Lutyens was altering for Adam Black.

I have found some very pretty blue linen and I have ordered a dozen table cloths. Is this good of me?

My own little love I do want you back and at home. I want you to see [Little] Thakeham and the Hoo.

I shall write again today sometime.

29 Bloomsbury Square   March 16.04.

How dear and kind of you to write me about Crooksbury. I am so glad you went over, saw it and liked it and the Chapmans have been such kind friends. That ingle nook chimney smoked awfully at first and we bored holes and did other things they have forgotten.[1] I do wish I could do things at Homewood for you to forget!

I have not seen Fastnedge [the builder] yet, I feel very cross with him for telling you there were differences between Homewood and Betty's. Constructionally there ain't. Floors, roofs etc. are the same as Fishers Hill.

An early idea for Fisher's Hill

It makes me miserable to think that you are not absolutely happy, absolutely content, absolutely comfortable in a house of mine! *You* of all dear people.

Homewood is much better than Crooksbury I think as regards architecture etc.[2] and when it all grows up and the sore places in the grounds heal up, it will look very well, but what do this matter if you are cold and draught ridden?

1. Lutyens's chimneys were notorious for smoking.
2. 'What gives such notable character to the whole design,' wrote Butler of Homewood, 'is the deliberate conjunction – in the high Ionic order and the rustication – of elements of palace architecture with elm weather-boarding and plain tiled roofs in the most vernacular cottage mode' (*Architecture*, vol. i, p. 31). Homewood was virtually ignored by Hussey, much to the indignation of Pamela Lytton whose husband had commissioned it. It became a second home to the Lutyens children.

Homewood. 'On the garden side the complex roof is cut away to reveal a small white classical villa emerging from a weatherboarded shell' (*Catalogue 1981*, p. 85).

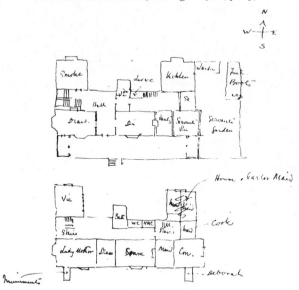

Sketch plans for Homewood in a letter to Lady Lytton,
2 August 1900

Buckhurst   April 23.04.

We have started the gardens at Hestercombe.[1] It is such a typical
self satisfied comfortable English sporting-squire of a house and
place. I shouldn't be surprised to be presented to porter and
oysters between meals – but one isn't. Breakfasts, luncheons,
teas, dinners, enormous vast quantities of foods and wines for
four persons – our number. Yet if Thomas is with me or a builder
I ask if they had got any lunch they shrug shoulders and say they
got a bit of cold curry or half cold mutton.

He spends his money on eating, hospitals and cattle breeding
and is, to boot, a real good sort (not mine a bit)! She, Lady
Bountiful and bazaar opener to the county and surrounded with
refractory puppies that never behave or are let behave. When
Lord Portman dies they will roll in gold.

Frank Bellville came in this morning rather perturbed on the
slow progress of Papps.[2]

Newnes perturbed about the endless difficulties with the LCC,
the Borough Council and the Bedford office, but we are starting
at last.[3]

Francis Smith [the family solicitor] came in to lunch and was
shocked at the big balance at the bank that I had. So I invested, on
his advice, £300 in Harrod's Stores. This makes over the £1000
saved! and I have even now in the bank £650 with £350 to come
in this coming week and another £150 next, so I ought to put by
another 500 or 600 next month. It is nice to think you will have at
least £1200 should I die, besides your own.

1. The celebrated Italianate garden built in collaboration with Gertrude
Jekyll for the Hon. E. W. Portman (1856–1911). Yet it is not every gardener's
garden. 'Under the influence of Miss Jekyll', wrote Harold Nicolson, '[Lutyens]
brought his architecture tumbling down into the garden, and we find the
unfortunate masonry of Hestercombe' (*Friday Mornings* (1944), p. 213).

2. Frank Bellville (1870–1937), who did little else but hunt, was the heir to a
fortune in Keen's mustard, thus giving a new meaning to the family advertising
slogan 'keen as mustard'. Papillon Hall, built on a butterfly plan – a typical
Lutyens pun – is a masterpiece of geometrical ingenuity. But Ursula Ridley,
reflecting the taste of her time, wrote to Lady Emily on 26 July 1950, just before
it was demolished: 'I feel rather relieved that it is going. . . . His very worst
Kingston By Pass manner in roughcast which is always ugly and a lot of half
timber bogosity.'

3. On the *Country Life* Building, Tavistock Street. Sir George Newnes
(1851–1910), Liberal MP and newspaper proprietor, was a business associate
of Edward Hudson's.

Kit Turnor[1] has asked me to stay next Saturday at Stoke and fish. I don't think I can go but I should rather like to see him in the middle of his many thousands of acres. He is so odd and mad, so full of original ideas, principally agricultural, quite clever, at least receptive, architecturally. The possessor of lovely drawings by the Italian and Dutch masters and to boot an admiration for my attempts! You know his father has renounced all the estates, money, everything, to Kit, so that he may still wander the world without responsibility delivering Plymouth Brother tracts in South America and the Antipodes generally.

29 Bloomsbury Square   July 24.04.

The Jameses sent their motor to meet me and I was whisked up to Monkton, seven miles in 20–23 minutes or less. All up hill, some 600 foot of solid rise.

They have been staying at the new house for some days, since the 15th. Mrs James was awfully nice about it and said she was sorry to have worried me about things and that she sensed she was wrong about her windows.

I left my pipe in the train so all day I was pipeless and James don't smoke.

The builder turned up about 2 and at 3 we all returned to West Dean. They have their Goodwood party there next week. It is a pure invention that the Wales's go there. My train left Pulborough 5.45, so I had a good two hours at West Dean – tried a new motor hill-climbing and then started Mrs James rearranging the big hall and left her with it half done. I managed with about three men to get rid of an enormous palm, two screens, a large white stuffed bear and an old sedan chair – and then there was enormously too much in the room.

I told Mrs J. about the Dolgorouki[2] woman. She says she is no one – vulgar, but kind and very fond of entertaining, to style her HH and that she would take any amount of it. That is all my James gossip.

1. Christopher Turnor (1873–1940), a leading agricultural reformer; he lived at Stoke Rochford, Grantham.
2. Fanny Wilson, a Lancashire heiress, who married in 1898 the Russian Prince Alexis Dolgorouki.

I bought two 8d pipes at Pulborough.

I got to Thakeham[1] about eight. A most divine evening. The great Downs bathed in reflected light and the garden wonderfully good. Blackburn is very slow apparently, but is really an artist and he does little at a time but what he does is singularly good I think. He has made the pergola delightful – in a way quite his own – with hollyhocks – and to enjoy the effect he postpones planting the more permanent things. His attitude is so unlike the general of people – like leaving a picture unfinished to enjoy the initial stages.

The children's gardens are very amusing. The four of them. There is no place for the fifth. Rather sad, and they say it was unkind of me. I retorted they could all be divided and so make eight. Aileen's garden was dull but tidy and fairly full. Sylvia's garden was rather wayward, Barbara's absolutely neglected, Aubrey's garden, aged 4 is really wonderful, he watches things grow, knows the names of all his plants and is thrilled and thrilling over it, so wise and sensible, picks off dead things, weeds, waters, propagates with sense and care. He has a row of sweet peas and roared with laughter at the idea of their climbing sticks, he put them in under protest, now in transport of delight, they climb! The lawn is covered with guinea pigs. I do wish we could have a garden and a country house and if only we could do that combined with sea and river it would be perfect.

In train from Ascot   July 31.04.

I dined at Ascot and must tell you about my day, amusing and I think successful. I write you in the train to tell you whilst my impressions are red hot, and to pass the time – a horrid excuse for a letter to my own particular pet angel.

I told you I caught an earlier not to be mentioned in Bradshaw train and so caught the Princess [Dolgorouki] unawares. I walked

1. Built in 1902 for Ernest Blackburn, the talented amateur gardener, Little Thakeham, Sussex, has a Tudor exterior containing a classical hall. 'Perhaps the enchantment of this house,' wrote Butler, 'may be summarised in its containing, within the vesture of a rough, solid, traditional Sussex building, an unsuspected jewel of invention in its principal room. In that way it resembles a distinguished old lady who lives in the country and, fading beautifully, wears her pearl necklace beneath a worn but well-cut raincoat' (*Architecture*, vol. i, p. 29). Lutyens described it as 'the best of the bunch' of his country houses of that date.

up and was in time to stop the carriage being sent for me. She sent a message down from her room to say she would be half an hour, and sent me a book of the Prince's sketches! awful things and exhaustible in two minutes. On her table was the July *Quarterly* and I had nice time to read the article on the Tsar, and which I very nearly bought so I felt I was earning six shillings by my wait, reading the notorious article. She came down about two minutes after I had finished it so I felt in a position to question her about the state of Russia. If she had not been shy, she said, she would have received me in her bedroom, of which she gave an amusing description with her bed cover of green velvet – how the train shakes.

Well, she came down and talked generally but soon started house.[1] It seemed hopeless. She not only wanted red carpets all over the staircase but – a red plush handrail!

Soon before lunch Hamilton Aide[2] came in and I would call him Augustus Hare! Most unfortunate as the two men were not on speaking terms! He left and in came a Colonel Cooper (was it ?) sort of relation with whom Hamilton Aide lives and has his 80 year old being. A more corpse like and resurrected roué than even Augustus Hare – I mean Aide. The Princess says I was the attraction which of course flattered me immensely, although I pooh-poohed it with excellent dissimulation. After lunch (a very bad one) we started off in a gorgeous Victoria – C springed and larded with royal crowns and those appalling liveries – blue with red facings and braid made up of crowns and arms – red on a silver ground – too awful – to view sites, and ended with tea with Frank Schuster[3] at Bray in a horrid little bungalow all frills and quite sexless. Some very pretty things, of course, and things I should like. I have never seen so many unmannish men in one day. I chaffed the Princess about her 'ITS' which delighted her. We called on Aide and Mrs Ross of Florence[4] was there, but I hardly had a word with her as she only appeared as we were leaving. I looked at a lot of Aide sketches. Quite interesting – to me – but not much as pictures.

1. Nashdom, Taplow, reminiscent of a palace outside St Petersburg, was designed entirely for entertaining; it is 'a particularly good example of Lutyens's fulfilling of his client's needs' (*Catalogue 1981*, p. 121).

2. Hamilton Aide (d. 1907), described himself in *Who's Who* as 'private gentleman, novelist and dramatist'.

3. For whom Lutyens had done work at Wimbledon in 1899.

4. Janet Ross, author of *Leaves from Our Tuscan Kitchen* (1899).

We got back to lodgings about eight, had dinner and then I got away to the station by 9.30. I can scarce credit it but we have actually arrived at a scheme in which *we both* have pleasure! I have got her over the plush handrail by putting the staircase between walls without a handrail at all! and managed her suites of rooms and the fitting of them to our mutual satisfaction. At times I despaired and wanted to throw it all up, if I had moral courage – more courage, ordinary – I should have, and now I thank goodness for my weakness which gives me such apparent patience. She seems on good terms with King and Queen and Princess Christian [of Schleswig-Holstein]. I asked her how it was she came to me. The Farquharson[1] that was in my office is her cousin and her relations wanted her to employ him, but he had done something she didn't like and thought not clever, and what would she do if he did little unclever things all over the house?! So my name was mentioned and she came against everyone's advice, as they told her that I build houses of my own type – a type not at all suited to her. But she said she couldn't get a clever man without a type of his own and she would rather deal with and get what she wanted from a clever man than from an ordinary man who did what she wanted and let her in for mistakes. It is rather wise, don't you think? and very flattering and I feel very pleased *now* that we are agreed on general lines and realise I can do what I should like and yet give her what she wants. She sticks to her fountain in the middle of the dining room table and in one or two other small things, but I get mine in all permanent things and things that will matter so long as the house stands.

On leaving she taught me to kiss her hand – all her nephews did it, she said. You would have laughed. I did. Specially when I found I couldn't keep my pointed nose from pecking it. I told her I could not do it before Hamilton Aide. She said I must, it would teach him manners!

My big news I keep to the last and that is that she has five miles of salmon fishing on the Dee and I am to go and fish there next year, and I may take Vic. This would be fun and save the long journeys to Norway. She has let it this year. She told me amusing things about her husband – how he was nearly a Mahometan ('She didn't mean that') how he won't ring a bell but calls and if he isn't answered after three low muttered appeals he goes

1. Horace Farquharson (1874–1966).

without. If a house is not comfortable or as he likes it, he says nothing but goes away! It sounds – and she nearly said so – Barbarian. I do hope it will all prove a success and it will bring in work.

29 Bloomsbury Square   Aug.4.04.

Drove out with Guest who met me at Rugby. He has been staying at Blenheim.[1] Saw the trustees' surveyor who has apparently an admiration for my work, which will make it easy. We played our town game – this time with Ashby as a site. We are going! to bring in the Grand Junction Canal in a lovely way – white horses on the tow path, rubbed green by the brass work of their harness; a great dock with heavy cranes made of oak – windmills – a lovely townscape with hall, houses, etc. The trades we shall start, encourage, and develop are – tapestry, wrought iron, barge building, waggon building, boots, weaving, linen, fabrics, clocks, etc. etc. Great fun!

Got all contracts signed. When I get back from Norway I am going to see Blenheim with Guest. This may be fun.

There is a great deal I do admire in Booton church, but the result is so painful in so many ways and so ugly and the way materials are used so unsympathetic and in my opinion wrong. So I suppose I don't like it.[2]

Your wedding letter came tonight. Darling you have made me happy and it is you that have enabled me to give you happiness. It is darling of you to say so and I do love to hear it and cherish the thought. No joy so great as that of giving one's best loved real permanent happiness.

1. Ivor Guest (1873–1939), who succeeded as Lord Wimborne in 1914, was a Liberal politician. Known as 'the paying Guest' on account of his immense wealth (and vulgarity), he was a first cousin of the Duke of Marlborough. Between 1904 and 1938 Lutyens made a series of additions to his house and gardens at Ashby St Legers.

2. In 1902 A. C. Benson described Booton as 'an extraordinary church with two towers recently built by Elwin, Editor of *Quarterly Review* – designed by himself. Hideous in the extreme – towers set lozenge wise to the church, all thick where it ought to be thin, and thin where it ought to be thick. I never saw a more pathetic place. It must have cost £50,000 and is designed in a sort of bastard Gothic' (David Newsome ed., *Edwardian Excursions* (1981), p. 87). As Lutyens remarked, it was 'very naughty but built in the right spirit' (*A Blessed Girl*, p. 22).

In train to Market Harboro'   Feb.4.05.

I work much later when you are away which is good, and I go up
at 12 and then read for an hour so I sleep bang through without a
stop till Whitney comes with tea and paper, later with letters and
then breakfast. I blow the lift whistle when I go to the bath for
Boch, and return to find my clothes laid out and am down by 9.15
which is good. I sorely miss nursery distractions, but by working
late and by being a little earlier there are few moments of absolute
and immediate pine for you all.

I wrote Mrs Franklyn[1] last night a short letter. I wrote one out
first, what I call a beautiful letter, but 2nd thoughts reduced it and
left out all the beauty spots. I said 'To be quite frank my first
thought on reading your letter was why you did not consult me
about the work and about an architect' – she said she wanted a
man young enough to take an interest in the work but old enough
to be trusted – so I said 'I am old enough alas to be no longer
young, I can lay no claim to fame and that I am "so busy" as I have
often heard repeated may do me harm and end my business'. She
said about being busy and about fame. George thinks she wants
me and so does Thomas. I proposed an interview and said that
I didn't know the men she mentioned, and that I could not well

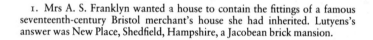

discuss my architectural colleagues in a letter. I shall tell
you what is the result.

Yesterday afternoon I
spent at [the *Country Life*
building] Tavistock Street. Sir
George Newnes said very
little, nothing nice, nothing
nasty. Hudson is very nervous
with him. It will be a great
thing if he is pleased, if he isn't it can't be
helped. I don't know whether I shall be
pleased.

I funk the chimneys and they are going
up up up and the two of them will look

---

1. Mrs A. S. Franklyn wanted a house to contain the fittings of a famous
seventeenth-century Bristol merchant's house she had inherited. Lutyens's
answer was New Place, Shedfield, Hampshire, a Jacobean brick mansion.

enormous, like two campaniles perched on my big roof and if I reduce the height a–b it throws the proportion c–d all out and wrong looking. I am nerving myself for some decision on Monday.

I must go to Bumps and to Ashby next week. Today I am going to the Bellvilles.

If you have a chance do go and see Bob Webb or get him over to Betty's.[1] I do feel we have neglected the poor old chap and he may think we are ungrateful and forgetful, for in his own particular reticent twinkling way he did help us and aid and abet his Mrs Webb of beloved memory.

I nearly forgot everything, money, papers and note paper. I remembered money at the last minute. I got this paper at a bookstall, but have left behind me various notes and papers I wanted for the job. A bore, but can't be helped.

Hudson will build at Huntercombe and I wanted it to be (as it must be) small, dignified, simple and precious, and to lay out to the glorious view across Oxfordshire.

Lympne will fall through, it would cost a lot of money, and everyone would exclaim about the small windows, which were absolutely essential to the character and archaeological bias of the place. You can't put plate glass windows in a fortress and yet keep it in its original state of defence, can you?[2]

Lady Helen[3] called yesterday but I was out. She do fuss me: we had a long conversation on the telephone after. She is sponge-cake or a lovely easter egg with nothing inside, terribly dilletante and altogether superficial. I feel cross with her and long at times to contrive that an elephant should give her a baby! (This is petulant and not all meant but . . .)

Herbert [Jekyll] is in complete agreement with me about Versailles and indeed all that work its *immense* inferiority to our English work. After the great schools of Greece and Italy nothing approaches English work. (Excepting the great French Gothic cathedrals superb and wonderfully glorious.) As a work of art

1. Lady Emily was staying at Fisher's Hill, Woking.
2. Neither of these Hudson projects materialised. Lympne Castle was eventually renovated by Lorimer for H. J. Tennant.
3. The wife of Sir Edgar Vincent (1859–1941), later Lord D'Abernon. Harold Nicolson described her as 'the most beautiful woman that I have ever seen' (*Friday Mornings*, p. 22). Lutyens designed the sunken garden for her at Esher Place, Surrey.

Versailles cannot be compared with our Hampton Court. This for a firm belief is very comforting.

It would be delicious to have a house of our own, but I want so much.

1st.   The best I know
2.   high ground for you
3.   a river for me.
This means
1.   £.s.d.
2. & 3. a large parcel of ground.
               total   <u>£.s.d.</u>

and that is the most difficult of all worldly things, the only worldly gift we haven't got and there is so so so much we have.

What fun it all really is, aren't you glad we are married, safely, securely tied up together, and no Badcock, debts or unnormal worries. Anxieties we must always have and by our love they become the very salt of life, my little sweetheart that you ever are.

Then I get so anxious in my work, the work that has been, the work that is and that which is to be or not! so many little half formed inexpressible almost unconscious thoughts of it surround me and it seems at times a barrier between us, it isn't really, except that it is mine and a failing though natural (such a convenient excuse) too, and if it was yours to share it would jar and become irksome and settle as some dead weight upon us both.

If real tribulation should ever overtake us it is you that will be the braver and *so* brave and then my gain will be untold. I don't want you to be cross over small things, over things which may generously and fairly be considered accidents (oh how they do annoy). It's small and unlike our real big self, little love (little is a term of *deep* affection). It makes me cross too and I hate it and think it wrong as bad as drink! What a scold! But I want you to show all your grace and Godfulness. You see I am an architect and it is by eye one judges my little pet. As I want you to be clothed with pearls and lovely raiment and have all around you and of you more lovely than is possible in this world, so I want your own sweet patient soul ever to shine and be present to the eye and not wrapped in your heart. Though I know it is always there and I know too! how to dig for it at any time and the briars you sometimes grow about it.

I just want to hug you and bless you and kiss you and oh to be so gentle, you know I *wish* that don't you? I wish I was strong and big and muscular, for the actions of strong men are always more gentle, it is always a weak man that upsets a garden vase or smashes the life sized marble group on the high pedestal and a strong man is quieter and less easily moved by impulses, at least I can imagine it.

It is such a lovely day. I long to get out of the train.

Your very own Emy possessed Ned.

This is Harboro.

Fisher's Hill   *Feb.5.05.*

I love your scolds and all you say. I know I am a bad cross thing. I will try. Thank God you are such an angel to help me.

29 Bloomsbury Square   Feb.10.05.

I have evidently hooked Mrs Franklyn

I wonder what she is like.

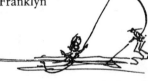

29 Bloomsbury Square   March 5.05.

Do go unless you really would rather not to dinner with Hudson Tuesday night. Sir George Newnes is such a dear man and I should like to get to know him privately, it might lead to a great deal too. I have only met Lady Newnes once. She is I think a plain housekeepery body. Sir George has a nice open face with a keen blue eye, a good sort of radical and without any side or pretension, very kind, very cool headed and unemotional. He might help you enormously too with your [good] works! and it would be such fun to hear your account of the dinner. It would please Hudson too.

You are such a darling to me and I am very very much in love with you. God bless you little one.

Homewood   *April 27.05.*

I have been thinking it would be such fun if we could arrange some small intimate evening parties for discussion of interesting subjects. The talk we had here when Mrs Webbe came down made me feel how interesting parties might be made if one could only talk on really interesting subjects. I am sure with Pussie and Ottoline[1] we could arrange it. I feel I could make that kind of entertaining a success.

29 Bloomsbury Square   April 28.05.

Yes, let us have dinners *amusants et instructifs*. I want one on St Paul's Cathedral, Herbert Jekyll, St Paul's architect, Hudson etc. I don't think it will do to announce a discussion on an interesting subject.

Old Rectory, Broadchalke, Salisbury   *July 21.05.*

Even Neville was quite smart yesterday in a grey flannel suit and white silk shirt and I did wish you could have something nice and

1. Lady Ottoline Morrell (1873–1938).

———

Lady Emily in 1905 – the young matron

clean and cool. Pamela said they had talked of your awful clothes for three days after the picnic! It is naughty of you not to take a little trouble to look nice when you have such a dear face. Hot stuffy clothes in hot weather smell and make other people feel hot and it is therefore selfish. But I mustn't scold you when you are away must I love, only you spend quite a lot with such very bad results because you don't take trouble and care.

29 Bloomsbury Square   July 22.05.

Went yesterday to Princess Alexis [Dolgorouki]. We drove out. She has found a really lovely site but quite unsuited to the house she insists on! She wants to spend £6,000. I told her it could not be done under £11 to £12,000, but she says it must and that I *can* do it and laughs and won't listen and says she doesn't mind if part of it doesn't stand for more than 20 years! I told her it wouldn't stand for 5 minutes and if it were built to last for 20 it would begin to come to pieces in 5 or 10 years. But she says Oh it can be done in an airy way. So I have arranged to see her man of business. I will draw out the house she wants but will not be responsible for the cost. She is very funny about it. She has the money but I cannot believe her serious. She is a rummun. I did not kiss her hand.

I am so sorry about my clothes. I should like George[1] and Victor to form a committee and set me up in clothes!

Princess Alexis read me letters from what she calls her Prince wherein he was expected to be attacked by miners and how the villagers patrolled his house and perturbed him. A government official arrived and asked the people if they had any grievances and they said no.

29 Bloomsbury Square   Aug.15.05.

On my way back from Ashby. No particular news by this morning's post and no letter from you.

A long letter from Mallet. He likes the sketches for the new Varengeville house.[2]

1. George Wemyss, married to Lutyens's elder sister Molly.
2. Perhaps *Clos du Dan*, a design never executed, or 'the dream house', *Les Communes*, built in 1909.

———

[Ivor] Guest quite nice and the same and all right. I had it all out with him and arranged a status quo over the accounts question. The cottages are to go on. I have got another £300 for them and a lot of stone and other material so the price has become possible.

He talks of going on with the house etc. and the garden; the house at some indefinite period, the gardens at once. There are one or two things he don't like and he is nicely outspoken about them and there is a great deal more that he does like. Marlborough seems to have been there again and approving. I do hope I get something to do at Blenheim, but I didn't like to question Guest.

He, Guest, had been over to Papillon Hall. He likes it and thinks it extraordinary clever etc., and sees the enormous difficulties that had to be met. He prefers Ashby, which is right. Lady Juliet Duff was there, who was she, a niece of Lord Pembroke's? [She was.] She talked of building but I didn't like to shove myself, as Guest was there! and might have snubbed. I say this just to describe my *arrière pensées*, my indefinite instincts of a sore being there. An excellent lunch.

A long letter from Madame Blumenthal,[1] breezy and amusing. She wants me to go to Hyde Park Gardens to see something, but says 'for heaven's sake let the caretaker know as she is apt to disappear in the attics to cut her toe nails and doesn't hear the bell'. This rather grued against my soul!

Guest knows Princess Stephanie they call her Stuffany and she likes being treated as Royal.[2] She has no money. Emperor of Austria allows her £10,000 a year, he may be building her a house. I hope so, as he has heaps.

Princess Alexis [Dolgorouki] telegraphed to me last night to come to Ascot today, important, but I couldn't go. I wonder what her game is now, a site she has found and for which she is about to offer half its asked for price.

---

1. Lutyens was altering Queen's House, Chelsea, for Madame Jacques Blumenthal.

2. A daughter of Leopold II of Belgium, Princess Stephanie (1854–1945) was first married to Crown Prince Rudolph of Austria, who committed suicide at Mayerling in 1889. In 1900 she married the Hungarian Count Elemar Lonyay. Later in 1905 Lutyens went to Hungary to alter their house, Bodrog Olaszi, Zemplen. 'This [is a] really terrible house,' Lutyens wrote when he got there, 'I walked about round the house and did it 7 times, blowing my own trumpet in the hopes that the walls would fall down, but they haven't' (6 October 1905).

Ivor Guest has bought 1 or 2 motors and has a heap of smart horses, polo ponies and a perfect army of men servants, with a groom of the chambers.

No other news. I have written a lot of letters. I go to Cromer tomorrow.

29 Bloomsbury Square   Aug.29.05.

I am very distressed indeed to see in the papers that Frank Bellville has been upset out of his car and fractured his skull.[1] His condition is critical *The Times* says. I do hope he will recover. I am really very fond of him and like and admire so much of him. I do hope nothing worse will happen and that he will recover and enjoy my Papps. It is odd the Papps prophecies and that this should happen. Everybody owning Papps is supposed to come to misfortune – the haunting red dog – the finding of a man and dog skeleton – the slipper legend – etc., etc. Do people recover from fractured skulls? Surely yes. He is so big and strong too and so really generous, patient and kind to his impossible wife. He does and thinks much that is not of the nicest but there is such a wealth of bigness and generosity and fair dealing about him and his faults are those of the untutored animal. He has a real good nature. However, I suppose my Saturday visit will be postponed and I am awfully disappointed. . . .

Saw Lonyay and Princess Stephanie. I go [to] Hungary [the] last week in September or first in October. Very kind and admiring but he don't think my scheme is possible and will cost too much. I must see the place. He wants me to stay two weeks. I can't. He talks of other houses to build and friends who want palaces etc., etc. I am delighted of course but it means nothing but the compliment of wishing to get me out there.

He told me Leopold of Belgium allows them nothing and that he has £3 million a year and is building a cathedral and a huge Palace, spending mints. Some money has to go to his family but he'll spend all he can. Lonyay has a place near Vienna where they would build, I suppose if Leopold leaves 'em money and he won't leave more than he can help. Wish I could build for Leopold! a job for £3,000,000 would set us up and give us at least £150,000 – in the mean time I enclose you £8.

1. 'his jaunting-car . . . struck a gate post. The horse plunged and the car was overturned, striking Mr Bellville on the head' (*The Times*, 29 August 1905).

In train to Alton, Hants   Sept.12.05.

I slept last night at Lady Hannen's, going down with Bo to see about the Columbarium for Ted Hannen.[1]

I am on my way now to Chawton – Monty Knight – an old house he is very proud of.[2] He restores a window or so every year or two. I am putting in two in the hall now and in opening out the old wall they have found some old beams and this necessitates my going down as it upsets the scheme and I don't want them moved.

Tomorrow I go to Marshcourt and will take my rod and have the last fish of the year.

Can you think of a really beautiful text for the inside of the Columbarium? Bo Hannen has found one – reported to me as being to the effect that the Lord is God of the Dead or God of the Living and it don't either way sound right. I have no drear emblems – I have praising angels, peacocks, whose flesh was held to be incorruptible and were taken by the early Christians as an emblem of immortality. Then I have various happy little thoughts and the building is surmounted by a cross enclosing the figure of Our Lord ascending and emblems of the evangelists. Commonplace but cheerful, hopeful and all easily read. Inside I want a fine rolling sentence – simple – of hope, faith and of an all pervading love. If the Bible don't give it I wouldn't mind a poet or philosopher – a good thought is always inspired. Rather like the messages in Bunyan's *Pilgrim's Progress* sent by those who crossed the river to those that were left and had yet to face the crossing. Do you remember them?

1. Nicholas (Bo) Hannen was an assistant in Lutyens's office from 1902 to 1910; he later became an actor-manager. The Columbarium was the Hannen mausoleum at St Mary's, Wargrave, Berkshire.

2. Chawton had been in the possession of the Knight family since the sixteenth century. Jane Austen often stayed there with her elder brother Edward, who had taken the name Knight.

The billiard room at Marshcourt

Marshcourt[1] at dinner   Sept.13.05.

Here I am at dinner alone – in state. The *big* red bed is ready for me. Rich oxtail soup. The next best thing to being with Emmieown is to write to her – a poor substitute I own. Filleted soul. I worked all the morning and then after lunch went out to fish. I caught 2 of 2½ lbs each and very good, and lost 2, and touched one or two more – all good fun. Then a hurried tea and out again. I missed one or two and caught two which I put back. Going down the river we saw an Enormous trout – after tea we saw the trout again – and Oh! coming home in the dark we saw him again. So I fished for him for the fun of it. Suddenly a dead steady pull at the line – and at a slow deliberate pace my reel

1. Marshcourt, Hants was built in 1901–4 for Herbert Johnson, whom Hussey described as 'the ideal type of Lutyens client', an ' "adventurer", stockjobber and sportsman' (*Lutyens*, p. 100). Built of chalk (as a bet), with a chalk billiard-table, Marshcourt is situated on the River Test, and 'there is a sense that the place was conceived as a great hunting lodge for a vigorous client' (*Catalogue 1981*, p. 107).

unwound. It could not be the big one?! The line slackened and I reeled in for all I was worth and there almost at my feet was the BIG (Roast lamb) trout. He came close up alongside and Baker and myself we gasped. He saw us and went off, not at any great speed but just at a good deliberate pace and my reel clicked out its merry song. I feared he was going into some weeds so I checked my reel – the speed did not vary – the weight of the fish was irresistible, it seemed, and then slack the rod straightened – he was lost! He must have been 5 lbs at least! It was too dark to fish more so I came home and played on the AEolian [pianola] – 'The dead march in Saul'. So endeth my last fish for 1905. Oh dear.

Pigeon and salad and then a savoury to come – coffee, port. Too much and it is such a bore alone and a lot of different courses – why not a soup and another fat partridge and have done with it?

Now I go round the house with Mrs Binns. It is a jolly warm evening so I have ordered a fire in the billiard room.

I am in bed and pray God Bless my darling.

29 Bloomsbury Square   April 27.06.

Pam and Vic came last night at 8 and left at 9. Such a wretched dinner they had they will never come again when I am alone. The cook knows nothing. I asked for spaghetti and grated cheese and an awful pasty doughy looking rice came up, for Convent Eggs horrid little half eggs with anchovy. I saw her for the first time, she do look a worm poor thing.

Homewood   *April 28.06.*

How could you expect to have a good dinner for Pam and Vic when you only order it an hour or so before lunch. There was no spaghetti in the house I expect, and the risotto dish requires many hours of preparation. Convent Eggs is a receipt in Pot Pourri *[by Mrs Earle] she has never had and of course would not know unless you found it for her. I am only glad you should realise the enormous amount of trouble required to teach the cooks. You don't know what I have to teach them all and the time I spend over it. This cook is dreadfully stupid and knows nothing, but she can do well from a receipt which is something and she is economical and honest and clean.*

---

29 Bloomsbury Square   May 4.06.

The Birds accept £7800[1] and more to follow and Mrs Franklyn accepts £9300 with more to follow, so I have got signed and sealed this week £34,600 which means £1730 for us. We shall be able to save this year! I *hope*.

Well, to go back to yesterday. I breakfasted downstairs and then at 9.30 had to go off with Hudson to buy rugs – so I did not see Lady M. [Mother] and Con off but made them affectionate adieu in their rooms, after breakfast. I went to Steinhardt and made Hudson buy 15 rugs for £130. One was a beautiful carpet and it is at B. Square at present, until he gets or builds a house. He didn't like buying so much, but he said he was awfully obliged to me. I said he wasn't really at all and he saw the joke and laughed.

I got back and there was an endless stream of people to see, scold and arrange with and then at 1.15 I went and lunched with the Dolgoroukis. He was there. I had not met him before, a tall thin man with a big plain rather coarse head, very proud of having walked from Portland Street to Chancery Lane, mild, simple, very greedy, paints – and oh how badly – talks quietly and very tentatively, adopting one's views as his own with calm assurance. She chatty and sparkletti (new word!) as usual, vague and definite on only one point and that is £15,000. Well that is a distinct advance on the original £6000! We lunched and lunched and then we talked and talked and she drove me to Glazier's office in St James's Street. I saw Pamela, Nannie [Butler] and Tony[2] and waved to them from the Royal looking carriage, I hope they were gratified. I was ½ an hour before time, so I walked up to Beale and Inman and ordered 12 pretty shirts, collars, bought some gloves, which I have left at B. Square (they are safe at all events), ties and some lovely handkerchiefs which will make envy. I shall now go to Hawkes and get some suits, sort out my under linen and then lie low again. Having done this I walked back to St James's Street where I saw Mr Glazier.

Mr Glazier is the Surveyor to the Westminster Syndicate, Jewish origin, very like Lord Battersea to look at but with dark eyes and a flatter and blander face. We drafted out a letter to send

---

1. William Bird (1855–50), for whom Lutyens remodelled Eartham House, near Chichester.

2. Antony, Viscount Knebworth, (1902–33), Lord Lytton's eldest son.

to the Syndicate. It puts the Westminster scheme on the shelf for a bit, if not permanently. Glazier gave me an enormous cigar, wrapped in gold paper. I told him it was a real gaud, which tickled him, but oh what odd folk I have to truckle with.

I went back to B. Square and saw someone and then dictated letters as I dressed for Birds. I was barely late for dinner in Cadogan Place. Bird is evidently well off.

Mrs Bird is a dear, and so is he and they do, especially he, so appreciate my jokes! He is a solicitor and goes big game shooting. He is her second husband and she is his second wife. She has a collection of most charming bric à brac and a lot of Chinese and Japanese objets d'art. Their furniture is rather bad.

I got back to B. Square about ¼ to 12! when Nobbs came in with estimates etc. and I didn't get to bed till past 1 o'c. and then and only then was able to read and enjoy your darling letter.

I slept well but too soon Florence [parlour maid] brought me up my letters and the awful Hemingway estimates, £17,000 odd the lowest! and then but little time to nerve myself to meet him. At 9 Muntzer[1] came, 9.30 Hedges the Dormy House[2] Clerk of Works and Steinhardt the carpet man. Hemingway[3] came at 10 and left at 2.30. He went carefully through the whole house and then quite nicely accepted the estimates. He told me he was better off than he had led me to believe. He had made £20,000 for the last 5 years and spends about £3000 a year and next year he will have a larger income as his partner goes out. He apparently has the money to pay him out. I got him to sign the contract and as luck would have it the builders came in and so I made them sign too.

Florence improves on acquaintance and she even put her head

1. George Muntzer, Lutyens's principal upholsterer.
2. A club house for the Walton Heath Golf Club built for G. A. Riddell, chairman of the *News of the World*, a director of *Country Life* and a friend of Lloyd George.
3. Ernest Hemingway was the Leeds businessman in the wool trade for whom Lutyens built Heathcote, Ilkley, 1905–7. Based on the architecture of San Michele, it is perhaps Lutyens's finest classical house. It was here that the well-known dialogue took place between Lutyens and Hemingway. 'I don't want a black marble staircase,' his client said. 'I want an oak staircase.' 'What a pity,' Lutyens replied. Later when they visited the house again, the black marble staircase was installed. The client protested, 'I told you I didn't want a black marble staircase.' 'I know,' Lutyens answered, 'and I said "What a pity" didn't I?' (Mary Lutyens, *Lutyens*, pp. 67–8).

into the room to talk to me whilst I was in my bath, a thing even dear Nannie hardly dare do! and it is such a comfort and helps to make everything easy!

This is all my news. It will be joy to have you back on Tuesday, and the children – glorious!

I shall be away all day Monday, Tuesday, Wednesday and Thursday and shall go to Holy Island on Friday.

We have got the raven,[1] it will meet us by the 10 train on Friday. It is a great blow the Barries[2] can't come, however it will be fun.

My letters seem so dreadfully egotistical, but my work is all I have to write about, but I do love you darling. Your Mother said it was a pity that we had not our work in common that she and your father had and did everything together but you can't mix up with my builders and men like Glazier, and Hemingway is weird, and all that. A political life is so different and as regards what I design and how I do it, I don't know. It just comes because I want it to, and if it don't I have to grip inside and make or force it and there is no speech that can describe it. My only words are foolish, quips and jibes, but you are there in all my work and whether you will or not are a part of and in it. And then it is so technical. The political life and those other professions are all based on literature of sorts. My work cannot be approached by literature, literature at the best produces a Pater or a Ruskin in the arts. I don't want you to be either of these!

Homewood   *May 5.06.*

What fun to think of you getting a new trousseau. Yes, do consult Vic, only I expect his clothes are very extravagant. Only you must not spoil your new things by scorching all the backs of the legs and spilling tea all down your front. Vic has very nice shirts always. I love your little grey suit and blue serges, only I never like your tweed ones. You might have a nice grey flannel for summer and some pretty shirts for cool – with soft collars.

I am glad you are home but do wish you were not so tired. I

1. He was taking a raven to Lindisfarne Castle.
2. Lutyens first met J. M. Barrie with the Groves, and he became a lifelong friend. In 1902 Lutyens had designed the scenery for Barrie's *Quality Street*.

long to get back to you but feel I must make the best of the time
here as I am afraid I shan't get about much now in London and I
get so tired of the Square – and people all stare at me and make
rude remarks and are sure I am going to have twins and it is a
bore. [She was pregnant with Elisabeth.]

In train, Stow [Abbotswood] to London   May 6.06.

The garden is not very satisfac. and I gave the builder a regular
doing. I was very nice to him afterwards but my words were as
much directed against Fenwick as against the builder. He alters
so much that everything goes wrong and awry, however he is
quite pleased, but it is good for the reputation [E.L.L.'s].

The Fenwicks have taken a house in London and are going to
give a Ball poor things. I advised them – when they expressed fear
as to sufficient young men – to send invitations en bloc to the
Athenaeum Club. A thing I am sure which has never been done
before and never having been asked before the members would
all come – the whole bench of Bishops and a galaxy of ancients,
and if they came, might I be there to see the fun.

Was it Friday's letter I told you what your Mother said about
us? I think I do wrong not to make the attempt – and force myself
to find language to describe building and my aspirations in my
work to you, my own best and v. true love and let the technicality
go hang and gradually we might get a language that we can
understand in and as my language improves your understanding
of building will improve too and then it will be a joy indeed and
we can sleep in each other's sleeves in happiness, surely an eastern
simile. I shall try and write you now something and then you must
tell me what you think, but don't be too critical.

I am very happy at all these jobs coming out right this week as
regards prices and it is only when they come out right and the
work is to begin that I wake to a horror that I have yet to work it
all out and they loom practical and into the realm of the
real-to-bes. The worry becomes greater – more, really anxious,
but then it is pleasant living the anxiety, and nothing dull.

The first place we stopped at this morning was Chipping
Campden, a dear old village – nearly town, the headquarters of
that most, to me, distasteful Ashbee,[1] new artist and furniture

1. C. R. Ashbee (1863–1942), who had his Guild of Handicraft workshop at
Chipping Campden from 1902 to 1907.

freakist. There is the ruin of an old house belonging to Lord Gainsborough, an Elizabeth or James house, destroyed by fire and never rebuilt, standing near its church, a fine example of a late period – how dull it all must sound to you. Fenwick knew the place well, but he had no conception of the picture that few remains could call up and had no idea of what the main lines of the house were. It was all of that delicious mad bad ignorant sort of architecture called Elizabethan, when the bad and curious attract more vividly than what is really good. The colour of the stonework was lovely, yet through all the colour you could see why some was better than the other, so much so that one could see the walls built properly and the difference between the day work mason and the artist. There are elaborate gateways, an *orné* cottage, two ample gazebos and a bit of the main house left. Yet what charmed me most was the building of a ventilator in the big barn, stones arranged quite simply, so, but every stone so most charmingly placed. The invention, simplicity and ingenuity charmed me altogether.

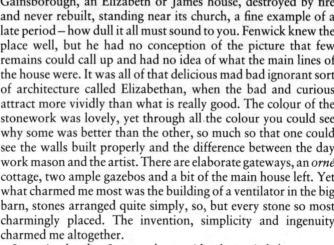

Later in the day I saw others evidently copied, but not as carefully thought out and proportioned as these were. You see the simple arrangement of three stones to make a charming pattern and satisfactory finish to a window or ventilator of absolutely no architectural (so called) importance, yet their function was so perfectly and so aptly fulfilled.

The general scheme was evident from the occurring buildings and the roll and furrow of the ground, distinct through fruit trees planted since but with their rows across the old lay out. A great long house facing south, onto a great wide terrace, terminated east and west by gazebos of some considerable importance, having painted ceilings, panelled walls and open loggias. These two gazebos now remain, one is a hen house, the other lost to any useful purpose, the loggias built up and made solid. The old gateway with its stone built flanking towers are there and the gateway itself is dreadfully bad and inconsequent, gables of many curves even now destroy to a great extent the dignified plan.

The church is admirable but does not bear close inspection. There intermediate buttresses divide at the top into arches and join again as pinnacles and towards the bottom split to pass right and left over the west door, an arrangement most disquieting and unhappy. Yet the general size and proportions and fenestration of the tower is fine and from a distance very good.

Dear old almshouses, but too many gables all of a row and too monotonous, but reprieved by the Gainsborough coat of arms and sun dial (that was charming).

The church tower was a great conception marred by detail and the almshouses a poor conception marring the detail – and it was all probably done by one man, long syne dead, and known no more.

Broadway is a village with charming houses, but I was frankly disappointed. It was self conscious and everything done was done just wrong. It was clean without being tidy, every old house had its sanitary necessities in glorious evidence, bad ugly curtains and other vulgarities grinned through old casements. The name boards on the houses (one was called Privet Lodge) is hardly fair criticism but no new name can fit an old place.

There was a new house near that made me start, and oh how naughty, a fearless copy of some of my work, yet dreadful and so foreign to the county and its materials.

Holy Island   May 12.06.

We arrived safely. Bumps not too tired. We have been moving furniture and I am very disinclined to write somehow. The curtains are not ready yet which is a disappointment but I dare not show it as they have worked so hard and well. The raven was an awful anxiety on the journey and carrying her on my lap across the sands.[1] However, we got her in the temporary cage and she seems wild but has eaten a lot of bread and milk and drunk a lot of water. She – or is it he? – mischievously upsets all its basins and plates and makes a fearful mess but she seems all right, and I have got two croaks out of her. Her beak makes a noise like castanets when she, he or it eats and drinks.

Bumps is quite charmed and so appreciative and we all had good nights.

29 Bloomsbury Square   Aug.31.06.

Hemingway asked about 'Mrs Lutyens' – would you like to go up there? You would have fits – a coursed breakfast in slippers,

---

1. Holy Island was only approachable over the sands at low tide.

boots put on in the sitting room sometimes used as a dining room and furnished as such – *en suite* but not so expensive as the real dining room. The ornaments – oh lor! and the walls of lincrusta with painted dado and frieze of flying sparrows, ferns and polyanthi displayed. And then a mass of modern prints from Academy pictures and electric light galore. The doors very shiny and painted in a curious way – brown chocolate, blue and gold. The drawing room is cut in two to make a cosy corner of half the room – white and blue walls and festooned lace curtains and armaments of albums and other such souvenirs. Photographs of the daughter posing as a professional beauty, but when you see her she is shrimpish – about 4 foot high, full of self confidence – adored by her admiring parents and her charm takes the form of giggles. 'Everything that money can do for her is done and being done.' A year at Paris, one at Berlin and now one at Dresden to complete her. A good school to start with. Can you not see the string out walking along a hot and stony esplanade from whence the heiress of my Ilkley imbibes her giggled charm? Mrs H. is very quiet, simple and dresses better than appears. Does nothing all day and takes turns with the cook to go out. The motor and motoring are a real joy to her and must prove an excellent and admirable institution for all that class of person. The boy – 17 – overnosed and very young and shy – very quiet – a passion for the motor. No initiative. He works hard and well but can not be got to take a lead. Spends no money. £50 a year he gets and earns another £60 and always refuses money offered by his father or mother. His father hopes his initiative will come someday – either through love or no matter what! He has been educated in Germany. Hemingway wonders if he has done right not sending him to the University. I was anti-University but now think I was wrong.

Holy Island   *Sept.6.06.*

Mr Hudson is lying on the green sofa reading. I write to you. We have both had a long talk about your competing for the County Council Hall and I do think you must try. I told him you said it would cost you £1000 and he said it was worth it and I think from what he said he meant he would help you if in difficulty. As he says, if you get it your fortune and name are made for all time.

You have Riley[1] and Norman Shaw favourable to you and I do think you must have a try. Go and see Riley directly you get back. Hudson says you are undoubtedly the cleverest architect in England! and they must think well of you to put you on the Council of the RIBA. Do, do, do think it well over and make a big dash for fame!

Hotel Metropole, Dublin   Oct.2.06.

I made my connection from Kingstown on to Rush from where I drove to Fargy's boat. Driving through Rush the Post Mistress jumped out of her cottage and said, 'Sur here's a letter for you I thocht you'd like to have it.' I should think so, for it was from my own Emy forwarded from B. Square. It was joy to get it.

Then across to Lambay we were nearly becalmed. It took 2½ hours to do the 3 miles, and had to row. I got there about 9.30. The Barings very cordial. Mrs Baring is a curious creature, a dear thing unlike anyone else I know. She is very strong and active, devoted to her babies and husband and quite happy on the island. She can be very reserved and stand offish, but now she is more like a girl and childlike in many ways. She is very American, very dark. She describes herself as a squaw. I *do* wonder what you would think of her. She gave a funny account of herself just before Calypso[2] came and she was big with her, deer stalking with Baring and how she could only get down the hills by rolling, she was so fat and round. I can't imagine everybody doing this, can you? Fancy her strength. He is very quiet. The children are dears but not *very* pretty. Awfully healthy looking and wear Dutch caps. Daphne[3] has a cap in white linen. The oddest thing.

29 Bloomsbury Square   Oct.4.06.

There is so much to do and everyone is pressing me so and so many places to go to that I feel almost hopeless about it all. I do

1. The assessors for the County Hall competition were Norman Shaw, Sir Aston Webb and W. E. Riley, the architect to the London County Council.
2. b. 1905. Married G. M. Liddell in 1926.
3. b. 1904. Married Arthur Pollen in 1926.

Lutyens at Lambay

wish I could get someone to help me. They are such idiots in the office and then they resent Thomas – some of them do. [S. H.] Evans is the head of the office and is really no real use. He swaggers and don't help when he can and then lords it and does the great man with the pupils. It is a bore. Such an arrear of work. Evans is on his holiday and leaves things unsettled and vague. I don't often grouse about my work, do I, to you?

Oh Ems, when I am office and work rid I do long to be able to go to you and sit by you even if it's only to play patience! But alone I can't get away from work and when I don't feel inclined to work and can't get away from it then I get miserable. I think holidays are a great mistake and that I ought not to have gone away.[1] The leisure and luxury of a yacht with no thought or care for the morrow is bad. I ought to have spent the time with you darling. We must get to do things together – won't we – but what? I think I am a bit tired and will be better soon. The one great radiant spot is our love.

29 Bloomsbury Square   March 29.07.
                                                        [his 38th birthday]

Oh such a nice quiet day. Been hard at it but not got far really [with the design for the County Hall competition]. Such a puzzle but it will gradually emerge.

No news. No letters. No telephone. Empty quiet house so I have no excuse not to work and I almost grudge writing to you! Time seems to go so quick and there is such an immense never ending list of rooms. Of the twenty I have not done one department and all the twenty have to fit and interfit. . . . I can't collect my thoughts. I can only think LCC [London County Council]. I shall write very little these first few days but do you darling write to me.

29 Bloomsbury Square   March 31.07.

At half past twelve last night I decided to begin all over again! That shows how I am getting on! Not so bad as it looks as it teaches me the conditions and requirements. But oh just as you get a department nice you find it has to be near somewhere else –

1. To the Baltic on a cruise organized by the Jekylls.

without an inch of space for 'em. So I shall have nothing really except generalities to discuss with Herbert Jekyll.

29 Bloomsbury Square   April 16.07.

Very busy over LCC. I have got the plan to fit all right but the innards are yet many, many, hours away from even approximate possibility.

The only news is that I have been elected to the Athenaeum Club. It makes my status good but is a horrid expense just now.

29 Bloomsbury Square   May 21.07.

Barbie's rudeness is such a trial. I wonder why our children are so rude? I was much impressed with Tony's obedience and good sense. He was playing with Victor's fishing box – fancy allowing Robert to play with my fishing rods! – and he did exactly what he was told to do and not to do. He came to see me in my room and told me he could make more noise than the whole of my family. I said not more than Ursula – he said No, not more than Ursula. Oh dear.

Crooksbury   *May 22.07.*

Our children are not really any ruder than others. I have heard Tony fearfully rude to his Nannie, but Vic has great authority over him and you have none over yours. You let them say what they like and don't ever reprove them. I have to do all the discipline and Robert badly needs other than female authority.

29 Bloomsbury Square   May 22.07.

I felt I should bring the parentship scold on my head when I wrote of Tony. You are quite right and my want of authority is the cause of half my troubles.

———

29 Bloomsbury Square   Aug. 12.07.

It is two days since I have written you, and I feel so miserable about it. I had such a busy morning Saturday starting early with Harold Brassey[1] and then back in time for lunch.

I had to catch the 2 o'c with Johnson [to Marshcourt] . . . well I couldn't write you in the train with Johnson there and some of his friends. Then when we arrived we went round the house making notes etc. and then off to the river about 6.30 and dined at 10.

Sunday was the same, notes and looking about and then the river. To comfort and console you I caught no fish! and the rise was a short one and what the fish were taking seemed somewhat of a mystery. Dined at ten again. I had with me the last piece of LCC planning and this took up my spare time and I have done it! A great and enormous relief. It is all polishing and drawing now. Oh dear, there is yet a lot of work and thought and I have to face the planning of all the machinery parts – heating and ventilating apparati – which have to be mechanical and the terraces do puzzle me.

In the early mornings and late evenings I am reading *Don Quixote* properly.

Church Farm Bungalow,
Rustington,
Sussex   *Aug. 14.07.*

I am so miserable but if Mr Chapman stays over Sunday as I expect he will, I really have not a corner for you. The house is already over full. I am so sorry and disappointed.

Arthur Chapman

1. Harold Brassey (1877–1916), for whom Lutyens had remodelled the interior of Copse Hill, Gloucestershire, in 1906. He was a grandson of Thomas Brassey, the great railway contractor.

29 Bloomsbury Square   Aug.14.07.

I am oh! *so* disappointed about Sat. and Sunday but I *quite* understand. Do darling assure Mrs Webbe I don't mean to be unkind and I certainly don't *think* unkindly. My one criticism of her is that her enthusiasms for her one point of view blind her to other points, but I do love and appreciate her love for you my sweet wife. (Hudson was so dear and nice about you today.) I am frightened of them at the same time for Emy, if moved, moves so very deliberately and with no equivocation and equivocation is a cousin germaine of tact. I don't mean to say or think that having no equivocation you have no tact, do you see, but do apologise to Mrs Webbe and say she is silly to think I mean to be unkind.

I should like to know Lady Pembroke for Wilton's sake, do be extra nice to her and so get her to ask us to stay there. I should love Wilton, the river! and oh the house, just the I. Jones part that touched the zenith of English architecture (with reservations I reserve). It wouldn't be me not to make reservations but then the PERFECT is not of this world except in my beloved Ems.

29 Bloomsbury Square   Aug.16.07.

Don't let him [Mr Chapman] or Mrs Webbe dream that there was any chance of my being able to come. Give 'em my love and say how really sorry I am I cannot get away – this LCC – and enjoy seeing them. Does Mr Chip Chap paddle? Think how kind he has been to *me*.

Bumps wants to be fairly comfy [she was going to stay at Rustington] as she travels with all sorts of things like Con, but not so much skin comforts as drawing boards and holdalls full of stationery and what nots to write and draw. Make her feel she may go to bed when she likes and don't let her feel 'out' of it. What a party of suffragettes!

Oh if I could only win the LCC I should be ladder top and then I should spend weeks with you at a time. I do really wish for a big house – about 12 dear houses under one roof and then the street would be one large and magnificent room used in the way St Paul's used to be used to walk about in and meet one's friends!

Give Chip Chap my love. Tell him the dear monument[1] is

1. Mrs Chapman's gravestone in Tilford churchyard, near Crooksbury.

dreadfully on my mind – a slab or lid to a brick box is so dreadfully cold and unthoughtful looking. I have drawn so many.

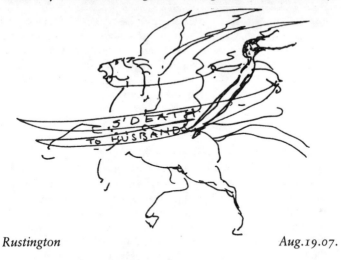

Rustington   *Aug.19.07.*

Mrs Webbe is in love with your picture of her on the winged steed and thinks it so clever and such a lovely figure that she forgives you all your unkindness.

Rustington   *Aug.22.07.*

How I wish you had been given the power to look through space and see Bumps and Emy drinking beer together and talking of Nedi! Soon after I finished my letter the motor sounded and I rushed out and there was Aggie [Jekyll] – looking quite sylph-like – and a young lady, name forgotten, and Bumps. Bumps laden with delicious funny odd luggage which she would unpack all by herself at once. Kind Aggie laden with baskets of fruit for me. We had tea and saw all round our abode and then marched off to the beach. Bumps in a most becoming capy shawl. The motor followed and then Aggie and friend whirled off again and Bumps and I had a little wander on the beach till we saw the babies and then Bumps said she would go back and rest a while.

Before dinner we did some wild flowers together but Bumps has forgotten her reading specs. We had quite a good dinner of

*soup, omelette, grouse, plums, junket, beer, and now Bumps has
gone to bed and I go too as the beer is doing its work and I can
hardly keep my eyes open much less write.*

*And now darling, I want to beg one thing of you, which is that
when you come you will try and not apologise all the time for
food, etc. I do my best and if you do you make everyone
uncomfortable. It is really such bad taste – quite unworthy of
you.*

29 Bloomsbury Square   Aug.23.07.

I long to see you – Bumps with the children.

Lady Battersea said you were such a dear etc. and I said I
thought so too, whereat she chuckled. She said you had great
with a big G good qualities and she said you performed your part
at the conferences so well. She agreed with me how great your
moral courage was, how fearless you were etc. *I* don't want to
encourage your courage in this way! I told her your criticisms on
the farm house [he had wanted to lease] small windows and beer,
it delighted her and gave her the chance of a good laugh at me.

Lord B. was present at all this and was enthusiastic that you
should come up to Cromer, so I said and Lady B. agreed that you
were not a bit his sort of woman and had no life blood for lovely
stuffs and houses – and Lady B. said, just like me, the house made
no difference to happiness. *I* think it the crown! of happiness,
even if it has to be worn round the neck!

Rather awful a couronne fermée
but that is better than a
bald place.

I am so happy at the thought of tomorrow. How nice to see
Aggie. Love to Bumps, don't let the children tire her.

29 Bloomsbury Square   Sept.10.07.

All my mind is on the LCC except that large part that is always with you i.e., yours.

There is that in art which transcends all rules, it is the divine – I use poor words – and this is what makes all the arts so absorbing and thrilling to follow, creating a furore. It is the same in the best of all man's work (G.B.S. shows it so amusingly (tho' he makes it ludicrous) in *Cashel Byron's Profession*,[1] applying the language of a painter to the mouth of a Boxer on Boxing). Then with inspiration rules are forgotten and some great immeasurable cycle of law is followed, unconsciously by some unaccounted impulse – in my own kind of work and with the moderns. There is I. Jones breaking through all rules when it suits him. He does it softly and it is hard to find out. Wren flagrantly defied them and he applied his ingenious intellect – he had more an intellectual than an artistic gift – yet with rules broken there was the great result, as you say, as there is with Carlyle in his work. There is the same effect produced on all and in all work by a master mind. To short sight it is a miracle, to those a little longer sighted it is Godhead, if we could see yet better, these great facts may be revealed before which the V.God as we can conceive him will fade dim. It is the point of view that ought to bring all arts, Architecture, Sculpture, Painting, Literature and Music etc. into sympathy and there is no ploy which cannot be lifted to the divine level by its creation as an art. And oh Wren, Jones are small besides Michelangelo and men like Leonardo da Vinci. They had this touch! and were able to apply it to every work and kind of work they touched, war, architecture, painting, sculpting. The thought of these men makes praise difficult to give and more difficult to receive.

No news.

Been very busy on the LCC.

Do hope my sermon on beauty won't bore you, but oh Ems loveliness is akin indeed to heaven and the thought of it to God.

If only the nations of the world would go for beauty with their whole resource and energies it would solve all difficulties and I do believe *all* sorrow and the millennium would be ours!

God bless you darling, huge love.

---

1. Novel by G. B. Shaw published in 1901.

29 Bloomsbury Square   Sept.11.07.

I retract the last sentence in yesterday's letter. I feel equally convinced today that nothing at least no one thing will mend the world. The schools of beauty would all quarrel and there would be more jealousies than ever.

Rustington   *Sept.11.07.*

Oh darling Nedi we have so much in common if we could only find the way to express it to each other. That is just the difficulty – the doors of my soul open to the north and yours to the south and 'never the twain can meet'. If one can only have soul communion over big things I think it would be easier to be patient over the little ones. The beauty that appeals to me is moral beauty, moral principles, moral ideals, traits of character. The beauty you know and care about I can't see though I know it is just the same – just as moral, just as great, but it is in a different form and that is where I think we fail to understand each other a little bit. I get cross because you are so critical and because you are troubled by the ugliness of much or most things and your horror of ugliness prevents you seeing moral *beauty behind.*

You think I should be more serene if all my surroundings were beautiful. I know that my great difficulty is a Puritan conscience with which I am always struggling. I should never be any happier for possessing. I should love a country home, a lovely Nedi built house, but I should like it very simple needing hardly any servants, with no priceless things that have to be guarded. I should like to have always a meal for a tramp, everything very clean, easily washed, and yet rather stern. I do hate the squalor of all our summer houses and yet they cost money more than I ought to spend and what else can I do? Where can I go? How can it be nicer?

I am so glad you liked the Carlyle a little bit. If only, only we could find each other in books – it is so much the easiest way and yet so difficult to manage. We can't even sleep at the same time! If I read after dinner I yawn and get sleepy and you are sound asleep in the morning.

Darling we have each our eyes on God but we just fail a little in reverence and understanding of how each wishes to attain it. But love will teach us – in time and I do love you darling as much as I know you love me.

Baby waves her hand and says Hooray in the sweetest little voice.

I am now going to bed so good night darling. What a letter!

In train to Ashby St Legers   Jan.11.08.

I wish I didn't keep on wanting to win the LCC. My chief feeling is a wish to get back [to] that office again and the excitement of the big work.

I had a good look at all the students' drawings at the RIBA today. E. George and Ricardo are with me on the committee to judge for the Owen Jones prize, colour decoration applied to architecture and they are drawings of old buildings where colour is applied. It was difficult to judge, only 3 sets and we finally chose the man who impressed us least at first look, which was odd. The students' work is very poor. I burned to be able to help them and point them the right way, my way! What a curious thing is conviction.

Mr Landseer Mackenzie called today! He is the nephew of Sir E. Landseer and wants advice in architecture and as his aunt, Landseer's sister, left me a £100, I must be very civil, and it was that £100 (which made me go into debt at once!) was the first cause of my getting on rather better than my brothers. It was a great advantage. Charlie and John had what money they wanted. I wonder if it is a good thing to give a boy a sum to start him – a fixed sum with no chance of more.

29 Bloomsbury Square   Jan.24.08.

I am afraid I have bad news. But no matter. E. C. Harmen, don't mention his name and do keep it secret, saw Shaw today. He said, their work was done and the result was a great surprise to him etc. none of the favourites had won. Harmen thinks he means the 8 selected ones by this, anyhow I was I am told a strong favourite. His [Shaw's] stairs and Webb's work was all done by Riley and his assistants who kept on measuring everything up, and disqualifying on the conditions. What tired him was continually walking up and down a quarter of a mile of drawings!

I really do now believe there is no hope and all my 9 months work is lost and the valued good wishes of friends go.

My own darling I do love you and you will be kind and not ask me to spend too much this year. Our dear little country home must wait a bit. All my little bits of work seem dull, but I shall soon pick up and be happy in it again. I am in plenty of good company. What I want is a nice big house to do and heart to do it well.

Homewood   *Jan.28.08.*

Oh! I am miserable and why am I away and not able just to comfort and love you. I would come back today only you are away all day and mother would be so unhappy if I left her. I think it is almost a relief to have it settled. The suspense is so trying and inevitable hope.

Homewood   *April 6.08.*

I see they are already docking Knott of some of the money for County Hall and also pulling about his plans. I am sure had you got it it would have been a curse and no good to your reputation.

CHAPTER FOUR

1908–1909

AFTER HIS FAILURE in the LCC competition Lutyens's wish for a 'nice big house' was soon granted in the shape of Great Maytham for H. J. Tennant and Temple Dinsley for H. G. Fenwick. But the most important visitor to his office, though he did not realize it at the time, is mentioned in a letter he wrote to Lady Emily in August 1907: 'The Hampstead Garden City solicitor came to-day, to consult me! and their architect came humbly afterwards, rather perturbed, I think.'

The founder of Hampstead Garden Suburb was Henrietta Barnett, an energetic philanthropist and wife of Canon Barnett, the first warden of Toynbee Hall in East London. The inspiration came to her when the London Tube reached Golders Green, within easy reach of her cottage near the Heath. Rather than suffer developers to erect 'rows of ugly villas' – the shabby suburban townscape so vividly portrayed in the novels of H. G. Wells – she decided to plan a community where 'all classes would live together under right conditions of beauty and space'.[1] In 1905 a trust company was formed which purchased 240 acres over which it retained strict control. As planner she appointed Raymond Unwin (1863–1940), a disciple of Morris and the planner of Letchworth (1904), the first garden city to embody the ideals of Ebenezer Howard.

In *Tomorrow* (1898) Howard projected a self-sufficient community, characterized by harmony and balance: balance between classes, between functions – home, market and production – and, most important, balance between town and country, between urban amenities and open spaces or green belts. Howard insisted that these ideals could only be realized if the land was held not by private landlords but by the civic authorities. Howard's ideas

1. Henrietta Barnett, *Canon Barnett* (1918), vol. ii, pp. 312–13.

owed much to William Morris, and the garden city was one of the most important offshoots of the Arts and Crafts movement.

Mrs Barnett was determined that the focal point of the community of Hampstead should be the Anglican Church of St Jude's which, together with the Free Church and the Institute, was to be placed on the highest ground, visible from all sides. It was these principal buildings and some of the houses surrounding them that Lutyens was called upon to design. Alfred Lyttelton was chairman of the Garden Suburb Board and it was probably he who suggested Lutyens's name to Mrs Barnett.

Lutyens, with his vision of great buildings and vistas leading up to them, and Raymond Unwin, who put the landscape first to such an extent that he seemed to regret every house that was built, were not a natural team. But it was perhaps because of these tensions that the result, with its architectural centre and meandering periphery, was so uniquely successful.

Though Lutyens welcomed the opportunity to build his first church, he soon ran into difficulties with Mrs Barnett. When she objected to his designs, he dismissed her as a 'philistine', with 'no idea beyond a window box full of geraniums, calceolarias and lobelias, over which you can see a goose on the green'.[1] But Mrs Barnett had a point. A towering magisterial exercise in discords, combining elements of the Gothic and the Baroque, St Jude's is a measure both of the distance Lutyens had travelled from the Arts and Crafts movement, and of his complete lack of sympathy with the William Morris socialism that inspired it.

When it came to town planning, Lutyens preferred dukes to committees, Tory paternalists and Liberal plutocrats to municipal socialists. It was with the millionaire Ivor Guest that he had played 'our town game', inventing a 'lovely townscape', in 1904; in 1908 he was excited by the prospect – which came to very little – of building a model town for the Duke of Bedford at Tavistock. Significantly, what he objected to about the People's Budget of 1909 was less the new taxes than Lloyd George's demagogic attacks on the dukes. To single out for vilification such a magnate as the Duke of Westminster was, as Lutyens pointed out, to ignore the fact that the Grosvenor Estate had by itself done more for London housing than any municipal authority.

If the effect of the Budget controversy was to confirm Lutyens

1. Letter to Herbert Baker, 15 July 1909 (Hussey, *Lutyens*, p. 190).

in his contempt for politicians, and indeed for parliamentary government itself, his commitment to classicism was strengthened and deepened by his first visit to Italy, in October 1909. That year a Royal Commission was set up to supervise the British contributions to the International Exhibitions at Turin and Rome in 1911, with Victor Lytton as chairman and Lutyens as consulting architect. Lucky by-products of his appointment are his letters to Lady Emily describing the buildings, the 'old friends' he knew so well. Soon after his return, Lutyens was commissioned to build the British Pavilion in Rome, an adaptation of the west front of St Paul's. Gratifyingly, it was later rebuilt as the British School in Rome.

Lady Emily was now emerging from total submersion in her family, having had her fifth and last child in 1908. Finding insufficient outlet for her energies within her marriage, she now sought occupation and interests outside. She became involved in the activities that occupied upper-middle-class women in the 1900s, such as social work and organized intellectual discussion. Being a radical, she joined the Women's Social and Political Union which had been founded in 1903 by Mrs Pankhurst to campaign actively for female suffrage and which, under her leadership, was becoming increasingly militant. Lady Emily was an energetic member, chairing meetings, addressing conferences and writing several well-reasoned letters to *The Times* making the point that, because of the justice of the case, happily married women could be ardent supporters of the women's cause.

It was through Lady Emily that her sister, Constance Lytton, became interested in the suffrage movement. In *Prisons and Prisoners* (1914), Lady Constance describes herself as 'one of that numerous gang of upper class leisured class spinsters, unemployed, unpropertied, unendowed, uneducated, without equipment or training for public service',[1] and as such she was, perhaps, a natural suffragette. Like Lady Emily she was a hero worshipper and it was under the influence of Mrs Pethick-Lawrence and the charismatic Pankhursts that she became convinced of the case for militancy. Lady Emily, by contrast, never condoned violence; indeed it was over this issue that she resigned from the Women's Social and Political Union in September 1909.

Earlier that year Constance Lytton had had her first taste of

1. Op. cit., p. 39.

militancy when she joined a deputation to the Prime Minister in February 1909. She was manhandled by the police and arrested in Parliament Square; after spending a night on bail from Bow Street at 29 Bloomsbury Square, tended by Lady Emily, she was sent to Holloway for a month. In October 1909 she was jailed in Newcastle for throwing a stone at a car containing Sir Walter Runciman, a cabinet minister. Emily Davison, who in 1913 threw herself under the King's horse at the Derby, was arrested with her.

In January 1910 she was jailed in Liverpool. This time she disguised herself as Jane Wharton, a seamstress, so as to avoid preferential treatment in prison. She was forcibly fed and owing to a weak heart her health was permanently damaged. In London Lady Emily heard a rumour that her sister was imprisoned and, with the help of Arthur Chapman, discovered where she was. Constance Lytton tells how Arthur Chapman 'went to see my sister who was dining out. Without a moment's hesitation and dressed just as she was she caught the midnight train to Liverpool.'[1] She brought Con back to 29 Bloomsbury Square, where she recovered, but some months later she had a stroke and remained partially paralysed.

Jan.25.08.

I am in the train from Botley. Mrs Franklyn was very nice to me. She attended a funeral in the afternoon, she apparently goes to all funerals in Shedfield. The builder's foreman told me she was 'terribly imposed upon'.

I have finished *Father and Son*.[2] It does seem odd to write of one's own father and it is more difficult to realise in this case than with Barrie and his *Margaret Ogilvy*.[3] Gosse's story is so like my own – the home part. Darling Mother's evangelism and Father's Venetian Secret.[4] It is thrillingly interesting. If I had been Father's

1. Ibid., p. 297.

2. By Edmund Gosse, published 1907.

3. The book Barrie wrote about his mother, who belonged to the strictly puritanical sect, the Auld Lichts, published 1896.

4. Charles Lutyens's 'Venetian Secret' was an ancient formula he claimed to have discovered 'for obtaining a particularly luminous shade of red used by the great Venetian masters. He offered to share his secret with members of the Academy and was bitterly hurt when they did not want to hear about it' (Mary Lutyens, *Lutyens*, p. 7).

only son! But then I don't think Father would have taken things to heart as he always loved good fellowship and horses and with loss of money and hard times friends left him. A book like that, if I could write it, I should leave it in my will to be published in fifty years – not *now*.

I don't like the Botley house [New Place] very much. It is a sort of Elizabethan pile, that may be nice in 50 years and always curious. The first house I designed was much better, it was £500 or so too much and then I designed the one as built and it has cost nearly as much and is not near as good. However, people go and photograph it already! which is rather cool. But it is not Nedi like as Bumps would call it, a bit. I must show you more of the drawings, darling.

I hope the Clutterbucks will build but she wants an Elizabethan house and my sympathies are not at all with that period at present. I want to go for the higher game, at least what I hold to be higher.

I am wondering whether I ought to have a drawing made of the LCC design for the RA. It would be another £50 and it is all speculation and not really justifiable. What do you say? It might appeal to the public to advertise, but it may not. [The drawing was exhibited that summer.]

29 Bloomsbury Square   April 22.08.

So glad to get your letter today. It has been a horrid bitter cold day here, ending in snow, rain and sleet. No news.

Frank Bellville looked in. His chauffeur and engineer has been killed in a motor smash and he wanted to know how to find another.

Sangorski[1] the book binder came in and told me how he had built a room himself with his own hands and made me roar with laughter. How he is going to build himself a house! and wanted advice on the buying of land. He won't put an upper floor in case it or the staircase gave way, and said the maid would have to sleep

---

1. Francis Sangorski (1876–1912), founder of Sangorski & Sutcliffe, the London bookbinders. He bound the Lutyens family bible in 1905. The firm bound many of the miniature books for Queen Mary's Dolls' House in 1923–24.

with a rope round her waist, tied to the roof and in case the floor fell she would be hung up safe!

The painters will be out in a week easily, the stair carpet will be a month. I am having the pantry papered and dark green roller blinds put up.

Next week I go to Ilkley Saturday to Walton Heath and perhaps to Munstead for the Sunday.

Here is a picture for Ursula called 'Ursula galloping across the Downs with Giles'.

Mells Manor, Somerset   May 3.08.

Got here about five, had tea and then walked about the village to look for a site for a memorial to Mark [Horner], then to the church. Raymond and Katherine Asquith, Jack, Cecily and Lady Horner are here.[1] She is awfully sad but all like talking about and of Mark which makes it easy. They are all rather skiffy coffy over the Pamela McKenna marriage.[2] I haven't got a present yet. Jack

1. Mark, the second son of Sir John (Jack) Horner of Mells, died of scarlet fever at the age of sixteen in 1908. His sister Katherine (1885–1977) married Raymond Asquith (1878–1916), the Prime Minister's eldest son, in 1907. Cecily Horner, the elder daughter, married Hon. George Lambton, the trainer, in 1908.

2. Pamela, daughter of Sir Herbert Jekyll and a niece of Lady Horner, married the Liberal politician Reginald McKenna (1863–1943) in 1908. McKenna, who in 1908 was appointed First Lord of the Admiralty, became an important patron of Lutyens's.

Horner is deafer than ever but a dear and so cheerful and nice to Lady Horner, it is rather touching.

They wanted to put an altar tomb in the middle of their chapel here, with a figure of Mark on the top and I am against it as it is too prominent a position for a small cadet of a house. It was rather difficult to explain but people are so apt to overdo that sort of thing at once. Like the Duchess of Rutland who is going to put her second boy[1] in the middle of the Haddon Chapel. I tried to stop that. It means here that they would have to turn out of their seats and would leave little Mark alone – that was my instrument in the destruction of the idea.[2]

It was joy to find a letter from you when I came down to breakfast.

Lindisfarne Castle, 1906

Lindisfarne Castle, Holy Island   July 3.08.

I have been so bad about writing. All Thursday we slaved to get the Castle tidy looking, arranging furniture, flowers and then the Princess [of Wales] came.

1. Like Lady Horner, the Duchess of Rutland was a Soul. Her eldest son, Lord Haddon, had died in 1894 at the age of nine.
2. The memorial eventually took the form of a public well in Mells village. The lettering of the inscription is by Eric Gill.

It has turned cold. Barbie seems very happy but quiet and seems to have little initiative of her own, so I try and instil selfishness into her! She is very affectionate and a darling altogether.

I must tell you about the Princess etc. From the battlements we saw a procession of 8 carriages come across the sands, and at 12 o'clock they arrived on the island and we heard the cheers of the islanders faintly and afar off.

The Prince was awfully bored apparently with the lecture given by some archaeologist and looked at his watch every two minutes. They drove over here and walked up the drive, 6 carriages in pairs up they came and I sent Hudson down to the bottom of the hill to receive them with Barbie. I waited at the portcullis.

Bigge[1] was walking with the Prince and I heard him say, you know Sir this place has been rebuilt by E. Lutyens. So I hollered out High Stop, I'm here. The Prince nearly had a fit of laughter. He said, how verry goode, ha ha and told everybody.

When I told him how I had proposed to drain the Castle with a gun etc. he said 'oh yes, drains, of course drains' without a smile.

He was terribly alarmed at the gangway up and wanted a wall built. I told him we had pulled one down and that if he really thought it unsafe we would put nets out. He thought that very funny.

The Princess couldn't bear the cobbles, they hurt her feet. I told her we were very proud of them! The only thing she specially admired were some fleurs-de-lis on a fireback.

Hudson said he was dreadfully nervous and I think they made each other stiff. The Prince was awfully anxious to get away when he found the tide was rising, for a sailor I thought him over nervous.[2]

Lords Crichton and Howick were the only appreciative people. Mr Chaplin[3] was only conscious of his bulk. [The Duke of] Northumberland was very demure and a good deal bored. The Ladies Percy took snap shots – Hudson with Princess me with

1. Arthur Bigge (1849–1931), created Lord Stamfordham in 1911, was Private Secretary to the Prince of Wales, later George V, from 1901 until his death. He bought Warren Lodge, Thursley, which Lutyens had built for Robert Webb in 1896, and in 1909 he commissioned Lutyens to add to it.

2. Kenneth Rose cites this incident as evidence of the frayed nerves of the Prince of Wales(*King George V* (1983), pp. 69–70).

3. Henry Chaplin, 'the Squire' (1841–1923), weighed at least 18 stone.

Prince – stole flowers out of the house and picked wild flowers in spite of notices.[1] We walked down with the party to the gate and off they went.

Hudson and I had a sleep.

The most wonderful sunsets and light all night! Today it is grey and cold and a sea fog early this morning which I thought might prevent my getting away.

A picture enclosed for Betty of Hudson, Barbie and E.L.L. going to bed.

I went over to Morpeth, Jimmy Smith met me at the station with Mrs Robert Harrison (Lady Ottoline's friend)[2] of Shiplake sister of Mrs Eustace Smith's husband. Mrs E. Smith[3] is a widow, 4 boys and a girl, *very* rich, and all monies left to her entirely.

Colonel and Mrs Cookson, the owners of Meldon Park, where Mrs Smith now lives, came over to lunch, to meet me. They have come in for a fortune and want me to build them new gates and lodges, which is good.[4] Mrs Cookson seems a nice woman, her son married Harold Brassey's sister so it all hangs together.

1. Those who knew the Ladies Margaret, Victoria, Mary and Muriel Percy maintain that this must be a case of mistaken identity.

2. Lady Ottoline Morrell described her as 'an intelligent woman caring for books and art, and their house was filled with beautiful things, Whistlers and Sargents' (*Early Memoirs* (1963), p. 128).

3. For whom Lutyens built Whalton Manor (1908), 'an extraordinarily ingenious conversion of four adjoining houses along a Northumbrian village street' (Hussey, *Lutyens*, p. 135).

4. The designs made for these in 1909 were not executed.

Mrs Harrison is *very* kind about me and she and Mrs Smith liked my suggestions and jumped to them at once so much better and wiser than those idiotic bishops! However I can laugh at them for though they rankle they are very funnily absurd. I cannot, at least have not yet arrived at a church, which is depressing.

Whalton Manor, built 1908

In train, Ilkley to Leeds   Aug. 5.08.

We have had such a day – plans, plans, house, house [Heathcote] – 8.30 till now. Curtains, carpets, gardeners, electricians, door handles, carvers, and now I go to Leeds to see the furniture makers tomorrow. Then to London to see my own, own, Emy and 'Edith Penelope Mary' [born 31 July]. Tomorrow night I dine with Fenwick and Friday I go to Victor, Saturday to Marshcourt and then I hope for three days of peace and Ireland and the Barings loom close on me which is an awful wrench for I hate to leave thee and long to see our bran new pet. But I must do my work and get it done with credit.

I am going to the Queen's Hotel. I hate hotels. The misery of them and in summer one can't even have a fire which is the only solace an hotel ever gives. With a fire one can build anew one's own surroundings – an empty paper-frilled grate is more than cold – a sort of frozen hades. Ugh.

Renishaw Hall, Chesterfield   Sept.17.08.

Here am I (in bed).

I arrived here just before dinner last night, a big rambling house with no electric light few lamps and huge fires.

I have a vast apartment which is called the Duke's Room and I feel sure is haunted, though they swear not.

Sir George Sitwell[1] is very courteous very civil and affects all that is Italian, a male Pamela. Lady Ida[2] seems a darling. She is under 40 and has a tall daughter of 21 [Edith] and two boys, the elder one [Osbert] has just gone to school and I have not seen him and the younger [Sacheverell] goes tomorrow, so there is a shadow on the house. They want me to do the Garden, the Ball Room, Billiard Room, Great Drawing Room and Dining Room etc.[3] The house is full of pictures, some quite, some very good.

Sir George wants to build a little water palace one room on the lake, which would be a delightful thing to do and to build a house in Sicily which would be fun, he is going to take me to Italy! I can't get away and I have again put off that poor Princess [Dolgorouki]. I have sent her the most grovelling telegram and sorrow etc., but I must look to work.

This morning I spent in the house and gardens, looking and thinking and pondering and this afternoon we went over to Hardwick. The Duchess of Devonshire[4] sent a message to say how glad she would be if *I* came and hoped to see me. She was alone and received us and took us all over Hardwick everywhere, it was kind of her. Sir George said he had never seen anybody pick a man's brains so completely, but I like being picked by a Duchess

1. Sir George Sitwell (1860–1937), Conservative MP for Scarborough, 1885–86 and 1892–95. His increasing eccentricity is chronicled by his son Osbert in *Left Hand, Right Hand!* (1944).

2. Daughter of the first Earl of Londesborough.

3. 'With the exception of the decoration of the ball-room at Renishaw, and of the design of the unfinished Pillared Room next it,' wrote Osbert Sitwell, 'even in the earlier days the many alterations that Lutyens planned for my father came to nothing. Nevertheless, year after year, my father would regularly start a new hare to be coursed by the famous architect, but in the end would inevitably employ in his place a local architect, who would more readily fall in with his patron's ideas' (*Great Morning* (1948), p. 25).

4. Evelyn Duchess of Devonshire (1870–1960), 'a great restorer and preserver . . . a perfectionist, she once sacked a housekeeper for half-glazing some chintz' (Duchess of Devonshire, *The House* (1982), p. 43). She and her family were staying at Hardwick while Chatsworth was being made habitable.

of Devonshire and it is such a wonderful and lovely place and so full of gorgeous work and labour that to do service to it in any way however humbly is and must be merit making. She is doing the place up herself poor dear and spends the day chivying inept plummers and workers about the place. I *do* wish they would hand the place over to me! but it was a chance not to be missed – and it is lovely. I do wish you had been with me and Ursula too to see all the great fairies that live in and about the place.

It is awfully spoiling for me to be here and treated with deference! The house party is an amusing one, there is Sir George, a young and old, old-fashioned man like a character in a Disraeli novel and a look of the Duke of Argyll, Lady Ida still young and remains of great beauty, of the Lady Pembroke type, rather, but much more graceful; a tall daughter more like her father than he is to himself if you know that type of likeness; a son, evidently with character, as he cannot go to sleep without everyone in the house including housemaids and guests attending his bedside; a major,[1] very common, an ex-crammer and failed is given a sine-cure of overlooking the cook's (an Italian man) account. An old Col. Morley, approaching the decrepit, here because he likes it and worked for Sir George in some election or other. He is the roundest person you ever saw, with an absolutely round red face, I have termed him the setting sun with great success. A tutor to the boys, rather stiff and good looking enough to allow his mother to flatter him! and a very set university manner, horribly puzzled by me. He received a telegram and I said, 'Well refused again?' It was evidently far more pointed than I should have dared point any remark. A Miss Eve Fairfax,[2] a great friend of Lady Warwick. She was ill all day but she received Lady Ida and me in her bedroom this evening, she in bed! quite easy and natural and the sort of ease of tutoring I love! without any thought unpleasant. A nice Miss X[3] a musician and professional singer,

1. Major Viburne, a blimpish factotum of Sir George, who 'treated the Chesterfield tradesmen – with some of whom we had dealt for several generations – as he imagined, in a mind permanently inflamed with imperialism, that an officer in the Regular Army would treat a low-caste Hindu accused of chicanery' (Osbert Sitwell, *The Scarlet Tree* (1946), p. 50).

2. Eve Fairfax (1871–1978). A beauty, sculpted by Rodin, and a professional house-party guest, she continued to play bridge till she was 100.

3. Helen Rotham, a gifted musician, who joined the Sitwells as governess to Edith.

nice, artistic and very understandable and can follow me down all my bypaths, by which I can only follow main roads, so exasperating to people of what is called common sense by them!

Lady Ida says if I can persuade Sir George to abandon standing for Parliament she will allow his building in Sicily at once! He says to me it will make very little difference. So there is a lot of fishing for work beside the actual work on the tapis.

I shall now come to Storrington [Sussex] before I go to Braemar [to the Dolgoroukis] so as to get a rest and I do do do want to see and be with my own dear love. This fighting with the wolf for work and working for the work's best sake does tire and I do want so darling to be with you without any thought of trouble or anxiety.

Goodnight.

Renishaw Hall, Chesterfield   Sept.20.08.

It was perfect joy to get your letter here.

It was the new Duchess that was at Hardwick trying to get the workmen out of the house, to make it habitable with hot pipes and oh what a pity it is to put 'em in.

Today we go to Haddon.[1] I wired Rutland Lady who answered yes cordially. They have no horses or motors here, but hire taxi cabs from Sheffield. It is funny to go to Haddon in a taxi.

I telegraphed and got sample colour and stuffs here for the Ball Room and they have proved a huge success.

Sir G. is rather sticky about the garden as he isn't really an artist, but has seen a great deal too much.

I am so sorry you didn't get a proper sequence of letters from me, but don't darling be cross with me for that, specially when I am away I am sure it reacts on me in some bad way! I want your blessing always.

1. The medieval castle belonging to the Duke of Rutland.

The quiverful, 1908
Left to right: Ursula, Robert, Lady Emily with Mary on her lap,
Elisabeth, Barbie

1954, Lady Emily's 80th birthday
Left to right: Ursula, Robert, Barbie, Lady Emily, Elisabeth, Mary

Sept.21.08.

I am in train to London. Yesterday we motored over to Haddon, we were late in starting, lost our way and got there, in pouring rain, a little after 5. The whole party except Lady Marjorie [Manners] and Cecily Horner awaited us – those two tired of waiting had gone home. Pamela was there! the Duchess, Cust (!)[1] and the rest of the Manners family except the Duke. Pamela was *so* nice to me and affectionately demonstrative. Lady Ida was rather shy, as we had to cross a bridge and walk some hundred and fifty yards up a hill to where the party stood awaiting us! She acutely feels Sir George's change in politics[2] and is pathetically miserable about it, and Haddon is in the constituency he is on the verge of fighting for (West Derby). I tried to comfort Lady Ida and made her laugh a good deal over it without real effect.

I had one or two goes at Sir George and tried to persuade him that he, as an artist, would be a far better and happier man outside politics. I told him too that Lloyd George was going to tax coal. He said was that so! Then I said, yes, but it would be forfeiture of mineral rights, and that they would not dare to touch the coal interests yet, but would first seize the tin mines, or some of the smaller interests.

Miss Fairfax and myself rehearsed a conversation to terrify Sir George, but I had not the courage to do it, as it was *so* good, though I say it! that I believe it would have been believed and have been written in the great book as a lie!

What Sir George wants is recognition i.e. a peerage! His reason for change is vindictiveness only and that is not enough to justify him making his wife unhappy! *I* shouldn't do it darling.

I have had a very funny time and all the time Sir George has kept me hard at work, in the garden and in the house.

1. Henry Cust (1861–1917), a Soul and the acknowledged lover of the Duchess of Rutland. In 1892 Lady Emily described him as 'a great flirt, and I think an odious young man. He is frightfully patronising . . . I long to box his ears' (*A Blessed Girl*, p. 172).
2. 'Sir George Sitwell has got the hump and is going over to the Liberal Party,' Lutyens wrote to Lady Emily on 19 September 1908.

Homewood   *Oct.15.08.*

Poor Grannie in an awful state of distress yesterday at hearing Con had gone to the Suffragette meeting in Caxton Hall, and then in the Daily Mail *it stated that she had taken warm clothes to the prisoners at Bow Street.*[1] *Poor Mother talked of the disgrace to her name and you would have thought Con had done some real crime. She was quite ill over it and is still very seedy and upset. I am truly sorry for her, but I feel more sorry for Con that at her age she may not follow her own principles. Life is very difficult.*

29 Bloomsbury Square   *Oct.16.08.*

Such a nice story, did I tell you? of the German Crown Prince: The conversation was astronomical and he said 'We know all about the stars.' 'Why, what do you mean?' 'Why they are the decorations my father has showered upon the Almighty.'

I long for Con's letters but I do feel mightily sympathetic for angel mother, Connie being mixed in print with such a crew of notorious rioters – and I sympathise Connie too, but Mrs P. Lawrence[2] is *so* very very second rate and I suppose they are all like it.

29 Bloomsbury Square   *Oct.24.08.*

I wish I had three or four great jobs in London and just two or three big country houses so I have not to run about so much.

I have written to Baker. I have never shown you his letter. The proposal is that on a joint income of £3000 he takes £1000 and I take £2000 and then as the income increases he takes 1500 – 2250; 2000 – 2500; 2500 – 2750; 3000 – 3000, and then equal. He puts in a plea for £300 a year to start with as a living wage

1. After the arrest of Mrs Pankhurst and her daughter Christabel on 12 October 1908, Constance Lytton acted as their intermediary with the Home Secretary, Herbert Gladstone. She also brought them bedding and rugs.

2. Mrs Pethick-Lawrence was treasurer of the Women's Social and Political Union, of which Mrs Pankhurst was chairman. Lutyens had designed the Billiard Room at the Dutch House, Holmwood for the Pethick-Lawrences in 1904.

which is fair I think. He is coming home and then we can talk it over.[1] Then for us there will be the question of Bloomsbury Square, whether we move or the office moves as B. Sq. won't be big enough for both. We could keep the second and third floors – that is your bedroom for our sitting room, a bedroom and bathroom. The top floor for Barbie or anybody or perhaps Baker – and then we should have a house elsewhere. Where shall it be? You taboo Hampstead and Knebworth. I can't go far afield. Bedford Square is too tame, Queen's Square too disreputable. Or we might move the office, which would give us a big house but not much more room except the dining room and pantry would be bedrooms for Robert and the girls. Thomas's office – pantry, office – dining room. My room would be my room still: that would be exciting. We must have a good talk about it. You see the house is not really too small, only I do want to get bigger work and not such a mass of little stuff. I am getting old enough now to do big work.

Bedford Hotel, Tavistock   Feb.24.09.

Here am I alone and absolutely distrait with that distraightness that only can belong to an hotel – an English one. I arrived about 8.15 yesterday, had a good little dinner and at 9.15 Rundle, the Duke [of Bedford]'s agent, called on me. A meeting of this sort always makes me uncomfortable. I imagine all sorts and kinds of a horrible, ignorant and unsympathetic man and, though they very seldom are, yet I don't have the confidence that they will agree with my rights and wrongs. However, we were soon closeted over maps and a map is a good diplomatist dealing in facts without a policy. At 10.30 I went to bed. It was cold and as there was no fireplace in my bedroom I waxed strong and got one – on the top floor! Why? as the hotel is unexpectedly large and quite empty: but for three other gents of awhatonearthwonder-whatyouare sort! But with a fireplace (in the bedroom) and a fire! slept sound and woke early. Had a regular 8 year old's nightmare a man I *tried* to make appear, with a goat's face and beard who leered at me till I hollared and would have hollared could I have

1. This plan for a partnership with Herbert Baker (1862–1946) came to nothing, as Baker's South African practice continued to grow.

found my voice – a hoarse croak, which sounding, woke me to find myself hollaring. I am glad I was by myself and those three gents were away on the floor below me.

This morning of course I was not called, my boots not cleaned, no bath prepared – I had not said! So I got three housemaids and I harangued them in my skutum with only my nighty under – as how I expected everything I could get without need of asking. Does a gent bathe? Does a gent have cleaned boots? etc., etc. I got a bath at last but one of these three gents spits in his! I hate hotels and felt messina[1] towards this one. At 9.15 I went to the Bedford office, got plans and then began a long, long walk. How pleased you would be! to see me walk, walk and climb hedges, ditches, gates, etc. We – Rundle – his clerk Bliss – most intelligent and happy in his place – and self. We saw the building estate, quarries available and unavailable, and round the town. The WHOLE town belongs to the Duke. A derelict mining centre, now without the mines, rows of squalid houses with unwashed glass holding people who do nothing and nobody knows how – grasping on the fortunes of a tourist season. Not one old building left and everything bad modern 50 years old and unkempt at that. The Town Council in a twopenny Ducal Town Hall built by Rundle's architect father, hereditary agent to the Dukes of Bedford – at – Tavistock kind of thing.[2] Full of portraits copied from originals at Woburn by Lady Arthur Russell ✿ to which I add the signs of the Passion (on Ash Wednesday) for safety's sake. Absolutely at the Duke's Mercy yet Bumbledom buzzing where'er it can to impale and mar. Rundle is a good sort, likes his master and sees the humour of his foibles. A socialist at heart – i.e. a good Christian without a church allegiance. Free Trader in spite of ducal Tariff Reform. Lunched with him (Rundle) alone. No wife. A daughter 15 years at Eastbourne. Is he a widower or what? I *longed* to ask but didn't. This afternoon we drove in a two horse landau, much more comfortable than the motor whose carburettor leaked, to Endsleigh – a place with 20 miles of drives in it

---

1. Destructive. In December 1908 an earthquake destroyed Messina.
2. The object of Lutyens's visit was to lay out a housing estate for the Duke of Bedford at Tavistock. The project came to nothing. A Tariff Reformer, and later a Diehard peer, the 11th Duke of Bedford (1858–1940) was the type of client whose feudal outlook appealed to Lutyens's imagination. Edward Collins Rundle succeeded his father as steward in 1896, remaining until 1926.

and a river![1] But the house! it isn't a house at all. A conglomeration in the style Mary Anne. The estate of Endsleigh was church
loot in Henry VIII. An abbey which is commemorated by a mitre
displayed here and there in odd places in conjunction with the
ducal coronet. A plaster Strawberry Hill Gothic with wood
window frames painted to look like granite – a local material!

They are making now an arboretum of piney horrors and two
gardens for butterflies! That is a garden composed of butterfly
loving plants.[2] Then there is a bird oasis and a fishing hatchery
with millions of small trout with the egg still sticking to them – an
enthralling sight – and one salmon four years old hatched and
bred there knowing no sea, no river and fished out for my
pleasure and I suppose everyone else's – by a net. Poor God-
forsaken beastie. A pond full of rainbow trout and a river full as
only a Duke can fill it with trout. I shall pray to fish.

The Duke is going to rebuild the village nearest Endsleigh.[3]
What a chance! if one got his ear and the town leases here are
falling in. But oh it wants industries and raisons d'être beyond the
tourist one.

The Duchess[4] apparently does nothing and sees no one and is a
mere name. A great pity. The boy Tavistock, now twenty, is also
kept out of sight, is very shy and watches spiders by the hour and
hours together, but takes no part in the town life and is not
known even by sight. What can you do with chances like this
missed! thrown away? That the Duke spent £70 in repapering a
room 13 feet square at Endsleigh to get it as it was before –
hideous – to avoid a change – frightens me. I don't mean the £70
but the obstinacy of it.

The Duchess rides hard and that is why there is only one boy
and they come here for three weeks in the year with a whole
township on their knees. Yet he is a very conscientious and land
proud landlord, patronising small oo-ologies on a large scale and
keeping no proper records. Last few years 200,000 rainbow trout

1. Endsleigh was built by Wyattville in 1810 with grounds laid out by
Repton.
2. The inspiration, perhaps, for the butterfly garden at Delhi. The Duke was
President of the London Zoological Society.
3. Milton Abbot, where Lutyens built a terrace of cottages, was the only
commission for the Duke that materialized.
4. Later known as the Flying Duchess, on account of her record-breaking
career in the air.

were put into the river and no one allowed to kill them. Now anybody killing one anyhow is a benefactor! I like the experiment but there seems to be no record, method or definite and reasoned why given.

Lawrence, the last London agent, was his contemporary at Oxford, and Prothero,[1] Lawrence's successor to the Chief Stewardship, was tutor to them both. This I like: it seems affectionate and picturesque and I should have loved to have shown continued confidence in my dominie – had I ever had one.

I wonder if Rundle pumped me as I pumped him. The gross rental of Tavistock alone is £36,000 a year and another £4–5000 on royalties of sorts. Now how does Tavistock without an industry manage to pay that? and the nett rental is less than nothing thanks to the Poo Poohological digressions.

Tomorrow I go to Hestercoombe and will get an hour or two at Exeter, a town I have never seen.

I have made some headway with two of my fellow guests. It *must* be the third who spits in his bath.

It will be joy to get home on Friday.

29 Bloomsbury Square   *Feb.24.09.*

What we have been going through!

Betty had gone out to a play and I was trying to keep awake for her return, when at 11.30 in walked Con. I said jokily 'Are you arrested?' and she said yes. She was in an awful state of exhaustion and collapse with a racking headache, but happily we got her hot water and bottles, and she recovered. I can't tell you now all she had gone through, how she did it all I can't imagine. Betty came in at 12 o'c. and we had a good talk till about 1, when I went to bed, and we put Con to bed, but I am afraid she got no sleep, but Bets rubbed her and was with her, and we were so happy we could be together.

Bets went off with her to Bow Street at ¼ to 10. I waited in case of Mother coming, but she decided not to, and Vic went down to

---

1. Rowland Prothero (1851–1937), was a Fellow of All Souls 1875–91, and agent-in-chief to the Duke of Bedford 1898–1918. 'The care of a great estate in its widest implications appealed to him as the opportunity for constructive work in administrative and social fields' (*DNB*). He was created Baron Ernle in 1919.

her. I am afraid she will be heart broken – and I can't bear it. Con
made a little speech in court and said it was the proudest day of
her life. Chippy and Betty went and saw her in her cell.

29 Bloomsbury Square   April 7.09.

Alfred Lyttelton came to see me about Mrs Barnett and the
Hampstead City. The majority of the Board supported my
scheme and Mrs B. is apparently awfully upset about it. I want a
certain height of building in a certain place for the general effect.
Mrs B. is dead against this certain height on the ground of the
other houses near being overshadowed. They would naturally
like not to disappoint Mrs B. who is the pioneer of the movement
and Mother of Hampstead. I quite *feel* this and hate going dead in
the teeth of Mrs B. The hard thing is that the board refer the
matter back to me, in the hopes that I may see some way out.

The Tenants Co-op, tenants of the H.G. City Trust, go, as
Alfred Lyttelton says, to their crack architect and do all that he
tells them and then the Board tries to refuse. He, A.L., says it is
absurd. He thinks Mrs B. is a dangerous woman – in that she is a
woman! and would not be loyal to a vote, but work up a rumpus
at Hampstead about it. Unwin warns me that it will make things
difficult between me and Mrs B. in the future. She evidently won't
forget it. There is a good deal of ill feeling in Mrs B.'s chest for the
Co-op Tenants and Vivian,[1] she thinks they are getting too
powerful on the trust.

Alfred L. was quite in agreement with me and awfully nice
about it and enthusiastic over my scheme. I feel you will have no
pity for Mrs B. as I do. He says I will be building all over the
country under the New Towns' Planning Bill and will speak and
has spoken to J. Burns[2] about me, and I wouldn't be surprised if
A.L. didn't go to the Local Government Board in the next
administration which would be good for me.

If I could see a way out of it I should be glad but I won't move

1. Henry Vivian (1868–1930), Liberal MP for Birkenhead 1906–10, was the
Chairman of Co-partnership Tenants Ltd, the financial administrators of
Hampstead Garden Suburb.
2. As President of the Local Government Board, John Burns was responsible
for the pioneering Housing and Town Planning Act of 1909.

that way unless I *do* see a way, a real good or better way than the present scheme shows.

The Barnett quarrel will rest I suppose until her return in about three weeks' time.

On board ship for Holyhead at last   June 10.09.

I do long to hear of your speech [at a suffragette meeting] and all about it and I do wish I had heard you. I am sure it will be a great success though your nervous trepidation will spoil and waste it for yourself.

I felt rather hopeless about all governments and the very small glimpse I see of Ireland emphasises it. I distrust *all* statesmen.

The Barings very kind, very amusing is the life, the children affectionate and nice to me. The house all pulled to pieces and they live in three cottages up the hill and I slept in a room near the harbour so I had a long walk for my meals. How you would love Lambay. The cock rhea is very busy sitting so I only saw the hen. The Japanese cranes now fly around which is an amusing and weird sight. They have imported a Dutch bull which is free as yet and out and about with the cows! much to Fraülein's[1] alarm.

The Barings, *mère et père*, occupy one cottage apart from the others, the children and govy another and the servants a third. I do envy them their life and oh what fun it would be with *you* and you would love the air and freedom of it all – all four square, sea side, mountain to yourself and family.

29 Bloomsbury Square   June 10.09.

My meeting quite a success last night. Hall very full, enormous majority of men, who were all very friendly; one or two interruptions but nothing much. My speech lasted above five minutes, but I felt it was most flat and pointless and I was sick with fright. Mrs Pankhurst spoke for an hour and was splendid.

---

1. 'Dicky' Baur. 'She wore a black and white striped shirt with a tie and had a gold watch pinned to her bosom and a steel buckle to her belt' (Daphne Pollen, *I Remember I Remember*, privately printed 1983, p. 3).

---

29 Bloomsbury Square   Aug.3.09.

Mr Gaisford, inheriting Lord Howth's property,[1] takes the family name of St Lawrence and he wants a family handle. He is a Roman Catholic and would build a chapel which would be fun, especially as he would get the Host there – a piece of ecclesiastical snobbery, wonderful too in idea. But I was near to explosion when he said that the Elements – a sort of Christ chop – were not perpetual, they die once a month and have to be reconstituted by a bishop with, I suppose, a special faculty from the Pope. I don't see how else they could work it, as if they were considered perpetual heaven knows into what hands the consecrated wafers of true blood etc. would fall. But the phrase sounds odd. 'The Elements are not perpetual.' How can one expect justice, goodly living, when men start life on such absurd contra-nature fallacies. No church seems able to exist unless it is built on some dogmatic rock and no man can devise a church of common sense – common understanding. I can understand the artistic side being satisfied by these abnormalities.

Am home very late very tired. I had a most lovely passage with a great moon over a still sea.

29 Bloomsbury Square   Aug.5.09.

You addressed your mother's letter to me. I am forwarding it on. I read it! It was longer than mine, but you say you will write today. You see I still love you well enough to be jealous!

About Lloyd George – *The Times* is full of it today[2] and Bendor has written himself which I think is a pity especially as the letter is a bit involved. So there is no need for me to make explanation. Lloyd George attacked the Duke of Westminster and branded him as a robber. He has a regular letch for this sort of thing.

But the Grosvenor estate of all people! Some twenty years back

1. In 1910 Lutyens built a chapel and made alterations at Howth, near Dublin, 'a romantic house with a courtyard, where a family curse decrees that an extra place be always laid at table for the unexpected guest' (Hussey, *Lutyens*, p. 192).

2. Lloyd George's Limehouse speech (31 July 1909), in which he pilloried 'Bendor', 2nd Duke of Westminster.

the old Duke spent so much on public improvements on his London properties that the banks very nearly sold him up and for a few hours it was all touch and go with him. Even now Bendor is pulling down a large block of valuable London buildings to let sun into the backs of some cottages and mews.

Look at the roads he made and money he spent around Eaton Square! and [William] Bird told me the other day he himself had shot snipe in Eaton Square! If Eaton Square, etc. had not been developed in the spacious way the Duke did it do you think Gorringe[1] would have had the opportunity of developing the same business he now has made? It is a matter of speculation if you will and Gorringe and the Grosvenor Estate are partners to it and it has nothing whatever to do with anyone else.

Any man dealing in anything wherein he stands to lose and win, if he wins is called a robber, and if he loses he is robbed.

For another instance look at the money the Duke of Westminster threw into the gutter by insisting on the south side of Mount Street being kept low so as to let the sun into the street.

I should say that no great estate had ever been so humanely administered as the Grosvenor estate and this is the estate that that cad L. George instances – as a robber Duke. His terse contemptuous phrase goes the whole length and width of the country as an utterance of a Crown Minister and who will read Bendor's letter?

Compare the Grosvenor estate methods and the Croydon Town Council dealing with the Whitgift hospital.[2] If Croydon was the Duke's that awful block of *hideous* shop buildings would go at once and the old hospital be opened up.

Look at Eaton – Chester – and then think. The estates of all the 27 Dukes in England could be bought up for some thirty millions. Carnegie could buy the lot and the whole of their combined fortunes would, if seized, only pay the deficit on the budget for two years.

The whole thing is childish, having no sense of proportion, simply the letch to distress and annoy folk more gentle than himself. Bah! This is what our democracy and vaunted Mother of Parliaments is bringing us to.

1. Gorringe's Stores were in Buckingham Palace Road.
2. Almshouses, built 1596–9.

I went down to Maytham[1] yesterday. By way of saving time I went to Appledon where Mrs Tennant was to meet me in her motor. Her motor man was ill so we had to drive 8 miles in a dog cart and then I had to drive 12 miles to catch a possible train to London as I was dining with the FABS.[2] So I spent another day drifting about between trains and only had a rushed half hour of the job. Such a worry and such a bore.

I have another small worry and I hate it. In the profession there is a great deal of feeling for registration, etc. As in all else the bounders and rotters are in the majority and they try to interfere with other people's affairs. There is a vacancy in the RA for an architect now, so these bounders must needs send out voting papers amongst all the architects as to who should be the next RA architect. No self respecting architect could have taken notice of it. My papers went into the waste paper basket at once. But the horror of it is that the result is now published and *I*! head the list. It is d—d cheek.

This is another long peevish letter.

Darling love I must work.

Southwold   *Aug.6.09.*

Betty is beside me in bed talking delicious funny language. Barbie is also in bed counting out her money. She has sold her bicycle for £2 and is so delighted – she is poring over her wealth . . . . Here I was interrupted to hunt for a large flea that was hopping about the bed. I can't tell you what a state we are in. Barbie is covered with bleeding sores and I with large red weals all over me. I must get some Keating's powder.

I had such a longing last night to escape from my educators and fly to my Nedi. Mrs Webbe reads me Esoteric Christianity[3] *all the morning and we have* Jane Eyre *at rest time after lunch and a George Meredith novel in the evening.*

1. Great Maytham, Rolvenden, Kent, which Lutyens was building for the Liberal politician, H. J. (Jack) Tennant (1865–1925), was 'Lutyens's version of the traditional Whig seat . . . a careful and somewhat uninspired example of the "Wrenaissance" ' (*Catalogue 1981*, p. 122).
2. The Foreign Architectural Book Society, an informal club within the RIBA, which met periodically to dine or visit old buildings.
3. By Mrs Besant. Published in 1901.

Southwold   *Aug.9.09.*

We had an agitating morning on the beach as we had decided to try and sell Votes for Women.[1] So after bathing we started along the beach with palpitating hearts. I sold two copies and entered into a long conversation with each buyer. Barbie sold nine copies and Robert two and Mrs Webbe two but she sold more on the way home and in the afternoon and by evening we had sold our thirty copies. I feel we have thoroughly established ourselves as Suffragettes. Pussie and I had quite a quarrel in the evening because she said she should write for more and go on selling them and I said much better wait till the new number and not bother people to death. She was so positive and said we were all wrong and I felt so cross with her.

I had to launch out this afternoon after the children's resting time and Jane Eyre, Chippy said to me 'I think you ought to do a little hard reading now'. I just told him and Pussie how I felt about being so much educated and not a moment to myself or to write a letter and then to expect me to read hard the one spare time of the day! Chippy was rather sorry for me I think and took the trouble to come down to the beach to make up a little.

29 Bloomsbury Square   Aug.9.09.

I am sorry you have been selling *Votes for Women* and you were quite right to stop when you did and after all you had done and if you have to sell them far better sell another number and try to gradually increase your circulation instead of exhausting yourself and the patience of your maybe purchasers. I always did think Mrs Webbe a little unwise with little sense of proportion and liable to let her ideas burn themselves, her and everyone near her.

I had a talk with McKenna about Suffragettes and told him one or two facts he didn't know and which he would never have learnt or received if shouted at him through a press-gang-press or a megaphone.

I am sure more good is done by quiet means than by civil-war methods.

Yesterday Muntzer called on me and took me to see his house

1. Edited by Mr and Mrs Pethick-Lawrence.

at Guildford and then came back to tea with Bumps who was very well – for her – but oh! her life now –

Breakfast at nine
   sausages
   cold bacon
   eggs
   coffee
Beef tea at eleven!
Lunch at one – Beef steak pudding, beer and stuffed tomatoes – to bed 1.30–3.30 – coffee
   Tea 4.30
   Dinner 7.30
and it was 365 degrees in the shade!

I dined with the Jekylls. Herbert Jekyll is much happier. He has got his money and office for the inquiry from the Government into the London roads question.

At the rate we are going – and London is increasing by 100,000 people a year – she will throttle herself and will not be able to supply herself with food. Paris is much smaller, has 42 great roads into her – London has only 20. They are going on building and buildings will have to come down and roads widened and new ones made, for it is quite possible – a blocked road – and London would be in a state of siege.

Our methods are wonderful of quite untaught and irresponsible municipalities, elected by an ignorant and untutored electorate, to simply throw away money in expensive local improvements which are little else than vulgar aggrandisements, with no state scheme linking them all together as they have in France and Germany.

This is where big estates like the Grosvenor estate with their advisers and continued policies pan out so much better for the public good. Even better than the Crown estates where political exigencies alone dictate the appointments and where men act as trustees only and not principals.

No work is done best where the men's interests are put first and not the work's. And this, I believe, is the big difference between, say, feudalism and democracy. I will spare you any enlargement of this theory. Feudalism only fails 1) where the lord is bad and 2) more generally when the vassals have democratic leanings and work for themselves. Democracy in any case must fail by this one reason alone.

The train is very jolty today – an old carriage I suppose. My own, own darling. When am I to see you? Do write and tell me about yourself. And write me more about Robert and don't be angry with anything I may say or be worried by it. I write, often in a hurry, and say just what is passing through my mind at the moment and all I say is subject to what you say as my life is subject to yours and my heart in complete subjection to your sweet self, Angel Love.

Southwold   Aug.10.09.

I think there is much wisdom in what you say but I think your gospel of work and its glorification somewhat alters where the work is ground out of you by a cruel employer. I don't think a sweated woman making matchboxes would feel there was much beauty about her work. (Betty has just announced to Chippy she has been in a big way on the beach!) But I think the ideal socialism is to give and not to take. Wisdom should begin with those who have and not with those who have not – but this is a slow process. If all possessions were regarded only as a trust for humanity and never for the benefit of the individual conditions would soon improve.

Darling love, come soon and I will soothe your irritations. I have never known you so angry about politics before and yet you own the Budget is a good one.

In train to Newcastle   Aug.10.09.

I am so glad you struck at hard reading and I do want *you* to enjoy yourself and take everything joyously. I don't see the good either of a dilettante storage of knowledge which can only make a banquet for the worms after dissolution – a dilettante it can only be and no fun for the worms. Reading is only second hand acquirement – worth nothing except it is frankly for pleasure which in your case it is not. Or as an auxiliary in the pursuit of some definite object.

Nor would I describe you as a patron of the fine arts! A good patron is a fine, a very rare thing. For a young man at a university who generally has absolutely no end in view he had better read hard than do nothing and it ends as often as not in his drifting into a school master or parson: they being the only two professions the universities attempt to fit a man for. And some stick in the meshes of the sieve and become dons and professors of mostly dead subjects – whilst ugliness and poverty, misery and crime abound.

When at Bumps' I was much amused by reading in the *West Surrey Times* that a certain gardener was exhibiting in a certain flower show 'peas in purple pods – a variety little seen now'. Oh for a pea in a purple pod and we giggled and Bumps has sent me the enclosed pome:

> Oh for a pea in a purple pod;
> For this I labour and turn the sod;
> And trench it deep for many a rod;
> And carry manure in bricklayer's hod;
> All for a pea in a purple pod!

I have got to stay in an hotel tonight and *hate* it 'The North Eastern' and I get there between 11 and 12 p.m. A lovely evening and I might be sitting cool with you somewhere and seeing the children go to bed and they will soon be all too old. I don't seem to see how I shall ever see you again at Bloomsbury Square. I have the office and you the children and wherever you are the children are and we can't go away together – you hate travelling. Nor could we do any 'hard reading'. Our sleeping and waking hours are reversed. Yet I do so r..ss you darling and long for you every moment. I so want to see and hear the family. Your friends seem little use to me and mine to you. Yet I so love to see you happy and to be near you when you are. You know nearly all my faults and scold me dreadfully: and I love you for your candour and the freedom I can give you.

You are such a perfect mother and such a dear true wife and I love you and I know you love me and nothing else can matter. And I only growl and say cross-cut things because I am so miserable being away from you.

Darling sweet heart.

          Your own very very loving Nedi.

Do say you love me. Say it in unexpected places – between lines and overleaf sudden like – just to please me darling.

---

29 Bloomsbury Square   Aug.14.09.

I didn't get back [from Maytham] until 11.30 last night. Very tired and no dinner, bread and cheese lunch and no breakfast. But it is good this hot weather – better than Bumps' beef steak.

Knebworth. Pamela's sitting room to be done with bead tapestries. The Tudor corridor a puzzle indeed.

I am down early, 9 o'c. to see a man who hasn't come so I write to you. Dr Bond[1] comes and then I go to Knebworth.

Mrs Tennant[2] was very much herself yesterday and goes into the most minute details of costs etc., which means awful delay and then everything is upset by some unforeseen and trivial affair and everybody is exasperated. Myself I am rather amused and entertained and I chaff her and she says it *is* her besetting sin she knows, and then plunges deeper into a mass of minutiae.

29 Bloomsbury Square   Aug.16.09.

Just back from Knebworth. Last night we were all talking of death and of course we all had different views, some minding and some not. Gerald [Balfour] was particularly above the possible, if any, discomforts and death. So I asked him what would he do if a skeleton walked into the room (we were at dinner) clothed with all the paraphernalia and trappings of death and walked round the table and said –

> I have a little coffin and it's not for you
> it's not for you
> it's not for you
> I have a little coffin and it IS for you.

We all giggled and laughed and I got no answer.[3]

Gerald was very judicial and interesting about the Suffragettes. He does not see how Asquith could take any other line now, than the one he has taken. He owns it would have been wiser for the

1. Henry Bond (1853–1938), Cambridge don and Master of Trinity Hall 1919–29, for whom Lutyens built Middlefield, Staplefield, Cambridge (1908).

2. May Tennant (1869–1946) was appointed first woman factory inspector in England in 1893 and after her marriage in 1896 she took a leading part in promoting the cause of women's work and welfare.

3. After his retirement from politics in 1906, Gerald Balfour devoted himself to the cause of Psychical Research.

sake of a quiet life if he had seen them at first. He has said all he has to say and would not say more. He does not think the agitation is sincere as if they saw Asquith they would start another grievance and another agitation. He does not think the vote would do either the good the pro-Suffs think or the harm the antis think it would. He put it all very well. He thinks the cry is not of first rate importance by any means – that it is very difficult to get anything done if the lines of cleavage are not on the party lines – and unless the differences are on party lines no Government can or will take a question up.

He did not think with all the work before them, etc. Asquith will introduce any form of Suffrage Bill and if he did it would be universal suffrage.

Arthur Balfour would probably do the same as Asquith and leave it to the House in the event of any sort of suffrage reform bill. The Ministers are there by reason of their party and for party questions and it is quite reasonable they should be allowed to differ on minor policies. He is not opposed to the women's vote because he thinks a vote is such a rotten thing: if the women came to have the majority of votes then he would reconsider arguments which he now thinks to be absurd.

If women had the great majority they might insist on a position or policy which they would not have the physical strength to eventually enforce.

He put it beautifully which is a great deal more than I have done. He thinks the Suffragettes are engineering their cause very badly now and he had no sympathy with law breaking. He was very Geraldian in his best mood. Victor did not press him.

He thinks Con is a saint upon earth and so say all of us, but that she knows little of the world and wants judgement. Don't repeat this, though we all know it.

Lloyd George is all right for some departmental work but as a Cabinet Minister he has put himself quite outside the pale. Gerald says he likes him: 'He is a nice fellow', but laughs at him. A parliamentarian rather than a statesman.

The Budget is all right. The land clauses are a bit raw and he don't know much about land and if the socialists want to nationalise the land let them if they can. But it is not for a Chancellor of the Exchequer to introduce that sort of revolution into a budget. I think it is a pity but it is not this side of it that has worried me.

———

29 Bloomsbury Square   Aug.26.09.

Just got back from Ashby where I had an exhausting time battling
with the commonalities of Guest, and Mrs G. don't help me and
follows him blind, in a way a wife ought NOT! However we have
arranged a scheme, but did not get my way with the big simple
direct lines I wanted and have had to put in a good deal of fuss
fuss to please I. Guest.

He has also got into a hump with the old parson there, over a
matter of £40, and I had to fight the parson's battle as it affected
the reparation of the old church. Guest's policy is that the parson
would get into debt and so become dependent on him (this in a
radical). I boiled over, but did no good. In the meantime the
parson goes to a local architect who straightway makes proposals to ruin the old church tower. I had a good talk to the parson
and stopped a lot of the work, and now I may have the bore of a
professional etiquette question. It was very good of me really and
folk generally are only fit to be slaves and talk of enlightenment is
humbug.

29 Bloomsbury Square   Sept.1.09.

I had to go to Ireland.[1] The job was very small, but it will be as big
as Hestercombe gardens or bigger when all done, and just at the
start it is very important to go over and see how they were going
on so that no irreparable damage was done. The matter was
trifling perhaps but the principle of it was the kernel of the whole
thing – d'you see? The bother is I could not work in Lambay and
Howth too, but on the other hand it is almost quicker to go to
London and back than the Irish cross-journeys.

It was quite cold last night and I would have been glad of
another blanket.

I go to Renishaw today, back tomorrow and on Friday go to
Temple Dinsley[2] and then Saturday!

1. To Heywood, County Leix, where Lutyens was designing gardens for Col
E. Hucheson Poë (1848–1934).
2. Where Lutyens was building additions three times as large as the original
eighteenth-century house for H. G. Fenwick, a distant cousin of Mark Fenwick.

29 Bloomsbury Square   Sept.16.09.

I saw Lady Battersea who was in great distress about her maid,
having been found to have been married to a footman. The maid
had a babe and had to produce to Lady B. her marriage certi-
ficate. The maid had to go and the footman was sacked. Of course
it is secret and horrid of her, but not really wrong and I told her
she would have to be godmother to the babe. It would have
delighted me. I gave Lady B. fits.

I am so distressed about things in Ursula's hair. They can't have
got established, but that girl ought to be publicly branded. It's
dreadful poor darling all of you.

God bless you and keep you

Overstrand   Sept.17.09.

*Poor Lady Battersea: why did her maid demean herself to a
footman? Is it the foreign one here who is so civil to me?*

In train   Sept.17.09.

The Duke of Manchester is next door. What a toad he looks.
Even if he built a castle by me! I could hardly forgive him for his
looks.

Talking of Dukes do you see the whole of the Devonshire folk
have been poisoned. This is I believe thanks to Lloyd George's
silly utterances – as a Cabinet Minister – and some idiot has taken
him seriously.

Sir George Sitwell called yesterday.

Dr Bond who loves his house,[1] especially the inside and the
south side. He likes the north side but it frightens him. He would
like it right enough if it belonged to somebody else. I have, for a
little house, got an extraordinary amount of dignity into it. Oh
when can you come? and see my houses! with me.

---

1. Middlefield. 'When it was done,' wrote Lawrence Weaver, 'Mr Lutyens
had done nothing more austere, or any building which relied so entirely on the
qualities of mass, symmetry and proportion' (*Houses and Gardens by E. L.
Lutyens* (1913), pp. 232–3).

I am very tired and do wish I had an ordinary bed to go to but am glad to get away from the office for a bit.

I was at Cumberland Place this morning at 9.30 (Lady Battersea's house).

The footman may be alright – it is not the German – and you ought not to talk of demeaning. What I don't like about it is not the marriage of a footman (he may be a butler someday, an Admirable Crichton, a butler to a lady's maid, a footman to a lady's maid is the same but a mere question of age), but the maid who was so beloved by Lady B. deceiving her and then trying to get the babe out during her holiday and come back again and never to tell.

I do want you to miss me darling and to love me and forget my crossness and waywardness. Angel darling goodnight.

Overstrand   *Sept.21.09.*

Fancy Lady Battersea's maid was the nice housekeeper who was here to receive us and the child was born the following week! The whole village knows about it.

I am very miserable because I have almost made up my mind to leave the Social and Political Union. I feel so sure they mean murder that I must make my protest while there is time though it is heart rending. I feel it dreadfully but I must do what I think is right.

Overstrand   *Sept.24.09.*

I should love to go to Knebworth with you on Sunday as I feel I cannot see Con. I have such a wonderful letter from her this morning. It makes me weep, but does not alter my resolution.

29 Bloomsbury Square   Oct.9.09.

Out of the *Westminster* tonight:

> Suffragettes at Newcastle. Four suffragettes were
> arrested at 12.30 this morning at Newcastle on Tyne for

throwing stones and breaking the Liberal Club windows. They were subsequently brought before the magistrate and sent to prison for fourteen days. Another suffragette was taken into custody this afternoon for throwing a stone at one of the windows of the Palace Theatre where the meeting was being held.

That's all, darling, to catch post. This is all the suffragette news. No women were allowed in the building.

Loving
Nedi

I see in the stop news that Conny and two others have been arrested in Newcastle.

29 Bloomsbury Square   Oct.12.09.

Mrs Barnett was vanquished and the church reduced, is agreed to, but Oh I do want more money for *my* church. I was not present for an hour and there must have been a tussle. I have not heard yet but will tomorrow. The Ecclesiastical Commissioner congratulated me on the design. The church is to start at once.

As regards the houses, the resolution Mrs B. had passed was that if the Co-partnership people could not get plans they wanted out of me they were to employ another architect. To surprise this resolution on me *when their last instructions* were that I *was* to *make* the Co-partnership people carry out *my* plans – is very shabby and unbusinesslike – a complete volte face without giving me any notice or intimation.

29 Bloomsbury Square   Oct.15.09.

I telegraphed to you, I start for ROME tonight.

I went up to Hampstead to find out about the meeting yesterday during the time I was out of the room and to see the church site, etc. and Hampstead is in full swing. Mrs Barnett was furious about the last meeting which settled everything without her, but she had to give way and did it with grace. But what they talked about for an hour I don't know. The resolution she passed

Lady Constance Lytton, journalist, 1897

Constance Lytton about to throw her stone, Newcastle, 1909

St Jude's Church, Hampstead, preliminary sketch

authorising the Co-partnership people to go to another architect when the delay and fault was on her side is a preposterous piece of cheek. She gets panics and won't let anybody do anything but herself and I believe the bottom of it is that a Ratepayers Association has been formed against *her*. She is a bore. Bourchier[1] I think means to do the whole church but where he is going to get the money I don't know.

In train Genoa! to Roma   Oct. 18.09.

I rushed through Genoa to find what I knew and with little time I found but little I didn't know of. One palace I didn't know and don't now by name, with a duplicated cornice to its Doric order which was very happy. The morning was grey and misty and except for the many little Pre-Raphaelite hills and trees it might have been Scotland. But on arriving at Genoa the sun burst out

1. The first vicar of St Jude's. The church was only completed in 1933 as a memorial to Bourchier.

and it is the first summer day I have seen this year. Real shade compelling bright day.

The architecture, a very little I have seen, cries aloud for sculpture and good housemaiding. The Rococo muck in the churches (the three I have seen) is dreadful. The lavish use of marble as stone, the splendid waste of space in the buildings and the economy of it in road ways makes the place. The very reverse of what we lay down as right in England. The lavish space given away in staircases makes me sick with envy. But the streets are too narrow for the palaces that stand upon them, from any point of view. The effect is not really great or happy. I don't refer to the gaps between them with long up climbing stair roads. This is fine and in a way beyond my criticism in that they were not *designed*.

I want badly to keep my head here.

Another thing that astonishes me is the fact of the small amount of window area required to light a room – brilliantly well.

The architecture, a good deal of it, is very badly finished off. Thoughtless, which would make me wild if it was mine.

The great buildings on the hill tops I see excite me fearfully, high, high, up against the sky. And how the devil do they get to them – still more at them to build them.

The picture oxen so mild and clean in pictures are poor old wrecks – mostly cows. Suffragettes! A mule with paniers full of cabbages and tinned things came well. The modern work too awful for words but the sun absolutely prevents one seeing them.

Great aloes in the railway cuttings give one a feeling of seeing something unreal and not seen before and palms in the villa gardens. I don't think I shall ever like a palm. *Then* I have seen a tree I don't know, so I am abroad. A sport of Pre Raphaelite monkey puzzle. We are going down the sea coast. Some painting in the palaces was jolly, but most of it was bad (almost as bad as Fontainbleau), one ceiling was ingenious and good in colour. I don't like the aloes. My insularity *shall* stick to me. I have seen both cypresses and poplars here. I have not seen cypresses as I have pictured them yet but the poplar so far holds its own. They are nearly as lovely here as they are on the Thames! The sea might be Brighton and but for the door handles on this carriage door I might be there or anywhere.

There is a delicious effrontery in the planning of their buildings – national rather than architectural.

I do wish I could have come with Wren.

They, the Italians, have fine ideas in scale. Stone thus ☐ instead of thus ☐ to build with. Then the great thick rolls of the little bricks and roofs as thick as the furrows of a plough *blazed* with light and great shadows from it. I look forward to twilight and if I am in some happy place along the railway I shall watch for magic. . . . I have seen cypresses up a hillside black in the sun amongst the grey foliage, *good*, just enough to make me realise my dreams of them may yet be true!

Nearing Spezia – nothing but tunnels. My eyes are full of dust trying not to miss the occasional glimpse of little town spots between the tunnels growing up out of the sea. The pity is that the habit of trains is to stop in the stations and not outside of them which latter system would be far more amusing.

Just past the Carara mountains where the white marble of that name comes from. There is lots! left for me! I have seen some quite nice picture book oxen and one or two characteristic little churches and a castle or two but nothing of red letter count. The next excitement in three quarters of an hour will be Pisa.

Pisa just got and oh so too short a glimpse of the white marble buildings with *lovely* red roofs against great blue hills lit by a setting sun . . . lovely. Just what the world *ought* to be. The cathedral, leaning tower, baptistry, then a glimpse of the Arno with some bridges and quiet buildings, pink and green, and now I am locked in the embraces of a station, with all that loveliness outside. If only they would back the train a quarter mile and let it stand there.

Had dinner – tried to get into conversation with an Italian that looked like Barlow who is travelling round the world – but not south of the equator! for pleasure. But I can't get further. He looked a bit wild and madly odd and I hoped he was an architect or something exciting enough to quicken the journey for it is now dark. I can see nothing and I have no book, having finished – long ago – my extravagance of buying *Ann Veronica*.[1] I keep it for you to read. It's good reading and I simply burn to know what you think and say of it.

Well, I, to the astonishment of this weird Barlowitalian, drew a map of the world and he traced his voyage. Since when he has retired. I think he is frightened of me or I have insulted him. There

1. By H. G. Wells (1909). A moderate statement of the case for women's liberation.

was a lady French with a husband – both so fat I cannot help thinking what they must look like *en masse* together – *au naturelle*! She conversed through dinner to her husband *at* me – do you know the feeling? So I put on my spectacles and she said something about Oh God look at that man and I wouldn't let the husband look at me by my looking at him! So you see what I am reduced to in an eleven hour journey. No papers to read and dark. The washing pit in the car is awful. No water, no soap, no towels – and a WC so low that everyone misses and messes it. The buying of a railway guide with maps, etc. is a great consolation but now the train is late I don't know where I am.

Oh that you were here but how tired and bored you would be. Railway travelling tires me just as much as being locked in a room with nothing to do and I am almost too old to fidget, at least to fidget for an occupation.

It has been an exciting day for me but now it seems long and endless. Genoa thrilling. Pisa – the glimpse of it lovely. But nothing nor anything in Italy can come up to my darling wee Emy in London alone.

Your own own very very very loving and adatorri Nedi.

Rome   Oct.21.09.

I have not written to you since my arrival. There is so much to see and with the short time here there is about 3000 things to see more than there is possibly time for. And then the first night – Tuesday – we dined with Count San Maritimo and his *lovely* bride – he is head of the exhibition to be here – and last night at the Embassy. It is all very wonderful and to see the things one knows from illustrations. . . . down a little street and then a corner and lo and behold stands some old loved friend in form of a doorway, staircase or palace. I recognise some of them by their backs – backs which I had never seen.

I don't know where to begin or how to describe what I have seen. St Peter's, various churches, the Capitol, Medici, other palaces, the Forum, and as I was looking down over the Forum what should sail overhead but a dirigible balloon, fish-shaped of bright aluminium. Such a contrast to see the Forum and a dirigible both for the first time at once.

The weather is too glorious for words, a blue, blue sky, lovely gorgeous sun and a breeze which makes life perfect. Directly the sun sets it is dark and the sky goes dark velvet all over. There is no twilight – a darkness comes up as though it is going to rain and then it is night.

Today the Maritimos are going to motor us to Tivoli, the Villa d'Este and Hadrian's Villa. Tomorrow the Vatican and Saturday I start home. I cannot tell you what I have seen and what not. The hotel is so comfy and our little suite of connecting rooms makes us all together intimate and very comfy. I do wish you were here. Victor has had bad doldrums but I think he has reason and I have been able to sympathise with him on the wee new coming.[1] I do *do* wish you were here. The cabs are so cheap and we just drive about for Rome is small, very squalid and few streets have pavements separate from the carriage ways so walking is one continual escape from gesticulating Jehus. Victor goes to the office every morning and then I and Pamela go off sight seeing and at 12.30 we have a gorgeous *déjeuner* of macaroni, etc. and drink Tears of Christ (which is a claret) but now I know things I try to keep her from doing too much.

Do thank Thomas for his telegram about Hampstead. It is kind of him to telegraph and say all is going satisfac.

There is so much here in little ways of things I thought I had invented! no wonder people think I must have been in Italy. Perhaps I have but it was not Rome. I have no internal ronge[2] and nothing comes in the least where I expect it. My old friends stand about in the most unexpected places and in the oddest relation to each other.

Rome   Oct.22.09.

Yesterday at 10 the Maritimos called for us in their motor and away we went through Rome – the awful dirty squalor – awful, prodigious! across the Campagna and away to Tivoli. Fancy being at Tivoli. There were lots of sportsmen shooting sparrows and game of that size, and there were lizards and odd grasshopper things that scuttled across the road. Droves of sheep and mules – the mules with paniers and one mule had its paniers full of little ee

1. John Lytton, b. 11 March 1910.
2. According to Ursula Ridley, a family word meaning memory, or to be reminded of.

wee lambs – 5 to a panier, with their heads and front legs out all of a row. Too funny and touching for words.

The first thing we saw was the ruins of Hadrian's great Villa, set amongst olives and great cypresses and ilex. It must have been an enormous place and really fine and impressive – a vast mass of ruin and here and there a little decoration of ceiling or pavement still left. Then lunch at Tivoli, after which – which was very *bad* – we went to look at the cascades. A great mountain range and then the sea flat Campagna, grey and everything is grey here, *black* and then the crown of blue sky – such blue sky and sweat hot sun. All grey and velvet black. Just what I like and no bright offensive colour except in the modern man's work and that is awful.

Then the Villa D'Este, lovely, grey again and wondrous cypresses and then great silver distances. Some of the work – the terrace balustrades – lovely, but more of the work was horrible and ugly than there was beautiful. It wants to be seen with great discrimination. Yet there is real god-given loveliness and oh if I could have the chances. But you can see in the work when vulgarity prevailed over good taste and sense, the same then as now – if only people could see. Inside the palace the decoration was horrible, and outside a river is taken through the garden and played with *ad nauseam*. Over it all is a great cloak of decay.

There were great masters and bad ones and the patrons could have had little real appreciation of what was right and what was vulgar.

Then home, across the Campagna, facing the setting sun and how disappointing a pimple is St Peter's Dome. Today we start early. I go to see the exhibition site with Vic and I have to make a sketch for him. They have got into difficulties and they are obliged to ask architectural advice and I am going to do it Honorary because if I take a fee and do not build the Pavilion then it will look bad for me. I do not want to appear to take any advantage over them by forcing myself on them when they are in difficulty.

The modern Italian architects are of just about the same bad degree as ones in England. Oh Ems how can God love us? If you were always dirty, every thought of yours was vulgar and pretentious could my best love for you hold? Yes, I should love you for what you were and cling to you ever so but the sorrow of it and that is the feeling one has here – a great pervading sorrow for the people and the land. The more so for the intermittent glimpses of real noble beauty. I *must* stop.

CHAPTER FIVE

1910–1912

THE YEARS 1910–1911 represent the high-water mark of what Hussey has called the 'flood tide' of Lutyens's career. Early in 1910 he received his biggest private commission yet: Castle Drogo on Dartmoor for Julius Drewe. In November 1910 he visited South Africa, and gained his first insight into Empire and its architectural possibilities.

In May 1910 a telegram arrived from Mrs Lionel Phillips asking Lutyens to design the new Art Gallery in Johannesburg. The wife of Lionel Phillips, a partner in Wernher Beit and an associate of Cecil Rhodes, Mrs Phillips had conceived the idea of providing South Africa with an art gallery, financed by 'Rand-lords', that would fulfil Rhodes's cultural ideals. Her artistic adviser was Hugh Lane (1875–1915), the Irish collector and connoisseur, for whom Lutyens had designed a garden in Cheyne Walk. She had acquired a site in Joubert Park, Johannesburg, and when in 1910 a competition for the design failed to produce any convincing local talent Lane advised her to call in Lutyens. Hence the telegram.

The South African architectural scene was dominated in 1910 by Herbert Baker, Lutyens's friend since student days, and he was Lutyens's companion and guide during his visit. With its post-Boer War ebullience, its unlimited wealth and its grand opportunities for constructive imperialism, South Africa went rather to Lutyens's head. As well as the Art Gallery, he designed the Rand Regiments Memorial; there was also talk of a university, a town plan and a great church, none of which came to anything.

Lutyens found in South Africa a new field for the High Game. A meticulously classical building, the Johannesburg Art Gallery reflects his theory about building in countries which are not part of the European civilization. He was convinced that, because there was no craftsmanship indigenous to the country, it was necessary to be more than ever accurate and strictly classical. He wrote about this to Baker: 'in *old* countries you can use *rough materials*, where you find old men instinctively handling it from boyhood and unconsciously weaving lovely texture into it. In a new country it is impossible to expect any help of that sort . . . reliance can only remain in the best *thought* – the harder and purer the better.'[1]

Castle Drogo could hardly have been more different. Julius Drewe was a self-made businessman who, having made his fortune in Home and Colonial Stores, had traced his ancestry back to the Norman Drogo de Teigne, bought land at Drews-teignton (Dru-his-town-on-the-Teign) and wanted a castle to boot. This was the first time Lutyens had been asked to design a conventional country seat from scratch. The trouble was that Drewe wanted not a 'nice big house' in the Georgian style but a castle proper: a castle which, by contrast with the island retreats of Lambay and Lindisfarne, was to perform all the functions of the great house.

Partly because of his client's insistence on solid granite walls six feet thick, only one-third of Lutyens's original design for Castle Drogo was actually built. Yet, in its truncated, asymmetrical form, perched on a rocky promontory overlooking Dartmoor, Castle Drogo represents a high point of Lutyens's dramatic romanticism.

In 1909 Lutyens paid several visits to Varengeville in connection with *Les Communes*, a Y-shaped house he was building for Guillaume Mallet. When he returned from one of these visits he told Lady Emily that the Mallets were Theosophists, and that there was a secret locked cupboard in the music room at *Le Bois des Moutiers* where they kept their religious books. Lady Emily was intrigued, and when she stayed at Varengeville in the spring of 1910 she was initiated into the secrets of the cupboard by Madame Mallet. On her return to London in May 1910 she joined the Theosophical Society.

The Theosophical Society was founded in New York in 1875 by Madame Blavatsky (1831–91), a Russian émigrée, and Col. H. S. Olcott, an American Civil War veteran. In 1882 they moved their headquarters to Adyar, on the shores of the Indian Ocean, now on the outskirts of Madras, but set in an exotic gardened

1. Hussey, *Lutyens*, p. 209.

landscape. In India they gained considerable support amongst educated Hindus.

Theosophy is an eclectic cult, combining elements drawn from all religions, particularly Buddhism and Hinduism. Most Theosophists believe in reincarnation. But perhaps the most fundamental tenet of Theosophy is a belief in the equality of all religions and the brotherhood of man.

Within the Society Madame Blavatsky had founded a secret inner society, the Esoteric Section, which Lady Emily joined in 1911. Its members aspired to enter on the Path of Discipleship under the occult Masters of Wisdom, Kuthumi, Morya and others, who lived in Tibet. One of the Masters might consent to take an aspirant on probation as his pupil, and later accept him for training, leading after some years to initiation. The Masters could be visited on the astral plane in sleep, though the aspirant could only learn what happened on the astral plane from a clairvoyant.

Madame Blavatsky was a controversial character and an aura of crankiness hung about the Esoteric Section from the beginning. In 1885 Madame Blavatsky's celebrated psychic powers were exposed as fraudulent by the Society for Psychical Research. Far from receiving letters from the Tibetan Masters as she claimed, she was accused of inserting forged letters through a sliding panel at the back of the shrine at Adyar. C. W. Leadbeater (1854–1934), an ex-Anglican curate and the chief exponent of Theosophist doctrine after Madame Blavatsky's death, was forced temporarily to resign from the Society in 1906 when he was accused of homosexual relations with the boys in his charge. Though the charge of homosexuality was unproven, Leadbeater freely admitted to encouraging his pupils to masturbate: an admission that discredited him in the eyes of Theosophists – one requirement of the advanced stage that he had reached on the Path of Discipleship was complete sexual purity – as well as bringing disrepute upon the Society as a whole, at a time when masturbation was still widely held to induce madness.

That Theosophy flourished in spite of these scandals was a measure of its ability to satisfy the spiritual cravings of a generation for whom the old religious certainties had been shattered by the onslaughts of science. One way out of the conflict between science and religion – the solution favoured by the more intellectual of the Souls – was to turn the weapons of science upon science itself. Arthur Balfour questioned the philosophical foundations of disbelief; his brother Gerald devoted himself after 1906 to the Society for Psychical Research, which endeavoured to subject spiritual phenomena to scientific proof. Esoteric Theosophy offered another solution: an escape from the moral and rationalist preoccupations of the nineteenth century into the realms of the psychic and the occult.

After Mrs Besant became President of the Theosophical Society in 1907, she and her colleague C. W. Leadbeater (whom she had reinstated after the scandal) put forward the idea that the great spiritual being, the Lord Matreya, was soon to come to earth to found a new religion to help humanity along the path of evolution. The Matreya would occupy a human body just as two thousand years ago he had occupied the body of Jesus and some two thousand years before that the body of Sri Krishna.

Leadbeater had psychic powers, and in 1909, on the beach at Adyar, he saw two Indian boys with remarkable auras. Convinced that the elder, Krishnamurti, was the chosen vehicle for the World Teacher, Mrs Besant adopted him and his brother Nitya and proceeded, with the help of Leadbeater, to prepare him for his vocation.

In January 1911 the Order of the Star in the East was founded to proclaim the coming of the Lord. This led to a revolt of the German Theosophists, who broke away under Rudolph Steiner and formed their own Anthroposophical Society. But to many, and Lady Emily was among them, a new and thrilling dimension had been added to previous beliefs; indeed, without this messianic element Theosophy would have been for her just another cause. For the next twenty years she believed that, in the Order of the Star in the East, she had found her heart's vocation.

When in 1911 Mrs Besant brought the two boys to England, Lady Emily was among the Theosophists who met them at Charing Cross Station. 'I had eyes', she recalled, 'for none but Krishna, an odd figure, with long black hair falling almost to his shoulders and enormous dark eyes which had a strange, vacant look in them. He was dressed in a Norfolk jacket.'[1]

Lady Emily threw herself wholeheartedly into her new calling. She took lessons in public speaking and travelled the country

1. Lady Emily Lutyens, *Candles in the Sun*, p. 303.

lecturing in draughty public halls, staying in dreary suburban houses, emphasizing the need for self-preparation to be ready to serve the Lord Matreya, who was expected to occupy the body of Krishna when he was about thirty. Despite her shyness, she became an accomplished public speaker. 'Even today', she wrote in 1957, 'I would much rather give a lecture than attend a dinner party'.[1] She and the children became strict vegetarians, subsisting on a diet of nut cutlets, and the food at Bloomsbury Square, which was never good, became worse.

Feb.7.10.

I am in the train back to Dublin from Heywood – Colonel Poë. I got on a great deal better this time, Colonel Poë was in a more amenable mood, but his cross period has damaged the garden as there is, I think, evidence in my work of my attitude or despondency towards him. And then these Irish people are so difficult to make work. The foreman is a nice man, terribly underpaid and quite unaccustomed to this sort of work but has done wonderfully well considering. However it is a pity and I don't know whether I'm wrong or not. The job is in a very rough stage too but they don't appreciate anything good. Ears wide open to all criticism which they report and I really lose all sense of proportion. I wonder!

I am going to control the planting which is good and I have sanction for lots of manure which has made the gardener – such a nice man – very happy. But they are all nice men these Irish.

The mad Poë boy[2] was at Heywood. He shouted at me to say I had quite spoilt the place and his poor mother nudged him and tried to quiet him. I think he didn't mean or could mean anything he could say but had got hold of what someone said parrotwise. Miss Paton was much amused and told me what he said as he was difficult to understand: 'Yar sil sill silly, yar qui kite spaw spaw-ilt th' the pl plaice.' At present it does look like it. Don't repeat this as it is rather unkind. I suggested to Miss Paton they should try mesmerism – he can't read yet. I do think Colonel and Mrs Poë are wonderful. They never hide him but always do what they can to bring him out and make him one of any party there may be

1. Ibid., p. 16.
2. Hugh (1889–1958).

there. She is only half there with anybody – the other half watching Hugh to see he don't become impossible. They all, Colonel, Mrs, Miss and Miss Paton go to Paris for the winter to finish Miss Poë. Colonel Poë, you know, has a wooden leg and he sits on a chair and watches the men lay stones – stone by stone – and finds endless fault. I couldn't stand it.

So difficult to write. It is getting dark.

I finally telegraphed Lane 'Impossible abandon work here immediately consult Baker partnership'. Twelve words with my name and address. I could go and leave you darling for six precious weeks, but it shows I may be faced with that sort of a question either to Africa or America or somewhere and it might be very difficult to refuse.

Knebworth House   Whit Monday [May 6.10.]

I *did* get, with joy, your letter this morning, and I never wrote because I too thought no letter would reach you and the telephone is a bore and not comfortable to talk through.

Oh I do wish you had come down. Yesterday divine and today too. Just going off to fish.

I seem to have no real friends, just the people I build for, and then when the building is done I never see them again. I wonder if I am managing my life very badly and it is awful not being more with you. In a few years' time the children will be more or less independent of us and we will be thrown together as we are now thrown apart.

Mothecombe House, Plymouth[1]   July 30.10.

My train on Friday was over an hour late reaching Tavistock, so I had dinner and then went up to the building sites and saw my house.[2]

1. Mothecombe was the home of Alfred Mildmay and his sister Beatrice, unmarried cousins of the Barings, who were spending the summer there. It was a Queen Anne house, the style and period of architecture most admired by Lutyens at this time; he based Ednaston Manor upon it the following year. In 1923 he added a dining-room wing to Mothecombe and altered the house and garden.
2. Little Court, Tavistock, for Major Gallie.

The gloaming is the best time to see a house so I was happy for it looked all right – promising. A wet day – Saturday I was up early and met the builders and all the other people and had a very busy morning and got through my work by 1.30 which enabled me to catch an earlier train and I had an hour at Plymouth looking at it.

Oh the horror of the place – its ugliness and it must once have been so delicious. Great warships in the harbour always impressive, but the buildings and people all equally hideous.

I saw one beautiful face – a young mechanic of sorts. I should like to have known him. A face exactly like a young Michelangelo. He was delightful to a drunk sailor.

The Duke of Bedford is going to sell all Tavistock except my 300 acres or so when he has embarked on this building scheme. The townspeople are rather aghast. They all growled at the Duke owner who never turned anyone out for non payment of rent, and gave this and did that etc. Now he is selling, the very people who complained now say it is scandalous to sell, etc. It will make a great difference. It means that rents will have to be paid and value given and it will probably wake the place up and give energy. But it will be a new town of new people.

He will keep Endsleigh and 800 acres. He may rebuild his own village and the agent – such a nice man – Rundle, spoke to me about it. It would be an awfully nice job and he, the Duke, does speak about rebuilding Endsleigh, which if I could get it *would be good*! But the Duke is apparently a funny, cranky and absolutely tasteless man.

This is a delicious place, a nice old square stone house surrounded by woods and deep lanes and the sea quite close through a wood, a sandy bay, tree girt. It is so much lovelier than the barren villa beset East Coast. Here it is real England, great trees and the sea thrown in.

I go back to London tomorrow.

East Runton, Cromer   *Aug.2.10.*

I quite agree with you that the east coast is very bleak and ugly; but then the climate is perfection and I would far rather feel well in an ugly place than ill in the loveliest spot on earth and I do feel so well here.

Chippy plays golf all day and reads Theosophy to me in the evening.

In train Tavistock to London   Aug.1.10.

I wrote to you yesterday morning. Did I tell you how we netted a salmon and lost a salmon Saturday evening and how Baring threw himself into the river to save the escaping fish, got very wet to lose the fish.

We went for a walk Sunday morning – a walk you would have liked as they have a botany craze on. We all started in a wagonette to lunch at Flete, Frank Mildmay's[1] place. A great house built by Norman Shaw 31 years ago. On our way up Baring and Mrs had a socialistic talk. There had been some difficulty between the servants and Sheila the nurse and Mrs B. was upset about it. She began to cry and Baring nor I did not realise how much she was upset. To change the subject, I saw a heron, and we began talking about birds and in a few minutes hello! says Baring and we found Mrs B. had slipped out – had disappeared. She hated going to a big house too full of servants etc. Baring went back, found her but left her alone and we went on without her. I was sorry. We had lunch and went over the house. The house is awfully *nouveau riche*. Shaw elaborated too much of it and old Aldham Heaton[2] had done the decorating, oak yellow and carved and the ceilings, carpets, walls and everything were agog with patterns, a pity.

We got back and could not find Mrs B. anywhere and then got in about 6 to find her quiet and serene at tea. Kissing and friend-making made me happy. I guessed a secret and they were both delicious about it but nothing can happen before February and *you must not say a word* as no one knows but me – a real padlock.[3]

Sheila says Bloomsbury Square is the only house where people are natural with her and don't talk Kings and Queens.

After tea we went up to Pamflete where the Bulteels[4] live

1. Brother of Alfred Mildmay. A country gentleman of the old school, Frank Mildmay (1861–1947) was Liberal Unionist MP for Totnes from 1885 to 1922.
2. Shaw's decorator, from whom Lutyens had rented 29 Bloomsbury Square in 1897.
3. Rupert Baring, now Lord Revelstoke, born February 1911.
4. Cousins of the Barings.

nearby. It belongs, as Mothecombe does, to Frank Mildmay, and they played lawn tennis until eight. We got back to dinner and dined about 9. Caught a baby bat but I fear it will die. This morning we made an early start to go to Cothele – a delicious old house belonging to Lord Mount Edgecombe – full of beautiful things and furniture, a heavenly place, and then a tremendous rush cantering across fields in an old wagonette and crossing a river by punt. We got no lunch but the ferry man gave us an excellent meal of bread, butter, cream, raspberry jam and tea. I left the Barings at Berealston and changed at Tavistock and caught this empty 3 o'clock. I love Mothecombe.

Everyone about is full of Crippen [the murderer] – even the boatman who had not seen a newspaper had heard of the arrest. It is horrid and yet the papers make one read it.

East Runton Aug.3.10.

I loved your letter about the Barings. I think they are a dear couple and I long to see more of them. I longed to clasp hands with her over her little temper and hatred of the big house. I wish I had been with you as I should have enjoyed it.

Barbie is very upset about Crippen and it is horrible the way everyone gloats over the details. But I tell Barbie we can have kind thoughts for him which we may send to help him.

29 Bloomsbury Square Aug.3.10.

Don't forget that Mrs Baring's secret is very padlock as the wee bit has only just started. I feel so for her through you for the antipathy to the big house and all it means from one point of view. I look at the big house from the other and best point of view. A centre for all that charity that should begin at home and cover, hen-wise, with wings of love those all near about her that are dependent, weaker and smaller. A house with the soul of a Wilton gives me a choke of veneration and its unending possibility of giving and receiving love. Neither the loveliness nor the love of such can be bought – not by all the millions in the world. There!

God Keep the Feudal and preserve all that is best in it and the result is love and loveliness. But I see too Mrs Baring's point – yours. Should you make all arable, grass? because some by neglect grow thistles.

Tuesday I was busy all day and at five I went off to Mrs Hunter's Hill Hall, Epping. A delightful old house round a courtyard and arranged in an amusing way. A mixture of [Lady] Battersea and Pamela – i.e. Mrs Hunter.[1] Sargents galore, Mancinis and other modern artists. Italian furniture and silks. Alas, Blomfield is the architect and if they do want me to do the garden my position might be a difficult one with Blomfield.

Mrs [H. G.] Fenwick's mother was Mr Hunter's sister. Mr Hunter said he would like to see Temple Dinsley and off we motored to lunch there today, and just as I was starting for home up came Mrs Hunter with Tonks the painter[2] and Oxenden the collector man, so I waited till a later train. Temple Dinsley is having a *succès fou* and Mrs Fenwick is *so* nice to me about the house and everything.

I came home with Tonks and allowed him to wash and brush up here as he was dining with the Protheros. Tonks is a nice man, met Father and rather thrilled by him. Loved Temple Dinsley.

Mr Drewe writes a nice and exciting letter to go on with drawings not more than £50,000 though and £10,000 for the garden. I suppose £60,000 sounds a lot to you but I don't know what it means. If I look at Westminster Abbey it is an absurd – trivial amount. If I look at a dear little old world two roomed cottage it merely looks a vast and unmanageable amount. Only I do wish he didn't want a castle but just a delicious lovable house with plenty of good large rooms in it. I have had an amusing week with appreciation in three counties.

I gave Mrs Hunter fits. The gardener was talking and referred to something Mr Hunter had said. I said 'Who is Mr Hunter?' I quite forgot the name of my hosts! Wasn't it awful? She did

---

1. Mrs Charles Hunter (1857–1933) was a sister of Dame Ethel Smyth; her husband was a wealthy coal-owner. A typical Edwardian – 'a fine woman' – she was painted several times by Sargent. 'Mrs Hunter is dead,' wrote Virginia Woolf in 1933. 'Died standing eating drinking dressing penniless, ruined discredited, having got through 40,000 a year, not all of her own; but they say she was a great hostess and all is forgiven – rightly I think' (*Diary*, vol. iv (1982), p. 145).
2. Henry Tonks (1862–1937), Slade Professor of Fine Art 1917–1930.

laugh. Mrs Hunter is depressed about a billiard table she has to get. I have suggested one in the court yard, a marble table with heavy India rubber balls. Why not? Rubber cushions, ivory ball would be the same in effect as an ivory cushion and a rubber ball surely.

East Runton   *Aug.5.10.*

I quite agree with you about the good points of the feudal system, only I have a good right to know about the other side for I lived in it half my life and it is oppressive – difficult to be natural – that is why I hate it. It is all unreal.

In train   Aug.4.10.

Just had dinner in train for Southampton and to spend the night in the *Balmoral Castle* Mirrielees' new boat, it may lead to my doing the next one! but he says it would worry me to death.

No news. I expect we will move the office[1] next week and then B. Square will have its full dress put on and I must find two twin tables one for you and one for me, good, square, wide knee-hole tables, some proper table lamps and two comfy arm chairs each wide enough to hold two!

Oh Emy darling I do so love to hear you say you love me! I should die if I thought you didn't and burst if I knew you didn't.

In train for Stroud   Aug.6.10.

The last time I wrote I was on my way to Southampton. I reached Southampton all right and then I drove to the docks and found Mirrielees on board with a lot of men and Flockhart the architect.

There was a singer man on board who sang love songs and comic songs. I do think it silly for a lot of grown men to sit about and listen to second class music and I was dying to go to the very bowels of the great ship and see how she came to her being. And the decoration was all so vulgar and silly and where there was no decoration, just building, a feeling of veneration – at least respect

1. From the ground floor of 29 Bloomsbury Square to 17 Queen Anne's Gate, next to Edward Hudson at No. 15. The telegraphic address was Aedificavi, London.

– was given. Directly they tried to do something artistic, either architect or engineer, as sure were they to go wrong. It is very depressing and gives me a feeling there can be no God.

29 Bloomsbury Square   Aug.8.10.

The black cat has just caught a mouse and is playing with it. I feel ill at the cruelty of it . . . it has escaped . . . caught again, I hear the squeaks. Oh dear. . . . I have killed it and feel horrid, a beast, ugh. She plays with it now, so gently, to bring it to life again?

I got to Stonehouse[1] Saturday evening about nine, just as they were finishing dinner. They asked me if I had dined in the train. I said I hadn't, but would pretend to have done so if they liked. Stonehouse is the house that was burnt and they rebuilt it themselves without architect, a decorating builder person. It was a very odd feeling, like going to stay with Barbie's husband after *he* had married again, everything just wrong and caricatured. I was very nice and Christian and behaved *very* well!

Went for a walk yesterday with another Mrs W[interbotham] a cousin. She thought I knew the way and I thought she, and she was a great walker and we went miles, lost ourselves and the party and oh, wasn't it hot. We walked for two hours instead of a mile to an old house.

In the afternoon we motored to another old house. An old house that has not been lived in for years and years and nothing ever done to it just melting away, it is *cruel*, far worse than cat and mouse.

And then to tea to B. Winterbotham the brother. He breeds pigs and a most extraordinary thing happened t'other day.

NOT TO BE READ ALOUD

The old boar was so heavy that the hind legs of a sow broke off!

I came up this morning. [Herbert] Johnson came in this afternoon. No news. It is so dull never to see you and I can't help being jealous of Chippy who has no living to make and all his spare time!

1. Lutyens had made alterations to Stonehouse Court, Gloucestershire, for A. S. Winterbotham in 1906.

East Runton   *Aug.10.10.*

Now I must tell you I think it naughty of you to be jealous of Chippy not having his living to get when you remember the years he has spent in working far away in India without wife or home and every penny of his money is self made. Also I must just say this: every man however busy can afford the time for a holiday if he really wants it. A little determination and a little management. But you know perfectly well that nothing bores you so much as to come away with me and the children. You have no occupation, no interest outside your work and consequently you are thoroughly bored whenever you are not working. Chippy is supremely happy with his golf and reading to me and playing with the children. You would hate it.

Your story of the broken legged sow is too horrible. A tragedy of sex indeed.

A sketch of Lutyens's standard garden seat, on the back of a letter to Lady Emily dated 20 August 1910

17 Queen Anne's Gate   Aug.22.10.

Reginald McKenna has bought a site in London and I *do* hope he asks me to build for him. Pamela is for me, and the whole Jekyll family.[1] I saw Bumps who sent her love. She is difficult and Aggie don't help her.

I went to Thursley — saw Father, Aileen and Francis, Nan's boy, Lionel, Lucy. Father very well. Painting a black Venus to elevate the blacks in the eyes of the whites! Venus is Aileen black all over laying up against a Surrey bank with a parrot in a nutbush and some geraniums under the hedgerow to give colour! It is really awfully funny and I did not dare laugh. I saw dear old Nannie.

1. He did, and the result was 36 Smith Square, built by Lutyens in 1911, an elegant and finely detailed town house built in the Georgian manner.

I am writing from Q. A. G. and dine with Hudson next door so don't get back to B. Square till late. They have begun work there. I *do* long for you to be home.

17 Queen Anne's Gate   Sept.9.10.

The McKennas have written and telegraphed over and over again asking me to go to join them at Sheerness aboard the *Enchantress*[1] (my beautiful white clothes can't be found by Mrs Tribe[2] and Robert has spoilt my yachting cap)! no matter. So I go, to talk new house in Smith Square for 48 hours.

I spent last night at Sidmouth. The Drewes wanted me to go and to discuss their castle with them quietly at the hotel there, so I came up from Sidmouth this morning instead of from Exeter last night. He wants to build a large keep or Commemorative Tower, to commemorate the first Drogo, and this will be over and beyond the £60,000 castle.

An early sketch for Castle Drogo

1. The Admiralty yacht.
2. Mr and Mrs Tribe were caretakers at Queen Anne's Gate. Each morning Mr Tribe filled six small pipes and laid them on Lutyens's drawing-board with a big box of matches.

Lutyens and the clerk of the works at Castle Drogo

Lane is very anxious I should do the Johannesburg Art Gallery, so I shall write Baker offering to share it. So you see there is a lot of work to do and coming on, but we must be careful.

I do so long, ache to see you my own sweet darling. Crabbet[1] wouldn't have bored me and with you it would have been joy fun.

I hope Sir Herbert Jekyll is there on yacht.

I don't know why I am writing in such a fearful hurry, but I have been in it and the flurry of it is still on me.

Wednesday I went down to Exeter and then took a motor out

1. Crabbet Park, Sussex, built by Wilfrid Blunt, was where Neville and Judith were living.

to Drewsteignton, Hall[1] was with me. We went to the site and then Mr Drewe arrived with his three nice sons and Mrs Drewe who is a dear. He changed the site of the castle again, wisely I think.

Next day, Thursday, I trained in to Exeter and then motored out to Drewsteignton and took a tremendous walk over hill and dale, stream and fence to locate the best position and line for the new road. I then explored the stream (salmon?) and had a fearful rocky climb, perfectly lovely and very hot, and Lord! I sweated. In between whiles I was staking out the Castle with Hall and two assistants. They, the Drewe family arrived at 1.30 and brought lunch. Then Drewe told me of his dream of a Commemorative Tower or Keep and this we planned and plotted and he was mighty pleased and proud. We went back and instead of my going to London from Exeter I went on to Sidmouth to talk more castle that night. We got on famously.

Then I started early this morning from Sidmouth to London. My GW Railway ticket did for the SWR which was a save. My expenses in motors alone was £5.5s. Drewe travels and hotels en prince. I get it all back of course.

In bed   Sept.10.10.

Enchantress. A name which conveys my darling to my soul.

It is great fun. Pamela the only woman and a lot of men all in uniform all calling each other 'Sir' and a general feeling of Gilbert and Sullivan, which is delightful to my humorosities.

We steam at 5.30 this morning for Devon where we will inspect things that go on and under the sea. My jokes have had an enormous success with these green sea side minds.

The McKennas like my plan for the house and McKenna thinks my staircase a miracle, he has spent months at it himself. So it is fun. Scoring at one's own game.

I was foolhardy enough to ring a bell when a man suddenly appeared all red coated – a lobster! and saluted. Of course the apparition rendered me speechless and I shan't ring again.

---

1. E. E. Hall was one of Lutyens's most valued assistants 1902–33.

Crabbet   *Sept.13.10.*

Judith and Neville are very kind and their life very happy and interesting in its way – but I am afraid I get a little irritated at their supreme indifference to the rest of the world and contempt of every opinion but their own. Also Neville's portraits of himself as a Greek God rather annoy me because he has such a crooked nose and sallow complexion – and yet the pictures are like him too. It is all a mutual admiration society but I suppose everyone has their eccentricities and we all like our admirers.

[Lutyens arrived in South Africa on 7 December 1910 and stayed two days in Cape Town.]

In train for Johannesburg   Dec.10.10.

5.30. It has been very hot and the country is supposed to be unusually green now! It is bare parched rock and shingle and looks more like a newly planted place where heather won't grow. Every plant stands separate by itself in a desert of its own. Distances impossible to judge – everything clear and nothing lost in half tones. It is all there as though under some wide lensed microscope.

Get a cart load of road rubbish stones dirt – mostly red – and scatter over a floor. And then collect the sponges in the house and space them about the floor – then you will get the Karoo.

Villa Arcadia, Johannesburg   Dec.12.10.

Arrived here last night. Mrs [Lionel] Phillips seems very pleasant and cheery but they are having difficulties about me – my position here, which will be amusing to watch.

This morning I went to the Art Gallery and the Joubert Park where the new gallery is to be built. The Rand Memorial site where the Duke of 'Cannot' laid a foundation stone is an

 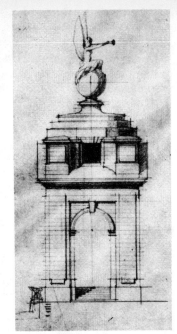

The Rand Regiments Memorial

impossible place.[1] The site for the church and back to lunch –
French chefs with fresh food is a great relief. Am now sitting on
the stoop under the shadow of one of the big posts with a cool
south breeze – all else blazes with sun.

The black people interest me enormously. Their faces, the soles
of their feet and their white tongues and it is so odd to see them
doing their work quite unconscious of my absorbed interest.

They affect Miss Jekyll type of gardening and it is so odd to see
great ugly cactus growing up in a Munstead border. I have
remarked that on the garden wall I find written 'Mene, mene,

1. The Rand Regiments Memorial, 1911–12. The foundation stone was
laid by the Duke of Connaught, but the design remained undecided. Lutyens
sent out his design in 1911 and it was carried out the following year in a slightly
altered version. It was his first war memorial, anticipating the great triumphal
arches of the 1920s.

Jekyll, upharsin'. My silly innocent jokes have a great success yet am warned by everyone never to make one, yet I haven't met anyone who don't giggle and seem glad to.

The town council etc. are all dead against Baker and they want to rope me in without Baker. This makes my position difficult – Baker is as good and generous as gold and I must be careful not to hurt him however advantageous to myself. There is a meeting of the town council with Phillips and Lane. I have refused to go. I can't argue my own case etc.

I *do* wish you were here to talk things over – people and policy. Everyone is dreadfully war conscious and the evil is they want more! t.10' not in Africa.

It is so difficult to realise I am not in some county – one I have not been into before – the 6000 miles I can't count. There is this villa decked land standing above a squalid town with here and there big buildings, a sort of Birmingham without its smoke and every other block of buildings razed to the ground to appease some appalling angel. Then beyond miles of chimneys belching black smoke and weird cat's cradle erections . . . the mines, mines of gold, the very heart of a modern world, and beyond the veldt wasting for hundreds of miles. They want me to go down a gold mine but I don't want to go down their man-built holes and see the miners and the pthysis the dust gives 'em – though water jets and every modern contrivance possible to minimise the evil is adopted. Yet it is there and I don't like men digging for potatoes they may not eat and gold they may not spend. Yet all this! rather than not be let build marble cathedrals and great towers to the glory of the sun.

Dec.13.10.

No wonder the Boers fought for their country. Tonight the moon is a revelation. No wind so it is warm and oh so soft and all so gentle and a view to the mountains 30 miles away.

This morning went and met the Archdeacon about his church and settled on a new site – far better and works in well with my Picture Gallery, etc. so as to make a bit of town planning on a big scale. In the afternoon did work in a room that has been devoted to me but the sun was all a blaze ⊤ no wind so it was hot and down on the table went my head and I slept for an hour and woke by pins and needles all over.

The Archdeacon loves my idea of a great campanile with the song all the way up it in layers – beginning at the bottom with Ananias, Mizael etc., and ending at the far top with a magnificent O Praise for the Lord and magnify Him for ever. Then by altering the town plan – which I think I shall be able to do – we can get an open air pulpit with a great public garden.

Tomorrow I believe I am going to be caught with an interview. I am horrified this morning by the daily newspaper having a column headed 'A great architect'. This was an article devoted to me and in language which made me sweat. All that part of it is *horrible*, but I like the deference paid me though, never forgetting the funny side of it all and very funny it is.

It is difficult to realise there was nothing here 23 years ago but limitless veldt – no building but a Kaffir hut.

The mosquitoes are singing tonight. I have seen some fearsome insects that turn one blue all through – ugh! and moths as big as haystacks and as witless.

Dec.15.10.

It is very late, so I cannot write much.

Directly after breakfast I started to work and at 11.30 went down to a meeting in the Mayor's Parlour about the Gallery. It was a purposes committee and I have got sailing orders to go on with the design but the town council have not ratified my position, but they will do so. I must get the designs inside before I go for the Gallery, its extensions, the laying out of Joubert Park and a wide bridge across the railway and connect the Union ground with it. They are all very kind and pleasant to me.

I have offered to go over the whole town plan of Johannesburg! with the engineers and architects and suggest revisions of the plan and also revision of the by laws! The Rand Committee have met and I believe that is all right, for me, so I am *very* busy.

1. University, Cape Town.
2. Pretoria – lay out.

Johannesburg

> 3. Rand Regiments Memorial of the Park.
> 4. Art Gallery. Joubert's Park and Parade Ground.
> 5. The great Church.
> 6. Mr Phillips's garden.[1]

It was such perfect joy to get your letters to day. I have read and reread every word and it shall be the last thing I do to read them again before I go to sleep.

Miss Phillips's birthday, had a long talk with Mrs P. and begged her to give Miss P. her young man for a birthday present. I have been half successful but I think it will be all right.

Broadlands [Health Farm], Hants   *Dec.30.10.*

I don't know how to wait till you come. If I had at all realised what it meant I could not have let you go. It seems just as if you had walked out of my life – and oh! darling, darling I want you so.

Our great excitement was a dance we gave at B. Sq. on the 22nd. We cleared the dining room and polished the floor and had refreshments in the schoolroom, and decorated everywhere with holly and green and it was such fun. I hired a piano and a lady to play. There were 45 children in fancy dress, and five of your clerks came dressed as plough boys in smocks and large sunflowers in their button holes and long clay pipes and they made such fun and seemed very happy. The dance was from 7 to 10 but all stayed till 11 and I could hardly get them away.

The next day we left for Knebworth pausing first at Homewood to get Mother's presents – such lovely things. Pamela was quite cordial and asked me if I had been seeing much of Gay (Lady Plymouth) as she was so fond of me! I felt I had gone up miles in Pamela's esteem!

After dinner one night she talked to me about Theosophy and was quite interested and wanted to read Mrs Besant's book [London Lectures (1907)] that first inspired me, so I have sent it to her.

1. Only two of these were executed by Lutyens, the Rand Regiments Memorial (1911) and the Johannesburg Art Gallery, begun in 1912, to which he added in 1929, and which is still unfinished.

Now I must tell you of my adventures here which have only just begun.

This place is very high up and little wooden huts divided up by high palings, three huts in an enclosure. A central bungalow where we eat and a sitting room. My hut is about the size of the bathroom at home. The stove is very warm. I slept last night with all three windows wide open but confess it was chilly. . . . At 6.30 a girl in a mackintosh and sou' wester called me and lit my stove. You are supposed to have an air bath early. I had one before lunch attired in a flowered muslin chemise and sandals. I could hardly bear the thought of it but I am bound to say it was rather delicious and I felt so hot after. I am supposed to do it three times a day. I am wondering if I shall have courage to go tonight. You run hard or do exercises. The company consists of Miss Behuke, Miss Clyde the manageress who superintends the treatment, a Miss Bell, a suffragette broken down in health, quite nice and interesting. A lady who is suffering from a nervous breakdown and who looks abjectly miserable and never speaks, only sighs deeply from time to time. Her daughter, who is a nurse, looks nearly as melancholy.

I am enjoying myself awfully. It is all so funny and new and such a rest having no one to think of but myself.

Lyons Buffet, Paris   March 29.11.

I have to represent the RIBA in Rome[1] as well as myself and I shall have to go in broad daylight in evening dress and an opera hat! It is too awful! and ass-making.

Dolgorouki wrote and asked us to Nashdom for Easter. Do write (if you can't go) cordially for me to say you are going to the c side. . . . Oh how those letters of ours ronged me, we must read them again sometime.

I have ordered my dinner it is all such a surprise it turns out so dull. French names sound so beautiful and good and just the dry old friends (or enemies!?) turn up. It is two hours before my train goes.

Everyone says the King's Memorial will be all right but there is a lot of opposition and it is a pity it got out so soon though if it

1. At the British Pavilion at the Rome Exhibition.

does go through it strengthens my position, but I do feel nervous. It is such a wonderful chance![1]

I see the King's coronation procession goes through Hart Street, Theobald's Road, i.e. Bloomsbury Square. Don't you think we ought to have a committee and make Barbie chairman and the whole family and Nannie a committee. You may have to call in professional advice – which is me. The children must vote the money and say if it is to come from house accounts or a special account or by subscription. Then the professional adviser (if he is called in) will upset doubtlessly all the committee's calculations and the professional (I hope it will be me) will be politely asked to leave the room.[2]

I am worried and angry too. Eight of my houses have been built at Hampstead and they have been so pulled about by the Co-partners inside that they are found to be, as I always said they would be, unliveable in. It is depressing but I shan't let them interfere again. Vivian very nice about it but it is entirely the fault of his own people. Don't say anything about it but if you hear anything you can say Oh well of course!

Goodnight my own most darling heart.

In train from Maytham   April 14.11.

I was glad to get your telegram and more glad to get your letter. Yesterday I had a very busy day, seeing people and a rush designing the great cross, altar, reredos, pulpit etc. for St Jude's. That evening I dined with the Barings at the Rendezvous and then went back at 10.30 to meet Hudson and go to Riddell. I slept at No. 15 [Queen Anne's Gate] last night as he, Hudson gave me a lift in his motor down to Maytham, so I was saved a tedious train

1. This was one of the schemes for the King Edward VII memorial which was to include a stone bridge, designed by Lutyens, across the lake in St James's Park: but the prospect of 'mutilating' the Park provoked so vociferous an outcry that the scheme was dropped. Another scheme, for Trafalgar Square, was also abandoned, and eventually, in 1912, after considering several more schemes, the Committee settled on an equestrian statue in Waterloo Place, for which Lutyens designed the plinth.

2. On 22 June Lady Emily and Barbie watched the procession with the McKennas from Admiralty House, accompanied by Mrs Besant, Krishna and Nitya. Lutyens stayed at home cutting crowns out of orange peel for the dolls of his younger children.

journey, one I am now doing on my return. He, Hudson, was awfully pleased with Maytham.

PRIVATE: Riddell and Hudson want me to prepare anonymously a King Edward Memorial scheme for Trafalgar Square at once and they are going to boom it like anything – sort of *cri* – a demand from the public for it. It will be rather exciting and amusing and we talked it over last night.

Had a long day at Maytham. Mrs Tennant is pleased with the admiration the house is receiving and I think listens to me more. But she do argue and talks me dry – dry to parch – but has charm in that she is always ready for a laugh or a diversion though it is seldom one can switch her off altogether from any point.

J. Tennant and she both asked if you would come down. I said you would not leave the children which meant I should have to bring five – a thing I could not afford. Would you like to come? Would you come next Sunday? It is a delicious spot but I am afraid you would not face it.

I sent off yesterday my Rand Regiments Memorial drawings to South ·Africa. I sent off plans for Drewe's revised castle in Devonshire. Next week I have to go to Ireland. Tomorrow I go to Mells and am to be taken to Longleat and to show Lady Horner my Bath scheme. And then there is the King Edward Memorial flare-up. The Tennants and Jack Peases thought the St James's Park cry too silly and undigested and that the newspapers were mad. J.T. did not think it possible for the committee to chuck me but I know committees and their methods better than he!

Hudson thought Maytham *most extraordinarily cheap*!

You see I am very busy but Oh! it is dull to get home to B. Sq. and find it empty and soulless. Emy my own darling one – I don't think you know how much I want you and the happiness I have in our home – if only to watch you all and take no part in your ploys and doings.

I know you hate leaving me and that the time will soon pass, but it will all pass so quick and then – shall I say it – years and years and I shall be your daughter and you my father – a relationship I don't think I shall at all appreciate!

I hear St Jude's church is splendid for sound. They tried the choir and Canon Barnett was there exclaiming 'How beautiful, how beautiful'. There is an awful row (secret) going on between Mrs B. and the church committee and as far as I can gather she is not to be allowed in at the opening ceremony to meet Princess

Louise and the Bishop. This will make awful scandal. She is a silly woman though she is nice to me now. The committee was called by her only to annoy me and make my work difficult and has now turned as an old nemesis of the sea upon her back. And Oh what a committee – a committee of bank clerks and curates. I attended the last one and nearly burst when they put questions affecting the appearance of *my* church to the vote – their vote! Luckily it went my way and I was saved from a declaration of my true opinions and beliefs.

Don't overbicycle and overtire yourself and don't do meetings and speeches and don't belong to committees which burn your faiths in fires of compromise.

29 Bloomsbury Square   April 15.11.

A long letter from Sir Rennell Rodd[1] saying the Sindic. of Rome (this is all death head secret) so pleased with our Pavilion they are to *give* the site – a valuable one and Rodd wants me to get the RIBA to buy the building and to fit it up as the British School at Rome. I must write to Stokes and Simpson[2] and get it done somehow – beg, borrow or steal £5000. The RIBA is hard up at present but they have had some money left them.

There will be a good deal of criticism about my building and its adaptability. A letter from Baker just come. Wildly enthusiastic about the Edward VII Memorial but alas it is all over! Oh dear and the agitations may militate against me out there as they could never guess the true facts.

Sandacre Lodge, Parkstone, Dorset   *April 16.11.*

Such joy to get your letters and such exciting possibilities. Is it quite fair for you to be designing memorials anonymously? I suppose it is all right. The Committee certainly haven't treated you very well.

How thrilling for you about Rome and shows your Pavilion is appreciated. You must not be depressed by criticism. It is only a sign that you are becoming a public man!

1. Sir Rennell Rodd (1858–1941), Ambassador in Rome 1908–19.
2. Leonard Stokes (1858–1925), President of the RIBA, and John Simpson.

I never saw the interview in the Morning Post, *do send it to me.*

I know that we were made for each other even tho' we have such different tastes. I love you more than I can ever express, and tho' I fear you are worried at times at my oddities, you are really responsible for them, because it is your fostering love and care that have helped me to develop my nature in its own way. I am afraid I sometimes seem ungrateful, but indeed I love and appreciate you from the very depths of my being and am very very proud of you. If I don't help you by society touting and planning it is really because I know it is unworthy of us both, and you know it too in your real moments, and you would not really love me if I was the kind of wife you sometimes imagine I ought to be.

I am afraid this letter is a good deal mixed up with sand as the babies come bounding over me.

Goodbye my beloved. Your Emy who loves you entirely.

April 18.11.

Here I am in the night mail for Dublin, Howth. Oh why do you go to Bath? You said or I said you weren't to go to any meetings at all during your holiday. You might easily have come to Mells! I shall be two nights running in the train and boat and the wind blows and I feel tired and Oh I want you so much.

Mrs Lionel Phillips called at 17 Queen Anne's Gate today. It was great fun seeing her and she was very cheery and talked 300,000 to the dozen.

The Raymond Asquiths came on Monday to Mells. He looks thin and worn, losing his looks. She all right and two dear little girls – 3 and 1, Helen and Perdita. They all think Perdita[1] frightful and I won Mrs Asquith's heart by sticking up for it – a frail little speck with a fringe of fine fine golden hair standing up on its head like an auriole. I thought delicious and pathetic and heart holding.

Jack Horner is deafer than ever. Edward[2] – with his face all scratched and torn from a fall from a horse. We met him at Salisbury and his face was plastered up all over – an awful clown freak sight.

1. Married William Jolliffe in 1931; he became Lord Hylton in 1945.
2. Edward Horner (1888–1917).

I talked Theosophy to Lady Horner but nothing appealed to her. She is in a sort of Aunt T frame of mind and a future without her present consciousness does not appeal to her. Nor does it to me, except I hope there is a wider consciousness of which my present will become a part. My real consolation is that all nature – call it by what name you like so long as it is healthy and of good being – is joy and God-given. So come what may the life will be held as dear.

Went to Longleat yesterday. Have you been there? A fine big house but cold and inhuman in its falsities – its cold callous adoption of Italian art. Sort of Lord Brownlow type of work that palls.

Lovely ground – park – trees – sky and views. The whole place empty and given over to hordes of Easter Mundites.

Sweet darling, Mells is so near to Bath. *Do* be very careful what you do there on account of my King's Memorial. I hope it is not political and the Vicar or Rector whatever he is is one of the most important members of the Town Council. Would you like a letter to the Mayor? Why do you go to Bath?

Sandacre Lodge, Parkstone, Dorset   *April 20.11.*

I wish you could see that a visit to Mells would have been torture, but a visit to Bath on my own with sympathetic people is a great lark for me. I am sorry if I annoy you. I can't help it. I know I am odd and perhaps getting odder, but so much happier and so loving of my darling husband. It is no use asking a flower that grows well in one soil to be happy in another, it is no use expecting me to lead a society life, I feel just like a flower that has been living in a cold clay soil and is suddenly transplanted into sunshine and congenial soil, and now I feel daily as if I was opening out and growing and stretching glad petals to the sun. I know you understand and don't really mind though you do sometimes wish I was a peony instead of a wallflower!

In train to Torquay   April 20.11.

The excitement of the day has been my seeing Aston Webb who is enthusiastic about Rennell Rodd's proposal about the Pavilion at

Rome being made the permanent home of the British School. He also talked about RA[1] in a nice friendly way. If it comes off – the Rome affair – it will be a great feather in my cap. Webb says he has seldom been so excited.

I wrote very hurriedly about Robert [nearly ten] this morning and in the middle of it thought of my youth – all my faults I see originating when I had nothing to do and was bored and the days were long – no school, no one to direct me, interest or help me – until I thought of building then the days became too short. But I do think I should have done better if my mind had been disciplined. I should have had more moral courage and my mind is dreadfully apt to rush about and I want the power of concentration. That is to say with a lot to do I sometimes cannot apply and concentrate my mind on the one thing for thinking of the many others. It is waste of tissue and tiring. How far this temperament works for good – it may – I don't know, and all this like Robert I feel.

He seems to have no friends and he is always second or third fiddle at home. His scout business may do him good, but his vegetarianism and unboylike antipathies won't help him. I should like a man like Herbert Johnson to take him up for summer holidays, endless exercise and a bit of a disciplinarian. O so unlike me. I have thought often of taking him about with me but would have to neglect him for hours in draughty muddy buildings.

Sandacre Lodge, Parkstone, Dorset   *April 22.11.*

We [E.L. and Arthur Chapman] were sitting on a sunny bank when winding up a little hill we saw a procession. A donkey with a little girl led by a tall man in a sombrero hat whose face seemed familiar. Following him a tall lady in a rather old fashioned velvet dress, purple woollen coat, a very bare neck with strings of pearls. Her hair in a plait down her back, and a coloured scarf round her head. Can you guess? Ottoline [Morrell]! looking just like a gipsy queen. She was so surprised to see me and walked a bit with us.
Mrs Besant sails today from Bombay. She is bringing Alcyone[2]

1. Lutyens was elected an Associate of the Royal Academy in 1913.
2. Name for Krishna in his previous incarnations. These were described in 'Lives of Alcyone', articles in the *Theosophist* in 1910.

and his brother with her did I tell you. I hope they all lunch with me on June 11th so keep that date free. The Bishop of London comes after lunch to see Mrs Besant.

April 22.11.

Now I am in the train to Maytham. Oh! these trains. Have designed my memorial for Trafalgar Square and am happy about it.

Letters of sorts with money came in, so I shall pay your dressmaker. Darling it is *so* little.

An enthusiastic letter from Webb, Sir Aston, about Rome. He telegraphed in my name to Rodd to say there would be no doubt that the architects would agree. There were many letters but your two dear ones were the first I read. You are not a bit like a wallflower and I don't want you to be a peony. I just want you to be my own Emy. I want you to be happy, well and full of *joie de vivre*.

I am not fond of crinky-cranky people. They amuse me certainly, but I don't think they help much and make many shy who might by other means be taught to do more.

I feel I want to write a Psalm to you and I am sure David had my sort of feeling when he said things like

All my bones are broke

My ribs are fallen apart, it is simply longing longing for the coming of his beloved one. You are my beloved one and I long for you so I write growls and depressed utterances glowing all the time for you, for my love of you, darling, my darling.

It is no real fun your coming to a place like Maytham until you have some common ground with Mrs Tennant, you would find lots, but with a client I cannot help having my mind on their pulse all the time.

I must try and help Robert and you must help me. It is scolding I can't stand and then I find it difficult to realise in real sympathy an opacity of intelligence, no matter how natural. I don't mean this in any conceited way, heaven forbid! I just utter what appears to me as a fact, as I write. None of my letters to you, darling, are thought out. I just write, blessing you for the sweet privilege I have.

Lady Horner is going in for some Social Committee work!

———

Teaching mothers or something, a new line for her. She is a social climber and has had a personal success, a patron of arts would describe her, and a political intriguer. She is political, her bias born of friends and not conviction. That side of her leaves me cold, but I like her artistic intuition, leanings. It is very funny her grandchildren call her 'Frances'. She does not altogether live for pleasure and slaves for her family, up early, to bed late and does everything. Ridicules poor Aggie Jekyll [her sister] for whom I always stick up.

Les Communes at Varengeville

In train [returning from Varengeville][1]   Aug.8.11.

My own sweet darling

A lovely crossing and I did a lot of work in my cool draughty cabin and I could have done nothing at all if I had sat on deck or in the terrible smoking room. One cannot work like reading a book.

I am tired – worried perhaps, and it is always a strain getting things done before a holiday as it is not only my going away but

1. Where Lady Emily and the children were spending the summer holidays, in lodgings; Krishna and Nitya were lent *Les Communes* by the Mallets.

the whole office goes and then I count the minutes to see your face and I do not get you alone – no real welcome – just a strain. Madame Mallet, though I love her, then the custom house contretemps made me cross. I couldn't talk to you a bit so I got inside myself and smoked (a form of meditation!) to be scolded, and then I said things sounding and affecting cold – longing, aching all the while for a wild hoorah to say I loved you.

You talked of divorce and we no doubt both, as little children do, each attended our own funerals. Then I went away and then you cried. Then I went all pink with compassion for the darling wife I love, have loved and always will love, that I was so unkind and so unhelpful to. I am so sorry for my bad temper for that is what it is – very very sorry and so ashamed, and now I am away from you I feel wretched, yet I don't want to be back, to see you at odd, abstracted moments, living away from you and seeing you only amidst nursery broils. Even our delicious walk felt guilty and stolen not free and natural with the full inclination of us both.

Why couldn't we have gone to the pine hill in the moonlight and had, with a lovely world at our feet, a talk and got down to the depths within each other?

You were Nannie, and I was Mallet conscious, and the today wouldn't forget the tomorrow and there was no real unself-conscious *joie de l'âme* in it.

Then the other condition – our rare encounters find my body self rampant, aggressive, horrid, so there seems no time wherein the physical inprickles can be forgotten and laid aside to our common happiness. We have no common occupation.

I cannot forgo my work with its overpressing claims, and you your interests with their compelling claims. Your Theosophy has brought us closer perhaps than any other subject. Its breadth is great but I dread the definitions and their articles and the isolation from the world of men's affairs to which I by necessity and will, must belong.

Why need we suffer the tyranny of creeds and the narrowing beliefs of men in men? The fencing in of God with palings to his ways.

Darling of course I love you. I love you dearly, very dearly, altogether whole heartedly, but I do feel the time will come when you will pass me by, so kindly, but pass me you will and I shall be so lonely and the empty house I go to is as a sign – a prophecy of what will come.

I have been so cross to everyone in my office lately and being cross with you frightens and depresses me. I must be more careful, more guarded. It is half the battle to realise it. It must affect my work and its quality too. Now I have told you a lot that is in my mind and I shall look forward to your dear and loving letter in answer.

Varengeville   *Aug.10.11.*

Your darling letter has just come and I am longing to answer. Such a sweet darling beautiful letter and it touches me to my soul. Darling I only wish I could put into words all I feel for you or make you understand how entirely I love you. You are quite wrong in thinking that I am leaving you behind, I am only beginning very very slowly to grow up to you. You were not cross the other day, you never are – it was only me and you being tired took my crossness too seriously. But it hasn't hurt, it is only a thunderstorm which has cleared the air and now the sky is blue and calm – only for the little cloud that my darling is not with me. How I wish I could make you understand how much I love you – only you will count by kisses, and lip kisses especially, and I can't pay in those coins. I can't even kiss my little baby on her lips, it is a horror to me. At the same time I am so happy just walking hand in hand with you and laying my head against your arm. Coming to me also I should like so much better if it was just natural and occasional as it should be at our age, and not the intruding presence every time I hug you.

Theosophy has made me feel you much closer, it has taught me to understand you and admire and appreciate you more than I have ever done. But of course it is ousting every interest from my mind, or rather I should say every other interest is coloured by it. I am one of those people to whom hero worship is the greatest joy of life. I want to be always at some one's feet. In my early youth I poured out all the devotion of my being on the thought of the Christ, and now the thought, the hope, the belief of His return absorbs me sometimes to the exclusion of everything else.

There is no creed in Theosophy – no fencing of God's ways, but some take little, some more of its teachings.

17 Queen Anne's Gate   Aug.14.11.

I was so glad to get your letter in answer to mine. Such a darling letter that I (and that's the worst of it) long to kiss you on those angel lips which I may and can never kiss again! No, I couldn't sleep that Tuesday night. I lay awake for hours thinking of you and realising that I must have lost your love through my own thoughtless ill doing. And I wrote to you in a spirit difficult for me to analyse – a spirit of childish wilfulness – almost resentfulness but I wrote straight from the heart and hardly know what I said through my love and anguish of love for you and I thought, having posted it, that you would – must – resent it and had I lost you I should have had no salvation in it at all at all. And then I could not see but in a scold-wise way you could have answered. I felt wretched and in the early morning I seemed to realise this and I wept softly as a child might cry and felt miserable.

I am so weak, so worldly, and oh Emy so devoted to you. If I may write to you as I feel and say cruel, hard things and you think those things I say sweet and beautiful, well then thank God. I have nothing to fear, but oh I do want to kiss you on your lips! Don't be feared I won't but . . .

Of course I was cross, bitterly cross that other day and you were as I know you were and together we built a bonfire that flared and thank God has burnt itself out to leave the softest of white grey ashes. And these ashes I wore upon my head and shoulders and worshipped you the while.

I know you dread the body physical and with me it flares and burns and behind it all there is my steady white light that belongs to you. The nearer things of the body cannot come natural somehow and we must help each other. But then it is difficult you know darling and must know though you cannot realise how such a thing can burn so long.

I have kept Mrs Besant for the last. She drank tea! and said she drank gallons. Yes I *do* like her but any occult power frightens me like world without gravity, effects without customary causes – makes my hair bleach. We had a long talk. I am still shy of her and feel as selfconscious before her as if I had no clothes on!

Varengeville   Aug.17.11.

*Your darling long letter came last night. I had gone to bed with a
bad headache and I loved it and slept with it under my pillow so
as to feel you quite near me.*

*I have been trying to think quietly over the three things which
make little rubs between us. Our married relations, the smoking,
and Theosophy.*

*Now about the first I want you just to try and see my point of
view. Remember that I married you, loving you and wanting you
physically as much as you wanted me, every bit. I don't reproach
you for one instant for what happened after because you were
just selfish and I was silly too. At the same time you can't believe
the nightmare the thought of my honeymoon is to me – a
nightmare of physical pain and mental disappointment. I was in
constant and unceasing pain and discomfort and you never left
me alone. We tramped about all day sight seeing when I ought to
have rested and at night I lay beside you crying with pain,
weariness and disappointment.*

*I know and fully sympathise with the disappointment you feel
but remember I have never refused you except when I was having
babies. If I could not respond to your feelings at least I have let
you come to me quite as often as my husband has a right to ask.*

*Then about the smoking. I have never asked you to give it up.
All I ask is – don't smoke when it means that the smoke must go
down my throat which sickens, and don't take your pipe out of
your mouth and then ask me to kiss you, and wonder that I say
no.*

*Now about Theosophy. I do want your help here very much.
Don't let me grow selfish and too absorbed. I know it is a
temptation, help me to fight against it.*

*You are by nature sociable, talkative, amusing and conse-
quently a social success. I am not by nature sociable, amusing or
talkative – consequently a social failure. I don't insist on your
coming to Theosophical meetings with me, you must not insist on
my paying visits or going to dinner parties where I am hopelessly
out of place.*

*Darling now don't take a word of what I have said for a scold –
it is not meant so for a moment. I have nothing in my heart for
you but tender love and immense pride and the longing that all my
children may be like you. I don't think you know how proud I am.*

In train for Rye[1]   Aug.18.11.

It will be such joy seeing you on the 1st. I got your letter today just
before starting. I am awfully hot and sticky, no porters to carry
my bag and we were a long time getting out of London.

Mrs Besant couldn't come today, so I wrote her a letter. I will
see her next week.

The three things. Smoking, that ought to be easy, if you will
help me. Married relations ditto. Theosophy ditto, it is just being
together and patient and kind voiced, but we love each other and
we have our children and we must talk it all over quite close and
each feeling for the other. There is so much I want to say to you.
Oh if there was a garden to go to over Sat to Monday. I wonder if
Bumps would lend her cottage. I fear no. How can I help you
darling? with your Theosophy. You will probably get calmer
about it when Mrs Besant goes away. I do think I have given up all
idea of your being a social success! though you are in your own
way, but I do want you to meet some special friends of mine half
way – at times. I don't want you to go to dinner parties but do let
me have friends, at home, naturally and with apparent welcome
on your part.

You can't really want our children to be like me, do you?

Try and forget the honeymoon and remember our first letters
and then remember I had anxieties and disappointments too.

I think I have told Mrs B. of my fears of psychic matters. I will
again. You cannot I believe fulfil your duties in this world and live
in another. I am not at all sure of the morality of preparing for a
future world to the sacrifice of any real duty in this – the pleasures
of this life pertain to the duty of it. It is a pity in the path of all
religions, to acquire self safety. But I long to help you darling and
you must help me.

17 Queen Anne's Gate   Aug.23.11.

Mrs Besant who came to see me today has accepted the land, at
£1000 a year and is going to start a building at once [for]

1. To Great Dixter, Northiam, Sussex, an early timber-framed house, which
Lutyens was restoring for Nathaniel Lloyd, the architectural historian, whose
history of English brickwork contains several references to Lutyens's work.

£50,000.[1] It will take some time to get the site conveyed, but as September 3 is astrologically a very favourable day she is going to lay a foundation stone in the North East corner. There is no time to lose. How she is going to raise the money I don't know. She says she has £3000 and has written to Miss Dodge.[2] She seems quite certain about the money. I showed her how she could get the plan on the site but she preferred my last one. The building will look like this.

I gave Mrs Baring lunch today. She goes to Lambay with Cecil for ten days. *She* can't leave him, but if it is too bad without the children she may go back. Poor darling this is not a scold, but just a pang and I have been so X in the office today I feel miserable.

Mrs Besant said she [would make me] an honorary member of the Theosophical Society. She will erect a tin hut on the site at once.

Varengeville   *Aug.25.11.*

I am so fearfully excited about the Headquarters Building and all you tell me, of course I must be at the laying of the Foundation Stone on September 3rd and so must you.

I am longing to hear more of your talks with Mrs Besant. Do you say she is making you an honorary member of the TS? Are you going to design the building for half price or nothing? I hope so and yet I know it means a large sum for you. But oh! it makes me so proud to think you have it to give – I wish I had as much to lay at my Master's feet. I shall be so excited to see the plans.

1. The Theosophical Society Headquarters in Burton Street and Tavistock Square. It was sold, unfinished, to the British Medical Association in 1923 and Lutyens completed it on a more modest scale and without the cupola in 1925. It has since been extended by another architect to Tavistock Square, with symmetrical wings joined at the front over an arched entrance.

2. Miss Mary Dodge (1861–1934) was converted to Theosophy by Lady Emily, who described her as 'an immensely rich American and, without exception, the most nobly generous woman I have ever met' (*Candles in the Sun*, p. 33).

The British Embassy, Rome   Jan.10.12.
[Where Lutyens had brought plans for the
rebuilding of the British School]

Yesterday afternoon we spent at the Medici[1] – thrilling – and they, the Directors extraordinarily kind and helpful. It is a wonderful life and tradition which I hope we may build up here – but I hope with better results. The Germans and Americans are going to start schools too. I am sorry one cannot start a wide world school with one common library. The amount of waste that goes on in the archaeology departments and history. The multiplicity of libraries is such awful waste – and why all this bone racking when everything produced is so hideous.

There are the English, German, Prussian, American, French and God knows how many more establishments. Then there is our own Records Office under another management. The saving in Bibles and *Who's Who*s would keep a student. Then there is the British Academy which has degenerated into a sort of elementary drawing class and some sheepish old maids who imagine they acquire Art by gazing at a nude man with pertinences improper.

Mrs Arthur Strong is in a very querulous and yah yah mood. I think she thinks our school[2] is going to be too big for her and she is terrified of the rough architectural students. Why she picks out the architectural ones I don't like to think. The Cambridge Benson – A. Benson?[3] – came out here and upset her. He is the man I inadvertently reduced to angry tears when with the Donaldsons at Cambridge. He sort of talked art-soft about stencilling his chapel, whereupon I told him that I thought stencilling was permissible in a tweeny's bedroom, but applied to a house of any God one believed in was beneath contempt, etc.

1. The Académie de France was at the Villa Medici.
2. Founded in 1901 as a school of archaeology, the British School in Rome was expanded in 1912, after the 1911 International Exhibition, to include the fine arts. Mrs Arthur Strong (d. 1943), the assistant director of the school from 1909 to 1925 and a distinguished classicist, was known to her colleagues as something of a stormy petrel.
3. A. C. Benson (1862–1925), Fellow and later Master of Magdalene College and prolific writer.

CHAPTER SIX

April–June 1912

THE YEAR 1912 MARKS A TURNING-POINT in Lutyens's career. Early in that year he was invited to serve on the Committee of Experts to advise the Government of India on the site and town plan for New Delhi. This was the beginning of a connection with India that was to last until 1931.

The decision to move the capital of India from Calcutta to Delhi had been announced by George V at the Coronation Durbar at Delhi in 1911. The reasons for the move were political. By far the most urgent problem confronting Lord Hardinge when he became Viceroy in 1910 was unrest and sedition in Bengal, stemming from Curzon's ill-advised partition of the province in 1905. The chief troublemakers were Hindu Bengali Nationalists, who resented the division of their community, as well as the creation of a Muslim majority in East Bengal. It was to conciliate the Hindus that in 1911 Hardinge resolved on the reversal of the partition. But this would swamp the Muslims in East Bengal, and it was to placate this element that Hardinge proposed to transfer the capital from Hindu Calcutta to Delhi, the capital of the Mogul Emperors.

Lutyens agreed to serve on the Delhi Planning Committee with alacrity, partly because he saw in the project an opportunity for the big work he hankered after. The other members of the committee were J. A. Brodie and Captain Swinton, the chairman. Brodie, 'a broad, matter of fact, midland, middle-class thing', was the City Engineer of Liverpool; Swinton, an expert on the town planning of London – though in Lutyens's view a verbose dilettante – had thrown up the chairmanship of the London County Council to come to Delhi. The triumvirate arrived in Delhi on 15 April 1912, and embarked on an exhaustive and exhausting survey – much of it conducted from the back of an elephant – of the possible sites for the new capital, the main contenders being a superficially attractive hilly site to the north and a healthier and more practical southern one. On 20 May they adjourned to Simla where, after consultation with the Viceroy and officials, their report was written, recommending a site south of old Delhi, between Malcha and Indrapat.

Lutyens recorded his impressions of India in a series of letters to Lady Emily which really amount to a diary, punctuated by the weekly mail. 'I give you first prize for letter writing,' wrote Lady Emily from London. She saw that, though his appointment was still far from certain, Lutyens was already looking at India through the eyes of the architect of New Delhi. He was struggling to grasp its strangeness and complexity: to distil the life of India to its very essence that he might reflect it 'through the medium of art'.[1]

What struck a chord with Lutyens was not the Indians but the Raj. For him, the Indians, whether Muslim or Hindu, were 'children', their architecture mere joinery in stone, without intellect. In the Raj, on the other hand, he found the ideal of an enlightened imperial despotism, dedicated to public service. Lutyens who, like many of his generation before 1914, was disillusioned with parliamentary government, found the idea of the Indian Civil Service attractive. But he was appalled by the civil servants' lack of taste and by the buildings erected by the Public Works Department. His ambition to achieve great work was strengthened by a determination to supply the Raj with an architecture fitting its lofty ideals.

What the style of that architecture should be seemed to Lutyens at this early stage quite obvious. Classicism was the style that he found both most interesting and most aesthetically satisfying; that it was, and always has been, the architectural expression of an élitist society was an additional point in its favour. As Christopher Hussey put it: 'The classical Orders, like those societies that have successfully employed them in their buildings, connote the authority of an autocrat, omniscient or benevolent or neither.'[2] In the Indian Empire Lutyens found the perfect field for the High Game.

---

1. Hussey, *Lutyens*, p. 166.
2. ibid., p. 123.

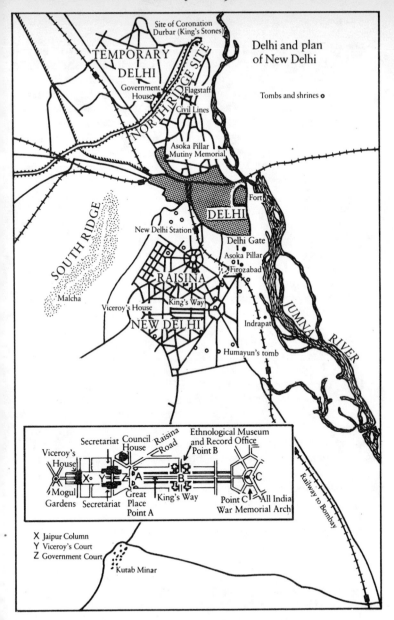

Delhi and plan of New Delhi

Site of Coronation Durbar (King's Stones)

TEMPORARY DELHI

NORTH RIDGE SITE

Government House

Flagstaff

Civil Lines

Tombs and shrines o

Asoka Pillar
Mutiny Memorial

SOUTH RIDGE

DELHI

Fort

New Delhi Station

Delhi Gate

Asoka Pillar

Firozabad

Malcha

RAISINA

King's Way

Viceroy's House

NEW DELHI

Indrapat

JUMNA RIVER

Humayun's tomb

Secretariat   Council   Raisina
              House   Road

Ethnological Museum
and Record Office
Point B

Viceroy's
House

X   Y   Z   A

B

C

Mogul
Gardens   Secretariat   Great
                        Place
                        Point A

King's Way

Point C   All India
War Memorial Arch

Railway to Bombay

X Jaipur Column
Y Viceroy's Court
Z Government Court

Kutab Minar

Bombay   April 12.12.

Here I am in Bombay and real hot and sticky all over, in a perpetual bath of sweat. I am writing before lunch at the Yacht Club with the Chairman of the Bombay Improvements Trust. Somebody else is going to motor us around after and then dinner at Government House. The Municipal Engineers tomorrow and then Delhi by the night mail.

Last night we had high high jinks, danced and had musical chairs. Mrs Brodie who weighs 20 stone or more was the most energetic and youthful of the party and broke two chairs entirely and many a scrimmage and wild shrieks.

This morning went to the tailors. My vests and suits not near thin enough and I have got a reach me down of tusser silk and larger topee and various other things like spine protectors and bedding. Cox's for money and back here to write.

12 p.m. went with the chief engineer and architect to see improvements! sic! Awfully boring. Same old story of blind committees and half measures and eventual waste and loss. Sir G. Clarke[1] very friendly and nice in a very quiet dry way. There is a big scheme on with a new Government House.

In train for Delhi   April 14.12.

I had no time to get p.c.s in Bombay. So many people wanted to show us what they were doing. Not worth seeing and as in England everything made 40 times more difficult by past mistakes, false economies, and want of imagination. The French and Germans are far ahead of us in town planning.

The mango trees are green – large round apple shaped trees and some sort of acacia is in leaf. The wheat has been cut and directly the rains come everything will start afresh and more crops. The thing that surprises me is the likeness of everything to quite different parts of the world. Hampshire is the mother of many scenes – Africa – Italy. These and other animals are satisfactory objects for curiosity to feed upon.

There is the old club with fine simple upstanding rooms full of the ghosts of choleric old Indian Bob Webbs who lived and died

1. Sir George Clarke (1848–1933) was Governor of Bombay 1907–13; he was created Baron Sydenham of Combe on his retirement.

and growled with their hearts in England. And the building with all its artistic faults held the soul of a gentleman – a great quality and one that syndicalism don't help. India – like Africa – makes one very Tory and pre-Tory Feudal! and the rot of party and votes seems like some slow sweet poison to spoilt children.

Have seen the corn being reaped, the oxen unmuzzled treading it – the black man winnowing it and the chaff blowing away – all like Old Testament stories. Blazing hot in the train and the wind like a dentist's hot air dry tooth squeezer.

Delhi   April 15.12.

Here we are at Delhi.

Mrs Brodie has had a heat and nerve collapse and shrieks when a silent black man walks into her room. I can't think what she will do when it goes up in a few days to 105 or so – it is only 94 today.

This morning we motored over the Durbar site and up to the Flagstaff (we walked this) but the distances are great and it will take weeks to see it all properly. In to breakfast about 10 o'clock. It was pretty hot and then bath and dress and breakfast and then out to the office. We have a large bungalow for an office which is being organised for us. De Montmorency[1] one room

Swinton	"	"
Brodie	"	"
me	"	"

Then we each have an engineer attached to us and we each have

1. Geoffrey de Montmorency (1876–1955), the Indian Civil Service officer assigned to the Delhi project.

two clerks, four typewriters and various odd people with odd names who do all those things that bore the white man.

This evening, 5 o'clock we motored out 5 miles to tombs (I can't get hold of names yet). The dust, and saw wonderful things full of strange ideas and stranger ghosts. And such a crew on the roads. The well-to-do farmers in their bullock carts going to a *fair*? a wedding party. I can't attempt to draw them from memory. Their methods of construction and their unconsciously obvious shams that shocks my Western sense of truth.

The wonderful astrological Mogul erections, the Italian influence and the riot of baby brick nonsense, and occasional lapses to really fine proportions and great simple conceptions. I thought I should be able to describe glibly but it is all baffling, people and objects. The love everywhere of animals. I saw a man call his sheep out of the way of our car and he kissed it – sheep's mouth to man's mouth.

De Montmorency is a nice thing – very keen about trees. [T. R. J.] Ward – an irrigation engineer. Chase – an RE [Royal Engineers] subaltern, with about 25 men surveying for us so we shall soon be busy.

I am to have a Government architectural engineer attached to me besides draughtsmen so I shall be well equipped. It is an awful bore having to get and spend monies and to write the endless letters in answer to letters and messages received.

Going out to see the river. The sun is high and fierce and the Hindus worship in the river bathing the while. They are a cleanly people but their methods require nerve and habit: A man is doing those things you do not speak about – a corpse may be finding its way to Heaven – bullocks wallowing and a live man is bathing and brushing his teeth with his fingers covered with river mud and no matter or difference whether he is up or down stream of fearful contaminating procedures.

Tomorrow we start our elephant excursions. We were up at 5 this morning. Deliciously cool but by 9 the old enemy was swearing at all animal things from his chariot in the skies.

Swinton and I dined alone and I got him to try his hand at designing Delhi! It was so funny. All his talk waffled out to nothing at all. The Residence building placed with no aspect in an old garden – the Viceroy's untutored selection without any relation to anything else within or without 20 miles. I gave him his head and then went for him as he went for us last night. I am afraid he was rather sick and finally said – well, it is for you to design it! However Brodie must tackle him and I in the meantime will flatter him up again.

Jaipur   April 20.12.

I have come here first to pay my respects to Sir Swinton Jacob[1] – an architect of renown! here; he is leaving on 1st May for England for retirement – and to see Jaipur as the Maharajah – a hundred years [ago] – left Amber and built a new city.

After lunch we were called for by Jacob and went to see parts of the Palace but did not see much beyond great astrological instruments. To the Albert Hall – a rather shoddy museum built by Jacob[2] and what thrilled me most was a description of a wonderful reception held there by the Lyttons.[3] A garden party – a farewell to Sir Swinton and Lady Jacob whereat were many people and a very few white men. I talked to as many Indians as I could and there were two dear little Rajahs – boys. But want of language made it difficult. One nobleman I investigated and to his great amusement found out how he dressed down to his black skin. We got back to Delhi about 11 p.m., very hot, very tired and slept sound to be called today Monday 22 at 5.30.

Off in motors to the other side of the railway to meet our elephants. Oh the green fear of me when I saw this great beast shy at a train. However we three got on. A whack on the head sent him down on his knees and then a chair from which we had a fearful scramble to get up onto the pad (not a howdah) and oh the feelings of mine going down steep ravines into nullahs and up again, over stony places.

1. Sir Swinton Jacob (1841–1917), a leading exponent of the Indo-Saracenic style, had served in the Public Works Department 1862–96, and was Chief Engineer of Jaipur State.

2. Murray's *Handbook for Travellers* (1918 edn) describes the Albert Hall (1875) as 'a sumptuous modern building', and the museum it housed as 'an Oriental South Kensington'.

3. The Lyttons had visited Jaipur in 1879 when Lady Emily's father was Viceroy (Mary Lutyens, *The Lyttons in India* (1979), p. 168).

This evening we went out north west nine miles from Delhi by motor and tomorrow at 5.45 we start a long elephant journey to view the land south of the city which we cannot reach by motor, or by cart. Just wild country.

The animals I have seen are buck of all sorts, baboons, monkeys, jackals, hare, porcupine, water snakes, great fish, giant tortoises which eat babies, snake, bats, flying fox, vultures, weird birds and many lovely ones. A lizard of sorts, yellow and dry, three feet long. *The* elephant. Tigers at Jaipur – fresh caught and angry, a black panther, hyena, and then a host of tame birds and animals – a tame partridge for instance. I saw a beautiful wild boar.

Tuesday night   April 23.12.

Another long day. 5.45 we started and motored out to where we were to find the elephant. Mrs Brodie came too to snap-shot us. Swinton got on first and then Brodie. He weighs 16 stone 11 lb. The elephant, and it is a large one, laid down in a ditch and yet the pad was a good 6 foot above the ground. Brodie took a run and jumped on coming tummy down. The shock made the elephant trumpet and he nearly got up to run away but the mahout whacked him and talked to him as though he was a bad child and it laid down quietly again – for me! Think of my feelings and how gently I got up! We had a very long morning and went miles on the top of this fearful and beloved creature and we went over very rough ground and there were some awful moments going up and down into nullahs.

We got home to breakfast about 10.30 and then 11.30 to the office where discussions and reports took place until 3. We were all dead tired and vowed to sleep but we got talking again until it was time to start out in motors again at 5. We explored the east banks of the Jumna and saw many odd sights. Indians fishing, a wedding party in bullock wagons, monkeys, jackals etc., etc. and back at 7.30.

I think we are settling on a site. We are all agreed at present that we may come home earlier but nothing will be settled till we see Lord Hardinge[1] next week. He comes for the day on his way to Simla. The reports we are receiving are voluminous and in quantity. When we can  begin to do constructive work seems far off yet.

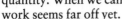

1. Charles Hardinge (1858–1944), created Baron Hardinge of Penshurst in 1910, was Ambassador in St Petersburg 1904–06 and Viceroy of India 1910–16. He married in 1890 his first cousin, Winifred Sturt, daughter of Lord Allington of Crichel. She died in 1914.

April 25.12.

Another elephant bout this morning and it was rather awful going along canal banks with overhanging trees. The ground looked rotten and you could not see the path on which Elephas walked.

The Mogul architecture is cumbrous ill-constructed building covered with a veneer of stone or marble and very tiresome to the Western intelligence. Some of the work is lovely, but then it is from some outside and possibly Italian influence. To fit it you must squat on your haunches covered with jewels, and little else in the way of clothing.

April 29.12.

Yesterday the Viceroy and Lady Hardinge came to Delhi. We went to the circuit house at 10 and talked some 2¼ hours. He was keen that we should have settled on a site as it affects the building of the Tin Delhi[1] which is to cost some £500,000! and wherever they put this Delhi it may be in our way.

Afterwards saw Lady Hardinge who was very cordial and pleasant and we all went up to tea at 5 and I had a good satisfactory talk with Lord Hardinge and an amusing one with Lady. He agreed to our coming home directly the monsoon breaks to come out again in December, so if it rains come June 20 I shall be home by July. However we shall see. The sooner I get back the better and then out again.

Our early starts and late discussions take it out of one but now that we have practically had our first general survey I hope for a less strenuous time. People of all sorts flock to this hotel with a view to catching any one of us. Architects and marble merchants make for me and engineers and plumbers for Brodie.

I had a row with Swinton and told him not to talk so much and waste time. He became exasperating with his flow of general useless talk when either Brodie or myself wanted to get to bed-rock on some one point. He, Swinton, was furious but he has been better since and personally no ill feeling or ill will is left. But

1. 'Tin' – officially Temporary – Delhi was built in 1912–13 to house the Government of India until the completion of New Delhi.

it is impossible to work or think even whilst he babbles and bumps his fist on a map.

Brodie is excellent – perhaps too slow and methodical and I know what the results of our selection will be. Brodie insists – and rightly – that we are driven to it by reason in spite of ourselves. So I am between two extremes. A map bumping illogical jumper and a brow furrowed slow-pacer. We do but little sight seeing but we do occasionally see a Mosque or a Temple or something or other. But it is all more curious than any real beauty. The atmospheres and colours etc. are lovely but these are not the works of men.

May 5.12.

Now we shall begin work investigating the various sites which are possible and one in particular on which I think we shall settle but it depends on water, subsoil and a host of technical questions.

Everybody looks very tired and worn out here – far away tired eyes. There is none of that restlessness here that there is in South Africa.

The I[ndian] C[ivil] S[ervice] nearly all young men is tape-ridden no doubt but [a] wonderful machine and within its tapes wonderfully free to the individual and men are keen and absorbed in their work. Ward, the chief engineer of the irrigation dept attached to us and to Brodie in particular is a quite excellent man. De Montmorency is a walking encyclopaedia. They are, I believe, the two crack men in the Punjab service.

It seems a pity they cannot start a civil service for Africa. Milner, I suppose, tried it but the parliamentary system and vote-cadging makes it impossible. Everyone seems to ridicule the Public Works Dept and it has the same character as the Office of Works in London. Taste and any sense of art is here as there non-existent. Everything is on the one basis of a fixed profit and a 25 years purchase – a method of no faith and of a foresight whittled to a point with the same amount of divinity as there is in the bill of a woodpecker.

Swinton still persists in giving himself away but I leave him to Brodie who in a slow lawyer-like way carried his statements point by point to their illogical end. It would make me sweat if Brodie did it to me.

I am keeping quite clear of disputes and going my own way. I have made up my mind as regards site but not how to treat it yet.

I am not impressed by the intellectual sides of any religion I have seen here but it is difficult to get at. In the Mosque here they have a hair from the beard of Mahomet, his sandal and his footprint in stone. I should like to meet Mrs Besant in India some day as she would understand it all sympathetically and this East I can't yet see – so weird and far apart and money and that saving of money, i.e. squalor, pervades here as well as anywhere. The only true God is a kind of Bank Rate creation and the alternative is a God of War.

Baker is very depressed about Africa and the want of hero worship. He is like you in that – but he wants his hero to be a dictator – your hero is a teacher. It comes curiously to the same thing in the end.

The housing of people here seems extraordinarily unintelligent – both for the whites and Indians – and sanitation is nil. The absence of drains is all right but the eventual disposal of things is awful. The milk, butter and supplies generally pass along the same road as the open carts carrying all horror and the baskets of filth on the heads of women so that flies move freely from one conveyance to the other ad lib. The natives can do nothing without making a mess of it and have no idea of appliances, of economy or any sort of cleanliness – apart from their own bodies which they seem forever washing but with water, and water from sources so obvious that it bleaches me to watch it! I have seen a few beautifully built men, one or two pretty women exposing themselves publicly in palanquins! a curious custom. The purdah to the open palanquin by day! seems further than an English home from Piccadilly.

May 7.12.

Brodie and Swinton had a flare up. Brodie said he would not be taught elementary engineering by Swinton and got off the elephant and walked! So I have had the chance of being peacemaker. I made a plan to show all their talk and quarrelling was useless as the scheme they fought over was a silly and needless expense and there was no need to move the railway at all. Brodie is very unhappy over Swinton's gas-bag nonsense but it doesn't matter a bit really and if we can harness him he may be very useful and pointful.

Tomorrow morning I am going over some native houses. I must find out exactly how they live.

If Mrs Brodie goes back to England before we do you must receive her. She is a dear, fat, wayward thing. Very wayward and teases Brodie who is awfully proud of her and nice with her. She's Scotch and a good deal of good fellowship about her, and girlishness in spite of her mountainous figure. When well her energies are wonderful. Directly it gets warm she crumples up, groans and goes red all over. At least I imagine it's all over and her diaphanous clothes show a good bit of her – more than one is accustomed to see. She has a nice round wide face and must have been very pretty.

May 9.12.

Yesterday I went off early in the morning through the public parks and gardens etc. to look out and identify trees and shrubs with Montmorency and Locke the gardener. In the evening went with Rai Bishambar Nath Sahib [engineer] to see typical Indian houses in Delhi. Now Bishambar is a Theosophist! He had sent away his women so as to have his house clear for our inspection. I gathered he had only three wives but the subject is an absurdly difficult one and my tendency to drop-jaw[1] questions might lead to embarrassment.

It was a tiny house with a tinier guest house facing it and an old house alongside for servants (4) and the cow and her calf, nice white Brahmin beasts. It was all spotlessly clean and full of ingenious and amusing devices and a very good ventilation arrangement of his own invention with double walls. An open court in the centre with galleries round and a swing for the ladies in hot weather to cool themselves! a see saw being like a swing which gives the most appalling motion.

1. Mary Lutyens quotes an example of a 'drop-jaw' question. 'One day a shy young man called Mr Weston came to lunch. In the middle of the meal Father leant across the table and asked him in a loud voice whether he was any relation of the Great Western. "Er – er – I don't think so, sir." Everyone laughed . . .' (*Lutyens*,p. 205).

There was a great deal to charm but our host's taste was appalling and of a mad-child order. In this court they cooked and washed up, store rooms and little hanging baskets for milk pans, etc. out of the reach of cats and dogs. It was approached by a little lane very long and very crooked, 6 foot wide at most, entirely built in with houses.

He has texts and mottoes. God is Love. Know Thyself. No Religion greater than the Truth, etc. His own bedroom and there were two and only two beds in it was a paradise of hanging lamps about the size of our bath room. A large glass chandelier in the centre, four other hanging lamps of a vase like shape and some six other large hanging lamps.

The pictures were the most dreadful chromo prints of smirking women covered with a sort of small pox of lustre sequins in many colours to represent nose, ear and lip rings and beads of jewels like a Brock's benefit display. Room on the roof and flat roof where they slept in or out as to weather. No fireplaces but braziers were used for cold weather. There was a funny little meditation room with a figure of a Goddess – an idol in a mere dark cupboard.

If Ursula had arranged the dolls' house with the same method and preciseness and cleanliness she would have top marks, so looking on him as a child I found him good, clean and wise.

Then we went to a rich Hindu's new house – a large one. Here dirt. Pucka stone outside, inside dirt filth squalor horrible. Ugly and without charm and here the naughty child played a game of stupid chaos. It is not worth describing except at the top you get a wonderful view over Delhi. The man himself was of the most evil countenance it has ever been my lot to see. A yellow cringing Mephistophiles. Head for ever on one side with eyes glittering obliquely up at you and a smile that cut the face sharply in two with attenuated horns at the end of the smile and large yellow teeth. A fat podgy son who had been to England – ugh! Dark and ill smelling and a glad-to-be-away-from place.

It was getting late but we thought we ought to go to the 3rd house if only to say that we were late. It was an old house belonging to a rich Hindu much added to, so much so that all coherence in plan had been destroyed. Here was a wedding being celebrated and there were some 500 guests in the house.

It was approached by a long narrow street that smelt all the smells that dirt can evoke. The entrance to the house was covered by an awning of evergreens where a band played pipes and tom toms. Feasting was going on inside the courtyard, covered by an awning and a large wood fire in one corner where everything was cooked.

We went to the top of the house to look down into the court and on to the many people and food – weird pickles, salt cakes, sweets, curries etc. were brought to us and lemonade in earthen pots. The complication of entertaining different castes and religions seems appalling. The food was very strange and frightening. We were given a bit to bring home which we looked at and gave away to our bearers.

They prefer their houses huddled and hidden and approached by these long tortuous alleys and they feel comfortable and safe in a house built in on all three sides with only one narrow entrance face.

Our Theosophist paid bearers to keep his alley clean and it made a great difference. The cows go out every day to the Bela lands for 8 hours and then home to the stables inside the house so you have to pass animals in these alleys. The bulls go where they like and wander and if the bull eats the contents of your shop you are a happy and blessed man and the bull may do what he likes and when. But I am a long way off realising what the people's organisation is in all these matters.

The second house of the evil man is to have an observatory on the top and we were introduced to the Astrologer who was also as far as I could gather an architect.

The Mahomedans have some central authority but the Hindus seem to have no central authority. The whole country is larded with shrines, temples, mosques, and wherever you take a line across it some, several, tombs, shrines are in the way and will have to be moved. The Mahomedans you can arrange with but the Hindus are more difficult as it is difficult to trace ownership of particular monuments.

No 2 of the evil face had a shrine in his house on the ground floor with a terrible gilt idol – a creature with 4 arms and as many legs and his property was registered in her, the Goddess's name. I long to ask if the Government could proceed against her to recover any just dues and what happened? This sort of thing makes improvement difficult though the Government here would be willing to remove and rebuild. Little shabby nameless tombs you find everywhere and apparently anywhere, the great majority absolutely neglected and in pieces. Some are kept tidy in the care of some holy man by a green cloth spread over and flowers, and then at night you find little lamps burning in the mud headstone and they are all cenotaphs so there can be little but sentiment. I do hope some way is found to deal with this question without being ruthless and appearing unsympathetic. Mrs Besant might know some good and simple way and how to do that which has to be done without hurt. The great thing is to win the people's confidence and having won it not to let them down.

May 12.12.

Did I tell you the talk I had with a rich Hindu about housebuilding? A lion shaped house is very bad and unpropitious and you are warned in old Sanskrit writings against them and he has known several instances of people dying who built themselves lion shaped houses. Whereas a cow shaped house was most propitious and you lived happily and well in it.

A lion shaped house is one whose front is wider than its back. A cow shaped house – a cow is a sacred animal – is one whose front is narrower than its back. All most seriously said and the front must be North.

Brodie and Swinton are still at daggers.

May 15.12.

When I talk Brodie and Swinton it means there is no news. Our days are spent obtaining and reading reports on water, malaria, making suggestions and plans evening and morning, going over the land on elephants and digesting the maps and their contours.

Hardinge is adamant as regards Lanchester[1] coming out, seems fixed on an Oriental style of architecture and probably a competition. Lanchester will support him in this like anything. I hope the London Indian Office will intervene!

1. H. V. Lanchester (1863–1953), architect and town planner with a large Indian practice, came out in June 1912 as consulting expert to the Delhi Planning Committee. He had been canvassed as architectural member of the Committee and Lutyens saw him as a rival for the building of New Delhi.

May 16.12.

I am harassed by the squalid suburbs that have been allowed to grow up and about old Delhi. Incoherent collections of mud walls, thatched roofs, with a decent house here and there which are assessed at an absurdly high figure. All crowded together, narrow non-paved streets, 6 or 7 feet wide and every other house a ruin. They ought to be burnt but the deputy Commissioner frightens us about the cost and the rehousing of the inhabitants and the litigation that would follow any attempt to do away with them. The population is not known but is assessed at 12,000.

If the British Government rehouses the Irish it had better rehouse these people too and make the purlieus of the new city clean and wholesome. £100,000 would cover the whole cost I believe over a period of say 10 years. The purchase of land would repay itself. If the old city develops as they expect, 25,000 every decade, building is cheap here and the native wants so little, a cow shape plot with a yard and a covered room surrounded by a wall. They don't want window frames or any fuss of that sort – just holes, and they live practically out of doors in their yards, and a nice mess they make of them. Their fuel is cow dung plastered on their walls in cakes to dry in the sun. Kites and hawks and jackals do the scavenging and oh the smells.

Natives walk about with pet sheep – sheep with horrid fat tails nearly as big as sheep themselves. They paint their animals in spots of various colours – their sheep, goats, dogs, cows, horses etc. How the children would enjoy an animal tame enough to allow them to paint it.

May 20.12.

The horror of India has not gripped me at all. A cockroach one may meet anywhere. I think I met them first in London. The difficulty is to grip India, not the physical side but the people and their minds, thoughts and habits and what they are driving at in thought.

Today we go up to Simla.

This morning we went early to the Fort to see the fountains play. I requisitioned it so as to see the effect of water – sight and sound – down the carved cascades. To my great pleasure I found the dear old Hindu Theosophist engineer in charge. I long to go and stay with him in his little clean house in Delhi city. But I fear the publicity of his guest house in an alley where I should be gazed upon by the young and curious Indians. And then the purdah question might be awkward as I should be bound to try and find out too much.

Old Rai Sahib had a caste mark on his forehead this morning. I think I shall start one – if I can wear one better than you can – if you get a better one than me I shall vote it rot!

Here in India I am most dreadfully Aunt T-ish and I ask questions galore but am told they answer to please and flatter you or themselves. 'How old is that tree?' (probably 80 years) '300 years.' 'How do you know?' 'My father was a hundred when he died and the tree was there then.' You don't get much forwarder.

There are no coroners here or death certificates and if the chief man of a village happens to be a Brahmin he will only register the deaths of his caste. A lower caste is not worthwhile he says – they are of no count. And on this sort of evidence the death returns are made up. There are no doctors who can diagnose a disease except the ICS men so all deaths are attributed to 'fever' if any cause is mentioned at all.

The irrigation is a fearful difficulty. You bring water to a desert and it is irrigated. The wells are not worked so the ground surface water rises until the place gets so unhealthy that the people get, as a whole, sickly and weak and they become poor and wretched. The Government then has to stop the irrigation and lose the revenue irrigation brings in to re-establish proper health conditions.

Grand Hotel, Simla   May 22.12.

It is very cold here, a hot bath and a fire in my room were a joy. Yesterday it poured with rain and hail. The rickshaws are amusing but I felt rather ashamed of myself being pushed up here in one by four panting men. Paid official calls yesterday afternoon and went through some of the work Hall[1] and Capt. Roberts have been doing here for me. Went to the Club to acknowledge my presence to the Secretary. Dinner at 8 and then a

---

1. E. E. Hall accompanied Lutyens on all his visits to India.

long talk with Hall and bed soon after 10. Dare not open my windows, a huge monkey came into Brodie's room. I have an irrational dislike of our cousins.

They say Simla has grown very much. The hills and depths below one are heroic, the buildings and conception of the place by the P[ublic] W[orks] D[epartment] mind is beyond the beyond and if one was told the monkeys had built it all one would have said what wonderful monkeys, they must be shot in case they do it again. It is inconceivable – and consequently very English! – to have a capital as Simla is entirely of tin roofs, and then the tin roofs monkeying better materials and reducing the whole show to absurdity.

Hardinge wants to separate the Town Planning from the Architecture, an impossible thing to do . . . with any success, but we shall go for him on Saturday about it.

May 24.12.

I am rather perturbed about Hardinge still insisting on Lanchester coming out. Do find out from Lionel[1] if you can what Crewe thinks and whether he will back me and not Lanchester! to *do* the work. There is no one here who can design at all, it is awful what they do.

May 26.12.

It is exciting about the RA but there is so much jealousy and Poynter[2] is so much agin me that I have little hope. However, hope I will till the very end if only to keep up a face.

The public don't know and don't really care a dog's leg about architecture. Some may like to talk about it but few can or care to pay.

Hardinge told Montmorency that he would not discuss architecture at all and that it had nothing to do with town

1. Lionel Earle (1866–1948), youngest son of Aunt T, had been Principal Private Secretary to Lord Crewe at the Colonial Office 1908–10. In 1910 Crewe became Secretary of State for India, a position which he held until 1915.

2. Sir Edmund Poynter (1836–1919), painter and President of the Royal Academy 1896–1918. Lutyens became an ARA in February 1913.

planning. I wrote a minute to say you could not consider a plan of a town without knowledge of the size, heights and dispositions of buildings and their properties and relations to each other – the parks, open spaces and vistas. He apparently remained obdurate in spite of it.

We had put down some twenty points for discussion and my special point was No 5. When my turn came and I had to speak up I spoke and Hardinge agreed! to everyone's surprise and said he quite saw my point and thought it reasonable etc. The interview was in fact very satisfactory and lasted two hours and he liked my first rough plan and was wise about it looking at general lines and not picking out details and making them difficult. He took a broad wide view – never committal to himself or anyone else as the whole question is full of difficulties. Engineering, political and malarial etc.

I lunched today with the Butlers. Sir Harcourt Butler[1] is Minister of Education. Lady Butler is referred to here as 'Her Weariness'. She is a nice, tired little woman and he is a nephew of the Trinity Master Butler – rubicund, roundabout. I asked him if men were in the habit in India of discussing affairs in public. He said yes they were. I asked him if he did it. He said no. If he had he wouldn't have been in his present position.

I asked him about Mrs Besant and her college[2] etc. He told me that she had, he thought, lost influence with the Hindus since she had become a recognised Theosophist and said there were ugly rumours about the boys at Adyar but he did not think it could be true. He did not refer by this to Alcyone [Krishnamurti] but he evidently thought the position might prove dangerous. This must be very unsatisfactory to you as I cannot tell you more and he made no committal or definite statement and I didn't really want to hear anything unpleasant.[3]

India – well man's work is so vile that it depresses me. This

1. Harcourt Butler (1869–1938), distinguished Indian administrator, was educational member of the Viceroy's Executive Council 1910–15. From 1918 to 1923 he was Lieutenant Governor of the United Provinces.

2. The Central Hindu College at Benares, founded by Mrs Besant in 1898.

3. In October 1912 Leadbeater wrote to Lady Emily: 'Krishna's objectionable old father has at last filed the suit against Mrs Besant which he threatened, professedly in order to recover possession of his sons and to remove them from my evil influence' (*Candles in the Sun*, p. 52). Mrs Besant lost the case and also the appeal in the High Court of Madras. She won an appeal to the Privy Council in London in 1914.

does not mean that I dislike the country and I am pleased when I can recognise a likeness to a Hampshire down, Scotland, Italy or some homey place! There is very little careful horticulture that I have seen.

God's work – country – is always beautiful and marvellous no matter whether it is a Himalaya or a Lincolnshire fen and there is always the magic of it to inspire and wonder at.

The natives do not improve on acquaintance. They are children without the charm of heaven, and there seems a lot of carnal! pleasures. And the caste rule rules out any broad line of Christianity.

I am awfully impressed by the Civil Service and the unselfishness of our Government here. I wish they would abolish the House of Commons and all representative government and start the system in England. My principal quarrel is that there is no taste and love of the beautiful at all at all. They will admire snow mountains with a rhododendron in flower in the foreground and they will go home and tie up a terra cotta flower pot with a pink drapery, so I guess their admiration is not for the beauty of the mountain but for its distance and size, and its imperturbability moves some animal chord in their being. Then it is always safe to admire nature!

This hotel 'The Grand' the messy food and people are depressing, though there are nice men and nice women. But the atmosphere of a mock Carlton – bad food, bad music – is stupid.

At the horse show yesterday I was much moved. Jumping competition. The only man who went over clear and without a fault was an Indian on a real nice animal, riding beautifully. And the men and women and children, English and native, gave him an ovation. This gave me the choke and I had to hide a tear and pretend the dust was in my eyes.

I don't think you would find that spirit in Africa. I didn't see it and I feel sure [you would find it] in no German or French colony. I don't think I am 'glamoured' of India as an altogether, though I am happy, forever amused and find an enormous amount to admire and love. I am a little afraid of the monkeys – they are such unpleasant mimicry. The very low intellects of the natives spoil much and I do not think it is possible for the Indians and whites to mix freely and naturally. They are very, very different and even my ultra wide sympathy with them cannot admit them on the same plane as myself. They may be on a higher plane or a lower one than a white man. But the very ether of their planes are different to ours and for one or the other to leave his plane is unclean and unforgivable.

Some of the men – a few – are very pleasant to look at, but the higher castes or the richer ones all go in for the soda water stomach and by the time they are 30 they lose all shape and just puff out into shapeless globular wanton creatures.

Tuesday [May 28.12.]

Swinton and I dined with the Butlers alone last night. We talked Theosophy. Lady B. said the usual things that Mrs Besant had no beginning or end to her lectures and that they left nothing behind, but said she was sympathetic to the whole line of thought. I ran out the postulate theory. Butler's grievance is Leadbeater and that old story and Mrs Besant's defence of him. I made my usual defence but one has to own to their extraordinary want of all knowledge of the world. But I was glad as nothing was said against Mrs Besant.

This morning I went up to see Lady Hardinge. She was very kind and Lord H. came in and I had a good talk about Delhi and architecture and it was all quite satisfactory and I am to make sketches for Government House and Lord H. is quite keen and agreed with my view as to the architecture of the country and how the problems should be met.

He said he wanted the two cities one and not *two* – the new and the old – so I scored all round and feel very happy. I asked Lady H. about Lanchester. She said he was only coming for a month and they had to be tactful to him. I asked her if there was any chance of my doing the building. She said Yes, of course – who else! This doesn't commit the Viceroy but it does, I hope, point to the mind wind.

I have been asked to send in a sketch for Clare College, Cambridge by July![1] This will fill me up. The amount of buildings required for Delhi is colossal! Great fun.

1. The design was not executed.

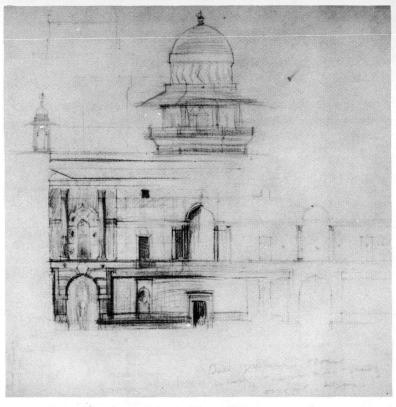

An early sketch for the Viceroy's House

June 3.12.

I saw Lord Hardinge this morning with sketch plans for Government House and Lady H. after. They were very kind and appreciative and I think I have got their ear and I talked to H. as himself and not Viceroy.

There is a lot of wire-pulling going on somewhere about architect etc. I lunched there today and am to lunch there on Wednesday. It is fun being received without the others! There is Indian opinion to be satisfied and all sorts of political conditions which is a bore and militates against the best, at least the best to look at.

Last night I dined with the Carlyles. Lady C. is very pleasant, Sir C.[1] is head of the PWD and one of the people to placate. He is hurt the Govt not putting Delhi into his hands altogether and Begg the architect[2] is also hurt, but if they did they would get a rotten vulgar show.

I must have answered your queries – charm of India, architecture of India. With *all their good* qualities an absolutely tasteless governing class cannot create charm.

Architecture – this is practically nil. Veneered joinery in stone, concrete and marble on a gigantic scale there is lots of, but no real architecture and nothing is built to last, not even the Taj. The Taj and some other of the tombs have charm. They are empty of people, quiet, square, simple and green, and this is only when money is spent on repairs, upkeep etc. When in ruins the buildings, especially the Mogul, are bad and have none of the dignity a ruin can have that has been the work of any great period.

June 4.12.

Last night the King's birthday banquet. There were some 78 gallant men in gallant uniforms and only Brodie and self were in black – two crows to 78 popinjays making 80 in all.

I had pleasant companions but too near the band and my tooth raged until nearly the end of dinner when I had peace till bed time and then an awful night.

I sat next to a little native in waiting to a Maharajah, examined his clothes, explained to him what a drop-jaw was, and then asked him endless personal questions about his life, wives – he had only one and was satisfied with that. He knew all about Mrs Besant and was eloquent in her praise. The number of natives, Rajahs and others of all sorts that I have asked to B. Sq. will – if they all accept and come – fill our black drawing room with a black population. There is always everywhere someone who knows John.[3]

1. Sir Robert Carlyle (1859–1934).
2. John Begg was Consulting Architect to the Government of India.
3. During army manoeuvres in the 1880s Major John Lutyens of the Royal Engineers was alleged to have 'misled Sir Frederick Roberts and 20,000 men as to the unfordable nature of the Delhi Canal through omitting to discover on a reconnaissance that it was, in fact, no more than a shallow drain at that season' (Hussey, *Lutyens*, p. 260).

There is a fearful battle going to blow over the architectural style of the new city. I have already got papers and attacks on the European schools, but the whole thing is useless and beside the point. Just tongue wagging and any arguments can be returned with equal cogency.

Personally I do not believe there is any real Indian architecture or any great tradition. They are just spurts by various mushroom dynasties with as much intellect in them as any other *art nouveau*. When Italians came over they brought with them some loveliness but never anything more than two dimension work and they imported no architects or craftsmen. They knew the Italian mouldings and used them. Nor can you do a portrait statue of King George in Mogul or Hindu style. First of all figures by the Mahomedans were not allowed and there is no space for sculpture within their lines of architectural deviation.

And then it is essentially the building style of children. At the Fort in Delhi, the most admired of Indian examples perhaps after the Taj, behind the white throne – a throne whereon or in a man can only squat cross-legged – is a lovely black wall painted with arabesques of birds and beasts in colour. Lovely and one panel is Andromeda and Perseus! It is all tommy rot.

I shall try and start an Indian school and Western tradition must be there. As Englishmen we cannot help it and then send the Indians straight to nature and let them invent and con-ventionalise to fit given spaces and teach them to think in three dimensions (a bed quilt is a design of 2 dimensions, a table has three) and to build in stone for stone and in wood for wood. When they build it is exactly like children's bricks and they put stone beams in tension.

Take the Fort at Delhi. The stones (marble) are like this. How does A stick

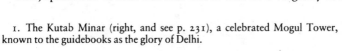

up. Nonsense by gum! Towers this shape.[1] Why should we throw away the lovely subtlety of a Greek column for this un-couth and careless unknowing and unseeing shape?

Cost, splendour of size: but that can as well be a vulgarity as

1. The Kutab Minar (right, and see p. 231), a celebrated Mogul Tower, known to the guidebooks as the glory of Delhi.

the one incentive to any art. Colour they have – or God gave them – when the earthquakes and convulsions made the stone. Marble of a most lovely texture brought by bare feet and hands – a quality our butlers once had in the balls of their thumbs and expended on our spoons.

300 years ago and for a period of 150 years the Moguls produced their architecture. 150–200 [years] is and must make an *art nouveau* and gives no space of time for any tradition.

Sir Harcourt Butler the Education Minister here is awfully nice to me and gives me sound advice and warns me what to do and how to meet the Hon. Members and tells me to leave everything to Hardinge. This is all private and must not go about.

June 9.12.

I think things are working out very well and I get my way and make my plans without disturbance and with right help, etc. Lord Hardinge was very pleasant today and he has written to Lord Crewe that I should do Government House and the Great Place in front of it. The Secretariat buildings come in and would eventually form part of the scheme and I may get them too – if the competition bugbear don't frighten them but Lord H. is not prepared to commit himself and a *great deal depends on Lord Crewe*: everything. Lord H. is delightful to work with, wide viewed, non-fussy and autocratic! Lady H. is very pleasant and all their ADCs etc.

I saw Begg the government architect who has a grievance and he asked me to come and has turned from cryptic utterance to flattery. He is no use (as an architect). I tried to show him the lines on which to tackle the Town Hall he is to build here, instead of starting off in a silly picturesqueness which isn't got and doesn't face up to the problem squarely. His grievance is that he, as consulting architect to the Government of India, has not been consulted about Delhi, so I told him (nicely of course) that he had been foolish as a government servant to write to the papers practically attacking Lord Hardinge's speech, for if he gives his opinions in the press what need is there for the Government to consult him, and then if he complains for ever how over worked he is to everybody how can he expect them to put even more work on his shoulders? He said, 'I never thought of that point of view!' But he would be lost in a job the size New Delhi means.

That evening there was a state ball and I went but didn't dance. First I was not in uniform and then I dared not shake my tooth.

The ball opened by the Viceregal party dancing the Lancers with propriety in a roped off area, all the rest looking on, and they knew it not at all and it was all *faux pas*. Some of the uniforms – specially the Indian cavalry ones – are very good indeed. Rajahs dressed well as only Rajahs can dress, but they don't dance which is a pity but the only possible solution to the horror of seeing a black man embrace a white woman.

We have started our preliminary report on the choice of site. This will be a weary quarrelsome affair as Swinton likes embroidery words which mean nothing but Montmorency is all right and will write it and keep us straight. The site is settled and is published – south of Delhi near Malcha. It is a beautiful site – aspects, altitude, water, health, virgin soil etc. right and views across old Delhi and that wilderness of ruined tombs that form the remains of the seven older Delhis. I suppose it won't cost less than a million by the time it is finished.

We had the Bishop of Lahore to lunch with us yesterday. I wanted to know how game he was for a big church – cathedral – £2000 or £3000 a year to endow it and it would want £500,000 for the church *if* it is to be placed in any big position. He funks the money part. Government won't or can't help to establish a church! and there are no rich whites in India. Calcutta, if there is a rich man, won't help as they are mortally affronted with Delhi.

Mr Mount turned up and called on me. A lieutenant sapper. He did the light railway at the Durbar very well. Now he is put on to build a large theatre and concert ballroom at Lahore. It is extraordinary madness the way the Government of India treat architecture. Here is a boy suddenly told off to build this thing. Absurd drawings of a huge vulgar structure have been made. The building is started and is out of the ground. Nothing fits or is considered architecturally or even in any form of sequence. His job is to build it and get it done – no one cares how.

He is a nice young man, very keen and alive to the responsibility and difficulty and very anxious to do the right thing and not to put up a monstrosity and he came to ask me what to do. So my rooms are all pinned up with these terrific drawings and he comes in before dinner and talks them over. I try and show him how to get at it but it will be a funny business.

June 18.12.

This is the last letter I can write you in India. The work here goes on. The Brodies have left. Brodie's want of taste and slow powers and Swinton's quick miscarriages have enabled me to get all I want – my site, my lay out, etc., so I am pleased. Brodie and Swinton wrote the report and how they quarrelled! I went on with my work and only looked in on them now and again and suggested a word or something and when I heard words flowing at too high a cadence a joke came as balmy. Swinton loves the flowery paths of language and Brodie a plain Lancashire statement. Brodie cannot make any statement without a long paraphrase on Liverpool and what they do there. It is wonderful the report ever got wrote, but it is at the printer's now and will be out in a day or two. I shall miss Brodie here to help rob Swinton's orchard of meaningless vocabulary.

I have to see a rich Parsee in Bombay. He wants me to build him a house in Bombay. He is very rich so I shall see him! and if he looks tame and will spend money etc. then it would be fun but if he looks difficult and won't spend money then I shall be polite and say no pleasantly.

CHAPTER SEVEN

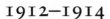

1912–1914

LUTYENS RETURNED TO LONDON from India in July 1912. Though his country-house practice still flourished – work on Castle Drogo continued, and in 1912 he made important additions to Folly Farm – it was Delhi that absorbed most of his energies between 1912 and 1914. He made a second visit to India between November 1912 and March 1913 and a third in the winter of 1913–14. During the intervening months in London, as well as the long weeks on board ship, he worked on with his designs for the new capital.

Lutyens's first concern in July 1912 was to secure his appointment as architect of New Delhi. Though he had the backing of Lord Hardinge, Lord Crewe, the Secretary of State, remained unconvinced, and there was still talk of a competition. The autumn of 1912 found Lutyens energetically lobbying, interviewing India Office officials and paying court to his patrons at Balmoral and Crewe House. It was partly in order to facilitate his own appointment that Lutyens pushed for Herbert Baker's engagement – the work involved was anyway far too great for one man – and in October 1912 Baker agreed to collaborate. By November 1912, when he left for India, Lutyens's appointment with Baker was virtually in the bag, and it was officially announced in January 1913. At the same time it was agreed that Lutyens was to design Viceroy's House and Baker the Secretariats.

On his arrival in India in December 1912 Lutyens was plunged into the controversies surrounding the new capital. There were two main points at issue: the site of New Delhi and its architectural style. On both of these questions the Viceroy's decision was crucial, and matters were seriously held up by the attempted assassination of Lord Hardinge on 23 December 1912, in the course of a State entry into Delhi. During his long convalescence Hardinge's judgement often wavered, much to Lutyens's exasperation. Though Hardinge made a full recovery, his relations with Lutyens were never the same again, and they were to deteriorate further after the death of the sympathetic Lady Hardinge in July 1914. It was to her that Lutyens made the famous apology: 'I will wash your feet with my tears and dry them with my hair. True, I have very little hair but then you have very little feet.'

The most pressing question confronting Lutyens in the winter of 1912–13 was the choice of a site (see Map, p. 229). Though the Viceroy had initially approved the flat southern site near Malcha recommended by the Delhi Planning Committee, he soon changed his mind. In August he caused consternation by calling for a reconsideration of the North Ridge site. In November he changed again and urged a new southern site, on Raisina Hill, which had the advantages of height and proximity to the existing city. In January 1913 he executed yet another volte-face and, bowing to pressure from London, issued orders from his sick bed for a return to the North site. Not until Lutyens and his colleagues on the Delhi Planning Committee had exhaustively demonstrated the disadvantages of the North site – lack of space, problems of health and sanitation – did Hardinge eventually approve the site he himself had first selected: Raisina Hill.

Still more contentious was the question of style. Lutyens's initial preference had been for pure classicism. This was what he had envisaged on his first visit to India, and his first designs for Viceroy's House, made in 1912, were strongly Renaissance in character. The Viceroy, on the other hand, pressed for an Indian style, and in particular for the Indo-Saracenic – that loose amalgam of Mogul and Gothic elements that had characterized the architecture of the Raj since the Mutiny of 1857.

Hardinge's reasons were as much political as aesthetic. To stamp the new capital with an alien, Western style would be to negate the entire political purpose of the move to Delhi: the conciliation of Indian, and particularly Muslim, opinion. The virtue of Indo-Saracenic was that it expressed the Raj's aspiration, in the aftermath of the Mutiny, to work in harmony with the old native élites. With this purpose Lutyens was in sympathy. 'Architecture,' he wrote in January 1913, 'more than any other art, represents the intellectual progress of those that are in authority. . . . To express modern India in stone, to represent her amazing sense of the supernatural, with its complement of profound fatalism and enduring patience, is no easy task.'[1] But Indo-Saracenic was beside the point. A formless riot of carved decoration and – what was anathema to him – pointed arches, in his view it hardly qualified as architecture at all. Instead, Lutyens set out to achieve his own synthesis of East and West: to translate the language of Western classicism into an Indian idiom. 'My everlasting prayer is for the greatness and help of a Wren or Newton,' he wrote. Yet he was certain that 'if Wren had built in India, it would have been something so different to anything we know of his that we cannot name it'.[2]

At Viceroy's House Lutyens's prayer was answered. 'For the first time,' wrote Gavin Stamp, 'Lutyens's architecture transcended that of Wren by going beyond the mere employment of the Classical orders and grammar.'[3] The geometry, the handling of space and the vertical forms are classical. But these are brilliantly assimilated to elements from the Indian architecture which Lutyens had initially so despised. From the Moguls Lutyens took the handling of colour and shadow, which he deployed with such effect to emphasize the horizontals of the building. The *chujja*, or sharp projecting stone cornice, throwing deep bands of horizontal shadow, was a Mogul device; so too was the use of contrasting coloured stone – at Delhi bands of sandstone of 'rich rhubarb-red and ivory cream'. Capping it all was the great copper dome, that 'shout of the imperial suggestion' – 'an offence against democracy, a slap in the face of the modern average man' – which was inspired as much by Mogul and Buddhist influences as it was by classicism.[4]

By the summer of 1913 this design was on the drawing-board. But Lutyens's work at Viceroy's House was bedevilled by the question of cost. In 1911 Hardinge told the British Government that the building of New Delhi would cost £4,000,000. Curzon, who in any case considered the building

Lutyens's Delhi Order. Corinthian, with stone bells that cannot announce the downfall of a dynasty.

1. Hussey, *Lutyens,* p. 280.
2. ibid., p. 297.
3. *Catalogue 1981,* p. 40.
4. Robert Byron, 'New Delhi', *Country Life,* vol. lxix (6 June 1931), p. 710.

of the new capital a pointless extravagance, attacked this figure in the House of Lords and suggested that £12,000,000 would be more accurate. In March 1913, after stringent reductions by the Public Works Department, a figure of £6,000,000 was sanctioned. Lutyens maintained from the beginning that this figure was too low and that Curzon's estimate was more realistic.

In the first round of cuts after March 1913 Lutyens had to reduce the original plan of Viceroy's House by ratio from 13 to 8½ million cubic feet, a task made more difficult by Hardinge requiring the dome to be higher. By the following winter Hardinge had changed his mind about the dome: he now wanted it lower, but he also wanted more accommodation within the building – for the Viceroy's secretariat, a printing press and thirteen bedroom suites. The cost grew again, and between December 1913 and January 1914 Lutyens began the Herculean task of recasting the whole plan to come within the Public Works Department estimate. Baker watched him: 'I marvelled at his amazing industry in his efforts to reduce the scale of his elaborate and monumental plans without sacrificing his cherished proportions. Night and day he worked, while I developed my detail drawings, waiting impatiently to go home before the hot season set in.'[1]

17 Queen Anne's Gate   Aug.26.12.

This must be a very scrappy letter. Swinton and Brodie came to B. Square on Sunday and we spent all day together. Hardinge has volte faced altogether and nothing can be settled until after Xmas at Delhi itself. We are all rather concerned and fussed but *don't* tell anyone. Brodie stayed the night at B. Square.

We all went to India Office this morning and saw Holderness[2] and Ritchie.[3] Ritchie took me to lunch and was very comforting and nice and helpful and fearfully anti-Lanchester. It may end in a battle between Crewe and Hardinge, but we are all right I think.

1. Herbert Baker, *Architecture and Personalities* (1944), p. 66.
2. Sir Thomas Holderness (1849–1924), ex-Indian Civil Servant and Secretary at the India Office.
3. Sir Richmond Ritchie (1854–1912), Permanent Under-Secretary at the India Office 1909–12.

Crewe asked us all to stay at Crewe on the next Monday, but as we won't have all news and papers from India we shall ask for a postponement – Swinton, Brodie, self, Ritchie and Holderness.

Stayed to dinner with Mrs Merton at Newbury[1] and came home late. She is such a dear and so kind to me. You must know her, and she wants to know the children. She knows Madame Blavatsky intimately[2] and stayed with her for weeks together.

I was rather unhappy yesterday, but write now much happier.

Royal Hibernian Hotel, Dublin   Aug.30.12.

Here I am after a day at Heywood with Sir Hucheson Poë as he now calls himself. The gardens promise well, but he is so cross to his workmen, to me and to all under him, and his wife, who is very rich is left alone and ignored almost. At least she goes her own way, ignores as much as she is ignored. She is quite happy and I have not yet found out whether she is brilliantly clever or half daft. We, Poë and self, are happy together – it is his manner. Tomorrow I go to Lambay and the Barings will call for me here.

The Hotel is FULL owing to Horse Show and Races. It is an awful anxiety getting away from Lambay but when there I forget all the world and I wonder if India will matter.

I am (this is *private*) angry with Lanchester telling the Viceroy my avenues were too wide. It will come all right but I do not want Englishmen to grow mutilated trees in their great streets. I want the trees to grow free as God made them and not a European acropolis – I am rather nervous too about the King who wants Mogul architecture, etc. Fancy Shakespeare being asked by Elizabeth to write an ode in Chaucerian metre, etc.

---

1. Wife of Zachary Merton (1843–1915), wealthy mine-owner and philanthropist, for whom Lutyens was adding to Folly Farm in Berkshire. In 1906 he had enlarged a cottage at Folly Farm for Mr H. Cochrane in the style of William and Mary. In 1912, contrary to his usual practice of adding in a later style, he reverted to his early Surrey style with conspicuous success. In 'the 1912 wing of Folly Farm,' wrote Weaver, 'every detail has been perfected so fully that even the vegetable racks in the scullery are more interesting than the fittings of many a great library' (*Houses and Gardens by Edwin Lutyens*, p. 281). The hall had black walls, like Bloomsbury Square.

2. Presumably on the astral plane, as Madame Blavatsky had been dead since 1891.

One thing I am glad, my troubles – and troubles will come – come that way to me through my work and do not immediately affect my own sweet wife.

Of course darling go to Genoa and love it and have no qualms or doubts.[1] Be happy, healthy in body and your mind will be true. Such is the way of God. Do go to the old town and pay my respects to the Palazzo Balbi, the University and some other palaces in that wonderful street. Don't bother about a Royal Palace. A King set on a throne by a Garibaldi has no taste, no tradition and is raw as an uncooked carrot (to you) steak (to me).

In train to Ballater   Sept.6.12.

I *do* hope all goes well and
I shall be able to satisfy
the King's Mogul taste.

 You can't dress
the King like this,   or

   like this bare
                                                 tummy, legs
and the Queen   and a veiled
like this,   countenance.

I have written to Victor who is at the Beattys' next door and I hope to see him, which would be fun. If we met in Royal presence I should get the giggles, which would frighten him dreadfully.

1. Lutyens had at first protested against Lady Emily taking Barbara and Robert to Genoa to meet Leadbeater, who had not been in England since the scandal of 1906.

No news and I have only that beloved story now old, of how much I love and want you darling to be home. I don't think you know when I say things I think, and when I write them they get fixed somewhat and a word may mean more or less of what I mean and the emphasis gets wrong. Darling, here the train is stopping, so I shall shut up to post.

c/o Lord Stamfordham, Abergeldie Mains   Sept.8.12.

Had a comfy journey and a breakfast basket at Aberdeen, arriving here at near ten. A Royal carriage it was that met me at Ballater with two hired horses. The King gives Bigge [Stamford-ham] all he wants in that way and uses the Royal liveries.

Went for a walk around and met Lord Stamfordham riding home from the Castle for lunch. I went down the riverside and saw the river – an occupation that always fascinates me. After lunch went and wrote my name down and Stamfordham and Miss Bigge played golf and I went off with Lady Stamfordham to see views but luckily the rain came on and I went home.

Some amazement has been caused – Friday night all the flags on the golf course had been destroyed and suffragette flags put in with mottoes on them. They evidently thought Asquith or Chur-chill was at the Castle. The men seem amused and rather shocked at the cheek of doing it in the King's own garden, but the womenkind are furious against their sisters! One woman has been turned out of the Ballater golf club for having accosted Asquith whilst he was playing. There are some absurd looking local policemen hanging about now.

Today we all go and lunch with the Beattys where the W. Churchills are and I hope Victor.[1] It is luck for I wanted to see Mrs Beatty.

Last night after dinner I showed Lord Stamfordham my Delhi sketches and proposals etc. He seems much impressed and Lady S. gasped and Miss Bigge would take no more transparencies or other amusing pictures. I think I am going to see the King some

---

1. At Invercauld, which the Beattys had taken. Lutyens had added to Hanover Lodge, Regent's Park, for Admiral Beatty (1871–1936) in 1909. Beatty was, in 1912, Naval Secretary to Churchill, the First Lord of the Admiralty.

time after lunch, at tea probably, so I shall have more to write to you later on, I hope.

King circles are not healthy or normal unless you have been born and bred in them. Their presence pervades too much. I shall be interested in seeing the boys.

Received the Indian mail of last week yesterday. Hardinge has a new idea for Government House and Lanchester's last plan is so weak as to expose his whole mental system of designing as a shop counter. Making of patterns and what people expect i.e. the commonplace with no imagination or invention just bores me to tears. I do hope the powers will see it.

Now it is breakfast time 9 o'c. Bigge goes up to the Castle at 10 and then on to church. I have no top hat or black coat. I said I thought it was only the Elders who wore top hats in Scotland.

I don't want to go to church and be conspicuous as the only man in day clothes and a soft hat.

Monday

I drew a picture on the above lines which Lord Stamfordham took to the King and I stayed here and did not go to church. They came back at about 12.30 and the Moderator – it sounds like a lamp but means a sort of Archbishop – preached a terrible dull sermon. We got into a motor – Lady S., Miss Bigge and self, picked Lord S. up at the Castle and went off to Invercauld.

I had such a nice welcome from Mrs Beatty and there was Pamela, Victor, the Winston Churchills and her sister. Pamela and Beatty said Oh such a good sermon, King and his people said Blimey rot.

I may fish in the Beatty waters which they say are better than the Balmoral. After lunch walked and talked and the weather was bitter cold. Motored back to Balmoral, walking part of the way and then tea rather late – 5.45 as men only came in.

Sir Walter Lawrence, influence with King on Indian matters;[1] Sir James Reid,[2] a whole lot of them and Samuel – a nice common looking [Jew] but [a] quiet one who went to church![3] They were all looking at Delhi plans on billiard table and I was being bombarded with questions when the King sent for me. We went, Bigge and I, to the Queen's room. There she was looking for all the world like one of her own photographs. She remembered me at Holy Island [p. 154] and I reminded her of her thin boots and the horrible cobbles. The King came in and the impression you get is two blue eyes and v. large moustachios carefully groomed. A kilt and sporran complete. Lord Crewe had warned him not to commit himself but he was interested and looked at the lay-out. Did not like the idea of shifting Government House on the axis line. Wanted King Edward's statue now existing in Delhi [in front of the south gate of the Fort] to be brought into the scheme but the stone not to be moved. I may shift the statue as on a pivot over the stone he laid on the Durbar site in December 1911. Very insistent and 'cut your head off' about it. He was pleased with a suggestion I made about it.

He liked Government House etc. and said it was 'beautiful'. Was exercised as to where the flagstaff should go – a point which frightened me but on which I was able to reassure him. The sizes of rooms satisfied – he thought they were too small perhaps but was satisfied.

I invited him to Delhi! and showed him and the Queen how they would be housed and begged the Queen to come and furnish it and watch the building which seemed to amuse her mightily. I did not give away Hardinge or anybody and said nice things of everyone. He asked as to whether Lanchester was going out again. I said I did not know. He wanted me to see Sir Walter Lawrence, so on dismissal I went to Lawrence's room and he came and we had a nice comfy talk. I smoking he not daring to as he thought his room was under the Queen's and I knew it wasn't!

And then walked home here to dinner arriving about 8.20.

Today I am going to fish and shall go up to London tomorrow.

I think it was all satisfactory. The Queen thought my great portico beautiful so I feel happy about style and those difficulties.

1. Sir Walter Lawrence (1857–1940). Ex-Indian Civil Servant and Private Secretary to Curzon as Viceroy, 1898–1903.

2. Sir James Reid (1849–1923), Royal Physician.

3. H. L., later Viscount, Samuel (1870–1936), then Postmaster-General.

Next week I must try and win Crewe and get it settled.

No other news. People were very amusing so I might write a novel bound in Royal purple and the bloodshot eyes for watchin' of 'em! Not unkindly or unsympathetically but amusing and perhaps a touch of jealous cynicism.

29 Bloomsbury Square   Sept.11.12.

I came down last night and who do you think I met at Ballata Station? I was seized from behind by Vic, and Pamela came soon after.

Stamfordhams very kind. He told me they were (all the gentlemen) all criticising and making suggestions to the King after I left, which was absurd as they only saw the plans for 2 minutes. Now King is writing to Crewe, i.e. Sir Walter Lawrence is writing a letter for Stamfordham to write and as they are both friendly to me· I hope it augurs well and that Crewe may say on Monday something definite, but I fear they are going to have a competition for the Secretariats.

However, the King has views I believe about this and it is astonishing how little power he has and how he is little more than a speaking trumpet. Stamfordham's last words to me were shouted across the golf course: 'I have no use for Mrs Besant except in her belief in the Divine Right of Kings.'

I was so shocked lunching at Downing Street when I commiserated with Montagu having to defend an action in the House of Commons he did not like and did not approve of[1] – Asquith laughed and said he had to do it every day of his life.

Bah! Politics! The greatest evidence there is of our degeneracy. It is such a low game. And now there will be silly crowing on one hand and explainings away on the other. What can a majority have to do with Wrong and Right although it can make one or the other? I think tossing would be a more moral and fairer method. I am glad if the dead hand of Gladstone becomes paralysed.

So much for politics. I have been very fair to both sides. Politics

1. Edwin Montagu (1879–1924), Liberal politician, was Parliamentary Under-Secretary for India, 1910–14. What he had to defend was probably Lord Crewe's policy for Indian self-government, which was more conservative than his own.

ought to be included within the Corrupt Practices Act and Whitaker Wright[1] was a soul of honour compared to the blarney of Ministers and others out on the cadge for votes.

29 Bloomsbury Square   Sept.16.12.

Don't forget my L-d-b-t-r warnings and keep clear of occultism. Do encourage Robert to see the buildings. The big stairways and halls in the palaces and the shapes of the blue sky seen up above between the cornices of the narrow streets. And go at twilight. Leonardo da Vinci said the twilight was the time to go and study the faces of people (I read it buildings) and buildings can have such dear faces. Solemn and sweet like my own darling Emy and when I have designed a building with the look my darling has then I know I have done a good thing. Still, level-eyed, clear and a brave quiet outlook as passive as a Holbein portrait. And these qualities words give no name for. I just bow. It is all very wonderful and what it all means I don't know, don't care, only it must be done or attempted and to be careless about it is culpable and to fail is sorrow. Perfection is ever beyond the reach of men.

The Greeks got it as near as anyone – there could not have been many of that excellence but many must have helped. And with their example they want me to do Hindo. Hindon't I say. It is not architecture – the best just clever children, though I own to some of their detail being beautiful, really beautiful, but just incidents and generally transparencies of sorts.

This is all about my work but Emyown runs through it all and her blue eyes are the woof of my life's warp.

Genoa   Sept.19.12.

I want to tell you my impressions of C.W.L. [Leadbeater]. Well, he is in appearance of course somewhat like his photo – a very big heavy man and yet wonderfully active considering his age – up early and seemingly never tired. He has a rather funny mincing

1. Whitaker Wright (1845–1904), the fraudulent company promoter, whose name was a by-word for corruption. Lutyens had built a bathing pavilion and boathouse for him at Witley in 1897. Wright's career was one of the inspirations for H. G. Wells's novel, *Tono-Bungay* (1909).

walk – a rather drawly parsonic voice but talks a great deal – very agreeably and naturally. He has a very courteous manner and has been most cordial to me – but under all one feels a mild contempt for all women and I feel I am only tolerated as the mother of Robert. He has a quite polite way of making you feel small and ridiculous which is not pleasant.

He has a slightly mocking way which makes me feel nothing is quite serious to him and that one could not bare one's heart in any way to him. One thing agreeably surprised me which is while all his followers talk a great deal about magnetism and vibrations and you mustn't wear this or that – he seems singularly unfaddy. *He belongs to none of the offshoots of the TS except Star in the East, and pours scorn on badges and ritual and dressing up. In fact I am having a bad time in one way. An idea came to me for starting a kind of staff amongst the OSE [Order of the Star in the East] members to really work and I spoke of it to Mrs Besant who promptly turned it into a new grade of the Order. I foolishly suggested another badge – i.e. a winged star which quite met with her approval and the scheme was published. Now C.W.L. evidently ought to have been consulted being co-protector of the Order with A.B. and he doesn't like the idea of new grades and hates the new badge and is full of ridicule about a winged star and I feel exceedingly depressed and miserable about it.*

Darling love please don't pass on to anyone what I tell you in confidence – only I must speak truth to you and to tell you all the truth I am going through a bad moment of disillusionment. Perhaps that is why I came here and it is very good for me and will at least show you that I retain my power of judgment! It is not that I believe the stories of C.W.L. I think they are probably horrible libels got up by the people whose feelings he has hurt. I think he may be a great psychic – I feel him to be big *but I don't feel him to be spiritual or a bit on a level with Mrs Besant and I realise that* both *can be very foolish on the physical plane and what is chiefly upsetting me that all is evidently not harmonious between them. He is absolutely loyal to her ruling as President but obviously does not trust her judgment just as we know she mistrusts his.*

Barbie and Robert are very happy. They are now being read to by C.W.L. a thrilling book called Dracula.[1]

---

1. Bram Stoker's *Dracula* (1897) was one of Leadbeater's favourite books.

Genoa   Sept.20.12.

*Mr L. was so charming with the children last night. He sat on a
sofa with one on each side of him and told them of the occult
government of the world. You may say you don't believe his
statements but to say the least of it they are more reasonable than
the statements an orthodox clergyman would make and quite as
likely to be true, and I suppose you would not have objected to
having them prepared for confirmation in the ordinary way.
Anyhow, he talked beautifully, reverently, simply with no
affectation or pretension and so that they could perfectly understand. He has a perfect way with children. He is very like a lion in
appearance and the way he walks. Perhaps being bare footed or
in sandals increases the wild beast walk. Then he is a mixture of
Wilfrid Blunt, Bernard Shaw and his Rev [Elwin] rolled into one.
I keep seeing each one in him.*

29 Bloomsbury Square   Sept.20.12.

Lord Crewe was nice and gentlemanlike but refused to say
anything or commit himself as to my doing any, all or none of the
Delhi work. But I hope it is all right. Lady Crewe said she was
frightened of my coming as she didn't like geniuses. That, silly as
it was, has comforted me: someone must have spoken well of me
and I think Crewe just bides his time. It is disappointing Crewe
being so reserved but it must be good as he does not discourage
me and then I told him of my difficult position professionally and
he did not warn me to be careful or not to count eggs as a
gentleman should have done. He is, though slow and non-
brilliant, a gentleman and said he realised the life of a professional man. Lady Crewe was nice, I think.

Crewe really don't know right and wrong and lives in a house
part old and part new, part good, most very bad, all very
elaborate and most out of scale.[1] Living at Crewe he must lose all
sense of scale and proportion and the Parthenon itself would look
through Crewe spectacles a foreign language, so little to be
understood as to be negligible and to appear quite impractical.

1. Crewe Hall, a famous Jacobean house restored by E. M. Barry in
1866–71. Mark Girouard has described it as 'overpoweringly high-Victorian'
(*The Victorian Country House* (1979 edn), p. 403).

Oh that one's patrons would live in tents, never to be taught to misread and miswrite. But for all this the beloved and unctuous Chippy class is responsible.

Dhar, Central India [on his way to Delhi]   Dec.16.12.

We came here, Dhar, at about 35 miles an hour including stoppages and bullocks in the way. Had tiffin – I cannot yet get accustomed to the affectation of these Anglo-Indian words. And then on another 20 miles to Mandu – the ruined city Lord Hardinge and Chirol[1] have been so enamoured with. I had a nice letter from Chirol and a mad excitable one from Swinton to say the Viceroy had gone clean mad on Indo-Saracenic again. I rather wish Swinton would leave my affairs alone, he has also been talking wildly and madly. [Sir George] Clarke is building a great Indo-Saracenic Gateway to commemorate the landing of the King and Queen on the Bunder at Bombay [in 1911]. Hardinge and Chirol both say that the opinion of the Princes in India is almost entirely in favour of an Indian style. But I say what on earth can an Indian Rajah know about architecture and its ethics. This is why we are touring round to see their cities – Mandu, Indore, Lucknow.

The ruins of Mandu – set in wonderful scenery in a wonderful site all ruined and gone to jungle. The swampy remnants of great tanks, the ruins of great baths. But behind it all the building is childish and quite inconsequent and built to destroy itself.

The Durbar Hall which seems to have particularly impressed the Viceroy is a great stone building with sloping buttresses and a series of huge stone pointed arches which once carried a flat stone roof (now fell in!) When you consider that the room 25 feet wide requires 36 to 40 feet of wall thickness to support it, it becomes ridiculous and an impossible type to adopt for any practical or secretarial purpose. And then when the roof was on would be as dark as dark could well be if you want the darkness visible.

The other buildings are Mogul with the old Hindu stones defaced and worked in, in a very haphazard way. Never con-

---

1. Valentine Chirol (1852–1929), author and foreign editor of *The Times* 1899–1912, was a member of the Royal Commission on the Indian Public Services from 1912 to 1914.

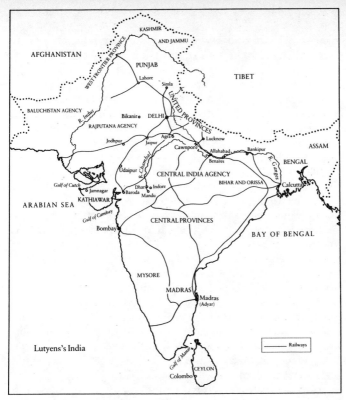

scious of using stone but treating it as though it might just as well be timber. A wonderful made picturesqueness but no intellect. The plans were fine – great simple rooms following each other and surrounded by galleries, passages and cloisters – quite unsuitable to anything of a practical nature except for a suite of entertainment rooms for those that wear no clothes want no furniture and have no real reason for a protecting building except for pomp and ceremony. Giant stairways leading to balconies where one man can squat and another may precariously stand to wave a flag-fair of peacock plumes.

Indore   Dec.17.12.

Went to Mandu and saw more of this once great city, now a
jungle enclosed by a wall 40 miles long with here and there a
palace, a tomb, a mosque ruined – and that quality of art so dear
to the literary mind – work done in a hurry by old war-worn
conquerors. Ruthless and squalid with no real nicety as the great
Westerns felt it. Freakish monstrosities most of them – their ruins
perched in high places mirrored in great pools – now full of coots
and suchlike fowl instead of Ranees bathing.

This is the Agent for Central India and is the Holkar's
country.[1] Holkar I saw in Bombay, tall, thin with a rather lovely
Eastern weak face, twenty-one years old, and no doubt in 10
years time will be a fat swarthy blackamore. His palaces here very
vulgar and his old palace in the city he does not use, except for
Durbar purposes. The building is of the Bombay Portagoose
influence.

We went before breakfast to see the Daly College by S. Jacob.
Very elaborate, cheap, and oh! absolutely in want of all that
Haldane has described as clear thinking. It was built by various
Rajahs and Ruling Chiefs of this Agency.

Then to see some more modern buildings in the Indo-Saracenic
style and then to the Holkar cenotaphs and to two more appalling
modern palaces belonging to Holkar.

Bounteous hospitality lines our way. Tonight we go to Lucknow and then on to Delhi.

This is a nice house – classical not very good but as good as I
have seen here and comfortable. The jackals made a great noise
just under my window (I am on the ground floor too!) and
turning over in my bed to sleep again the whole caboodle
collapsed. Oh I thought the jackals had got me. However, with
the help of a chair, I fixed my bed and slept soundly till morning.

I had a very kind letter from Lady Hardinge welcoming me to
India, but she warned me that the Viceroy for high considerations
of state felt bound to have an Indian styled city. She told me not to
listen to any suggestions I might hear on tour etc.

Sir V. Chirol also wrote a most charming letter but said he had
had many conversations with the Viceroy and other people in a

1. Both the Maharajah Holkar III (b. 1890) and the Agent to the Governor-
General for Central India had their residences in Indore.

position to know and spoke of the great political move in the construction of a new capital and the necessity of building it in sympathy with the new era of reciprocity between the East and West and the West must not dominate style. I fear me the Viceroy has gone back to consider an Indian style for Government House. Chirol speaks of a new style and so does Lady H. but how! It will want new blood to make one.

Everybody will bring some tit-bit which will only be conducive to chaos. Any new blood will be looked on with suspicion. However we shall see.

The Hindus knew little and the Moguls little more of any ethic of construction and art in relation to them. The Moguls took Italian forms and mutilated them. They will be suspicious of a Mogul form regenerated to the well digested section of an Italian moulding. But yet how can one knowingly mutilate a form to give it the appearance of a dead man's hand? In the meantime Swinton has been telling them I will not build if I do not have my own way and I think it is Swinton's excitement that has produced both Chirol's 2nd letter and Lady Hardinge's.

It is a question of high politics and not one of taste. My position will be easier and I with a free hand might bend but then it must be put on record that we English in giving the Indians our civilisation withdrew our great art traditions for reasons political. Of course it is absurd but it is the same calibre of literary influence that plants English Gothic buildings down here and in Africa in the form of churches. God help them. And they mutilate a man's capacity for a mere paper idea. Clarke in Bombay is on the same tack – a mixture to please all parties.

If they would only build well and consider the climate and conditions and realise that these are the paramount objects to aim for and not treat poor architecture as a mere wall paper it would be easier.

So I suppose I shall have a bit of a fight and for the rest it is just wait and see. I cannot allow the supremacy of the Eastern over the Western mind. The Chinaman is an exception perhaps, but the Hindus and Moguls are mere children at the game. The Devil stalks the world now and calls himself Education and were there ever such blind fools as we poor mortals?

It will be interesting to meet the Viceroy and have it out. I have written letters which I hope will prove tactful but the worst of Hardinge is that his FO training has given him little understanding in the way of doing and how to do things and I hear things at Delhi are getting rather messed up. However, I wait and see and I am sure of a kindly and patient hearing.

Lucknow   Dec.19.12.

Have had a busy day sight seeing. At Daly College, Indore – a college built for the sons of Rajahs and Ruling Chiefs by Rajahs and Ruling Chiefs. I asked to see the boys, dear little nigger chaps, and they were at breakfast. Some without clothes and all without shoes, sitting on their haunches eating a curious conglomeration of food out of plates with their fingers. They eat in sort of loose boxes according to their castes. Loose boxes in which one would not put a prize ox – a mud floor and no window, just a door which they kept shut and the doors fitted badly enough to let in a glimmer of light. One boy, because he had tea with the master was fined by his people 500 rupees. They have their own ponies and are very keen about games of all sorts.

One little blackamoor asked the master if he might send home for another pony as his had a little one in her belly.

We had the Chowk [in Lucknow] opened for our motor – the main trade street old and narrow and full of weird clothed people. Then the Residency – it must have been a pleasant building, well built and well designed. Lots of natives were going over it and I could not help wondering what they thought of the battered buildings and the stand we made.

Horribly pathetic and moving and, except for the original buildings built by some sapper of taste, all is ugly, vulgar. The monuments enough to turn any decent bodies in their graves.

The modern buildings here are awfully all filigree and silly nonsense and ugly to boot. But I guess I have written enough.

Delhi   Dec.26.12.

When I left off was at Lucknow. We went on from there to Cawnpore and went around the place. Lucknow and Cawnpore poured out their mutiny massacres and I got thoroughly sobered by the thought of suffering and the futile bravery. Massacre and then them that escaped saw RED. It is horrible and pathetic and the sly slime of the Eastern mind is repulsive. I have been reading a good deal of history out here and it is not black v. white. It went on before we were thought of and goes on now. I am building a theory that black and white means nothing – but the dark element here is inbred with treachery for countless centuries.

To our camp and my first night in a tent[1]. A comfortable tent too. Electric light, an oil stove but no other comforts. In the day time the outer flaps are all raised and oh it is beautiful the sunny weather but awfully cold morning and night and it is very difficult to leave in the morning one's cocoon of warmth to sit in the ice cold trickling hot water over one's bare body. Thick coats and my comforter early and late and oh! my yellow waistcoat is *not* here!

Sunday I walked out and ran into Harcourt Butler. He took me to his most luxurious camp and told me all the gossip. He (this is all private and might harm he, me or someone) is very angry with the Viceroy and the way he changes his mind and plays to the native gallery etc., and says every Viceroy after his first two years gets fed up with the adulation of the natives and their Ruling Chiefs and begins 'I' 'I' 'I' do this and think that, etc.

On Monday we were all gloomed over by the bomb throwing.

This morning Lady Hardinge asked me to go to breakfast and I spent an hour or more with her afterwards and her account of the squalid incident may be of most interest.

Directly after breakfast I went into her room – she was just finishing her breakfast. I showed her some plans and the things I had brought out and she was so natural and simple and then told me her story.

Half way down the old main street of Delhi – the people cheering wildly, an unusual thing for Delhi folk, she heard a report, not realising it was a bomb, but felt as though the elephant was wrong or there was an earthquake. She looked at the Viceroy and saw his coat was torn and put her hand up to close the tear to tidy him when she realised that a large bit of meat (that is not her language) was sticking out of the Viceroy's uniform. She realised then what had happened.

The Viceroy said someone has thrown a bomb – go on. She did not know how to stop the procession and thought Lord H. was probably mortally injured and another shock might hurt him

1. Part of the Government of India was under canvas until Temporary Delhi was completed early in 1913.

again. She looked round for help and then saw only one man behind them and he was dead. So she said we cannot go on with a dead man in the Howdah and the procession must stop. H. said I suppose it must, stopped it and fainted. She beckoned to Maxwell, Military Secretary on the elephant ahead and she does not know how he got down his and up their elephant.

The elephant behaved splendidly though slightly wounded – never ran or showed fear. Jolly beasts elephants. I love 'em. I have such a lot to say about elephants too – how one of them did go musty and how they punished him.

Motor cars were brought and there was great difficulty in getting Hardinge off the elephant into a car. They built a scaffolding in the crowd of parking cars and lifted him down. In the car he recovered consciousness sufficient to say the procession is to go on and the ceremonies to take place as though nothing had happened.

Lady H. never lost presence of mind nor did she squeal. She told me she had always been accustomed to assassinations and bombs in Bucharest, Constantinople and St Petersburg.

The C-in-C was blaspheming helplessly on the top of his elephant and Lor! what a helpless position an elephant top is.

But the people most infuriated were the natives – Pertab Singh[1] and the Indian troops and if they had been there, there would have been a massacre in the house from which the bomb came. The howdah, which I have seen, is an extraordinary sight – battered to pieces and soaked in blood and Lady H. was not touched.

I saw Chirol and had a long talk with him. I think things will be all right but the bomb will delay us. The Viceroy's fixed on an adaptation of the Indian style but I can't fight him yet and it just depends on what he means and what latitude he would allow. Talking with Lady H. it seems all right. The suggestion is that I, Baker, Swinton Jacob – the latter as a sort of walking dictionary on Indo-Saracenic art – should do the whole caboodle. This would be worth while.

We have been and are all in a fog of helpless rage. I only see the squalor of it all and fear that any political influences should be mongered. But it is rot.

1. General Sir Pertab Singh, Regent to his great-nephew the Maharajah of Jodhpur 1911–16.

And God damn the Pethick-Lawrence crew and all else who use the bomb as an argument. It is such messy work. What is the use of disembowelling a native servant in Lady Hardinge's presence? And the fear of the Delhi people is great. They expect reprisal not so much from us English as from their fellow natives. Hundreds hid themselves.

Delhi   Dec.29.12.

No news. Discussions day by day. Folk here instead of saying what is *best* hugger mugger away at expediency and at what 'they will say' and estimate with the result that they get something which is not cheap or efficient. Their imaginations are all of the destructive criticism order and not constructive. However, until the Viceroy is up and about again everything in the way of initiation in the country stops and as he is doing the new Delhi himself everything, as far as I am concerned, waits. However, the country is so large there still remain areas which we can investigate and buildings and always a tomb to be investigated. And then these endless pow-wows!

I suppose we shall give up India, leave our people in the lurch as they have done in S. Africa. The average Indian seems a hopeless creature. I wonder what will happen. They will reduce the native troops and increase the natives in the Civil Service and away with discipline. They will try and give them representative government which will no more represent them than our system represents us. Government will get into the hands of talkers and they will be governed by phrases as we are. And no one will be a whit the better and a good many a good deal worse. Then there may be more Eurasians, a hopeless, helpless class disliked by blacks and whites.

There is a story of Curzon. An Indian came up and insulted him and Curzon promptly knocked him down. The man lay on the ground and whined and said he would report him to the Viceroy. Curzon was furious and in a furious rage said 'Why by God! I AM the Viceroy!'

The clergyman here is talking about an English Cathedral – a true Christian Gothic one.[1] If he says any more I shall place the

1. The design made by Lutyens in 1917 for Delhi Cathedral was far from Gothic. But it was not executed and the building that is now Delhi Cathedral was designed by H. A. N. Medd in 1927.

Cathedral in an outer ring and give it the rank of a third rate building. I shall tell him with all its great beauty a Westminster Abbey is only fit out here for frying bacon.

Delhi   Jan.2.13.

The Viceroy is fearsome of not getting his way, but architecturally he knows so little and is so vague. He is a water colourist and his father was a friend of Sir Francis Grant[1] and Landseer and [his father] exhibited in the RA for twenty years. So you see [why] he said 'I know something about Art'.

Delhi   Jan.7.13.

The Viceroy changes his mind every time I see him. I am afraid he will make work very difficult. He has no idea of how to get things done and to get to work. And all he will think about [is] what the place will look like in 3 years time. 300 is what I think of. I mentioned 10 years in regard to something and he said it was so far ahead not worth considering! This is the building of an Imperial City!

Delhi   Jan.16.13.

The nationalist movement here is exactly as though the children of a nursery rose against their nurse – and if they, the children, would not wash and break everything in the room they had a mind to reach to.

The people are patient and contented and whenever they are left with an Indian Resident they apply for the reinstatement of an Englishman. Their tradition – clan against clan and treachery, a certain clever sliminess and vice – and it will be years before they are fit to govern themselves with any sense of justice or of fairness.

It is a terrible question and I can only foresee disaster even greater than what the young Turks have brought to Turkey. I am

1. Sir Francis Grant (1807–78), sporting artist and portrait painter, President RA 1868–71.

not sure but that the only gentlemanlike thing we can do is to leave India. But it would be to the grievous harm and regret of the huge mass of inarticulate peoples. The Bengali and people who [only] talk to grouse and to serve their own immediate fatuous conceits. And the extraordinary thing to me is that politicians come out here and preach the efficiency and justice of the vote! We have had the bronze age, iron age, stone age, etc. This surely must be the lunatic age. Government by phrases. It is mad. Poor India, she will have some iron-shod foot across her throat.

I cannot help laughing to think of all the millions we spend at home on education – an education that blinds and rots man's better sense. Never was there set up such an idol – set up by men for men to worship. Nebuchadnezzar's golden calf pales to tin!

Delhi   Jan.20.13.

Hardinge sent for Swinton on Saturday and told him that we must consider the North Ridge again as the site of the new city.

This after months of work on the other side, the south site, and after the Council, Viceroy and Crewe had all agreed!

Delhi   Jan.21.13.

Montagu[1] has got a full grasp of the situation, and thinks it is all very serious. The govt's *volte face* and pandering to an ignorant public without foresight etc. The only thing we can do is to make other plans etc. until such time as Hardinge is well enough. The Viceroy seems to have lost his nerve, and suddenly chucks a thing without instructions from home – and which he, and his whole council (except Fleetwood Wilson)[2] signed and sealed and got the home govt to sanction.

I am rather depressed about it all though the architectural part seems to go on well and may turn out all right. But then if I am in the saddle and the Viceroy wobbles and changes his mind and

---

1. Montagu was on an official visit to India from October 1912 to March 1913.
2. Sir Guy Fleetwood Wilson (1850–1940) was Finance Member of the Supreme Council of India from 1908–13.

---

interferes in details, it is hardly worth giving up the best of one's life to this work.

This bomb has been an awful bore. He gets threatening letters every other day. This policy of pacification and India for the Indians does not seem a very happy one and Hardinge is tremendously pro-Indian and this is his reward.

I have been trying to find a Buddha for you but can't get one and Lor! how ugly everything Indian and Anglo-Indian is – it is most remarkable.

Delhi   Jan.27.13.

Friday dined with Harcourt Butler.

Lady Jenkins – wife of a chief justice Calcutta. Amusing, and of a cheeky artistic sort. Gambles and shoots and breeds race horses etc. Pretends to have taken a fancy to me, and addresses me as darling etc. You know the sort. The slap and tickle kind. But very kind.

Butler drank too much for which I was sorry and I sat on till one, and Butler talked India which was thrilling. He has had a long career here and was our Foreign Minister [on the Viceroy's Executive Council] so knows all the ruling chiefs – and a good deal of my impressions are gained through his talking.

He seems to like them etc. – which the impressions I hand on to you may not seem to imply – but he does. He rather resents on political grounds that the chiefs here who grovel and place their head on the ground between his feet should when in London be placed beside the King and women curtsey to [them]!

Monday we dined with Fleetwood Wilson and learnt or heard a good deal as to how the Government and the bureaucratic methods of men delay progress and the doing of work by their methods and their eye for their own automatic promotion. Rather depressing. He is undoubtedly clever, keen – and knows of what he talks about. But there is ever a feeling of a game being played by a man who knows so well how a game is played!

There has been a sudden jump back to the north site.

All the week we have been planning, estimating etc. for a possible lay out on the north site. From a business point of view it is the right thing to do tho' it is practically all waste. Yet it will close this particular door ever being opened again to any hurt.

In train, Delhi to Bombay [to meet Baker]   Feb.5.13.

Monday I went to see Mrs Cotes.[1] Now Mrs Cotes is a clever lady here, a novelist – a correspondent to both London and Calcutta papers. She is one of the prime movers of the movement to get the site we have chosen moved onto the North from the South of Delhi. Well I went at 5 o' clock by appointment and found her alone in a clean little bungalow with a post impressionist picture over the mantelpiece – to give that touch of *dernier cri* in a most amusing way.

Tea things spread round a large brass kettle – cyphering – and sufficiently out of reach to give a touch of womanly bustle and to and fro movement of attentions so flattering to a man in another man's house. And we talked for two hours or more. She is a clever woman but a first-class ass! Her main contention is that a city built to the north – a small ceremonial city – with no chance of expansion could be built – whereas a city to the south would at the first war, famine and other national disaster be dropped.

Some fat blacks [have] occupied the only ladies' carriage – and you mustn't occupy a carriage they have used. They don't know how to use the lavatory basins, and they use them for all sorts of purposes. The poorer nations they taught to use a WC by putting a looking glass in such a way, their irresistible curiosity compelled them to sit! So that they had to use the thing properly.

In train, returning from Agra   Feb.16.13.

We saw the Taj by rain storm, then by moonlight, and last night a rare and heavy thunder storm and hail! It was amusing to see the little boys eat hail balls – a thing they had probably never seen before.

The gardens were delicious – clear western skies, gorgeous colours and dark glossy trees and the pools and water channels full. So we got full reflections with a great blue and white sky culminating high above.

---

1. Mrs Everard Cotes (d. 1922) was the author of several books, including such titles as *A Social Departure: How Orthodocia and I Went Round the World by Ourselves* (1890) and *The Simple Adventure of a Memsahib* (1893). She had speculated in land on the North site.

We spent a good deal of time with the gardener looking at trees and shrubs and finding out what will and will not do at Delhi. We go to building after building and over all the architecture pervades a childish ignorance which if corrected and put right so alters the style as to become no relation to it at all – unrecognisable.

The Taj by moonlight becomes so bald and indefinite, the patterns disappear and the arch-forms merge into a fog of white reflection, leaving the great turnip of a dome as a bubble poised in space. It is wonderful but it is not architecture and its beauty begins where architecture ceases to be. And so it is with all these Indian builders. Anything really admirable has been done by an Italian or a Chinaman. For the rest it is all pattern – just the same as on any carpet hung up, on ceilings, walls, inside or outside. The buildings are tents in stone and little more. Elaborated to howdahs. Stone buildings which when put up are carved and carved and carved without any relation to the stone, its purpose or location. The Indians of today have no sense of construction decorated.

We went through some stone yards where Indians were chipping away at hideous vulgarities without endeavour of better attainment. It will be difficult to find the men – Government ought to breed them! A job for the Eugenic Societies! I cannot yet see how we are to get together a school of craftsmen. The right way would have been – had it not been made a political question – to go one's own way direct to one's own great point and compelled them to follow and in following bent our ways to theirs by those games that have always been there when great styles are made. I feel sure it is no use blunting one's own sense of righteousness by stooping to the inefficiencies of an atrophied architecture. But! I am not in the mood to write now having got up very early after a wakeful night of continuous thunderstorm.

Delhi   Feb.18.13.

Baker is at present very much pro-North and goes for the position on the Kopje as he calls the Ridge and does not yet realise as we do the conditions that govern the health and sanitation of this weird variable climate, but it is great fun and comfort having him. I don't think he treats architecture as seriously as I do.

One thing I feel certain of is that a great Imperial city must be laid down on lines absolutely sanitary sound from a health point of view and if for the sake of a picturesque skyline or some scenic advantage the city is misplaced it will become yet another dead city with which India abounds.

I had a nice letter from Mrs Besant putting in a plea by its way for Indian architecture. Indian architecture is, to make a far reached simile, what a Surrey cottage *ornée* is to Westminster Abbey. A peasant's house to Chartres and a cave dwelling to the Parthenon.

Herbert Baker

Delhi   Feb.26.13.

We saw Lady H. alone – she is wonderful with the vice-crown on her shoulders, and I think she sees over the crown and beyond – as well she might being so much smaller.
We talked much and long
as is the Indian
habit so to do.

This sort
of thing
with
apologies
where
due.

Delhi   Saturday

The Viceroy is all for the south site thank goodness! for wisdom's sake. Tomorrow he has called all the pronounced pro-Northerners to meet him in consultation. But I have no fear now and we can begin to get to work soon I hope.

The Viceroy seems wonderfully well and full of his old vigour and courteousness. I don't mean he was ever discourteous but he has regained his presence of wit and no longer wanders in the midst of pertinent business. I hope by next mail I will be able to tell you that the site is settled and that this settlement is in the South, where you can build a healthy city for India and the Indians without putting the Britons in a plain by themselves with sufficient space of real healthy ground for any future development that may be ever possible, whether we, the Indians or the Chinese hold and govern India. All that matters is that the Government is *good*.

In train, Lahore to Delhi   March 9.13.

I had a long talk with [the Begum of Bhopal[1]]. She was thickly veiled and I felt I might have been, for all I knew, talking to Bumps, God bless her. I started suffragettes and she said if women in India did what the women of England do she would stop education. Education is her one great idea, and she spends heaps on it. She is going to build a purdah college at Delhi. She wants it near the river so the ladies can learn to swim. I wondered if crocodiles would respect purdah. I also asked her what about aeroplanes and we settled that a big hat or umbrella might meet the difficulty. Her grand daughter was with her with her veil up! She allows her grand daughters to go out of purdah when in a Lord Sahib's house, but is very strict amongst her own people the Mahomedans.

This morning Dane[2] motored us out to Jehangir's Tomb and the ruins of the tomb of the Empress, then on to the fort to see the wonderful tiled pictures of elephants, camels and men fighting, marching, hunting and what not. At the fort gate an elephant met

1. Nawab Sultan Jahan Begum came to the throne of Bhopal in 1901.
2. Sir Louis Dane (1856–1946), Governor of the Punjab 1908–13.

us and we rode through the old city on him and saw an Indian city in an Indian way, and so home to lunch.

I had asked Dane for his camel carriage and he said yes, little did I know! until I saw a sort of charabanc drawn by six huge camels – each camel being mounted by a man in red uniform, twelve red coated men on the box! Baker and I occupied this egregious equippage alone and went into Lahore for to see the museum again at our leisure. We got back to tea, and galorious I got my mail – your darling letter. I cannot see you reclining on Persian divans your cheeks rouged and henna on your finger tips, however a Lytton does change about with his or her moods! The charabanc we used was built for 'the Lyttons'! so their charabancs don't change at all events.

We gave Louis Dane a cheque for 75 rupees (£5) to start a competition in the art school for the best design in tiles of the King Emperor's progress from Aden to the Delhi Durbar. The result may be awfully funny and Dane is delighted with us in consequence.

I am so glad to have good news of darling Con.

I am longing to get home.

Harcourt Butler telephoned to us to say that the Council had decided on the south site. So that is all right. I am glad. Any other decision would have been fatal. Extraordinary how one distrusts any opinion but one's own in moments of crisis.

Chester   April 18.13.

Here I am waiting between trains. I had an awful rush to get off. I lunched with E[velyn] Shaw and Blomfield about the British School at Rome and then I had no sooner got back than Lady Norman[1] arrived. She is so difficult and wants impossibilities and never does a thing I say. She buys rubbish in Italy and wants it fitted in and expects me to design the noses of putti cherubs in places where cherubs should never go. Makes rooms larger than the site will hold and then wants to pack in anyhow essentials. An

1. The Hon. Florence McLaren (d. 1964), daughter of the 1st Baron Aberconway, married in 1907 Sir Henry Norman (1858–1939), coal-owner and Liberal MP. In 1911 Lutyens designed The Corner House, Cowley Street, and No. 8 College Street, Westminster, for her and her brother, Francis McLaren.

awful client, and typical of all overreaching and vulgar minds.

So I started in a cross-patch mood and arrived at Barrow nearer 12 than 11. Furness Abbey. And what avail is it to build at all when great buildings [in] a very few hundred years are in ruins in spite of their permanent methods of construction that is of no avail against destruction and neglect?

Very depressing. I saw the site for the Vicker Maxim Entertainment House I am to build[1] and then went over their great works and a great battle cruiser just completing for the Japanese. 13.5 guns and lots of them and a mass of men – English and a lot of Japs just arrived and amongst them a policeman whose appearance tickled me.

And now I am on my way to Ireland and I feel so bored shunted for 3 hours in an hotel. I do so hate being away from you darling and long to get back.

What a weird horrible tragedy the Oscar Wilde letters read in the Douglas libel action.

29 Bloomsbury Square   April 26.13.

I am so sad coming home and finding everybody and you away! and I with no engagement and alone.

Drewe was very pleasant and only wants me to do what I think right even about the stone! A very different attitude. The Grenfells were very kind and pleasant and have given in about the staircase sticking to the original plan.[2] So I am happy. I only wish Lord Hardinge was as wise and as understanding. But then he has never built before and cannot see things until he puts words to them and if he likes the words he likes the thing and they have no real connection whatever.

Varengeville   *July 12.13.*

I am glad Mrs Grenfell liked Robert. I have always wanted to meet her, but when have I had a chance? You have never

1. Abbey House, Barrow-in-Furness. 'Rather grim and impersonal, as efficient as a battleship, the work caught something of the mood in which it was conceived' (Hussey, *Lutyens*, p. 293).
2. Lutyens was adding to Roehampton House for A. M. Grenfell.

suggested asking me. Besides you know your clients only want to talk shop with you and it would bore them awfully if I came too.

Do you seriously believe that you know and like my friends better than I know and like yours? The irony of it all is that practically all my friends have been yours – only you cease to care for them. Chippy was your friend not mine. The Mallets were your friends not mine and through them all the mischief came. You are only interested in people while they are building. But darling I have always said you were far bigger in many ways than I am but you are training me!

Varengeville[1]   *Aug.18.13.*

I somehow feel that our holidays never come off. I am so horribly active and full of ploys and you just want to sit and smoke and cuddle, so we pull against each other all the time. At home it is different. However I love you always you must remember that and forget my bristles.

29 Bloomsbury Square   Aug.20.13.

Oh but darling I was conscious of no bristles. Were you very disappointed with me? Do you remember when we went to meet Badcock at that Welsh station, we were happy and expectant and when he put his head out of the window our spirits fell and our joy fled. Was my coming like that?

29 Bloomsbury Square   Aug.21.13.

I find by chance on your table a little diary, 1913, looking through it in an absent sort of a way I found 'Human Duty' recurring. Now I did not like *that*, but felt reassured when I saw it was as often when I was in India, but what is 'Human Duty'? Or

1. Lady Emily, now entitled to wear a yellow silk Indian shawl, as one of Mrs Besant's special group, had taken, on 11 August, her first step on the occult path and was on probation to the Master Kuthumi. Lutyens had paid a visit, but had to stay with the Mallets as there was not room in the farmhouse where Lady Emily was lodging with the children (*Candles in the Sun*, pp. 55–7).

ought I not to ask, however I ask and I cannot compel a reply.

Oh darling Ems I love you and Oh I am curious and that perhaps is an ingredient of what makes *me*.

Varengeville   *Aug.24.13.*

I could not help laughing heartily at your interpretation of 'Human Duty'. It is the name of my Masonic Lodge.[1] What weird ideas you do have!

In train for Ireland   Aug.22.13.

I have a vasty insight into things, somehow, but no authority, no education. I take paragraphs at a run. I hear things, see things, unconsciously almost, and store them and they turn up afterwards – from whence I know not. I believe I am more astral than you, but I have one huge anchor in this plane and that is you, incarnate, darling. You are more logical than I am, more determinate, consciously aspiring to spiritual things and having pleasure in the statement of them, so we are severally the two faces of a medal – the same medal.

I went down to Folly Farm this morning and back early after lunch, Mrs Merton's initial is A [Antonia] her husband's is Z (Zachary) her surname is 'M'erton, so I put on a fireback

MCMXIII is the date. It will look like a legend on a Huntley and Palmer biscuit, as made at Reading nearby.

We have bored an artesian well, a six-inch hole 200 feet deep and lo! and behold! up comes a stream of ice cold clean clear

1. In 1911 Lady Emily joined the Order of Co-Masonry, a breakaway group from the exclusively male Masonic Order, started in France in 1870.

water bubbling away and looks like a trout stream, a little river a day old which will never dry up is in its way a miracle.

I shall give your message of love to Mrs Baring.

Good night darling. I hope my troubled one will be a good one. How I hate changing to a boat in the middle of the night. 1 a.m.

29 Bloomsbury Square   Aug.27.13.

Friday night I had a perfect crossing. Went to Howth harbour where I found the *Shamrock* and we sailed to Lambay in two minutes under the hour, delicious!

We are going to build cowsheds, bothy, lengthen another 4′6″ the great Chinese wall, a sort of customs house, possibly cottages etc. I was very busy all the time. They are in love with the place again. They drink buttermilk. The rheas thrive. No mate for the chamoix yet.

Indian letters. A strong letter from Hardinge in favour of the pointed arch. So silly. However, I shall bide my time and take no notice. He says I am living in a London of round arches and forget Indian sentiment. My answer will be that I am working in the shade of Westminster Abbey.

Walters[1] is such a good plain cook, cutlets excellent, potatoes plain boiled, ragoût excellent.

The Theosophical buildings are going on all right. I am building up to the 1st floor and then getting renewed estimates. The additional land, increase in the size of buildings, have naturally increased the cost. So I shall let Mrs Besant know before she gets committed to anything beyond what she has calculated on. She knows the buildings are larger and this is all as was arranged before she left. But I am not going to do things in a hurry and live long to regret them. I say this for you alone so that you cannot repeat anything and a wrong impression get to Mrs B. before she gets the statement she asked for.

1. The parlour-maid, who valeted Lutyens and packed for him. The cook was on holiday.

29 Bloomsbury Square   Sept.16.13.

Getting on with Govt House and begin to see my way.[1]

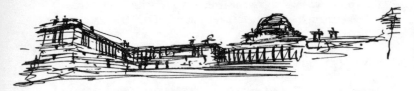

It is the mass of internal planning etc. that takes so much time in puzzling out.

Chattris are stupid useless things.

In train from Bombay to Delhi   Nov. 29.13.

I saw Lady Willingdon[2] whom I did not in the least recognise as she has got so much thinner and looks so much younger. He has aged like anyone else and seems very well liked and is doing well.

1. Lutyens was working at 7 Apple Tree Yard, his Delhi office from September 1913 to 1924. It was lent him by Gaspard and Henry Farrer, for whom he had built it as the mews to 7 St James's Square, which he had built for them in 1911. In the same year he built them The Salutation, Sandwich, which Butler described in 1950 as 'Sir Edwin's supreme rendering of the full Georgian idiom, touched with something more than had been achieved by his eighteenth century predecessors' (*Architecture*, vol. i, p. 37).

2. Marie Adelaide, daughter of the 1st Earl Brassey, married in 1892 Freeman Freeman-Thomas (1866–1941), who was created Baron Willingdon in 1910. He was Governor of Bombay 1913–18 and Viceroy of India 1931–36.

Lady Willingdon abused my old topee so and also my dress clothes! which had gone in the lapels! I wish Walters had noticed it. I didn't. I had to buy two [topees] a tidy one I lost somewhere at home and an everyday work-a-day one. I went to the bank, Hoare's, to outfitter and to the School of Art. The latter was very depressing and all on wrong lines, teaching the Indians to compete with English machine-made goods, tiles etc., and they have such good tiles in India in old buildings, it is so blindly stupid.

Lady Willingdon is very brusque and in her way rude. It is all done in high good temper – good intent and self-complacently. He is full of charm, ready wit and understanding. There is something very attractive about her and looking so thin has an air of appealing pathos about her. She was very miserable though she showed it but little to outsiders like myself, over the death of some little dog she had, very suddenly yesterday.

Delhi   Dec. 9.13.

I had a very few words with their Ex's. He likes Baker's elephants up upon his domes! I think them awful! He wants to cut down my dome but that I don't mind but he does not realise mine is 10 feet lower than Baker's as it is. He flew a small balloon 300 feet up in the air to see how high it would look. My dome is only 180 or so, so he said it was too high. It is all very mad.

Delhi   Dec. 10.13.

I went up to Viceregal Lodge to lunch and went through plans with Lady H. who seemed very pleased with them. I saw His Ex. too and had a comfortable talk with him.

I think the Viceroy likes the plans but he will not be able to do them for the money. The engineers cost them at a high rate. I am glad to have nothing to do with the cost and Keeling[1] says my conditions and the costs imposed by the Government of India are incompatible. It may mean making new drawings but if it is reduced in ratio it won't be the same trouble as making a new design which would take six months or more! Everyone likes the drawings which is something.

1. Sir Hugh Keeling (d. 1955), Chief Engineer for New Delhi, 1912–25.

This morning (Monday), we had to go up to the Viceroy to meet Hailey,[1] Keeling the engineer, Harcourt Butler etc. The Viceroy very kind etc., he would not look at plans, only at the perspectives which he criticised in small and quite nicely and deferentially. He don't like my dome and wants the Chattris 2 feet higher! He said he liked the design very much etc. but he would not allow one penny more of money, and that more money would jeopardise the whole Delhi scheme. £200,000 is what I want and the whole estimate is £8½ million, of which three only can be recovered in rents and rates. He would not listen that since he approved the plans he has raised it all up 30 feet and added onto Government House his printing press and secretariats quite big buildings in themselves, besides adding a lot of bedrooms etc. to the house, so I must reduce by a ratio, or by a new set of plans. It is a great bore.

They also seem very unimaginative about the control of the new city and are fearful of frightening people off if they put any conditions at all at all, so I am rather depressed and my tummy don't help. Tomorrow I had intended to take castor oil and stay in bed, but feel and am so much better that I don't think I need.

Guest House [of the Maharajah of Benares], Benares

Dec.28.13.

Yesterday we were up early and went down the river in the Maharajah's paddle boat. The paddles were worked by 8 men working a sort of tread mill. We were perched up high and made slow progress down what is the most wonderful prospect in all India.

The hosts of multi-coloured people bathing, the great steps, temples, many of them sinking in the mud their foundations being washed away by the river. Bulls, cows, donkeys, dogs – mangy ones, the holier the place the more mangy the dogs – goats, people washing, praying, bobbing, exercising, meditating. Yogis, fakirs, priests – every sort of black body doing every sort

1. Malcolm Hailey (1872–1969), Chief Commissioner of Delhi 1912–18 and as such responsible for the new capital. A dedicated imperialist, it was his practice when perplexed by the problems of India to commune with the grave of John Nicholson, the hero of the Mutiny. 'They were red-letter days', wrote Herbert Baker, 'when he was able to accompany me on my usually lonely early-morning rides watching the progress of the developing city' (*Architecture and Personalities*, p. 83).

of thing. A kaleidoscope of gesture and colour and the lovely morning light over it all.

Our motors met us at the other end of the town and brought us back to breakfast. After breakfast I went down to the Theosophical Congress and called on Mrs Besant.

We talked Theosophical buildings. She is anxious to get part done and I told her how glad I was. I introduced Baker to her who seemed impressed, but he was very sceptical of the whole Hindu philosophies. But Baker is curiously matter of fact and unimaginative on those lines. His world is bound by the range of a pom-pom gun.

After seeing Mrs B. we went into the town to view the temples. Oh my! The dirt, filth and the impossibility of bull, cow and monkey worship and oh the stench and the hideousness of everything. Barbarism in terms of evil smelling slime. A Juggernaut car to squash the whole thing seemed logical and desirable! I had a kindly feeling to the mild Hindu but Benares, his holy city, is filth and rotten filth almost beyond belief.

My bearer went to wash in the Ganges and then had to hold a bull's tail while they poured water over his hand with incantations. It made him very happy and cost him 5 rupees which I have promised to pay for him.

We saw the burning ghats. After lunch we went up the river to the Maharajah's palace and went over it. He had some beautiful Indian pictures which I had asked to see and they were had out for me. His engineer who does his buildings, gardens and photographs and painter too to his Highness! was alas not able to meet us.

You should see the pictures. He photographed the King, Queen and Maharajah and then did from the photo a huge life-size picture of this ill assorted bunch of peoples. My eyes! A picture to haunt you and capable of causing a miscarriage to any unfortunate individual to whom that calamity is a possibility. I asked the Maharajah why he had not got his man to paint pictures in the old Indian style. He said Oh he can paint a picture like that in a fortnight but it took a year to paint an 'Indian picture' – a picture almost a foot square and all the Rajah Sahib's family and forebears are painted *en suite*. One room this painter engineer architect gardener had painted was rather delicious. Uncouth, childish but it turned the whole room into a mango grove with birds, peacocks, serpents, squirrels adorning it.

In train from Benares to Delhi   Dec.29.13.

We motored out to Buddha Gya and there saw the place where Buddha attained his Buddha-hood.

There was the remains of one of those wonderful Asoka rails which I admire most of all India's work. A great stone fence some 7 or 8 feet high which Asoka, the Buddhist king, built round the shrine to protect it. The shrine itself is a restoration built by the British. The whole area around it is dotted with little shrines and temples of all sizes according to the money the devotee had to spend on them. Many fragments of Buddhas and other sculptures.

The general form of all these Hindu temples and Buddhist shrines is an elongated pyramid going up in steps and flanked with ever diminishing pinnacles, like a cactus or children's toy tree on a steep mountainside, decorated at the top with flags on crazy bamboo poles and bits of rag – offerings of the faithful. And God preserve me from the beggars and fakirs that line the approach to these holy places.

To describe them or to attempt to would make you sick. The deformities exposed, the rapacity. The painted faces and the ash covered fakirs . . . ugh. I spare you.

Delhi   Jan.1.14.

I have been very busy on what are practically new plans and I begin to see daylight through the wood. I wonder. I hear Hardinge has abandoned the Railway scheme.[1] It is sheer mad folly and spoils everything. It is all because he made, on the advice of F. Wilson, an asinine statement of the cost and now he has not the moral courage to own to having made a mistake. It is like a witch's curse that acts on future generations.

The Committee go to all lengths to make things fit Hardinge's preconceived ideas as to what costs should be. It is too silly and they all laugh at him and his methods. It is a great pity. However, I am cutting down vigorously but there is a point beyond which I

1. Hardinge cut the scheme for a terminal railway station in New Delhi as part of his attempt to reduce the over-all cost of New Delhi to fit his estimate of £4,000,000.

cannot go. Barrie was quite right when he said I should find Governments always aiming for the second best.[1]

Udaipur   Jan.28.14.

We arrived here about 12 o'clock. We went over the Palace and met the Crown Prince – a nice little man with withered legs – a cripple from hip disease.

Udaipur stands on a lake and I had heard much about it. I was disappointed. The lake was smaller and the glare at full blast. The evening is the time to see the place but that was not our fortune. It is barbaric and a large amount of glass tile decorations and our room was full of Dutch tiles!

The Maharana was away shooting. A fine old chief, the head of the Rajputs. The one man in India who would not make obeisance to the King and by right. They made him something-in-waiting but he did not turn up. Very old-fashioned and it was all old Indian Barbarian Feudalism with a flavour of the tourist about it.

In the palace at Udaipur we saw the Treasury and they were counting out the money exactly like the four and twenty blackbirds in a pie story.

The old Maharana would not go to Curzon's Durbar and to prevent his going his brother committed suicide so that the days of mourning would give an excuse. Unluckily the days of mourning came to an end in time and he had to go to Delhi where he took such a fearful dose of medicine he nearly died of it and every doctor had to admit he was too ill to leave his room.

The Rajput Udaipur blood is credited to be pure and has never mixed with the Mogul or other alien bloods. The Maharanee has only left the place twice in 36 years and will receive no European woman! Refused the Duchess of Edinburgh and the Queen did not ask to see her.

But the place from an architectural point of view I was

1. Lord Hardinge told a different story. 'I had no trouble with Baker, whose plans were admirable and within the figure prescribed for the estimate, but Lutyens's plans, though beautiful, were made absolutely regardless of cost and had to be reduced in every way, which created some unpleasantness. He told people, the Queen amongst them, that I had quite spoilt his plans, but I think I was generous in allotting to him more than half a million sterling to build Government House' (*My Indian Years* (1948), p. 96).

disappointed in. They are so childishly vulgar and their taste is for all that glitters. The cut glass furniture, chairs, beds, tables and huge looking glasses make one squirm. A four post bed stuffed with red made of white cut glass of the worst sort.

Delhi   Feb.1.14.

We got [to Jodhpur] in the morning.

After lunch, having rested a while, we were each given a tent, we called on Sir Pertab Singh, an old and rakish gentleman of high Rajput blood who has acted as Regent in the Jodhpur state during the minority of the [Maharajah]. He is over 70 and still plays polo and keeps all the young men in tremendous order. His house was more like a saddle room than a dwelling. He is a great sportsman and a man of enormous courage. He bathes and dives backwards with a double somersault into the water! Not bad for 70. He talks English very badly, has the wet *glissant* eye of an eagle. His great comment is that someone, indeed near everyone, is 'silly lookin' '.

Then we called on the Maharajah – a frolicsome boy of 16 just out from England where he has been at school at Wellington.[1] The manners of a fourth form boy, very cheeky and teases his elder cousins, smashing their topees, pulling off their turbans – a regular mosquito, and retaliation is not possible. Bikanir[2] took him to task and spoke of his duties and his position. 'Gar on, when you were my age you just jolly well slacked it I bet' was his comment. He is a good shot and shapes well for polo. He has been enthroned but has no power given to him yet. This depends on the Viceroy. His marriage is in contemplation.

We arrived Bikanir early Saturday morning. Bikanir was at the station himself to meet us. We motored up to the new palace in two A.1. Rolls Royces and had a great breakfast.

The new palace[3] the Viceroy admires so much would from an architectural point of view disgrace Putney Hill, nothing fitting, all just anyhow and every inch of it carved and carved badly, you never saw such a place. A great courtyard was pleasant but only

1. He died of drink soon after he assumed power in 1916.
2. The Maharajah of Bikanir (1880–1943), the most distinguished of the anglicised Indian princes and a crack shot with a rifle. In 1921 he became the first Chancellor of the Chamber of Princes.
3. Designed by Swinton Jacob and built of carved red sandstone.

so to a perfectly unseeing and uncritical eye and mind.

After breakfast we motored down to the old fort. A large barbaric pile with some good lacquer work and other decorations inside. Some of it was too awful for words. Gods, Goddesses, Kings carved and jewelled and painted – no gollywog could better it! Some fine jewels and beautiful arms – huge swords, quaint guns and many fearful instruments of torture. Swords none of us could scarce lift.

After the fort we changed into carriages. I was with Bikanir and the people all turned out and cheered him as we drove slowly through the town. They shouted Kharmah, a deformed Sanscrit word meaning in Sanscrit Pardon. And old ladies made gesticulations as H.H. passed, taking the evil eye from off him onto themselves. I was much touched and was glad to have had dark glasses to wear.

Delhi   Feb.3.14.

Just going to bed. A long day of hard work. Have sent in plans to the chief engineer, Keeling, and now I must wait until Saturday. In the meantime I am busy on the !ay-out wherein Hardinge takes no interest. Things move along all right. You have only to watch the indiscretions of engineers and the game is joy fun but when the Viceroy comes in all kinds of difficulties crop up and politics and diplomacy arrive though in other matters out of his ken politics and diplomacy are never thought of! Isn't it a funny world?

It is so difficult to design even a coal scuttle well but if they brought in politics and diplomacy then it is impossible.

Delhi   Feb.4.14.

My book by Weaver[1] arrived today. It does make me hot. I do wish he had not mentioned Delhi so often and Oh dear it is just a catalogue of mistakes and failures. Clients who when I first started – I don't mean Chippy of course – did not know enough to direct and afterwards enough to be led. So fares the world. The only attainment possible nowadays seems to be words, words, words.

1. Lawrence Weaver, *Houses and Gardens by E. L. Lutyens* (1913).

CHAPTER EIGHT

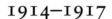

1914–1917

BY 1914 NEW DELHI HAD BECOME the centre of Lutyens's working life, and the pattern of winters in India and summers at home, which was to continue until 1930, was well established.

Meanwhile Lady Emily was becoming more and more involved in Theosophical business. She was deputy editor of the *Herald of the Star*, the magazine of the Order of the Star in the East, and was doing most of the editorial work. Her devotion to Krishna had grown during the three years that she had known him, and he was dependent upon her to an extent that was disapproved of by the Theosophists who were closest to him, particularly George Arundale, who was left in charge of the two boys while Mrs Besant was in India. In *Candles in the Sun* she described her state of mind at this time: 'My husband, my home, my children faded into the background; Krishna became my entire life, and for the next ten years I suffered all the difficulties of trying to sublimate a human love.'[1]

In the summer of 1914 Krishna and Nitya were staying with the Arundales in Cornwall, at the rectory in Bude. Lady Emily took a house nearby and spent September there with her children. Every day she went over to the rectory with Barbara and Robert to be with the Krishna party.

It was from Bude that Lutyens received her letter telling him that their physical relationship was at an end. To him it cannot have come as a complete surprise but nevertheless it was a devastating blow. To her it was not only the logical conclusion of a situation that had been developing over several years, but also a means of securing promotion on the astral plane: though perhaps the most important factor, which they neither of them admitted, was her love for Krishna.

---

1. pp. 59–60.

In 1944, when Lady Emily was rereading their letters after Lutyens's death, she looked at their marriage in a different light. She wrote to Ursula:

> I begin to think it is really very dangerous for me to let you read our letters, because I think you will end by disliking me as much as I dislike myself and won't that be awful! I am afraid I get worse and worse. Shall I stop sending them? But if they make you love Father more and more that is all to the good. His letters have that effect on me.

Lutyens's unhappiness was increased by their departure from 29 Bloomsbury Square. The lease had expired and the house was due to be demolished. While he was in India Lady Emily had bought a lease of 31 Bedford Square, a house he disliked. The move seemed to symbolize all that was going wrong with his life. 'Yes', he wrote in September 1914, 'I am very sad leaving Bloomsbury Square and so much else came along with it, a sea of surf and sorrow.'

His loneliness in Delhi was now balanced by a new loneliness at home. His health, which had always been excellent, began to trouble him; he had dysentery during the next winter in India, then painful and distressing piles. His depression verged on a state of nervous breakdown.

It was partly in order to mitigate the loneliness of Delhi that in the winter of 1914–15 Lutyens arranged for William Nicholson to come out with him to paint a portrait of Lord Hardinge for Viceroy's House. Unfortunately Hardinge was too busy to give the many sittings that Nicholson always demanded, and the commission was not a success. As Elisabeth Lutyens recalled: 'Spectacular Sikhs . . . occupied the foreground and the Viceroy could be seen as a tiny, insignificant figure standing on top of a stairway at the back.'[1]

Nicholson returned to England earlier than intended. When, in the summer of 1916, Mrs Zachary Merton – or Mère-toni as Lutyens called her – lent the family Folly Farm for the holidays, Nicholson stayed too. He decorated the dining room with murals and began the portrait of Ursula in a busby. It was finished at Apple Tree Yard, in the studio that Lutyens had found for Nicholson near his office.

1. *Goldfish Bowl*, p. 42.

Though the war had no immediate, traumatic effect on Lutyens's life, it brought money worries. It was obvious that private building would slow down, perhaps to a standstill. New work in Spain was therefore all the more welcome. Lutyens met the Duke of Peñaranda staying with Ivor Guest at Ashby St Legers, and was commissioned by him to build a country house near Toledo. In 1915 Lutyens stayed for a week at the Liria Palace in Madrid with Peñaranda's brother, the Duke of Alba, and his letters describe the exotic life he found there and the buildings he saw. Because of the Civil War neither El Guadalperal, the house he designed for Peñaranda, nor the one he planned for his sister, was built. One positive result of the visit was that Lutyens and the Duke of Alba became lifelong friends.

The following winter in Delhi saw the Battle of the Rise. In the spring of 1913 it had been decided, for political reasons, that Baker's Secretariats should share the top of Raisina Hill with Viceroy's House. In order to achieve this Viceroy's House had to be set back from the crest of the hill. This caused a dilemma. If Viceroy's House was to be seen along the whole length of King's Way, the gradient had to be very gradual, the slope including the area between the Secretariats, known as Government Court. If Government Court was not included in the slope, but level, which was clearly more practical, Viceroy's House would be invisible from the Great Place and from part of the approach along King's Way.

In March 1914, when work on the Secretariats was about to begin, Lutyens signed a minute saying that there would be no further alterations to the plans of Government Court and King's Way. At the same time he agreed that the approach should be of a maximum gradient of 22½. This figure had been chosen before the exact levels of the area had been decided, and Lutyens took it that it allowed for the constant visibility of Viceroy's House, as shown in the perspectives drawn by William Walcot in November 1913 and exhibited in the Royal Academy that summer. But. he was wrong, and its effect was to ensure that only the dome of Viceroy's House was visible from certain points on King's Way. How this very basic error in design went unnoticed by Lutyens is hard to understand. It was mainly a case of lack of communication, for which ill health and depression were partly to blame.

Not until January 1916 did Lutyens realize his mistake, and he wrote his first dismayed letter to Lady Emily describing the problem. It was a theme that was to recur again and again during the next eight years as it turned into one of the classic aesthetic battles in architectural history: aesthetic, and also personal. Lutyens maintained that Baker had agreed that Viceroy's House should be visible along the whole of the approach, and that in building his Secretariats on a slope which he knew would block it out he was not honouring their agreement. But relations were already strained. Baker wanted his Government Court to be flat, and he was in no mood to support Lutyens in his plea for a change in the levels. Lutyens's references to Herbert Baker change from mild disapproval of sloppy work to hurt fury.

More was at stake than a clash of personalities. At the root of the quarrel lay conflicting views of empire and of art. In South Africa from 1892 to 1912 Herbert Baker had drunk at the fountain head of the new Imperialism. In Cape Colony he succumbed to the dubious personal magnetism of Cecil Rhodes, for whom he built Groote Schuur (1896). In the Transvaal after 1902 he joined the young men of Milner's Kindergarten in the exciting work of post-Boer War reconstruction, and in 1910 he designed the Union Buildings in Pretoria, probably his greatest work. From Rhodes and Milner Baker derived a belief in the imperial destiny of the English-speaking peoples, and it was this that led him to Wren and the universal language of classicism. But for Baker architecture was less a matter of intellect than a vehicle for the expression of 'human and national sentiment'.[1] Through his architecture he sought to convey the ethos of the new Imperialism: that peculiar blend of the muscular and the sentimental, of early-morning rides, Kipling and Elgar.

To Lutyens this was anathema. Not only was he unimpressed by 'Kiplingese and the White Man's Burden', which he found tawdry and empty. More important, he was profoundly suspicious of Baker's literary approach to architecture. For him art began where words left off; to attempt to translate it into the medium of literature was to deny its very essence.

In the short run it was Baker who won. It was he who had the last laugh in the battle of the rise – an outcome that Lutyens, not used to jokes against himself, could neither forgive nor forget. Politically, too, the tide in India was flowing in Baker's direction:

1. Baker, *Architecture and Personalities*, p. 68.

1918 saw the first steps towards Indian self-government with the publication of the Montagu-Chelmsford Report, an advance that was welcomed by Baker's Round Table friends as the prelude to Indian membership of a British Commonwealth of Nations.

In the long run, however, Lutyens was the victor. Baker's Secretariats are 'Edwardian Baroque buildings with Indian details'; though they express the aspirations of Montagu-Chelmsford, there is no real synthesis of East and West.[1] At Viceroy's House, by contrast, Lutyens 'at last attained the sublime'.[2] The tragedy was that Baker was aware of this – so much so that he may never again have recovered his belief in himself as an architect.[3]

17 Queen Anne's Gate   Aug.5.14.

So war was declared last night. I heard it at the Athenaeum too late to telephone you and the morning's newspapers would tell you·as soon as I could. From the top balcony of the Athenaeum we watched the German Embassy but there was no demonstration – a few boys booed and perhaps 12 policemen moved them on gently and without effort. There was no stone-throwing. Rule Britannia very badly sung – the Marseillaise and God Save the King.

The crowd was an offshoot of the Buckingham Palace crowd on its return. I walked home and got into bed about 12.30.

17 Queen Anne's Gate   Sept.1.14.

I have written a long letter to G[ranville] Barker[4] suggesting that he should start touring companies – no scenery – actors on low scale of wages, full prices asked and the surplus to go to the P. of Wales or other funds. See Riddell, McKenna etc. Call them Queen Mary's own Star Co.! It will give salt to people's amusement if they think they are helping war funds and will give work

1. Gavin Stamp, *Catalogue 1981*, p. 38.
2. Mark Girouard, *Times Literary Supplement*, 27 November 1981.
3. Gradidge, *Lutyens*, p. 69.
4. Harley Granville Barker (1877–1946), producer and critic. Since 1912 he had been planning a National Theatre, for which Lutyens had made sketches.

to unemployed actors etc. It might be so organised as to eventually become the National Theatre. Repertory plays, no scenery to
speak of, houses where and if possible rent free, authors' royalties
given away too where not hurting. Don't you think it a good
idea?

17 Queen Anne's Gate   Sept.10.14.

I was reading early this morning a 'Star' pamphlet which has been
on my bed table. I do not like magnetised ribbons – blue or any
other colour! I don't believe they are 'magnetised' – do you?[1] I
thought Mrs Besant's speech funny and dangerous. Imagine it
happening at a convocation – after a speech by Lord Halifax – the
Archbishop of Canterbury gets up and says 'Whilst my noble
friend has been speaking I have been dreaming' etc. It does not
read well balanced indeed. It is rather funny and must harm her.

I cannot believe and I am sure Mrs Besant does not wish – the
coming Lord to bring with him sorrow and the seeds of pained
sorrow. No true religion can be based on hypotheses – it brings
priestcraft, popery and hypocrisy. My great sense of comfort is in
my belief of your moral courage and when your position becomes
untenable you will not find your boats burnt. If they are you will
paddle home!

Darling own Ems. However let us talk of cheerful things, let us
talk about the War!

I dined with Lady Randolph[2] last night. She was alone. She had
no news and seemed very unhappy. Winston hardly ever goes to
see her and Clemmy never. Her other daughter-in-law appears
very hard up and is cross that she, Lady R., should have spent
money getting into a new house. Winston, to please her, has given
her George a commission which depresses her, so he is happier
than he ever has been! and Mrs Pat[rick Campbell] has gone to
America to make £500 a week. She says George West is a rotter

1. The ribbon was for badges of the various grades of the Order of the Star in
the East. In 1912 Mrs Besant wrote to Lady Emily: 'About 3,000 yards of blue
ribbon will reach you from Paris – the right colour at last! Please set a lot of
people to cut it, or as much of it as is wanted, into ¼ yd lengths. Then ask
Krishnaji to magnetise it in bulk' (*Candles in the Sun*, p. 43).
2. Jenny Jerome (1854–1921), widow of Lord Randolph Churchill and
mother of Winston Churchill, married in 1900 George Cornwallis-West; he
divorced her in 1900 and married Mrs Patrick Campbell, the famous actress.

but she loves him. In her old age she is forsaken and has no friends – no strong arm to lean on. She was very unhappy and I was not too comfortable but did what I could.

Bude   *Sept.11.14.*

My own Nedi darling, I want to write to you of something which has long been on my mind to say and I have not known how. It is something which must hurt you but as you read it remember the love that has been between us for seventeen years – the love that still is. Think of Tuesday evening when we watched the sunset together hand in hand. The thing I want to say is what has been growing upon me for a long time and that is that if our love is to continue it can only be on my side by a severance of our physical relationship. I don't think this will surprise you. I think indeed you know it already. I must tell you exactly what I have come to feel. It is useless to go back over the past and its mistakes – but whatever the causes I have suffered intensely physically *during all my married life. There were compensations when I wanted the children and had them. But now we are both entering upon middle age. I have done my duty to you and my country as regards children and I could never face another. With that incentive gone your coming to me has been increasingly difficult for me to bear.*

I believe and hold firmly that a woman has the right over her own body. Where she gives it willingly the relationship is beautiful – where she gives it because she must *it becomes prostitution whether in or out of marriage and is a degradation.*

We have a great bond in our children – we will both try to find more common interests – to do more things together. You can only decide what will make it possible for you – I mean as regards sleeping arrangements. I am sure a double bed will cause you constant torment and now *is the moment when we could have single beds in a natural way.*

Remember I could not *go on into old age as your mother did and so it always comes back to the question – shall it cease now while I love you dearly or will it continue till my love for you is dead and with that will go all the rest.*

My Nedi darling forgive me for the pain I cause you – I cannot really help it.

17 Queen Anne's Gate   Sept.14.14.

I am so looking forward to your coming tomorrow.

I cannot write or do anything I feel ill and depressed.

You have indeed put a pistol at my head and though I accept and would do anything to retain your love yet the day may come when all I hold true may turn to dishonour and shame.

I cannot give up work. I should leave you and all dependent on me too badly off and yet all my confidence and hope seems gone to water.

I'm NOT asking your pity darling but just sympathy.

The thought of India so hopelessly far and alone for months without a friend, in a world of Bakers, makes me sick. Sick at heart am I.

My failure belongs to me alone and I must bear it. I almost wish I could go out and leave it all.

I feel further away from sympathy with Theosophy than ever I have felt before. I think I know what you feel better than you know what I feel.

I write this now darling that I need not speak too much of myself tomorrow and try only to show that I love you truly.

Your very, very sad and loving Nedi.

Bude   *Sept.18.14.*

Try not to be too miserable. I know you must think me very cruel but I have only done what I felt I must. The whole thing is so mysterious to me – how you could ever have found pleasure in what you knew I hated.

17 Queen Anne's Gate   Sept.19.14.

I have not the slightest wish to be miserable, it is misery! Yes, how could I? and how can I ever? But that I should be celibate seems, to say the least, a very strange condition.

I must in fairness to you and for my own honour sleep alone. I cannot become a child again. A child's kiss and the grateful warmth of a Nannie in a married bed cannot be withstood. I don't want to hurt or say unkind things they only add to unhappiness and endanger the possible or impossible future. How could I all this time do those things you hate and loathe? How could you darling be intimate and petting with the Krishnaji party. You know how I hate it. My fears. I have tried to be just kind and patient. How I have hated the large photographs, the constant chuckle at my discomfiture when what I hated was introduced into my house and home. I think the plane – if true – on which you and others occupy each other's minds and bodies is just as immoral – to me nauseous and horrid – as anything else. Do you hate 'me' because you think it prevents Vedas or what-ever you call them occupying you?

Heaven knows where (what I believe to be) your absorbing 'follies' will lead you. Further from, not back to me. In India I shall suffer and there it is – alone, I shall suffer most.

I looked into the club and read casualty list. It is very sickening and heartbreaking. No names I knew well.

I met Victor yesterday, he said Pamela could not have me,[1] she was arranging with Homewood for me to go there, so my plans are rather in what you might call the air or Astral Plane.

My poor darling Emy I do love you.

Bude   *Sept.21.14.*

Can I have a picture rail round the top of my meditation room or can I put nails into the wall?[2] I know my photographs irritated you and I removed them all and put them away before you returned from India to please you. I don't suppose you noticed. I have never had a corner of the house which was my own. Now it will be all right. You have been darling in giving me my little room and I need never have in other rooms the things which annoy you. I never meant 'How could you' in the sense you take it but there it is and as you say we won't discuss it.

1. Lutyens was building St Martin's Church, Knebworth, which was completed by Sir Albert Richardson in 1963–64.
2. Lutyens hated picture rails. The meditation room was built by him for Lady Emily at Bedford Square. It had a blue linoleum floor, and she sat there for hours, meditating in the yellow shawl given her by Mrs Besant.

Temple Dinsley, Hitchin[1]   Sept.26.14.

A perfect day and my heart just yearns and aches for you. I am so mizz and out of gear. Just had lunch and have escaped to write to you before starting for Hill End. Fenwick is away! and I am alone with Mrs Fenwick and Mrs Fellowes.[2] The wasps and bees hum on the window panes – a lone ticking clock all seems to annotate my left aloneliness.

Leaving Bloomsbury Square wring, wranged me. That is all past now – gone.

Temple Dinsley   Sept.27.14.

[Mrs Fellowes] said last night she would like to marry me! I was, she thought, kind and unlike other men. I assured her I was not really kind and she would find very little difference in me from other men.

They are intrigued as to what is the matter with me. They think I am in love. I wonder! Of course I am but it is always with the same person which is dull of me I own and very boring. So much so one does not talk about it.

I have to write out my RA subject today to get it sent off to-morrow. Oh dear my grammar and sentence making difficulties. I can put a thing in 40 different ways but never quite get said what I want to say and I have a feeling that a conjunction of 3 words should do it.

The style is to be one adaptable to all climates yet is to represent the ideal of British Empire. Of course classic is the only architectural language that can achieve this and I am sure it is better, saner, wiser and more gentlemanlike than the most sentimental of an English building bad Indian or bad anything else.

1. Lutyens was building cottages at Hill End for H. G. Fenwick.
2. Dorothy Jefferson married in 1900 the Hon. Coulson Fellowes, eldest son of Lord de Ramsey, from whom she was divorced in 1912. Though something of an adventuress, she was for a time a great friend of Mrs H. G. Fenwick, who commissioned Lutyens to build Hill End (now Langley End), Hertfordshire, for her in 1911.

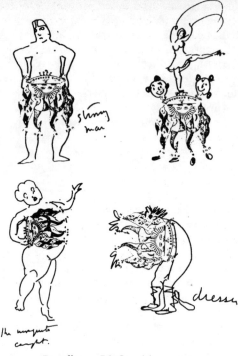

Doodles on P&O writing paper

English Channel off Plymouth [en route for India]   Dec.6.14.

I did so love your sadness when you walked away but was so wrung by it my darling.

I had time to speak to Hall and I have asked him to let you have extra monies when possible i.e. if money comes in etc. so you may enjoy taxis and some ease and you must have a really happy Xmas and New Year eh?

Try and arrange astronomy lessons for the whole family for the coming summer if you can without commitment. Try and get a mathematician and not an astrologer – a Cambridge don! rather than a curiosity-hunter. Do you know what I mean? The courses of the planets – their measurings and their relationships and weights. The naming of stars astronomy will walk in their wake. Also the soothsayings and what else and what not. But the mental focus should be the deliberate and provable knowledge of the mathematician rather than that of the assured speculator.

It would be useful to me and a fresh view for the children and an open door to wider knowledge and sense of proportion and true assertion.

But can such a man or woman be found because we range in intelligence from Mary! to Barbara! Between the farmyard and astronomy as I see it lie the philosophies of all the worlds.

One wants to understand the merry-go-round of the universe as though it were in the palm of one's hand. That we should attain anything – finality! – don't matter – we *won't* – but the endeavour to realise the universe as a lancer dance wherein our friends take part.

Does this add to your labours too much? If so don't darling worry about it and ache from it, and of course a genius teacher is wanted to see the essentials of my picture – simple and broad enough to build pyramids of knowing anywhere along the baseline of our thought. And I believe that you will find that any of these pyramids – be the baseline true – will reach up and meet at one apex – the very God of very God.

I don't see why you should not teach a child and we are all children or should be (bar naughty ones!) the meaning, view and intention of conic sections, the differential calculus, etc. etc. without the necessity of any sums or figures and without the puzzle world comprised within the numerals.

Delhi   Jan.3.15.

The Viceroy called on us. He motors himself. He is a pathetic creature and has felt his boy's death, we dine with him tonight, Sunday. Nicholson lunched with us and whilst the Viceroy was talking I looked round wondering if Nicholson was still there. On the sofa I saw a rug and from under the rug protruded a pair of boots. It was N. fast asleep! H.E. was much amused.

They are all very wild and angry from H.E. down with a certain Professor Geddes[1] who has come out here to lecture on Town

1. Patrick Geddes (1854–1932), biologist, sociologist and town planner, was in India from 1914 to 1923. He had proposed himself for the post Lutyens filled on the Delhi Planning Committee in 1912. His theories of town planning – which derived from his attempt to found a sociology on the basis of biology – were not calculated to cut much ice with Lutyens.

Planning. He seems to talk rot in an insulting way. I hear he is going to tackle me! A crank who don't know his subject.

One of his ideas is that all the roads of the city should be in the old *nullahs* (water courses). He says people don't walk out when it rains. Well if they went by *nullahs* they couldn't! He also lays down the law about *serais* (Indian inns). His plan was the most idiotically amusing affair. He says the coolie lines are incestuous and he wants to separate the men and women. I must say no money is wasted, but they are given long water-tight sheds which they divide off as they require. They come some for a few days only with wives, sisters, uncles, aunts, grandmothers and children and maintain their family lives and traditions. He wants to break up families and prevent women taking their babies onto the works etc.

Tonight we dined with H.E. He talked of Lady H. quite simply and naturally and referred to her wishes opinions and reports etc. Diamond[1] seems younger, more like a little girl, gentler and lost the brusque asperity of mama that did not become a child. I gave her the parcel with the photo frame and a box of wire puzzles which I bought on board, to blur the sentiment of the gift frame.

My bedding is not comfortable. I am short of two blankets and a rug. It is very cold and I sleep in my bag.

Today hard work and then the afternoon given up to the Delhi Committee, viewing plans and sites and conditions for the peons' quarters and the Indian and European clerks' quarters.

Oh it is difficult. Ancient prejudices.
               Modern   "
               Money. . . .

The Government of India decrees this – engineers that – money t'other, which leaves little else but 'Whys' for the architects.

However things are improving and we shall prepare the way for another Delhi. They are, the Committee, very nice and understanding but are harnessed between the Government of India's shafts who direct from consciences made by treasurers.

They cannot afford or see the essential differences of an arch carried on posts of sufficient calibre B and those which have the

---

1. Diamond Hardinge (1900–27).

bilious (thin) feeling A. Yet on paper in elevation they both look

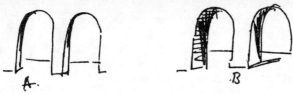

alike. Nor do they think it matters what the sweeper sees at the back doors and yards. Personally I hate to expose omissions and defaults even to a feather-numbered sparrow. Ow!

Delhi   Jan.17.15.

I have a great deal of designing to do. Parks, roads, buildings, etc. besides Government House and much work going on one must see to. It goes slow – the work. And they are not spending so much this year on account of the war. About £400,000 or £500,000 instead of £790,000.

Baker has been very troublesome and serves ever Mammon rather than the righteousness of good and what I consider fine building. He is very selfish too. It is a bore. He has great, good qualities and can be very charming and is to those in his own interests. I don't mind that if he didn't put it before the work. For instance – the placing of the King's stones.[1] I had my view and insisted. He protested – finally we made two sketches – mine and his. The Committee wouldn't look at his, took mine. He crumpled up at once and had nothing to say for his scheme and takes the credit for the scheme he bitterly opposed with me.

As there is no brass hat in India who knows or cares for beauty or would make one whit of sacrifice to obtain beauty it works hard. For when we pull together he will sacrifice the best for the opportunism of the bad, cheap and ugly. I dread to think how much depends on the next Viceroy and the shortly incoming Members of Council. I miss Lady Hardinge's help and influence enormously. This is all private.

1. The King's stones were moved to New Delhi, where they were incorporated in the retaining wall of the Secretariats.

Delhi   Feb.25.15.

 They want all my details up to the 729 level, that is about 15 feet out of the ground, a big job and difficult to do out here short-handed and before you can give the lowest stone you want first to design to topmost. A to be designed before you settle B sort of thing. This thought compels me to stop.

31 Bedford Square   *Feb.15.15.*

Poor Barbie is longing for conventionality and fashion and suffers agonies over my strange ways and our unconventional house. She wants white table cloths and silver salt cellars and says she cannot invite her friends home to such a house. It is not very kind. I tell her she must hurry up and get one for herself! She has done a good deal to improve things. She tidies up my room (too much sometimes), arranges the papers in layers, puts Kate [temporary parlour-maid] on her metal to serve things nicely and finally she and Nannie have given me two beautiful new blue glass bowls as an Easter present, Barbie a flat lake for the dining room table (she objects to the pestle and mortar) and the other a gigantic blue wine glass – both most acceptable and useful.[1]

We are forbidden to have lumps of cheese on the table at the beginning of meals but cheese is relegated to its proper course and handed with biscuits and butter in a triangular dish! In fact you will find on your return that whether you like it or not you are under Barbie's fashionable thumb and I hope you will be as amused as I am.

She is certainly very pretty and much admired wherever she goes – but then so is Robert and I think you will find he has your gift of social charm.

Homewood, Knebworth   *March 15.15.*

Chippy and I arrived at Bow[2] and found an icily cold hall and a

---

1. The pestle and mortar returned to their old place on the dining room table in 1920, when Barbara married.
2. In 1912 George Lansbury (1859–1940) resigned as Labour MP for Bow and Bromley and contested the seat as an Independent on the issue of votes for women. Though he was defeated, Bow remained a stronghold of the women's movement.

good sized audience about 150 of all sorts and kinds. We started proceedings by singing the Women's March and then a rather pretty faded lady with frizzy fair hair done out in a bun recited – a favourite poem called 'Lorraine, Lorraine, Loree' which I am sure you must know. And another about a man who loved three girls 'Ninie, Ninon, Ninette'. I nearly got the giggles. The chairman was a nice working woman – suffragette – who said that they were quite willing to spare a little time from their own important business (agitating I suppose) to listen to other people and so they welcomed me. I felt much more sympathy this time than last but still think it is very difficult for the West End to go and talk to the East End. There was the same aggressive atheist who put questions, but on the whole the meeting was more of a success I think. Chippy went into guffaws of laughter because my atheist friend claimed that the TS [Theosophical Society] was composed of the aristocracy!

Delhi   March 18.15.

This is my last letter to you from India this time. I want you to try and put yourself in my shoes – to try and remember what I have lost and how little without your confidence I have left of all I had most dear to me in this life.

I cannot go through again what I suffered last summer (I do not refer to body things nor do I expect ever to go into your room) but everything else seemed hard and crooked and I write you darling for the love you have for me to show some kindly mercy, some practical sympathy and perhaps sacrifice. But I will ask no sacrifice of you that you are not willing to give and unless you are happy how can I be?

Baker has not been any help architecturally and I have to fight him and the world to get anything done thoroughly to what I believe is right. It all seems right with words but when words become deeds they all go woolly and sloppy and nothing matters so long as people don't know and if you can't describe a thing it is a thing that doesn't matter – a gallery I can't play to.

I think an art begins where words fail it. An art has to be something which it alone can express in its own medium. Now how would you express it? I don't think you ever understood why that lovely Keats on a Greek Vase made me angry. It was silly of me but I will try and do better next time.

I have got rid of my tummy pains, but have had for the last five or six days bad headaches. I think I shall get better when I leave. I look to be refreshed at home with my Emyown's love and help.

Boulogne [in train to Rome]   July 2.15.

I count the days to be home again.

War with three committees, one in Rome two in England make the British School so difficult and everyone seems X with me! as though I could help it, and ascribe everything to my being in India. Then the Roman Municipality and their absurd drainage rules, Mrs Strong, Rodd and all and I suppose I have given them £1500 worth of fees at least, so my journey is heavy hearted and little by little the committee, which contains Aston Webb, a delightful fellow but no humanitarian taste in my sense etc. etc. etc., just spoils the building and don't save money or use it to the best purpose and does not make for lovableness in building.

[A. J.] Thomas has been tactless as usual and puts everybody in the wrong. Esher[1] is rude and brusque and ignorant. The delay is unavoidable but everyone is X and I hate it and can't do anything without sympathy and encouragement. There is a nice silly clerk of works Squire, a protégé of Lord Esher's, they give him £10.10 a week! quite stupid and useless. So you see the kettle – a sort of kettle your little fish Nedi is never happy in.

Just passing Le Touquet. There are two Canadians in my carriage, a man and sister and they have brought 100s of packets of cigarettes – they got them through duty free – and they throw them to the Tommies as we pass along. Great fun. Great excitement and the happy beaming faces are good to see. Now they have got to the sweets. I wish I had thought of it. I will next time, if the war lasts till November or if I go to Spain.

Some troop trains are in front of us I expect as the train is very late. I hope I do not miss the connection, but we are nowhere near Paris and are already overdue.

I shall post this in Paris and if you get this and nothing more

---

1. The 2nd Viscount Esher (1852–1930), *éminence grise* at court and a doyen of such committees.

you will know I have gone on to Rome.
    Oh Emy darling I do wish I could make you happier:-
    If I take no interest or care in what you do or how
    If I expect you to take none in me
    If I give up smoke and drink and meat
    If I can make enough money to free you
    From all worldly care now and in the future
    Believe all you believe and change my faith as yours
    may change
    I could not love you more and oh darling I grieve
    For very love of you I grieve[1]
    Oh darling own wife, Emy love. Your very very loving Nedi.

In train, Turin to Genoa   July 2.15.

We had an hour to wait in Turin so I spent the time in a picture gallery. Giovanni Griffier[2] – a name unknown to me. Two delightful little pictures one of an English home – a house by Wren and a garden by Le Nôtre. I wonder where. And Lambeth. A picture by Van Eyck of the passion and panorama of many scenes, each scene a station of the Cross. St Peter's cock was shown as a peacock! a new idea to me but probably a just view with the harsh cry of that bird. There were many pictures and ever so many frames and a series of wonderful names but nothing held me.

    The picture I liked best was an Italian adoration – its charm to me was that it was out of its frame and on the floor of an empty room leaning against the wall. It had a human interest at once and the spirit of reverence became accessible and a feeling that the painter might have walked in at any moment and been very cross at one's looking at it. It was unfinished.

United Services Club, London   Sept.8.15.

I am here as an Athenaeum guest. I have not joined the services!
    They all seem to expect an air raid tonight. Last night a bomb fell in Fenchurch Street and Mazzawattee's [tea] factory near

    1. A parody of Kipling's 'If', which appeared in *Puck of Pook's Hill* in 1907.
    2. Jan Griffier (1645–1718).

London's Tower was destroyed. I go down to Knebworth tomorrow for the night.

Get Miss Dodge or Lady De La Warr[1] to motor you over to W. Robinson at Gravetye. He has a wonderful garden and has done great things for the English Garden. You ought not to miss the opportunity of seeing him. Go with my name and kindest of regards. He has I believe a wonderful collection of 'blues' out now. He is a very old man paralysed not long in this world. W. Robinson is a full fleshy fruit but oh such a stone of such great size! This is to explain you his character.

Be happy. God bless keep and direct you.

17 Queen Anne's Gate   Sept.9.15.

I dined at the Club alone and heard much illicit gossip by overhearing soldier men talking. I took a taxi, picked up my bag at Apple Tree Yard and arrived at Bedford Square at 10.45. I no sooner was on the pavement than bang – crash-bang bing boom. And there sure enough up in the sky above the trees was a Zeppelin. The searchlights were on her and kept more or less on her and one could see the shrapnel bursting about her. But to me it looked like very bad shooting (a sort of trade-unionist shooting!) shots for their own pleasure and not much thought of the thing shot at.

Crash now and again as a bomb dropped and the sky lit up red to the south-west of No. 31 so I suppose there were fires. For 10 minutes or a ¼ of an hour I watched the great brute – a grey silver fish. The bursting shrapnel made red stars on the blue black night sky. Nothing of a firework order. An aeroplane went up but was soon lost to sight and nothing happened. How one longed to see her hit, doubled up and come down. I thought she was hit once but she was changing her direction which operation altered the proportion and for the minute looked like a crippling of the structure. She seemed quite unperturbed and inviolable.

1. Muriel Brassey married in 1891 the 8th Earl De La Warr; the marriage was dissolved in 1902. A sister of Lady Willingdon, she was 'small, wiry, smartly dressed and remote from her own three children' (Mary Lutyens, *Krishnamurti* (1975), p. 53). In 1911 she was converted to Theosophy by Lady Emily, together with Miss Dodge, with whom she shared a house. Lady Emily was staying with her and Miss Dodge in East Sussex.

I went in and wondered if the fearful noise of guns and bursting bombs had woke our maids but there was no sound. Then I caught sight of a light in the basement and I opened the kitchen stairs door and looked down and hollared 'Anyone there?' A timid chorus said 'yes' and there they all were in every sort of a garment, panic-stricken and crouching in the wine cellar.

I have told them to fill the baths etc. and not to cower like idiots and to get properly dressed and not wrapped up in bed quilts etc. You either see it coming and can engineer your safety or you are caught unawares – and then nothing but chance can save you. It is no use sitting miserably frightened in a cellar expecting to be buried at any moment in the debris of a destroyed house!

I do not think the maids ought to be left alone and I wish Nannie were not so nervous. But the chance of a raid may be over before they get back. I am wondering mildly how the maids found the wine cellar key!

Palacia de Liria, Madrid[1] [on the way to India]   Oct.23.15.

I have very comfortable rooms – a bed-sitting room, dressing room and a bath nearby. All of which I have enjoyed and an excellent breakfast served up here. Peñaranda has appeared in a dressing gown *très chic* and I feel clean and welcomed.

Peñaranda motored me into the town to buy guide books and to buy a motor for the rough roads to save his Rolls Royce. Then back to this place where I found Alba lying out in the garden. First class French cooking and multitudes of servants who I felt ought to be in the fighting line! The only really Spanish thing was a most excellent ham, the best I ever tasted, and was rather horrified to find, after, it was raw. Wild pig cured and then buried.

Peñaranda does not think he will begin building until after the war but there is much to prepare first – the plans – getting water – building huts for work people etc. that in no case could we start for a year or more.

---

1. Lutyens was staying with the 18th Duke of Alba and 11th Duke of Berwick (through his descent from an illegitimate son of James II by Arabella Churchill, who was attainted in 1695). He was educated in England and at school was known as Stuart. The Duke of Peñaranda was his younger brother, and it was he who had commissioned Lutyens to build at El Gordo.

Madrid   Oct.25.15.

We started for the Escorial. The great neo-classic church surrounded by Palaces, University and Monastery. All in granite. It
lacked in invention but the proportions were good, the building
good, the detail somewhat clumsy and a repetition of the same
features.

Motley's *Dutch Republic* helped me to realise the power of
which the Escorial was the centre. It is a wopping great palace, all
very simple and no fraudulent construction as our Government
of today insists on. The gardens were very pleasant – thick cut
box hedges in knots, stone niched walls and gravel. Grass is nigh
impossible in this country.

P. is a charming person – 33 – very young and simple in the nice
way, full of fun and life. My odd times I go on planning El Gordo.
Had a good go in with Taylor, an Admirable Crichton they have
here and an Englishman, about the offices of the new house. The
house everywhere is beautifully kept and very well run.

Alba is a Grandee of Spain 13 times over – i.e. he could sit in 13
seats in the Senate if he had as many sit-upons. He has only one.
He has the power of giving his spare Grandeeships away, so if he
had 12 brothers the 13 of them could, as far as I can gather, have
seats in the upper house. As it happens he prefers his seat in the
Deputies.

Alba's given me a ham, I shall give it to the Viceroy!

[Boat to Cairo]   Oct.27.15.[1]

We left Madrid Wednesday morning in the Rolls Royce and
reached Toledo. To the cathedral where the dead hand which
lays its hand on Spain is seen in flesh of very flesh! i.e. fat priests.

The building cannot be compared with our Northern Cathedrals – Chartres, Westminster etc. – but the wealth and elaboration is certainly impressive. The great coloured windows and the
most marvellous profusion of heraldry part hidden by great gilt
reredos and in front of these stand great iron grilles and grilles

1. Though dated 27 October, this long letter was written from the boat. On
31 October Lutyens wrote from Spain: 'The story of my adventures from
Madrid and on to El Gordo I must leave until I have leisure. I will not fail you.'
He then made two rough lists of characters and scenes.

again in front enclosing the choir. Precious stones and marbles, inlaid woods, carving.

The huge illuminated books that must take two men to lift. Each generation piling on the last some elaboration making a temple so sombre, so mysterious, that you can only think of the poverty stricken country outside with sadness.

They seem to have had good architects and Philip II was a purist! Grand conceptions but weak in architectural technique and when they leave the Doric order – which, by the way, they run to death – they come awful croppers. They seem to have no men of the calibre of a Mansard the elder and certainly no San Michele nor a Wren! The rungs of their ladders break by elaboration and they fall into veritable pools of ostentation.

Every village has one great church gaunt and half ruined, sometimes two or three. Monasteries and convents galore and here and there a Moorish fort on high ground dominating the roads – and oh the roads. Makes me realise what we have done in India. Labour is cheap and stone in plenty but you see men every 20 kilometres or so carefully filling in the ruts with dust from the sides.

The two bridges that cross the Tagus belong to Alba. Towers at each end – great buttresses, 4 small arches and one great span, all in granite. Huge.

We left Toledo for Ventosilla about 4.30 and away we went along the bad roads that stretch 'across the plain until they stand up to the horizon like chimneys.

And oh! the adventures with the motor and the mule teams. The tearing barking dogs, their barks and narrow squeaks. Luckily we only killed one. More Moorish forts and then down again into the valley of the Tagus we arrived at Ventosilla. We were met in a courtyard by a crowd of dogs, Dukes, Duchesses, children and a delightful Irish Nannie. An old house added to by their own labour, direct enough and shamelessly shoddy. Roomy, comfortable and as English as they could make it. A sumptuous tea and Nannie presided. We had time before dark to go round near about the place.

Santoña[1] and his Duchess, Alba's sister, are keen only on country life. They are independent of everything and everybody. Their own farm, bakery, they breed mules, pigs, preserve their game, make their own electric light and power for their farm machinery. A Lambay in a sea of Spain. She is his second wife and her money runs the place and reconstructs and has made the large additions.

There was a delightful priest – father confessor and estate agent loving the hunt, the shoot and spends his day in breeches and gaiters and for dinner he appears in his cassock with its 42 buttons (one was off). An adenoidal tutor. Motors in plenty and a delightful battery of servants. All friendly and friends of the family – each one a host in himself. Furious wood fires. Nurseries with toy room complete and such toys! and each little boy had a recess by his bed as an altar or chapel where saints and martyrs and the Mother Mary stood in the full panoply of Rome.

Dinner. The dining room – an uncomfortable room and a huge table with many faces round it. A scratch lot of servants. Very different was the food to that at Liria Palace in Madrid. At one end of the room was a table covered with every kind of cup, pot, coffee pot, plates – a display of silver – so mixed and so untidy as to give one the feeling that they were moving house. We dined at 9! Lots to eat in many courses.

The Duke is a quite genial creature suffering from gout. His hands were very bad. Living for sport and his farming. She very small – always in breeches and gaiters – more like a boy to look at than a woman. Has no nerves and rides astride, though in the evening she appeared gowned like a Byzantine queen in pelts, baroque jewels, some very good pearls and a net of gems for headgear. Dogs everywhere.

Transparencies and pictures generally a great success with the children and especially with the priest! A gaunt bedroom and yet

1. Lutyens designed a house for the Duke of Santoña at Ventosilla but it was not built.

---

more gaunt bathroom were given me in the guest wing. The family live in a wing by themselves and all seem a happy nursery party to which Peñaranda belongs.

Next morning we started for El Gordo – the Duchess, Peñaranda, the priest and myself.

El Gordo – a village reported to have 1200 inhabitants perched on a gentle mound, approached by ruts knee deep up a sharp hill, not cobbled but bouldered. A barren gaunt church and two small houses and Peñaranda's granaries formed a small piazza in which the whole population had gathered – 3 leading ladies in deep black, 3 bailiffs in black, the guards, the rest of the population in blue, the women with yellow shawls, some few with red and bare headed, the men with leather aprons – one to each leg and huge black hats, children galore. And they cheered our party, a great deal of handshaking, much talk to apparently very little purpose. The car to the children was honey to the bee.

We went into the principal house for lunch. The picturesque squalor of the crowd was emphasised by the 3 ducal footmen in livery that had arrived before us to make ready and no footman is allowed under 6' 2" and no ordinary Spaniard is more than 5' high.

We occupied two houses. A wide entrance hall without windows but double doors. A shady court in summer – a prison in winter. To the right a kitchen with huge fire and vaulted roof. Up 4 steps a suite of 3 rooms. Window arrangements most awkward. Great thick shutters panelled in many small panels and glass outside – all clapped into one frame. No curtains.

To the left a bedroom for the Duchess. To the right a bedroom for Peñaranda. No sanitary arrangements, no fireplaces and flies abounding.

After lunch coffee and then we started for the property and to find a site for the house. The Duchess on the money-lender's horse – such a jolly beast – astride. Peñaranda on Rosinante, the priest in gaiters looking stout and gallant on another. The 3 guides armed! And myself and the bailiff in a mule cart. The bailiff's brother and various oddities on mules.

Off we went and the roads got ever worse – ravines and *nullahs* crossed with prayer for bridges. The day was dull. We seemed to walk and drive miles viewing the possible and impossible sites, until dark, and then in the dark we all got into the cart – 4 of us – to drive back.

Next morning was brilliant and the whole panorama lay bare to us. The forest of old ilex, the Tagus at our feet. To the south a range of mountains beyond a plain and to the north snow-capped giants that seem to belong more to heaven than to earth. We ventured with the motor which was far better than the mule cart. We stuck in the sand once and had to be dug out. It was jolly.

The priest rode about searching for brick earth, lime and sand and returned gloriously happy and successful. Good sand, good clay, brick earth and plenty of stuff to burn good lime.

There are Roman ruins nearby and on the part of the estate near the river and on the site I want and on which I think we will decide are giant heaps of stones evidently collected by some ancient for a building – never started. Perhaps a Moorish fort before the re-conquest or a Roman one before that. No tool marks on the granite to make evidence.[1]

We lunched out doors at one of the guards' houses and after made more explorations. A surveyor from Madrid came out and I showed him where and what I wanted to do, levels, etc. On the river site – a cliff over the river – a curtailed view of snow mountains and the other possible site – high up with great views all round but no shelter whatever from wind or sun and no view of the Tagus. I want the lower sheltered site where the trees grow big and the river runs and you will get views beneath the spreading branches and not above as in an aeroplane!

The local people and the priest say hill top. It will look so fine! and be so well seen!

I had great fun with the priest who could only speak Spanish and I not a word, with pictures, transparencies and such like and he was such a good chap too – a sort of Bumps in orders. So knowledgeable about the country and the fabrication of buildings etc., farming and stock of all sorts, a good shot and fearfully keen to hunt.

So back to dinner.

---

1. The ruins were a prehistoric tomb and the site was moved two miles away. The final plan, made in 1927, 'envisaged a wing for the accommodation of the King of Spain as well as for the Duke. The plan of the house was now similar in general outline to that of The Viceroy's House.' Extensive outbuildings, however, still exist at El Gordo. These were built by Lutyens's foreman, Hinton, from 1918. See Gavin Stamp and Margaret Richardson, 'Lutyens in Spain', *A. A. Files*, No 3 (January 1983), pp. 51–9.

British Residency, Cairo   Nov.16.15.

The mosques are much better built than any I have seen in India. They are remarkable, with qualities of real building and not that love of dickey (shirt) front order so loved by the Indians (Moguls). Fine conceptions, finely wrought. The bazaars good too. The closed streets with serrated gleams of brilliant blue sky.

Cairo is full of Australians and is a hospital base too but owing to the impression on the native mind of the quantities of wounded they are now shipping them home as they cannot conceive how we can have any men left!

We went to the Egyptian museum in the morning by ourselves and in the afternoon with the director, a nice pleasant fellow and saw much that was beautiful, much that was odd, and those pathetic and horrible mummies that I hope some day will be reinstated in their tombs amongst the writings on the walls that were intended only for the eyes of their Gods to their own great comfort.

In the afternoon we went to the Pyramids, then stayed there with a good sunset until it was dark. I never realised that they stood on a plateau. The Sphinx . . . that speaks what all true men feel. With these colossal monuments the weariness of it, the ruin and desecration, the eternal strife, is very saddening and it goes on perpetual in both worlds.

We came home in the dark and started by an 8 o'clock train for Thebes. Mr Storrs[1], the secretary here made everything comfortable and we were met at Luxor station by a nice little Egyptian and taken to the hotel in his smart victoria, a few minutes after went to the Temple of Luxor. One of the obelisks before the pylons – one of a pair! – was given by Memelik to the French! and that is the one now in the Place de la Concorde. How any moral man could give or take such a gift is beyond the dreams of reason.

A huge mud-conceived temple in stone and granite, ruined, despoiled, a dreadnought beached. In the afternoon Karnak, a mile or so down the river. A good deal of the work is without imagination like noughts to a cheque, but much that was lovely, much that was impressive and the vast amount of material and the exact labours spent marvellous.

1. Sir Ronald Storrs (1881–1955), orientalist and collector, was Oriental Secretary in Cairo 1909–17.

We dined with our Egyptian friend in a large new bad French house overlooking the Nile. An elaborate badly cooked dinner of innumerable courses and a very sweet claret cup – a syrup to drink. Baker has had a tummy ache ever since.

This is a dull letter and terribly so when I try to focus the stuff that I have seen. Great God-fearing children playing with huge toy bricks and then telling their stories in picture words with no adjectives and childwise the man himself is ever the centre and adopts the godlike image and occasionally rising to a very high level of accomplishment little thought in this world but to meet the terms of the next and assure a perpetual happiness.

I hear Lady Anne Blunt is here.[1] I shall try and see her but she seems difficult of access.

In train from Cairo to Port Said   Nov.19.15.

[Sir Alexander Baird[2]] came to Lady Anne's with me. We went a bit by train and a bit by trolley stopping at a white wall and at a door in it.

This door was opened and revealed a large sandy court in which animals were tethered and jolly camels – a heaven made place for a wondering child. Lady Anne approached us from the opposite side in wonderful clothes. I had forgotten her charming voice and she looked so handsome. Much thinner but as keen as ever and her face suggested a very good looking walnut.

You know the kind of clothes better than I can describe them. But with the camels and her head man dressed on similar lines it made a picture fit to illustrate an Eastern fairy tale.

We had tea in her little verandah. Baird did all the talking and did not see very much. I should like to have gone over her new building she has built for Judith's children. It was quite matter of fact and as such Lady A. left it but I don't think she realises what a very able designer she is and how she achieves the obvious and simple and that with grace. She is a child innocent of her powers.

The sun sank quick and a good moon lighted and I left her in her court with her man and camels, mounted the trolley, boarded

1. Lady Anne Blunt spent the last two years of her life from 1915 to 1917 at Sheykh Obeyd.
2. Sir Alexander Baird, 2nd Bart (1876–1931).

the train and then motored home. I guess my sympathy and regret that she should be left alone was quite wasted. But to me her position seemed pathetic and she ought to have grand children all about her playing with her a delightful game of Noah's Ark day in day out.

Yesterday after more sight seeing went and had tea with Storrs, Secretary to the Chancellery. He has collected some very jolly things and some wonderful alabaster things of incredible age and he has reached that stage when the Greek sculptor dominates his preference above all else. It is bewilderingly odd why it is that every man is not able to concede this – the highest of all known human endeavour.

Government House, Bombay   Dec.3.15.

Lady W[illingdon] is softer but as energetic as ever. She still I am told believes her boy will turn up sometime, somehow.[1]

In the afternoon had the steam launch and a tea basket and went to the caves of Elephanta on an island some 7 miles out in the harbour. Rather wonderful and some evidence of real beauty. But how can you achieve beauty with a Ganesh and what do you think Ganesh is made to ride on? An animal, what steed? For the great soft fat elephant headed god . . . a mouse! Came back facing a fine sunset.

Yesterday the Aga Khan's agent called for me in a motor car whose chauffeur was dressed in crimson velvet embroidered and embossed with silver lace. Went over the site and the existing buildings.[2]

Delhi   Dec.24.15.

To woo you I can only think of how I could build you a house – I have only my craft you know, to use for good or ill – on a high sandy wind blown site surrounded by firs. A garden such as you might want might be difficult and grass for tennis etc. nigh

1. Her eldest son, Gerard Freeman Thomas, was killed in September 1914.
2. Lutyens did not build for the Aga Khan.

ARCHITECT'S OFFICE,
RAISINA,
DELHI.

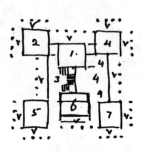

1. Hall
2. Sitting Room
3. Staircase
4. ... Offices.
5. Sitting Room
6. Sitting Room Children.
7. Dining Room
V. Verandahs.

1 – 7. bedrooms
B. baths.
b. balconies!

, bedrooms in roof.

Would that please you?

impossible. But such a site and a house with large airy canary cage windows and balconies everywhere, hot water, built like a hospital, pneumatic cleaners and rounded corners so as to have as few servants as possible!

This would be your room with six large windows on two walls, bed on a third, fireplace and doors to bath and the passage, the fourth, a red tile and polished floor and lots of hot water pipes.

What won't please you darling is the probable cost. House, land, garden, furniture, would break into £10,000 and if we do it for my honour's sake we would have to do it well and conscientiously – to give good example and to give to labour the dignity that belongs to it. It need not be luxurious or smart – just bare simplicity with good materials, good labours, so I fear it is not practical politics yet and heaven knows what difficulties the end of the war may not land us in.

Hot water, baths, lavatory basins, etc. and labour saving appliances are not cheap and generally cost more in capital than the value of the additional maid or boy. But it is an amusing game and may become possible at any moment! Say, darling, where would you really like it – Crowborough? Too far for me but that don't matter. Remember Barbie and Robert and the rest of the family down to Nannie and the possible grandchildren and say what you would like. Between us we have nearly the £30,000 saved.

Delhi   Jan.3.16.

Baker's very busy making out emblems for India, her Provinces and indeed all Dependencies, Crown Colonies etc. of the British Empire, so he has the rose for England, the leek for Wales, the five rivers of the Punjab and so on.

I maintain that an architect should always design in three

dimensions, it is his job, for why I want to give the star of India[1] six points as five won't work to be seen from all views as an entity, and yet it can be applied to a coat or shield.

Any animal (except a flea or a sole) is all right, a horse, lion, bull, talbot etc. The coronet has been conventionalised, in reality ![coronet] on paper ![coronet on paper]

The society of Antiquarians have adopted as their crest a four way lamp. To draw it correctly you can only see three ways – to make it right on paper they have to draw it so, in perspective, which is bad heraldry.

In Europe you can alway use a figure and emblazon your bearings on a shield, but a figure allegorical is not possible in India. First any figure is considered to be a king or queen, secondly, the Mahomedans disallow it.

In words (literature) you can describe any emblem and you are not faced with the difficulties until someone is prompted to execute them and it is the architect's job to do so, where possible and when possible to prevent lay folk embarking on a crest and badge that cannot be used by the people for all purposes without necessary contortion and vulgarity.

I do not think phrases describing physical features which cannot be portrayed in the round, and if in the round cannot be portrayed on a shield or flag, is good sense. Architecture should begin where literature leaves off, each depending on the other. It always has been so in great periods.

Baker says it is very difficult. I fear it is and all the more worth doing, and it wants too a Shakespeare. wit to ordain symbols which will hold people to them and hold water too.

Mother Church gets out of the difficulty by making figures hold their own emblems.

1. On top of the 145-foot column designed by Lutyens and donated in 1912 by the Maharajah of Jaipur to commemorate the Coronation Durbar. Lutyens submitted a perspective drawing of the Jaipur Column, coloured by William Walcot, to the Royal Academy when he became a full Academician in 1920.

St Barbara a town and for St Catherine a wheel, but a town on a post or a wheel on a post would mean little.

The Swastika cannot be claimed by any one province. It is very difficult to discover a system but it is certainly the duty of the architect to go the one better and stick to his all round – three – dimensions and let painters and writers do the others. The Lotus belongs to China and Egypt as well as India.

I should rather see an orb which means power surmounted by the star, six points, which can be drawn flat or round.

But tell me what you think could be used as emblems in India avoiding Hindu and Mahommedan scruples.

The Maharajah of Jaipur has I hear approved the Column (absurd to ask him as he can have no idea of what part it plays in proportion and progression in the scheme as a whole). But instead of the King in State and the King's Arms with Indian supporters etc., he wished to have bas reliefs showing the King at the Delhi Durbar and he and the Queen arriving at the Apollo

The Viceroy's House and Jaipur Column

Bunder[1] at Bombay. This would be a pity as it would degenerate to the *Daily Graphic* type and if true the King would look so insignificant as to be ill distinguished.

Delhi   Jan.7.16.

Mail has gone and Sir Chattur Sankaran Nair[2] has been and gone too but whilst his visit is fresh upon me I write.

He seemed intelligent over the drawings and then we went up to the site and up the observation tower, built on the centre axes of the Government Court to be. And then down along the Viceroy's Court to where the foundations for Government House are going on. He brought me back here but would not partake of tea. We walked and drove and talked of many things. He asked after Conny and was interested in Suffragettes.

I spoke to him about education – book learning and the present system producing unemployed lawyers, clerks and litérateurs, instead of educating people to appreciate and demand the best in all things and thereby producing good tradesmen, craftsmen, etc. men who could be proud of and happy in their work.

He appeared to sympathise and asked me if I thought it possible to start a school at Delhi in connection with the building of the new city for three months every year. I see the bristling difficulties but said Yes fearlessly and it might be a great thing beginning for India to raise the level of endeavour and make the principles taught in the lecture room visible and practical in the growing city.[3]

Delhi   Jan.19.16.

Keeling told me that the Viceregal staff houses cost more money than allowed. There was a fearful row last year because they were planned too small *to instructions* and the Viceroy intervened and

1. A wedding-cake arch of white plaster was built at the Apollo Bunder, the landing-place at Bombay, through which George V passed on a red carpet when he arrived in India in 1911. It was removed soon afterwards, and the Gateway to India was built on the same site in 1927 by George Witte.

2. Sir Chattur Sankaran Nair (1857–1934), education member of the Viceroy's Council 1915–19.

3. This idea came to nothing.

ordered them to be bigger but allowed no extra money for it! When you realise houses are estimated so cheap that no door or window has a handle or a lock! just a bolt you can imagine the pigstye class of work. . . . So the row will have to begin again and I shall get no redress if the plans – six months work – are chucked. It belongs to India I suppose, like Mrs Besant, who enlarged the TS three times, three sets of plans and then expressed surprise the cost was higher than estimated! But in this case H.E. was told it would cost more . . . of course it would and gave him no credit for common sense.

We heard the name of the new Viceroy and my guess was right. Baker had given so many wise? reasons why it could not be Chelmsford[1] and he was so frustrated I was amused. It makes my conversation with Chelmsford funny to think of when I said that Viceroys and Kings – only Kings and Viceroys – should have equestrian statues in New Delhi, he winced. No nice man can contemplate an equestrian statue of himself with equanimity!

They think figures on a plan are just put on to look pretty and if a wall is 3 foot thick they are likely to write 9 feet or 9 inches on it quite willy nilly.

Baker curiously tiresome and numb as to what lines and levels are right and what not in landscape and other gardening work. He talks in a way they seem to understand and which to me is drivel and is very strong willed. So I am up against a real difficulty and he is quite happy with inaccurate drawings and approximations – always playing for opportunism which is not conducive to good work.

1. The 3rd Baron Chelmsford (1860–1933), created Viscount 1921. His appointment was an unexpected one; he had experience only as Governor of two Australian states, and he was serving as a Captain in the Territorials near Simla when the offer was made. Nice but weak, his term as Viceroy (1916–21) was overshadowed by the Amritsar massacre of 1919.

Delhi   Jan.27.16.

I am having difficulty with Baker. You remember the perspective
showing the secretariats with Government House beyond.

Well I find he has designed his levels so that you will never see
Government House at all! from the Great Place.

You will just see the top of the dome! He is so obstinate and
quotes the Acropolis at Athens, which is in no way parallel. The
steep way is stopped by the Propylaia across it and we should not
have heard so much about the Acropolis if it had not been for the
super excellence of the Parthenon that crowns it.

I have now put a protest in to him in writing and he will be
angry and I shall have to carry it further. His perspectives are
imaginary and wrong and it is too naughty to mislead like that. I
do want help out here.

Delhi   Jan.31.16.

I took Lady du Boulay[1] into my confidence about my difficulty
with Baker, she was very sympathetic and duly shocked and
made me tell du Boulay. So I gave him my letter to H. Baker and

1. Wife of Sir James du Boulay (1868–1945), Private Secretary to the
Viceroy. Lady du Boulay had become close to Lord Hardinge since Lady
Hardinge's death.

his answers. I also talked to du Boulay about the houses for the Viceroy's staff and the irreparable pity of building too small for practical purposes.

I gather the Government of India are furious with my idea that Crewe took up and gave form to in a committee on the furnishing of Government House formed of people who knew India climatically and good things of various kinds.[1] They look upon it as interference with the rights of Government though not one of them can lay any claim to knowledge as to what is right and fit – from a picture to a clock.

As trustees of Indian money they are in my opinion bound to rely on expert advice which is not obtainable in India and there is wonderful little of it in Europe. Also discussed the horrors of the Englishman's home and English built India man's house in India and the reasons why, and instanced the Duke of Bedford's system of finance as against the Government of India.

Delhi   Feb.4.16.

I have been working on the Viceroy's wing again. It is full of memories of Lady Hardinge. I guess the new lady will want everything different. Have you met her?

The Committee has postponed until next Friday our discussion as to Baker self difference. Baker is meanly! basing his defence on cost and selecting the most extravagant way of meeting the difficulty. But why if Government House is not to be seen at all should they have spent so much money putting it on to a raised basement? However, I must wait. I do hate these fights, but the whole matter is a point where Baker fails and where he misleads himself with words. It is his love for Kopjes and shop window effects. At present the perspectives he has prepared are as much value as regards truth as a seaside resort council's station advertisement to show the amenities of their place.

There was no committee but Hailey etc. came to breakfast and the upshot of my grievous difficulty with Baker is that we both write our views and the Viceroy will give his opinion. This is a

1. The Delhi Advisory Committee on decoration and furnishing was set up in May 1917. The members were Lord Crewe, in the chair, Lady Minto, Lord Hardinge, Lord Carmichael, and Sir Cecil Harcourt Smith.

bore for me as you know how difficult I find it to express myself in a way that is acceptable to those who do express themselves by penmanship.

Delhi   Feb.11.16.

Chowdbury the Indian Sculptor boy came. He seems satisfied and he comes now to work on models until we leave on the 19 of March so as to prove himself. He has been taught in England at the South Kensington Museum Schools. He has been taught to model naked women and busts, etc. but never a word as to design and the relation sculpture should have to piers, bases, panels and their positions and height, their size, scale and all or any fact in relation to other facts.

Delhi   Feb.16.16.

Worked, worked, worked, worked and dined at home and worked. The mail coming in prevented me from sleeping and I was awake long before it arrived – if ever I slept – like a child before Christmas. But anxiety sat by my pillow.

Delhi   Feb.17.16.

I hear H.E. is disturbed that Chelmsford does not take everything seriously. I think that he, Chelmsford, has a sense of dry humour of which Hardinge has no spark, wet or dry. Also that H.E. wrote on the budget report 'I don't understand a word of this' which is true judging by what he says and does! Right mindedness in saying so. If he would only say these things in public he would get so much.

I am so glad you are reading Indian history. It is a wonderful story. The eternal wars, the multitudes of races, the strong man from the north stooping as a hawk on the sun baked plains. The raids, treacheries and government by the sword, except the wonderful story of Asoka. There are two Asoka columns in Delhi. One imported and set up by us on the Ridge and the other in Ferozobad set up by Feroshah. Ferozobad is one of the old dead cities that litter the bank of the Jumna and lies between the present city and Indrapat.

Shah Jehan built the Taj and parts of the fort at Agra and the fort here. He built the present city of Delhi.

People go head over heels with their admiration for the Taj but compared to the great Greeks, Byzantines, Romans, even men of the calibre of Mansard, Wren, etc. it is small but very costly beer, and alongside the Egyptians it seems evanescent. A grandiose plan laid out on geometrical lines, the making of endless intricate patterns with water, flower beds. The method gives great charm but it stops just where invention should begin to fruit. The third dimension seems beyond their philosophy and they never get beyond carpet patterns and their carpets – the Persian etc. – inspire their architecture.

The Taj is built on a constructively very extravagant plan, the space enclosed being smaller than the area of the walls enclosing it. Imagine a huge box of concrete octagonal

on plan enclosing five octagons, set up on a great podium or platform with a minaret at each corner – staircases are beyond them they are the most break neck affairs. Having got this mass built in concrete, each face has a carpet of marble and stone veneer stuck onto it, and then to further adorn the building they put on five domes. Four little and one big.

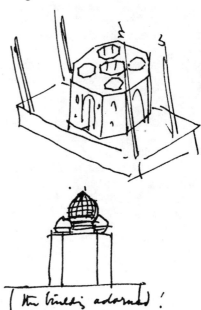

And then further embellishments with chattris and little arcades with toy drums in rows like pearls on a necklace.

Compare this method with a building like the Parthenon or any of the great French cathedrals – where the stones are the bones of the building and make by their construction their own decoration and then everything thought out relatively to make the whole design one organism approaching a work of nature. Do you see the difference? Some of the detail, such as the screens at Agra and Delhi are beautiful – the designs may be Persian, and certainly Italian craftsmen were employed. The Bactrians with the Hellenistic influence did wonderful work, and the Pathans (Afghans?) were influenced by it. And then the Hindu work which has degenerated to the most ungainly shapes and repetitions and monstrosities.

You will not get a fine art without great artistic discipline and discipline seems never to have been a strong point with the mass of Indians.

Now for my diary. Lady Selborne[1] took Baker away all day Saturday, Sunday and Monday. His time here has been one long holiday. I should feel guilty taking £5.5.0 a day for it!

I received a letter from the Imperial Committee refusing my plea that Government House should be visible from the Great Place. It is not fully visible for more than half the length of its main avenue of approach. It is not fine design. I have written to the Viceroy. He is against me I know but he may postpone the question for his successor.

Lady Selborne is a dear. She talks perpetual leading article and Baker does the same: very obsequious and tentative in his opinions. It amused me but I had no one to share the amusement with me.

I am to lunch with H.E. tomorrow. I feel rather nervous about the interview.

Later. Just back. H.E. will not go into the merits of the case. He says Baker and I are one architect and that I had agreed to a particular gradient. The only solace is that I may bring the matter up to Lord Chelmsford but his opinion is that what is agreed to, though he doesn't like it, is settled. I am very depressed. However it will be put right when it is built at great expense.

1. Lady Beatrix Maud Cecil (d. 1950), daughter of the 3rd Marquis of Salisbury, married in 1883 the 2nd Earl of Selborne. One of the 'Salisbury Plains', Lady Selborne had known Baker when her husband was High Commissioner in South Africa, 1905–9.

Delhi   Feb.24.16.

Ever so many thanks darling for the Egyptian book. Naturally it is superficial but the many pictures are what I like.

I am interested to see the method given for setting out the angle of the great pyramid is the same as what I used and thought I discovered for the setting out of my roofs.[1] But I am sure there are simple geometrical facts that make or mar any work. And 'Art' is a curse to mislead and give excuses for haphazard and slovenly work. Art comes subconsciously by very sweat out of very sweat. A god that can have no name must be right in idea. I wonder what their music was like and if it went so far as their other work.

I hear the Viceroy has decided against my contention in favour of Baker's. I shall have to write to H.E. officially. It is such a worry. Ought I to resign? It is such bad designing. It can be altered afterwards but at great cost. Chelmsford may see the point and realise the stupidity and ugliness of Baker's line.

Delhi   March 2.16.

Eddie Marsh[2] wrote to me. He says Lady Chelmsford is dowdy and that old Lady Wimborne[3] is in the seventh heaven with offspring on the thrones of India and Ireland. Do tell me about Lady Chelmsford.

31 Bedford Square   *March 1.16.*

Sunday we had a great family gathering at Fisher's Hill [the Gerald Balfours']. Neville looked gloriously well, and was in wonderful spirits – full of fun and not a grumble or thought for

1. 'In earlier days,' recalled one of his assistants, 'the angle of his roofs was 51.5°, that of the pyramid. But the angle of 54.5° . . . was rarely departed from in the last 30 years' (Hussey, *Lutyens*, pp. 488–91).

2. Edward Marsh (1872–1953) was a friend of Neville Lytton, who started him on his career as a collector of watercolours. He was assistant private secretary to Asquith, 1915–16.

3. Cornelia, Lady Wimborne (d. 1927) was the mother of Frances, Lady Chelmsford; her son Ivor, Lutyens's client, was Lord Lieutenant of Ireland, 1915–18. When her nephew Winston Churchill crossed the floor in 1903, the formidable Lady Wimborne ordered all her offspring to follow suit; only her son-in-law, Viscount Ridley, remained loyal to the Tory flag.

himself. It was his last departure before going off to the front. His creed of life is just to take life as it comes and live each day to the full and as well as may be. He has no belief in an after life but is going out to face death or worse with perfect courage and cheerfulness and I must say it is a noble creed and I admire him greatly. Robert was quite bowled over with admiration of his wit and charm.

Judith was her usual wonderful impassive self. A marvellous hairdressing of tangled curls – a wonderful pink complexion (I am exercising my mind as to its genuineness) not a line on her face or a grey hair. She is stouter but her figure wonderfully upright and vigorous. She was most cordial to me and seemed really pleased to see me and said we must meet when Neville left. Wonderful stories of family quarrels – her parents are reconciled and now both attacking her.

The war is to her a constant nightmare but she does not seem moved to take the slightest share in helping and Betty thinks it has entirely cut her life off from Neville's and made a big gulf between them.

Gerald looked thin and aged. He and Nora Sidgwick,[1] who lives with them, are wholly absorbed in psychical research. Gerald went over the Hampstead Garden suburb the other day and was most rapturous – especially about your church which he thinks shows more genius than any modern building.

We all sat round the fire after lunch and talked and after tea Neville sang with Judith to the guitar and also they had choruses 'Marching through Georgia' etc. and a big lump settled in my throat.

17 Queen Anne's Gate   Aug.8.16.

On reaching Apple Tree Yard a note to say the Queen was coming at 2.30. . . . I had to leave in the middle of lunch to get back here in time to receive Majesty. I made no jokes and feel a loser! She was rather prim and sticky and horribly shocked to find

1. Eleanor Balfour (1845–1936), Gerald's sister, was Vice-Principal and Principal of Newnham College 1880–1910; she married in 1876 Henry Sidgwick (d. 1910), philosopher and a founder of the Society for Psychical Research. In 1916 she came to live at Fisher's Hill, where she remained for twenty years, until her death at the age of ninety-one.

Government House had been cut down. I hope I made a good impression. The first thing she noticed was the plan different to what she had seen before and wanted everything Hardinge had knocked out.

Then soon after she left Baker came in. He has sent off to India plans of bungalows before the scheme is worked out properly and stolen another march on me. He is a bore and ought not to do it. I then went to see Austen Chamberlain.[1] I gave him messages from the Queen about the Committee and the reduced size of Government House. He was horrified at the idea of building without proper estimates and cutting the essentials to fit guess estimates etc. But it has already gone out to India as a cabinet order demands for a report on costs and how the estimates are arrived at. There is quite a good chance of the work being stopped altogether but they will wait for this report before making a decision.

He was very pleasant but I wonder. I feel that Baker is working against me and going for himself and not the work itself. However, Chamberlain said I was quite right to come and tell him anything I thought but I feel lonely and don't see how I can get the right thing done.

Sketch for the Duke of Santoña's house

Ventosilla, Toledo, Spain [on the way to India]   Nov.17.16.

We arrived here about tea time and received a very cordial welcome. Monday I spent pegging out the Santoña house on the

1. Sir Austen Chamberlain (1863–1937) was Secretary of State for India 1915–17.

low hills overlooking the Tagus near here. In the evening I made foundation plans, etc. so they could get on without waiting for the finished drawings. I worked like a slave. Tuesday ditto. Only one drawback – there was no water in the house and we had all to go bathless and other insanitary inconveniences.

. . . Wednesday we went to El Guadalperal . . . Thursday the King and Queen[1] arrived at 10 for the shoot.

I sat with the King in his butt and walked and talked with the Queen and had a very good innings! I was duly photographed in a group and alone with the King! We talked building and I told His Majesty many things he should do even as Napoleon did, etc. The photographer is a little lame man who follows the King wherever he goes. He is privileged. The fun of the man is that he carries his sandwiches and cognac, etc. in his boot which is made like a box to make the lame and the sound legs equal. So down he sits, opens his boot and eats his lunch!

The King has asked me to the Palace tomorrow and is going to take me over it himself which will be fun. He is having it all opened up from cellar to attic and the Palace architect will be there too. He asked a lot about Delhi, the prices and costs of material as affected by the war. He was very keen to see the El Guadalperal's plans and was awfully kind and appreciative. They have been a great success and Alba congratulated me in full and ducal pomposity on them.

They shot till near 5 o'clock and then a bounteous tea when I had another long talk with the King and after tea with the Queen. I must say another little baby hasn't done her any harm. She looks young and very well, very simple and easy, but bigger in build than the general run of Spanish women. But the King! He has really a wonderful personality, simple, charming, a mixture of boy and grand seigneur, very much taller than I expected for he is a tall man! Very thin and quick and energetic, a serious, thoughtful face with small eyes that twinkle yet full of fun and *joie de vivre*. Everybody seems to love him and count him friend. He is treated with enormous respect yet no one has the slightest fear or any feeling of self consciousness when with him.

He had his two loaders and three guns and shot like a maxim and they say he is a very good shot indeed but I hated the murder

1. Alfonso XIII (1886–1941), King of Spain from 1886 until his abdication in 1931. Queen Ena, whom he married in 1906, was Princess Victoria Eugenia of Battenberg (1887–1969), and a granddaughter of Queen Victoria.

of it all – the driven birds, hares, etc. The priest led and generalled the beaters.

My visit has been a great success. I have set out two houses, eaten a great deal, but I know a King and like the feeling of it. So very different to ours!

31 Bedford Square   *Nov.28.16.*

Your success with the King! It is too amusing and I feel Nedi's royalist tendencies have found a satisfying subject and you will soon get appointed architect in chief to the Spanish court.

I am a good deal worried about the Knebworth Church affair, and the heavy excess on estimates. I only heard of it yesterday from Barbie. It only shows there is something seriously wrong in your office. I don't want to bother you now you are away but some day you will have to face up to the question of Thomas [A.J., the office manager].

Now what did I do yesterday? Oh yes morning printer, also a lady who wishes to improve my powers of speech and so made me recite strings of words with a cork between my front teeth.

I took Ursula to Nicholson and saw the picture. He has not got the mouth right otherwise it is very like. He has decorated the studio in a most amusing way. Every shade of coloured paper cut in octagons! He did it for a ball he gave and for light had 150 bottles with candles stuck in them! He made £800 for the Red Cross at the ball. He had charming bouquets of velvet flowers. He is an amusing person.

31 Bedford Square   *Dec.19.16.*

I posted your letter on the way to my shop,[1] where I had my usual queer tea party, a mixture of social talk and the confessional. I got back at 5.30 to see little Lady Elcho[2] who had written asking if she might come and talk to me. She came looking so tragically

---

1. The Star Shop in New Bond Street, where Lady Emily often helped to sell books, calendars, silver stars etc. produced by the Order of the Star in the East.
2. Lady Violet Manners (1888–1971) married in 1911 Lord Elcho, who was killed in the summer of 1915.

*sad and we discuss.d the great problem of death and after and
especially Oliver Lodge's book[1] and she told me of some interesting messages received from her husband. I told her of my beliefs
about death and she was so nice and I thought it was one of the
wonders of this wonder time which brought that particular lady
to me for help. I am sending you Oliver Lodge's book as I think
even you will feel it is convincing.*

Delhi   Jan.15.17.

A command to dine at Viceregal Lodge on Monday. I started off
in our old car and half way there in a low suburb of Delhi the car
went bust and I was stranded. I got hold of a telephone and
phoned Government House and they promised to send a car to
my relief. So off I went walking to meet it. I walked at least 1½ to
2 miles when I was lucky enough to pick up a second class tonga. I
never met the car. I got to the house at about 5 to 9 (dinner at
8.15), found no one there in the portico, so I walked in. No one in
the hall so I walked on. No one in the inner room so I walked but
the band was playing. I entered the dining room. They had
reached pudding stage. Chelmsford very friendly and my place by
Lady C.'s side had been kept.

I had a sketch dinner beginning with soup and on – and
everyone waited. Rather uncomfortable and I had a great deal to
say to Lady C. too. She is not a bad sort but is fearfully
unpopular. I.F. they call her (Interfering Fanny). I told her I had
heard she did not like puns. She said she loved them and her
husband was always scolding her. But I was good and didn't
make any.

I had a long talk with them both after dinner – alone. I told
them about my King's visit and all K. and Q. had said. The only
difficulty is money and that is due – Lord Crewe won't allow it to
be [to] the Government of India – but to Hardinge.

They came out to tea here today and she was quite intelligent

---

1. Sir Oliver Lodge (1851–1940), physicist and philosopher of psychical
research. In *Raymond or Life and Death* (1916) he describes contact after death
with his son who was killed in 1915. Lady Wemyss was reading the book aloud
to her family in November 1916 (Lady Cynthia Asquith, *Diaries 1915–18*
(1968), p. 237).

about plans and really looked at them and into them. He is all for my star and not the one that makes a long nose at you seen sideways, and also about the carving on the [Jaipur] Column base.

Delhi   Jan.24.17.

Wonderful Lady Elcho coming to see you. One wonders if it is sincere! I know of course it is. They are clever and have nice points those Manners ladies and the war I suppose brings out qualities one didn't realise. I can understand great sorrow but it would never send me, I think, to the supernatural, the stars and sun and suns beyond seem an impenetrable fence to the mind. We want new – a 6th sense – which of course your friends claim. Well, I can't manage five, bless you.

I am looking forward to receiving Lodge's book.

Oliver Lodge

Delhi   Feb.21.17.

Yesterday we had the committee meeting to settle the bungalows. Mine came out, as I expected, as they rightly should, too high [in cost]. Baker's horrors came out too high but possible. It became a question of a scheme which they had previously decided on. I have a real jolly scheme. Baker has no scheme – just slap dash cocky olley anyhow orum. I said I would reconsider but must have time. Baker said we could get no help during the war and made the most of delay. So the matter was left.

The next point was the buildings in the main avenue at Point B where the four great Buildings must be symmetrical.[1] Baker wants all of these! I have done one and the main avenue. At this point I suggested that I should do the whole of Point B and anything within the State Avenue, Baker the bungalows. The Committee supported me. So I have resigned the anguish of building a certain number of jerry villas (oh the waste of labour!), and it was such a nice scheme, but I get the whole of the state approach etc. under my own control, which is good. This morning Baker is trying to kick against it as he always is on the wobble about any question. The first letter of his alphabet is B, B for Baker, and is such a bore. He is sure to muddle the villas and I shall be quit of responsibility.

I submitted my plan for the gardens of Government House. They – the Government of India – commanded a Mogul garden which means terraces, water ways, sunk courts, high walls, etc. etc. and have at the same time allocated sufficient money to plant a certain area with shrubs and no more. It is too Alice in Wonderlandish for words. However it will come in time.

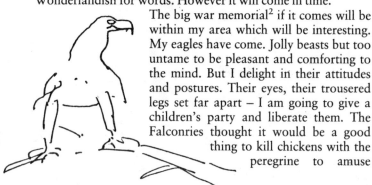

The big war memorial[2] if it comes will be within my area which will be interesting. My eagles have come. Jolly beasts but too untame to be pleasant and comforting to the mind. But I delight in their attitudes and postures. Their eyes, their trousered legs set far apart – I am going to give a children's party and liberate them. The Falconries thought it would be a good thing to kill chickens with the peregrine to amuse

1.1 The four buildings at Point B (see Map, p. 229) were intended to incorporate an Oriental Institute, a National Library, a Record Office, an Ethnological Museum, a War Museum and a Medical Research Institute. Though Lutyens made designs for three of these, only part of the Record Office was built (1922). Baker's bungalows were not built either.

2. The All India War Memorial Arch, built in 1920.

the children! I cannot imagine anything that would be more conducive to tears than to see a chicken torn to pieces by a hawk.

Delhi   March 13.17.

Monday afternoon I had a children's tea party – the children of Raisina and the PWD on the occasion of the liberation of the eagles. Lady Chelmsford came with her littlest – Margaret, aged 9,[1] a dear little child, most friendly. I did not warn any of the ladies that Her Ex. was coming to save an exhibition of fine clothes and would have spoilt the children's day and it all went off very well. The PWD ladies were flattered and the children were untutored to the Viceregal presence and were natural and good fun.

The eagles alone were disappointing. The first one, the big one, flew into a hedge and then burst his way through it and took a line across the post office building, flying very low, so was soon lost behind the building. But captivity had made him stiff. The other eagle rose better but went bang into some wire netting but flew low but went a long way which helped us to keep him in sight for longer.

Did I tell you the Baboo's poem on the death of Queen Victoria?

'From dust to dust and ashes to ashes,
Into the grave the Great Queen dashes.'
Can't you see Her Majesty?

Delhi   March 27.17.

I hear Chelmsford thinks the war monument should serve some utilitarian purpose! You cannot represent India in any monument of a utilitarian purpose with her multifarious castes, religions and nationalities. A war monument wherein all India can have the services of her great men commemorated would surely help and tend to bind the country to a common service and purpose.

1. Margaret Thesiger, b. 1911 (m. 1934 John Monck); she was in fact six.

Curtis[1] pow wows all day on Empire and what not and altogether misses, I think, the real points, but he has humour and don't mind my chaffing him a bit. Yes, he has a very conceited nature and very pompous utterance. He is very pro-Indian and I am I must say surprised at the set against him.

I must say to my own undoing that Indians understand me quicker than Englishmen and object less to my method of persiflage by which I find it easier to convey ideas.

I had a birthday dinner on the 29th. We dined under the trees in the garden at 7 tables with electric lamps, comfy. Everyone brought their servants and it all went well. The office boys dressed up in smocks and top hats and gave us folk songs, glees and jollies.

44 of us sat down to dinner – just Delhi builders. I wanted 48 one for each year. I had a cake with 48 candles. The night was lovely, warm and a new moon sky high. The Government of India has flitted and it is very quiet and no one here.

I have been designing St Stephen's College[2] and the University which Government will or may build here and as the buildings will eventually form one group it was important to lay down lines. Rudra is the principal, a Bengalee. St Stephen's College has been fairly successful in turning out seditionists – some of whom have been duly executed. It is so silly somehow.

This I think is very remarkable. Rudra's son enlisted as a Tommy! in an English regiment and has seen a great deal of most awful fighting in France. Being dark skinned he cannot get a commission. That is right at present, but it is a brave, loyal thing for any Indian to do and would help enormously to promote good feeling if it were only more frequent.

It is very, very lonely but this year I have been extraordinarily well and have worked really hard and I think to some effect.

1. Lionel Curtis (1872–1955), a member of Milner's Kindergarten, a founder of the *Round Table* and a prophet of the Commonwealth ideal. In 1916–17 he was in India to discuss the question of Indian self-government.
2. St Stephen's College was built in 1861. Lutyens's plan was not executed.

CHAPTER NINE

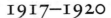

1917–1920

LUTYENS EMERGED from the depression of the early war years subtly changed. He was no longer the romantic young architect, living out his architectural dreams. Rather, with the approach of middle age he took refuge in a new dichotomy between art and life. The Ned Lutyens remembered by contemporaries and caricatured in his own sketches began to take shape: bald, cherubic, pipe-smoking and bespectacled, the inveterate punner, patience-player, diner-out and habitué of the Athenaeum Club – 'I like to wash my hands between two bishops' – and later of the Garrick Club. Yet behind the smokescreen of jokes and puns Lutyens's artistic vitality was undimmed. Increasingly intellectual, even abstract, his work was to scale new heights in his quest for the monumental.

Preoccupied by his own problems in India and at home, Lutyens had maintained an uncharacteristic detachment from the events of the Great War. Yet it was he, more than any other architect, who was to commemorate that war. In June 1917 Lutyens and Baker were invited by Fabian Ware, the instigator and Director of the Imperial War Graves Commission, to visit France in order to report on the construction of military cemeteries. It was this visit that first brought home to Lutyens the full horrors of the Western Front.

On his return from France Lutyens threw himself into the debate about the form of the war monuments, crossing swords once more with the hapless Baker. Baker was one of the many who favoured the Christian symbol of the cross. Lutyens by contrast envisaged a simple, non-denominational statement: the Great War Stone. Never one to be fenced in by narrow religious creeds, he saw humanist art, distilled to its very essence, as the ultimate means of glorifying God. In his broad approach, Lutyens was at one with Lady Emily and Theosophy, and over the Great War Stone he enlisted her sympathies as he had never done before.

Lutyens won the battle over the Great War Stone. Eventually each cemetery contained the Stone of Remembrance designed by him, as well as the Cross of Sacrifice, designed by Reginald Blomfield. In February 1918 Lutyens, Baker and Blomfield were appointed Principal Architects for France and Belgium, and work on the war graves began. In London, Lutyens's Great War Stone first appeared as the centrepiece of the temporary war shrine he designed in Hyde Park in August 1918.

Closely related to the Great War Stone in the classical simplicity of its conception was the Cenotaph, the monument for which Lutyens is perhaps best known. When in June 1919 he was asked by Lloyd George to produce a temporary 'catafalque' in Whitehall for the peace celebrations later that month, Lutyens dashed off the design for what he called the Cenotaph[1] in a matter of hours. This temporary structure was rebuilt in Portland stone – with significant refinements – in time for the Armistice celebrations of 11 November 1920. Deceptively simple in design, the Cenotaph is in fact a geometrical *tour de force*, containing no straight lines or flat surfaces. With this elemental classicism Lutyens contrived to capture the spirit of war sacrifice, as well as reaffirming the values of pre-1914.

Work on New Delhi was suspended in 1917–19, and country-house building came to a standstill as well. Lutyens's practice consisted largely of war memorials: between 1918 and 1930 he designed at least 65 in this country alone. Many of these were for private clients, and Lutyens toured the country commemorating the demise of the world that had brought him fame in the Indian Summer before 1914.

During and after the war Lutyens's patrons were to be found, not at dinner tables and house parties, but in government offices. Yet he continued to dine out, finding in the smart London society of the 1920s a much-needed relaxation, not to mention an escape from home food. Some of his letters read like the index to the biography of any socialite of the day – Colefax, Cooper, Cunard. But the old friends remained, particularly Pamela Lytton and Lady Horner. Then, from 1916, there was Lady Sackville.

Lady Sackville was the illegitimate daughter of one Lord Sackville by a Spanish dancer and the wife of her cousin, another Lord Sackville. In 1912 she had been left a fortune by Sir John

1. See above, p. 48, for Lutyens's early use of the word 'cenotaph'.

Lady Sackville in 1911

Murray Scott, for many years her admirer. When Lutyens met her she was fifty-four – eight years his senior – and her marriage, which was a tenuous one, was finally breaking up. Mary Lutyens remembers her in the twenties as having 'grown too fat', but 'still beautiful with a perfect complexion':

> Her slight foreign accent and her general ambience of deliciously scented opulence were a great attraction to me. She always seemed to wear a hat with a veil, even indoors, and to be dressed in sables, the softness of the fur emphasising the softness of everything else about her (except her will).[1]

1. Mary Lutyens, *Lutyens*, pp. 155–6.

She and Lutyens became instant friends, called each other Mac-Sack and MacNed, and, judging by the few letters that survive, communicated in a private nonsense language of their own. 'Joy fun Thursday, Hungry and Firsday,' he wrote. 'Roast Claret and toasted Kimmel sounds puffect.' (Lady Sackville's table was an excellent one.)

Lady Sackville had a passion for building, and Lutyens built or altered at least five houses for her. She found in him an architect to indulge her fantasies, and the relationship turned into a hothouse version of the game Lutyens knew so well how to play, of architect and client. But he could never get her to understand what he called the grammar of building. 'Now look here,' he wrote:

> You must brace yourself and swear never to commit an ugly construction or deed. It is no excuse to say 'I want it' or I know what I want or other emphatic phrase. Ugliness is the one great sin in this holocaust of a world and one must fight it. Sloppy umbrella architecture and mind means destruction of beauty in God's gifts and a lost world. No trouble by any individual just jazz and dazzle and small talk, and everyone at sea rudderless and bumping. *There*. This for your pipe for smoke.

Far from seeing Lady Sackville as a threat, Lady Emily welcomed this new addition to Lutyens's life. 'Mother was hugely amused by her,' wrote Mary Lutyens. 'When MacSack took Father to lunch at the Savoy she would send her chauffeur round afterwards to Mansfield Street with the remains of the Brie cheese they had had.'[1] Things were looking up in other ways as well. The hated house in Bedford Square was sold, and in 1919 the family moved into 13 Mansfield Street, the Adam house that was to remain Lutyens's home until his death.

---

1. ibid., p. 197.

Chapel Wood   May 19.17.

Oh dear, poor darling, Lady Sackville rang up and said may I bring Mrs E. Cunard[1] to lunch with you on Wednesday and may Lionel come – i.e. Lord Sackville. I said alas I am lunching out and she said May I not see your wife without you? To which I had no answer but a cordial affirmative. So will you write to her. I advise you darling to get it over and make the party an exception to the war rule but I am sorry. But I know you will collar Lady S. and her spare cash for the TS and become another Mère Toni [Mrs Merton][2].

GHQ, DGRE, BEF, France [near Montreuil]   July 12.17.

Each day we have long motor drives, being billeted in a château some way back from the front.

The cemeteries, the dotted graves, are the most pathetic things, specially when one thinks of how things are run and problems treated at home.

What humanity can endure and suffer is beyond belief.

The battlefields – the obliteration of all human endeavour and achievement and the human achievement of destruction is bettered by the poppies and wild flowers that are as friendly to an unexploded shell as they are to the leg of a garden seat in Surrey.

It is all a sense of wonderment, how can such things be.

Men and lorries – motors without thought of petrol – fat horses and thin men all in the pink of condition. Great in size beyond imaginations and all so inexplicable that it makes writing difficult and one dare not mention names of places etc.

One is seeing very little of all there is to be seen but the little is ominous of what lies beyond a battlefield, with the blessed trenches, the position of a machine gun by its litter of spent

1. Maud, later Emerald, Lady Cunard (1872–1945), society hostess, in whose box at the opera Lutyens had met Lady Sackville in 1916.
2. 'Middle-aged, rich, fat, plain and with a strong German accent, she was wonderfully kind and possessed the attraction of good grooming from a French maid' (Mary Lutyens, *Lutyens,* p. 130). Mrs Merton had been converted to Theosophy by Lady Emily, but despite her efforts to achieve spiritual promotion – she gave much of her money to the Order of the Star in the East – Leadbeater disliked Germans and he never spotted her on the astral plane.

Temporary British War Cemetery in Northern France, 1917

cartridges. The ruined tanks, the rough broken shell-hole pitted ground, you assume was once a village. A small bit of wall of what was once a church may stand but nothing else.

The half ruined places are more impressive for there you can picture what a place might have been.

The graveyards, haphazard from the needs of much to do and little time for thought. And then a ribbon of isolated graves like a milky way across miles of country where men were tucked in where they fell. Ribbons of little crosses each touching each across a cemetery, set in a wilderness of annuals and where one sort of flower is grown the effect is charming, easy and oh so pathetic. One thinks for the moment no other monument is needed. Evanescent but for the moment is almost perfect and how misleading to surmise in this emotion and how some love to sermonise. But the only monument can be one where the endeavour is sincere to make such monument permanent – a solid ball of bronze!

For miles these graves occur from single pairs to close packed areas of 1000s on every sort of site and in every sort of position, the bodies laid to face the enemy. In some places so close one wonders how to arrange their names in decent order.

We have a lot more to see.

The question is so big, so wide that the most one can do is to generalise. General Ware, the Director,[1] is a most excellent

---

1. Sir Fabian Ware (1869–1949). Editor of the Tory *Morning Post*, 1905–11. Inspired the establishment of both the Graves Registration and Inquiries service – of which he was Director, 1916–18 – and the Imperial War Graves Commission, which he served as executive Vice-Chairman 1917–48.

fellow and very keen to do the right thing without fear or favour of the present sentiment – a preference for the most permanent and perfect.

I am terrified of the censor. The mess here is delightful – a terrible château does not spoil it. A good view and fine trees. France – as France – is altered, becoming gentler and more sympathetic simply that they have not the labour to cut the trees so hard.

Tomorrow we go again to the battlefields – to a scene of obliterated villages, scarred soil and destroyed tanks etc.

17 Queen Anne's Gate   Aug.7.17.

The first person I saw [at the Athenaeum] was Bernard Mallet.[1] I told him of France – he said Cantuar[2] is upstairs why don't you tell him. So I went upstairs and there was Cantuar and some fellow bishop. I said I want to speak to you, Sir. He said 'All right, wait a mo'. So I waited a mo and up he came and I told him of my big stone idea as against the cross – the permanency, the non-denominationalism etc. He was very kind and said he was greatly and favourably impressed but would think it over.

In train to Abbotswood   Aug.23.17.

Such a rush. At 12 to General Ware who kept me more than an hour, full of sympathy and fight for the big stone, furious with Baker and almost at breaking point with him and Aitken.[3] Baker's last idea is a five pointed cross, one point for each colony. India, Ware pointed out, was forgotten, but what does a five pointed cross mean? Ware bids me courage.

Ware showed me Barrie's letter about the Great War Stones. He referred to me so nicely – I won't tell you what he said, you wouldn't believe it! he had never met a man with a greater imagination than what I had, better put and more of it! It is pleasant to be thought to have imagination.

1. Sir Bernard Mallet (1859–1932), Registrar-General 1909–20.
2. Randall Davidson (1848–1930), Archbishop of Canterbury 1903–28.
3. Charles Aitken, Director of the Tate Gallery.

Cavendish Hotel, Eastbourne　　　　　　　　*Aug.24.17.*

Baker must be dotty! A five pointed cross for each of the colonies.
Too silly. And India left out which will cause bitter hurt and what
about the Jews and agnostics who hate crosses?

The Athenaeum　　　　　　　　　　　　　*Aug.24.17.*

I got back to London about 6.30 from Abbotswood. I found two
letters from Lady Sackville. One all about Robert and what a
charming companion he was and how she implored him to give
up smoking until he was old enough when she would give him a
cigarette case! etc.

Mrs Fenwick is so much better – came down to lunch and
dinner![1] wheeled in her chair and she has regained her mis-
chievous twinkle and can talk again about greyhounds. Mark is
just the same but beginning to get very infirm.

He is going to do more building. I do wish people would say
what they were aiming at and intended to do. Alterations and
additions make in the end a sort of fool scheme instead of an
achievement creditable to the men that build it. You design a
house

and then you find they meant to add

with this result![2]

However I forgive much when they are kind and appreciative,
and I *was* glad to find Mrs F. so much better. She reminds me
very much of Mrs Barbara Webb though the two women are
quite quite different.

It *is* dull here. I am in a large room entirely alone and thanks to
the war the writing table where I may smoke has no light! Lady S.

1. Mrs Fenwick never recovered from a fall she had in 1909 jumping a swing
gate on the way home from hunting.
2. Mark Fenwick did not add to Abbotswood.

in her second letter wants to enlarge the London house[1] still more.

I have no news and feel very depressed and mis. Empty club, empty home, bureaucracy in India, divided counsel and compromise. The 2nd best in all things aimed at and a mild 3rd achieved. The beastly waste of war. The loss of life and happiness, the church faces which mark fraud and so on. Animal instincts, moral fences one can have no real faith in, knowing as one grows older how they are created.

I think I have induced Mark Fenwick to build decent cottages. There ahead of us is an awful quagmire of hideousness and discomfort, 1,000,000 cottages built by a government that can only work through compromise and leave their consciences in the hands of accountants. I wonder if Chippy would help. He has influence.

A cottage cannot be 'good' if the man building it is not happy and content in his work, besides this fact, pay – so long as he can live – matters little. I mean the veriest labourer. The government building rules – which they are bound to make – will be based on obsolete acts to save them initial trouble and get a 'procedure'. They will determine costs before they ascertain essentials. They will treat their professional advisers as being dishonest and in the process will make them so. Those in final power will be appointed for their very want of special knowledge and be more influenced as to whether there is a 'D' in knowlege or not! than the subject matter with which they have to deal, design and decide. And England where men have built and might yet build beautifully and sanely will be scarred and seared with innumerable habitations which will look as though man alone was the world's scourge.

This, darling, is an explosion. All this is the return of my having no news and tired just for the moment by all I ought to do. So like a man to victimise his wife.

I suppose the Sydney Webbs are a really [happy] couple when they have a common grievance and some common object to destroy.

---

1. Probably a house in Brook Street that she was thinking of buying and wanted to enlarge.

---

17 Queen Anne's Gate   Aug.24.17.

I will ask Montagu to make a point of seeing Mrs Besant, but she has rather cut her painter by her insistence on concessions against the judgement of a government in the midst of this awful war, which has not helped her with the official personnel. Also I hope she will refrain [from] receiving Montagu with bare feet. With all due respect they are, through no fault of hers, old and boot worn and it shocks sensitive Indians and Englishmen alike.

I met Blow[1] last night. He is doing no work! except a house for himself and living with Westminster running his house, a sort of bailiff and Maître d'Hôtel! as far as I can make out!

17 Queen Anne's Gate   Aug.28.17.

Yesterday Lady Sackville motored me to Bumps. She went to lunch with some Americans at Great Tangley, she then called for me at Munstead and motored me back to London. Bumps very *épris* with Lady S. They were funny together. There is to be an exchange of foie gras and pot pourri.

Bumps has written out great war stone idea so well.[2] Now she is taking up the monument idea. That the most beautiful sites should be selected not where the victories were and all that snobbery, for I hold that there is equality in sacrifice and the men who fell at Quatre Bras are just as worthy of honour as those that fell at Waterloo. I do not want to put a worldly value over our dead. They put 'killed in action' or 'died from wounds', 'died'. Died alone means some defalcation and shot for it. I don't like it. The mother lost her boy and it was in the interests of the country and she had to suffer – her boy. Do you see what I mean? But then I don't fight nor do I fight yet for the seemly sepulture of the Germans when they lie along with our men.

1. Detmar Blow (1867–1939), protégé of Ruskin, and Arts and Crafts architect. He built a lot for the Souls. In 1930, after seventeen years as agent to the Duke of Westminster and surveyor to the Grosvenor Estate, he was ignominiously dismissed, a blow from which he never recovered. His house, begun in 1914, was Hilles, Gloucestershire.
2. In a letter to Lutyens.

Homewood   Aug.29.17.

I am very keen about your stone. It appeals to my side of life – as houses don't and I see so much true symbolism in it. I do hope you get it through.

I am also entirely at one with you about equality of sacrifice and that all those who 'die' no matter from what cause should be honoured. I think it is too awful that the wife of a man shot for cowardice gets no pension. After all he is equally lost to her and by government orders. I think it is barbarous.

Too funny to think of Bumps and Lady Sackville together!

Homewood   Sept.5.17.

It seems as if your stones are going well and I do hope for your sake something will soon finally be settled so that you can set to and do the work. It would be the finest thing of your life if it comes off and I am entirely in agreement with you about taking no money for it. It is your war work. You should charge expenses – this you must do – but no fee. Of course it is anxious about money but we must manage somehow.

Did you see Mrs Besant has been elected President of the next Congress? Isn't it splendid? The finest answer India could have given to the government. I hope Montagu will arrive at some compromise by which they can release her.[1] I am sure he would if he could.

17 Queen Anne's Gate   Oct.14.17.

I went to the Geographical Society to borrow a book and photographs, as Mr Howland said they had photographs of great stone elephants[2] at the Ming tombs in China.

Afterwards went and saw Fabian Ware. He was 'shocked, grieved' at the Archbishop's letter – expected a neutral attitude not a narrow antagonistic view. He says the clergy in France are most tiresome – always trying to upset any and every kind of

1. In September 1916 Mrs Besant began her agitation for Home Rule for India. She was interned by the Madras Government in June 1917, and she became a national heroine. In September she was released.
2. Presumably for the elephants on the retaining walls at Viceroy's House.

applecart. But he thinks the 'stone' will win yet, and he may chuck the whole thing and let the Office of Works do it all with lych-gates[1] complete. He liked my grave head-stones and did not like Baker's and was cross at his being so difficult and petty. He said he would consult General Macready[2] and if he agreed would announce that I was appointed Hon. architect to the whole caboodle. He wanted to know if I could afford it.

The question of uniform was discussed – for me to be a 'Captain'. I said no – he thought I was right. I could not go about in khaki with straps of a sword I cannot and could not use etc.! It may mean I shall have to give up a lot of private work. I am rather vague about this and must think it out.

Saturday – got up at 7 and caught the 8.35 at Liverpool Street, my cold prodigious. E. Montagu, Mrs Montagu and Lady Diana.[3]

Breccles[4] near Thetford, an old tumble down house restored by Blow! in a tumble down fashion. I am glad I did not do it – as he did it! It made me feel lonely. They were very kind.

Montagu did not want to tell me but Mrs M. made him, how that Queen Mary's great stunt was mimicking me! describing the beauties of Delhi. He was very frightened lest it got back to the Queen that he had told me! She was kind about me so I don't mind, but I did not think she had the personality to do it.

Got back at six, my cold worse and I have stayed in bed all day.

Knebworth House   *Jan.1.18.*

I am wondering what Robert will say to the Honours List, which is out today.[5] I wish somehow you could have refused it, but I suppose it is difficult. Baker is not in it. I wonder if he refused.

1. 'Lionel [Earle] is all for a lych-gate and a rose garden. But there is nothing permanent in a lych-gate' (Lutyens to Lady Emily, 3 September 1917).
2. General Sir Nevil Macready (1862–1946). As Adjutant-General to the BEF 1914–16 he was responsible for the establishment under Fabian Ware of the Graves Registration and Inquiries organization.
3. Lady Diana Manners (b. 1892), married in 1919 Duff Cooper (1890–1954).
4. 'The house was extremely well repaired by Detmar Blow shortly after 1900 and added to and (less well) altered by Lutyens after 1918' (Pevsner, *Norfolk, North, West and South* (1962), p. 96).
5. Lutyens had received a Knighthood in the New Year's Honours. Lady Diana Manners wired: 'The King and I are agreed – well done.' Baker was not knighted until 1926.

In train Bordeaux to Hendaye[1]   Jan.1.18.

Happy New Year! A world of snow and snowing still. Spain will be impassable!

Did I tell you that an American in the train from Havre to Paris [asked] if I was Lloyd George. I said, 'Yes I am'.

A.   Well I guess you have put me in a difficulty now.
Me.   Not one of my seeking I assure you.

The little lady, rather pretty, on my right, enjoyed it enormously and I found out she was a traveller and travelled in veilings. I am sure she sold lots of veilings by the unveiling of her sleek little eyes. She was rather like a rubicund edition of Pamela McKenna. A little lady that travelled and was merry at it might prove a solution of many difficulties. I wonder what you would say?

My cold is immense and I use up handkerchiefs per kilometre and again it has gone to my throat. At the Bristol, nature having forsaken me for two whole days, I asked the waiter for a '*verre de selles Epsom*', he brought me an *oeuf à la coque*! I humbly ate it and wonderful to relate nature returned to me immediately, such is the action of God, who cares for people who are as children. My request for Epsom was taken as a prayer. Now if I was properly grown up I should on the next occasion ask for an egg, but then it would be with dire and contrary results without doubt.

I hope you admire my philosophy. However I got rid of pains, creeps and surges of giddiness which constitute the flu, and the fever too flew.

I wish I was at home to see the papers.

Liria Palace, Madrid   Jan.3.18.

Here I am at last. When God says s'no'w he seldom means yes, but yes it is now. Thirty two hours late and oh what a journey. We were snowed up at Avila, three hours from Madrid, in the mountains, snow banks in front a derailed train behind. Our fuel for warming the carriage failed, the lights went out and there for hours on a mountain top I waited, getting hungrier and colder

---

1. Lutyens was on the way to El Guadalperal for the Duke of Peñaranda.

---

hour by hour. Finally we got back into Avila station, but the Fonda (restaurant) was so extraordinarily unappetising that one did not get fonder of one's food. You see I can still joke. I felt thoroughly beknighted! However they sent a snow plough from Madrid to our succour, but why not keep snow ploughs in the mountain passes, passes my imagination.

Chartley, Staffs.   Feb.26.18.

I reached Shrewsbury in good time and was met at the station by Sir Bryan Leighton[1] and a parson friend Mr Phillips in a big American car and off we went. We went straight to Loton [Alderbury] church – a nice funny old church but spoilt with a very interesting tower, but it was too dark to see anything and the drive facewards towards a wonderful sunset did not help one to see in the dark.

However, I got an idea with the help of an electric torch and darkly visualised the Loton Chapel and came to a conclusion sufficient for my peace of mind that night. Then on to the house [Loton Park]. An old ramshackle place added to and embellished by fits and starts. Most of the starts don't fit! and very bad excrescences in Victoria's goodly age when Ruskin and hypocrisy preened its own aprons without the loss of any pelican feathers.

Leighton has been at the war flying. Apparently he got at cross purposes with the authorities, and they rather he went than probe justice. His job now is felling timber on his estate, for which he gets government labour and his other job is testing parachutes. Did you ever hear of such a job! He is very proud of having jumped out of an aeroplane at 350 feet, 1200 is nothing if your heart is good enough to stand the change of atmospheric pressure. How I should hate it. He says it is the most delightful of all occupations – ugh! Would you like it?

The house has been untouched and unhousemaided – there were no housemaids and I should think never had been one and it wants twenty – for years, and a litter of every kind of paper and thing – guns, rods, fishing tackle, bows and arrows, old furniture, beds, curtains, pictures and heraldry galore, shields and banners

1. Sir Bryan Leighton (1868–1919), 9th Bart. War correspondent in the Russo-Japanese War and in the Balkan War of 1913. Joined the Royal Flying Corps in 1914.

etc. The house shut up, save for his little den, a litter of every sort of thing, very warm, panelled, with a great fire and windows never opened, quite a good dinner of an old fashioned sort and lots of heavy port. Then back to the little room and we talked war monuments and I found it past one before I retired to a terrifying for ghosts bedroom. However I slept very well and woke to a stormy morning and the rooks ablaze with noise and clamour, thoroughly rattled.

Breakfast at 8 then to the church and out to another – a train to Stafford, where I met Hudson. A taxi drive here (to Chartley), an excellent lunch, then to Chartley Church to try how the monument[1] fitted – Billy Congreve – the model behaved quite nicely and satisfactorily. A walk back, tea, talk, dinner, and now this letter to you.

17 Queen Anne's Gate   April 22.18.

I was motored up to London by General Brancker[2] this morning and reached Apple Tree Yard by 9.30 which was good.

The house party was Mrs Astor,[3] Miss Astor, Lady Cunard, Lady Diana Manners, Lord Ribblesdale,[3] Vansittart (F. Office),[4] Duff Cooper, Knoblock[5] and self. Gen. Brancker came for Sunday night. A wretched day, Sunday, no news and no gossip. Everyone seems in arms against the politicians, and the army suffers as the architects do! only stones don't cry out like the blood of men.

I have lost such a lot of drawings by submarine – dead loss to me, and a worry and a bore.[6] These plans keep me very busy – no chance of my getting away Friday. Thursday, Friday and Satur-

---

1. A memorial tablet to William La Touche Congreve, killed in 1916. In 1927 Lutyens added another to Sir Walter Norris Congreve, VC (1862–1927).

2. Major-General Sir Sefton Brancker (1877–1930) was largely responsible for the expansion of the Royal Flying Corps in the First World War.

3. Ava Astor (1868–1958), hostess and beauty, with whom Lutyens had been staying at Wilton Park, Beaconsfield. She had been previously married to John Jacob Astor (d. 1912); in 1919 she married the 4th Baron Ribblesdale (1854–1925).

4. Robert Vansittart (1881–1957), diplomat. Created Baron, 1941. An admirer of Lady Astor's.

5. Edward Knoblock (1874–1945), playwright, connoisseur and a friend of Lutyens's.

6. A set of Delhi designs was torpedoed.

day are Varnishing Days at the RA and Friday is an election – the architects have settled to elect Scott.[1]

Lady Sackville has had a road accident, a taxi running into a wall at night, and she had to walk back to Knole in a half dazed condition having been stunned.

So long as lay committees manage professional men you will get time-serving professionals and on and on the war! There. It is true. There are ominous signs of various appointed bodies moving against the politicians – as such. What amuses me is that Valentine Chirol is aghast at the influence of the political chiefs with professional men. I wish he had believed that when he was at Delhi.

17 Queen Anne's Gate   April 30.18.

I had 1¾ hours to wait at Shrewsbury. I walked for an hour and came across that hotel, 'The Raven', designed by a great man called John Ruskin![2] His game was spoilt by thinking of what he had said and the result is a sorry business – and he would never have been allowed [nor] would he have attempted such a thing if he had not said so much. There are some remnants of buildings left when men still thought in terms of building when building. The modern buildings are putrid! A fit word – worse than Ruskin's! Nothing that I saw in the town acknowledged his assumed premiership. All he had done was to destroy the leadership of the older worlds and left it unreplaced, save by the anarchy of cheap advertisement.

In train   May 27.18.

Morrison[3] says bring laundry down if you like to stay. Saturday

---

1. Giles Gilbert Scott (1880–1960), elected ARA in 1918.
2. Pevsner calls the Raven Hotel 'a curiosity and warning' but does not attribute it to Ruskin (*Shropshire* (1958), p. 274).
3. Major J. A. Morrison (1873–1934), Unionist MP 1900–06 and 1910–12. He was the grandson of James Morrison (d. 1857), textile warehouseman and merchant banker, probably the richest commoner of the nineteenth century, who bought considerable estates in Berkshire, Buckinghamshire, Yorkshire Kent, Wiltshire, and Islay.

night I won through with the communal idea.[1] Sunday I lost it, Phillips the parson and self in a minority. Rural conditions difficult. The difficulties they have had even in only semi-detached cottages with the women quarrelling they say makes the scheme impossible. He would like me to bring Barnes[2] and Hyndman[3] too. I am not sure it is wise as they and Lansbury mean to upset any scheme qua building by introducing trades union and other questions and it will all get on crooked lines and mixed up endeavour. I shall be able to achieve nothing except trash of unions! There will certainly be a communal kitchen and a communal laundry, but it seems a communal building is impossible in the country. The villager will not be man-handled. As near neighbours the women quarrel.

The food culture at Basildon is very amusing. I wish the children could live amongst it. All rabbits, guinea-pigs, geese, turkeys, chickens of every sort and every experiment. Horses, sheep, short-horn, black angus, red devon, wonderful pedigree beasts judging from their money values. Pigs – you never saw such animals and such families. Goats – the children would adore their little model stalls. You know what I told you about women and curing bacon. Well the same thing happens with vegetables and intensive culture. They all go bad. This is why the tenants have had to give up their intensive gardens during the war.

Isn't it curious and difficult to understand?

9 Montagu Street[4]   July 31.18.

Then Barbara McLaren[5] came to see me. I told her of the difficulty I had with Fortnum and Mason,[6] how stupid they were

1. Lutyens prepared designs in 1917 for Major Morrison for an entire village layout at Basildon. The designs (now at RIBA) show a War Memorial Church to be surrounded with almshouses, an institute, communal kitchen, school, grave-yard, vicarage, village dwellings etc. A Walcot perspective of the design was exhibited at the RA in 1918 and was widely illustrated. But none of the scheme was executed, although Lutyens later designed Park Farm Cottage, Basildon, and a pair of cottages at Westridge Green for Morrison.

2. George Barnes (1859–1940), Labour MP 1906–22.

3. H. M. Hyndman (1842–1921), influential socialist.

4. The furnished house Lutyens leased after selling 31 Bedford Square in April 1918.

5. Barbara (1887–1973), elder daughter of Sir Herbert and Lady Jekyll, and widow of Francis McLaren (1886–1917), Liberal MP and brother of Lady Norman. In 1922 she married Bernard Freyberg, VC (1889–1963).

6. About a food parcel for Robert who had joined up though under age.

– suggested huge boxes of biscuits, no chocolate, no meats without coupons and so on, so I left them. Well I told Barbara of my difficulty and she said, why not consult Mrs Lewis (Cavendish Hotel lady)?[1] I did. She said 'Oh Fortnum and Mason are impossible. Go to Jackson's in Piccadilly mention my name and ask for Mr Chuter.' I did. Everything was at once forthcoming and I have ordered 10/- a week to go to Robert and Mrs Lewis said she would see Jackson's for me tomorrow. She is a woman you would not like, but she was so understanding, knew exactly what he wanted and suggested lime drinks, as drinks were awful, and knew all about everything.

She also said, but I have not told Robert, that if he ever wanted a room in London she would always give him a bed, a meal and a bath. She knows all the flying boys. She says she has given up her hotel to them and they have wrecked it! She said a Tommy or an officer it made no difference to her, so long as she could help them.

Then I went to see Lady Horner and then to Lady Sackville. Lady Horner about her chapel at Mells.

Merton Hall, Norfolk[2]   Aug.5.18.

I went over to Breccles yesterday for lunch. I walked! 5 miles there and 5 miles back! and then all over the house. Mr and Mrs Montagu, Birrell,[3] Scatters Wilson,[4] Mrs Aubrey Herbert,[5] Lady Diana [Manners]. I spoke to Montagu about India and Mrs Besant. I tried to tell him what you said – putting in my point of view to show good will and 'understanding'?! I asked him if he would see you. He said yes, any time. He said he saw Mrs Besant constantly. He is undoubtedly distressed but he says she has burnt her boats. I think you may be able to help a great deal. I wonder. However – it is up to you if you can. I hope I have not done wrong but that you will be pleased with me.

1. Rosa Lewis (1867–1952), 'the Duchess of Jermyn Street'.
2. Lutyens was staying with the Edgars, who had taken Merton Hall from Lord Walsingham. He wrote on 4 August: 'This is a house rambling – no light – no baths – the place of the Babes in the Wood, and my room, the one I am writing in, is called "the wicked uncle".'
3. Augustine Birrell (1850–1933), writer and politician.
4. Sir Matthew Wilson, 4th Bart (1875–1958).
5. Mary (1889–1970), daughter of 4th Viscount de Vesci.

17 Queen Anne's Gate   Aug.28.18.

I saw Kipling – Prothero.[1] Prothero sympathetic about cottages.
Kipling I feel unsympathetic. I don't like 'Their bodies lie
buried in peace but their names liveth for evermore.'[2] Someone
will add an S and it will read pieces. It is too material! (not bad for
me). Can't you darling find or think of something? To the
Brave-All's well. 'God created man immortal image eternity.'[3]
Too long. Can eternity be too long? How oddly my abbreviation
reads but it's a fine thing. You found it and I can't get away
from it.

Been working hard on the Hyde Park War Stone.

Church Stretton[4]   *Aug.30.18.*

*I quite agree about Kipling's choice of text. It is clumsy and
because of the pieces becomes ridiculous. My text, as you call it, is
I fear too long: 'God created man to be immortal and made him
to be an image of his eternity.'[3] Another I love: 'Certain is death
for the born and certain is birth for the dead, therefore over the
inevitable thou shouldst not grieve.'[5] There must be many beautiful sayings in the Bible. I will try and have a look but have not
an Apocrypha which is one of the most fruitful sources. When I
come back we will look together in mine. I have never said how
glad I am about the Hyde Park War Stone. I do hope you get it.*

*What could be shorter or more complete than 'Death is
swallowed up in victory'?[6] It says all there is to be said.*

In train to Muncaster[7]   Aug.30.18.

A lot of German prisoners are in the train. Some look pleasant
and some don't. The guard was very malignantly disposed, but

1. President of the Board of Agriculture, 1916–19.
2. Ecclesiasticus, 44:14.
3. Wisdom of Solomon, 2:23.
4. Lady Emily was at Church Stretton, Shropshire, where the three younger
children stayed from February 1918 to July 1919.
5. Bhagavad Gita, Bk 11 27.
6. I Corinthians, 15:54.
7. To stay with Sir John Ramsden, 6th Bart (1877–1958), at Muncaster
Castle, Cumbria.

was quite civil when they attempted to put pennies in the money box on the dog's back.

My pen leaks everywhere except at its point, so I take to pencil.

Yes, do think of a text or other phrase. My War Shrine [in Hyde Park] is thus

War Stone flanked by monolithic watching pavilions, or glorified sentry boxes carrying fir cones, the emblem of eternity. On these buildings will be carved your text

1.	2.
'Immortal'	'Eternity'
God created man in his own likeness to be immortal	and made him to be the image of his own Eternity.

Below the platform on which these structures and the great stone rest is a bench approached by six steps and a landing where wreaths may be laid.[1]

---

1. The pavilions were temporary.

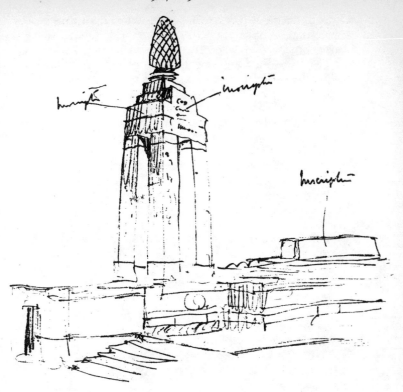

There is the inscription for the Stone.

Kipling: Their bodies lie buried in peace(s!) but their names liveth for evermore.

Kenyon[1] suggested the latter half would do, Their names liveth for evermore. But what are names? Even that is long to bear repetition thousands of times round the world's circumference.

You want a word like

Go losh

Though it suggests gums and slippers now it will mean *the* thing in the years to come.

1. Sir Frederick Kenyon (1863–1952), Director of the British Museum 1909–30, a member of the Imperial War Graves Commission.

Your other text, You live to die, die to live, does not appeal to me, it sounds helpless, hopeless and has the rhythmic action of a barrell organ.

(To those) (These are they) that came out of great tribulation.[1]

(For these) The trumpets sound from the other side.[2]

Barrie's 'All's well'.

Nicholson 'To the Brave'.

I was glad when I found both Waring[3] the donor and Mond[4] were anti Cross. I am coming to believe the Cross is the great anti-Christ of prophecy!

'Peace be with you.' Too churchy and Christian? There might be fine things in Bunyan.

The question is getting to a head, and if Kipling once says ?? [sic] the Royal Commission will say 'Yes' and there will be no retraction.[5]

And I want one phrase, one word and the same to ring the world.

is what I have put on the model, a block of alphabet, M to T with an O to begin with. It reads jolly well! You declaim it aloud. Nine letters. I can get them larger. Now a long inscription would not have the same effect at all.

One might get a phrase, cut it on the back of the stone, just the initials GMMTBI on the face and in time they will be known like the splendid Roman SPQR.

1. 'These are they that come out of great tribulation' (Revelation, 6:6).
2. 'All the trumpets sounded for him on the other side' (Bunyan's *Pilgrim's Progress*).
3. S. J. Waring, who paid for the Hyde Park War Shrine.
4. Alfred Mond (1868–1930), Liberal MP, was first Commissioner of Works 1916–21. Created Baron Melchett 1928.
5. The wording eventually chosen for the Great War Stone (Stone of Remembrance) was 'Their Name Liveth/For Evermore'.

Church Stretton   *Sept.2.18.*

*If you want only one word you should have Amen. It is the same
really as the Indian OM and the Egyptian A-Men is the sacred
word of the Aryan race – a name of God.*

In train   *Sept.3.18.*

In a very full train on my way back from Muncaster. I think I have
had a very successful visit. Ramsden likes my suggestion and was
interested in my making sketches there and came in and watched
me. I worked Sat., Sunday and Monday from 9.30 till 8 taking
occasional walks to see things in relation to the job and the
aspects of it to and from others. I think he will spend £100,000 so
it is quite a good job.[1] He is rather Gothic but pleased with sort of
Marshcourt stage.

   I have left all my sketches with Ramsden and he will digest
them, dig for rock foundations and get me samples of granite, etc.
and I will go up again in October. I expect it is a rainy district
amongst mountains – the chief Scaw Fell – the highest mountain
in England, a little lower than Snowdon in Wales. Just the sort of
country you would like. A magnified Church Stretton with sea
and river quite near by. But it takes 9½ hours to get there from
London. I wonder if Ursula would like to come. Bathing, ponies,
but they shoot and Joyce the little girl 11 or 10 years old so loves
the catapult![2]

17 Queen Anne's Gate   *Oct.27.18.*

I had a very successful visit to the Lewises, as regards making a
scheme and plan for adding to their house at Rottingdean,[3]
[William] Nicholson's old home (*how* he hates their being

   1. The proposed alterations to Muncaster Castle were not executed. In 1919
Lutyens built a tomb for Sir John Ramsden at Muncaster (into which Sir John
did not get until 1958).
   2. Mary Joyce, b. 1907, m. 1929 Major-General Sir Randle Feilden.
   3. Lutyens added to The Grange, Rottingdean, in 1920 for Sir George Lewis
(1868–1927), son of the famous solicitor. According to Hussey, The Grange
'typifies [Lutyens's] peculiar blend of sympathy for good existing work with
zest for his own' (*Lutyens*, p. 476).

there!). They have terrible faults – he specially – such ugly habits and feeds *très mauvaise* – but like most Jews very kind and hospitable.

The Athenaeum   Oct.30.18.

Last night I dined with E. Hudson. A dull dinner. Barbie had had a dinner too [at Montagu Street] and when I got back at 11.30 I found all had fled but Ivo.[1] I left them about 12.15 and asked Barbie to see me when she came up. Then I slept and woke and became restless, then noises and I found Barbie and Ivo were still talking. He left at 2. I was very kind to Barbie but told her it must not happen again or I should sit up and then turn everyone upstairs or out. She was darling and said she had been very wise and had much to say to Ivo as she had not seen him for a fortnight. I put my arms round her – at 2.15! – and chided her very gently, so don't say anything unless she speaks to you about it. He is young and so is she.

Church Stretton   *Nov.1.18.*

I was a little perturbed at the thought of Ivo staying till 2 o'c. as though I have every confidence in Barbie it is not fair to put him or herself into a position where a sudden rush of feeling may be too much for them. I am very glad you were there and told her what you felt. I hope she felt happy as the result of the conversation. It is all so strange to me that young men can go so far and yet apparently mean nothing.

17 Queen Anne's Gate   Nov.3.18.

I was very anxious about Barbie but she seems wise, and says she was very wise. I think they are tentatively engaged, Barbie feeling that he is too young and so much run after . . . and that someone

1. Ivo Grenfell (1899–1926), youngest son of Lord Desborough. 'His beauty is really very great, the real poetry of a youth's looks, and he has delicious manners and blushes' (Lady Cynthia Asquith, *Diaries*, p. 433). Barbie was working as a VAD; she was twenty.

Barbie as a nurse

after the war will turn up. She is not in love but would like to be. The boy is. This is only surmise and Barbie would hate my saying so much.

Another thing I scolded her for, prompted by fear. She went up in an aeroplane – without a hat – taken by a daring male child and looped the loop and made a spiral nose dive! Terrifies me! However it was apparently enormous fun, but it makes me realise that the parents – this one at all events – cannot run with his children!

The building prices coming in terrify me, they are so high that one wonders if there will be any building with a big B at all.

I am working with an engineer – Scott – for Hudson on some cottages. The economic rent has gone but yet the cheapest possible remains and the sizes they propose for rooms and will insist on are too small for human comfort. I cannot get anyone to see this except a Morrison or a Ramsden. The Local Government Board are doing dreadful things. It is not fair on the people and means eventually discontent, restlessness and the miseries of no home life.

The news is wonderful and perplexing. The wait for the Armistice terms absorbs one's patience.

The unveiling of the temporary cenotaph, 19 July 1919. The architect was not asked.

Lady Emily was not photogenic.

Thorpeness, Suffolk   *July 31.19.*

I had to send you a telegram I was so excited over the announcement that your memorial [the Cenotaph] was to be permanent after all. I was just planning a letter to Lansbury on the question of the Christian symbol. I long to read your letter which moved the Cabinet so deeply. I hope you have kept a copy as it will become an historic document, something which actually moved a government to do the right thing!

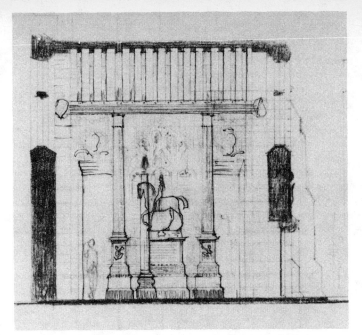

Preliminary sketch for Edward Horner's memorial

In train returning from Mells   Aug.4.19.

Just coming back from Mells. There were present Jack and Lady Horner, Katharine Asquith, Mrs Aubrey Herbert and Harold Baker.[1]

I took down with me Edward Horner's memorial tablet.[2] The train was very late and I arrived and found Lady H. alone, had tea and then unpacked the memorial and we carried it into the church – so there was no fuss and it was an excellent excuse not going to see a Shakespeare play in the Vicarage garden – *Cymbeline*.

1. Harold Baker (1877–1960), friend of Raymond Asquith, known as 'Blue-tooth'.
2. For the pedestal of the memorial in St Andrew's Church, on which stands a mounted cavalry officer by A. J. Munnings. 'One of Lutyens's best and most moving tributes to the waste of life in the Great War' (Colin Amery, *Catalogue 1981*, p. 143).

Jack and Lady Horner and Katharine met the villagers and walked round all the morning inspecting sites for the War Memorial at Mells, a funny procession. I walked miles Sunday morning with Katharine Asquith to have a preliminary survey. Found a perfect site in the centre of the village, which no one else found, or thought of, and with a little tact and patience it was carried by the villagers with acclamation[1].

Yesterday afternoon went over a house restored by E. Lister. A bachelor household full of virginals and other precious furniture and a lot of whitewash that was for ever coming off and whitening us and the inhabitants.

I was very funny! and with some success.

The evening I spent in the church, repainted the inscription to Raymond Asquith, for which they were grateful, so my weekend was as a spring day, fun and tears. All their young men are killed.

On board ship to India   Nov.13.19.

I was introduced to Tilak[2] today a funny little wizen, ill-dressed and rather difficult to understand. Like all reformers I have met he talked of the brim and forgot the hat. I got one or two laughs out of him. He said we had governed India for 150 years and Government had given them no library or laboratory to equal any of those in the big provincial cities or in Oxford and without appliances how could they progress. I said that Faraday had to make his own test machines and Watts's first engines were so ill made by hand that the piston was as much as $\frac{1}{4}''$ smaller than the cylinder bore, that elaborate apparatus was not necessarily a help

1. The stone and yew War Memorial is in the High Street.
2. B. G. Tilak (1856–1920), Hindu extremist and leader of the campaign for Indian Home Rule.

and if India showed energy she would get a volume of help outside the Government.

Rylands Library at Manchester and indeed most if not all libraries were the gifts of individuals. A hundred years ago a woman was hung in England for stealing a loaf of bread.

That is the root, want of private energy and patrons in useful directions. You want men, not appliances, men, not books.

Homewood   Nov.26.19.

Mother is living in a most cruelly Spartan manner, with only one fire of wood and an oil stove. She is really crazy about it. She has a most peculiar set of servants who shout and sing and talk all day regardless of anyone's presence. Con of course encourages them and has them in to sing to her.

Tilak is as you say nothing but a wizened little old man and I wondered much at his power and influence till I saw him at the Albert Hall when his management of a crowd was magical. He said nothing of any interest or value but he manipulated them with marvellous cleverness and I understood he was a born manager of men.

Nanny Sleath and Ursula at Homewood

The Dowager Countess of Lytton at Homewood. Note the weeds.

Delhi   Nov.30.19.

It is warm here and of an evening walls give off a warm glow you feel standing near them. The sun pulls the joinery to pieces and makes the work look ruined before it is finished and the Indian cannot finish or make anything fit. Nor can he make a moulding straight – yet the fierce sun casts their shadows and the shadows go wobbly all over the place. A straight line should throw a straight shadow.

I have worked on my secretaries' houses, the bodyguard building, Government House, the railway station, the arrangements and rules for Chiefs' houses, the big arch at point C terminating the central vista [see Map, p. 229]. The Viceroy says a war monument is too difficult. I expect he is a cross-man [i.e. + not cross-patch] and not being able to do that will do nothing else but Hailey is for a fine monument. The solution is another Viceroy.

13 Mansfield Street   *Dec.3.19.*

Lady Astor[1] is in for Plymouth, the first woman in the House. Barbie and her friends are delighted. I think it is just as well a woman of her type should be first, it will disarm criticism. Barbie cannot now object if I follow! Except of course that I should stand for Labour which she would hate and should be introduced by a couple of miners instead of the PM [Lloyd George] and A.J.B[alfour]!

13 Mansfield Street   *Dec.11.19.*

There has been a lot of Cenotaph talk and fresh efforts made to have it removed to Parliament Square,[2] but I am glad to say that

1. Nancy Astor (1879–1964), succeeded her husband as Unionist MP for Plymouth after he succeeded his father as 2nd Viscount Astor.
2. The permanent Cenotaph was built in Whitehall on the site of the temporary Cenotaph of July 1919, in the face of official objections that it was an obstruction to traffic.

when a grant of £10,000 was asked for in the House of Com-
mons, it was finally stated it was to remain in its present position
and that the eminent architect was giving his services, great
cheers! so you have been figuring in the public eye this week. You
will see it all in your Times when it reaches you.

That kind Lady MacSack sent me a cheque for £25 as a
Christmas present. It is really very kind and generous of her, only
I wish she wouldn't. If you write do tell her I told you of it and
how delighted I was. The worst of it is I don't know how to spend
it, there are so many ways and I shall probably end by spending
three times as much!

My weekend was spent in deadly dull Theosophical Commit-
tees which lasted most of both days. On Monday evening went
off to St Albans to speak for the Labour Candidate. Nannie came
with me as she anticipated rowdiness!

Delhi   Dec.24.19.

The Committee, when we met again, chucked Baker's scheme for
bungalows. They did it nicely and they will be done by the
Engineers' staff under Baker and my supervision, etc. This means
H.B. won't do any and all the gerry men will come to me. They all
liked my railway bridge and my big gate. I may get the big one,
though it does cost more, a lot more, but it is no use putting up a
little thing when a big thing will alone tell.

I think much of you and ours and I do hope Mansfield Street is
behaving itself in Xmas garb and Nannie is happy with it and
children too.

Delhi   Dec.28.19.

Are you seriously thinking of standing for Parliament – to stand
that you may sit! It is very expensive and you will hate the
hustings. Labour is all right and nothing could be finer or more
chivalrous, but Labour hasn't yet learnt to play a clean game and
have a very narrow view. I don't see, I own, how you can expect
them to do aught else as the selfishness and narrow views of the
middle classes, Church and other vested interests have given no

Homewood. West front. Watercolour by Ursula Lutyens, aged sixteen.

lead. The only class who have given a lead in unselfishness is the few old types like old Lord Salisbury and Devonshire – men beyond all personal advantages. They ought to have Labour Peers but they must be men who are A1 at their craft and insistent on the honour of craftsmanship beyond any dollar scope.

Delhi   Jan.13.20.

There was a Delhi Committee meeting here on Saturday about the Council Chambers and Princes' Chamber building that H.B. is doing. I gave Baker no trust and the design he put forward did not fit the site![1] so I said what I thought and in the end I got my points, the site and the shape of the building. I insisted on his designing the new buildings to mask the faults of [the] secretariats he is building now, and I went for his shape, and for one that filled the site he didn't like, but I won the day I am glad to say.

One façade was a dreadful untidy arrangement and his excuse was that he had not worked on it but that it would be all right. I went for him and told the committee that Michelangelo could not make anything of it nor could God himself unless he worked by miracle and against the laws that govern this world.

I am getting on very well with the boys – the younger architects – and they all bring me their designs and I go over them and Keeling has been awfully nice allowing them more money when I point out how greatly the building would be improved. And the architects in the town outside the PWD come to me too. I am sure it is a better way to help than just pie talk. H.B. is out of it – he don't care one little d—n about the craft of architecture – and I really do believe his work all centres round and built on phrases that will sound well with his Round Table friends! A little more of the T square and a little less of the Round Table.

1. 'I struggled long with a three winged plan. . . . But as the demand for accommodation grew I was forced to resort to a circular plan which Lutyens favoured' (Baker, *Architecture and Personalities*, p. 75).

Lutyens and Persotum

Delhi   Jan.21.20.

I asked 12 Bombay art students and their masters to dinner.
Baker was rather stuffy about it[1] but I warned Persotum[2] and we
all sat down 'to a devil of a jam' and oh such an extraordinary
meal. Persotum provided every sort of Indian delicacy. They were
all Hindus except one – a Roman Catholic. They ate vast
quantities and drank endless bottles of ginger beer and lemonade.
One tried to smoke but failed. None of them would take wine or
spirit. I ate betel nut made up in a green leaf greatly to their
amusement, and tried to make them sing but only succeeded with
one who sang a long dreary monotonous Maratta song.

After dinner I got them all going after a little while drawing on
the walls of the big room in charcoal life-sized representations of
the Hindu gods. I had a very fierce light to throw silhouettes

1. Lutyens and Baker shared a bungalow until 1921.
2. Lutyens's bearer. When engaged in 1912, Lutyens described him as 'an
old scallywag dressed in an uncouth dhoti'; he went on to become a devoted
servant and friend.

on the wall and I posed them. But the master Solomon[1] started off and drew out of his head and did not follow the shadow. However, when he started I got the rest to draw and for some hour and a half you could hear nothing but the scratch of charcoal on the walls and now the room is in a wonderful mess with a gigantic Ram and Krishna, Kalee, Ganesh, Siva and many others whose names are elusive to remember as a telephone number.

Then I gave them toys which did really please them, so the evening I dreaded was a great success and they seemed pleased – especially at dining with us. The masters wanted them to sit at a separate table to myself but I was obdurate. I had only one table – anyone who dines with me sits at my table. The God of Art was above all castes and creeds so there was no question of caste or difficulty of that sort. The boys came from all parts of India. They couldn't understand my jokes but when they did they cringed and grinned. My transparencies were miracles!

13 Mansfield Street   *Jan.27.20.*

I have been asked to stand for Parliament for Luton! as a Labour Candidate. However they require financial backing which I cannot do – beside I might get in which would be too horrible!

Lucknow   Feb.2.20.

The Duke[2] is a great bore, I refer to the Bunder Buss of preparation, clothes, rehearsals, instructions, palms and red carpets and the ritual of Royalty which petrifies and makes for self-consciousness and interrupts work.

Will Reading[3] be an administrator or just a lawyer who will lip indisputable cases and leave mischief at that? You won't understand one bit what I mean. Will he be ruled by his own logic

1. Director of the Bombay School of Art.
2. Arthur William, Duke of Connaught (1850–1942) visited India in 1920–21 to open the Chamber of Princes, the Imperial Legislative Assembly and the Council of State.
3. Lord Reading (1860–1935) was Lord Chief Justice 1913–14 and Viceroy 1921–26.

which does not necessarily fit situations? I cannot imagine him being as numb nippelly as either Ha Ha Hardinge or Ch Chelmsford. I am sorry for C. No one but myself, as a Christian, would ask Fanny to lunch now they are en route for OUT.

I have got my black table top and a lot of talc pencils, so I can draw all through meals.

No news of Nicholson, yet. What is Bumps' portrait like?[1] I do hope he softened the one I saw, and turned her from the Bumps that wishes to scold and correct (ME) to the sort engaging a problem or a joke.

13 Mansfield Street   *Feb.11.20.*

[Neville] talked a lot of Judith, who has a case on against her father with reference to the Stud. He said they were much alike, both loved quarrelling and neither of them was a clean fighter and would not stop at anything to score a point. The reading of the case is very painful as Judith seems anxious to drag in everything against her father that she can, even her own awful letters to him, apparently she has got her mother's diaries dating from many years with all her wrongs set down, and Judith is determined to make her father suffer as much as possible for his crimes. It is a painful and sordid story.

Unfortunately I missed Pamela the other day but Ursula took her over the house and she told her to say her eyes were black and her heart green with envy of this house![2] I was delighted as she had only seen it when we first got in and was very sniffy about it.

I was greatly amused at your account of your Bombay students' dinner. How glad they must have been to have you put them at their ease. I can see Baker stiff and solemn.

13 Mansfield Street   *Feb.25.20.*

I dined with Vic and Pamela. Pamela was rather amusing about Margot Asquith,[3] who is writing her memoirs and apparently she

1. Now in the National Portrait Gallery, it was commissioned by Lutyens.
2. Pamela Lytton was referring to the black walls and the green painted floor of the drawing room.
3. Margot Tennant (1868–1945) married H. H. Asquith in 1894. Her *Autobiography* (1920) is indeed outspoken about A. J. Balfour.

says that on putting down everything she knows about Arthur Balfour she is horrified to find how dreadful he is. She wrote to him and told him this and asked if he would care therefore to see what she had written before she published it. His answer was most characteristic, that he did not wish to see anything as he had every confidence in her affection for him!

Delhi   March 22.20.

Saturday afternoon the Rajah of Karika (?) came with four other gentlemen all members of the Legislative Chamber. Karika a Hindu and others were Moslems. Went over the site with them and showed them drawings.

There is a mosque ruined and abandoned standing in the middle of one of my water canals and opposite a tomb also ruined and neglected. I showed it to my Mahommedan friends but they say they cannot be moved. The tomb – yes if the family chose to sell it. The mosque belongs to all Mahommedans in all parts of the world. I offered £10 towards building a new one but it was no use. The Khalifat question is very uppermost and every suggestion I made was scored off. I got my own back when I said that the first Hindu Viceroy would destroy them. I suggested he should move them and I would put up a stone to record his public spirit 'and send me down to posterity as a tomb wrecker'.

One old gentleman would keep on praying. He had his carpet out 3 times. Directly they got interested he began his praying. I asked one of them if he had been doing anything particularly naughty that he should pray so much, and they laughed so much that the praying man was perturbed but after the prayer was over and I told him what my question had been, he joined in the laugh as much as the others and the laugh turned at me yet with me. But it is disconcerting to show a man Delhi when every time you get interested he prays and prostrates.

They are much more conscious of their temporal estates and powers than in any public interest or public achievement. I gave them tea. They will eat large quantities of very sweet cake and biscuits and prefer sweet lemonade to tea.

13 Mansfield Street   *March 20.20.*

Granny came up yesterday for the night to go to Neville's exhibition of pictures at Redfern's in Bond Street,[1] a great family gathering I believe. Mother lunched here and was very excited because a note came to say Queen Alexandra would go at 3 so she rushed off to receive her. I would not go, hating Royalties and imagine my feelings when at 3.30 I was told Queen Alexandra was downstairs! I had to rush down and there was the Queen and retinue. I bobbed and shouted[2] at her and tried to explain the mistake. A wonder I was not in an overall with my sleeves up! Neville was delighted with the first day and sold many of his pictures and was in great spirits.

In train, Jamnagar to Bombay   April 4.20.

We reached Jamnagar at 2 o'clock and there was red carpet on to which I lightly leapt, mildly thinking either that the Jam Sahib[3] was expected at once or possibly a further extension of the Jam Sahib's hospitality to me! But no – it was for the British Agent. I had got out too soon! However he stepped out with much more dignity and assuredness than I when they fired a salute of 13 guns uncomfortably close which gave me a sense of discomfort in having to do with a small power! A lump of army was there who saluted and did soldierlike things and a band played the Jamnagar national anthem which seemed to be a mixture of them all. Cadences of the Old Hundredth, God Save the King and bits of God bless the Prince of Wales – rather like broken up jigsaw puzzle.

    Motors met us, 3 or 4, and off we went to the guest house covered with garlands of jasmine and roses where a mighty lunch awaited us.

    After lunch we went over the palace which is in process of being built and [on] which H.H. wanted my advice. The secretary

---

1. In 1937 the Redfern Gallery moved to Cork Street, where it is now.
2. Queen Alexandra was very deaf.
3. Sir Ranjitsinhji (Ranji) Jam Sahib of Jamnagar (1872–1934), the famous cricketer. Despite much talk of building, only the bases of two statues in Jamnagar were executed; however, throughout the 1920s Lutyens gave advice on the Jamnagar Town Plan and they continued to be friends.

general, a young Indian, was my help and guide. He had been to Oxford and was proud of his degree. There are 3 secretaries who run the State and do all the ministerial duties for about £1000 a year each.

Well, we went all over the palace half built and over the store rooms where the Jam Sahib keeps the furniture and an odd collection it is. Silver and gold chairs and wonderful trick and surprise furniture that must have cost £s in Paris and London, and a lot of plate. He has, too, innumerable skins and stuffed beasts and some 400 R. Academy on the line pictures.

Then tea and at about ½ 4 when it was cooler we went off to see the city – just a first preliminary view, and to various shops to have a look at what the city could produce. King-cob stuff etc. like what they make at Benares. The state grows cotton and then the mild climate with its delightful and almost ever blowing sea breeze – oranges and plants we know and love instead of the usual Indian growth which is generally of a sullen and often angry disposition – offered a feeling of contentment. And the people seem more open hearted and with a gaiety of face and expression as though they lived to live instead of living to die – an Indian habit.

I got the state engineer to give me the plans of the city and of the palace which I studied till it was time for dinner.

Then [the next day] to the old city and went over the old palace – the ladies being locked up whilst I enjoyed their premises. There is some wonderful painting, much that was squalid and much to wonder at. One room had been left for 2 or 3 hundred years – no one would enter it – (I did!) nor clean it. The old Jam's bed just as it was, all falling to pieces. The quilted stuff on the ceilings and great painted red blotch on the wall stuck over with stamps of gold to appease the Goddess, for murder had been committed 200 years or more ago. I offered to clean it up but my offer, though meant, was not taken seriously. The Treasury, little courts and an absurd Durbar hall hung stiff with glass chandeliers and looking glasses. The Jam Sahib wants this all improved and modernised but I have persuaded him to leave it, to protect the paintings and to use it as a state museum and regalia, etc.

There is a great wall surrounding Jamnagar with many gates – all fortified – and two great forts standing in a lake with the wall running across the centre of the lake so that half the lake was within the walls to ensure a supply of water to a besieged population. Half this wall the Jam Sahib has pulled down and proposed to put suspension bridges between the forts. This idea I hope I have nipped in the bud and he said if I thought it right he would rebuild the wall.

There was a funny little painted watch tower which I hope to have saved for the time being at all events.

Then back to lunch or late breakfast at about 12. Afterwards I had the plans out and the engineer up and I worked about 1 till 4 on the plans and made a scheme – a tentative one. At 4 tea and then about quarter to 5 went off to see the city in view of my suggestions and its improvements etc. and to see the sites I had allocated to the various buildings required for state purposes etc.

I only saw the Jam Sahib from 9.30 till 12 when the lights went out. They have not got a proper electric supply yet. There are 1st rate oysters at Jamnagar.

I went through my plans. The plans for the two houses at Delhi which he liked. The plan suggesting the main roads and improvements to the old city. And then when it came to the palace I had to tell him that all I could advise if I was to help him was to pull it down, cut his loss and begin again. He said he was afraid I would say that and he was quite prepared for it. It means a 9 lac – that is about £100,000 loss, less the material we can save but I doubt if he has really spent as much as that.

He also wants three houses in various parts of his territory to save the bother of having to set up and go into camps. He will be home [in England] in May and June when I will see him.

E.L.L. in dressing gown given by Jam Sahib

Government House, Madras   April 8.20.

I arrived here yesterday from Bombay. Mrs Besant was at Bombay and came up to Government House to see Lloyd.[1] But I had to be in Bombay town keeping appointments with Colonel Meyer and the architect of the Baroda state.[2]

It was luck just catching the Lloyds. I gave Lloyd a lot of advice – architectural, and I think I shall be roped in to do the Bombay extensions which are to be on land reclaimed from the sea in Back Bay. I have pleaded for a Venice with sea ways, canals and lagoons, instead of the bay being filled in with bumps and lumps and no fun. It would be a glorious scheme.

Madras is – expectedly – quite different to any other part of India that I have seen. But oh the people – the scallywags. Awful faces, to me degenerate, very dark, very naked and awful habits of hair dressings. The bulk of the faces merely loony. Willingdon[3] says they are most unusually intelligent – so there.

The old houses built by the old Englishmen appeal to me as being sincere and with the souls of gentlemen and none of that horrible Eurasian architecture that our modern sentimentalists promote. I have seen Adyar [the Theosophical Headquarters] from a distance across the river. Willingdon adores 'naughty Annie'. Lloyd was sorry he did not think of asking her to lunch at Bombay to meet me and I her. It is amusing to find her hobnobbing and working with governors!

The Catholic churches here are pathetic. Good little buildings too with Italian influence, save the monstrosity of a Cathedral they have achieved. The river and sea here is good in combination but oh the chances they have missed, and the casual way they have of placing buildings – anyhow, anywhere, like parcels on a railway platform. Selecting sites where the foundations are easiest, leaving to the future impossible problems and costs that

1. George Lloyd (1879–1941), Governor of Bombay 1918–23, created Baron 1925. 'Lloyd, cursed by the prefix George, a Tory demagogue', was one of Lutyens's fellow-passengers on the voyage to India in December 1914; Lutyens found him 'a mannish man with streaks of niceness and gentleness about him'. The Bombay extension was not designed by Lutyens.

2. About a library he had designed in Baroda for the Gaekwar (1863–1939) which was not executed. Lutyens built him a palace in New Delhi in 1921–23.

3. Governor of Madras 1919–24. He had invited Lutyens to advise on re-planning the town, but the project did not get as far as the drawing-board.

are bound to militate against good building and honourable labours.

However, I am going to have an up and at them about the absurd size of compounds – so large that they cannot be kept up or clean and as wages rise the sanitary standard is bound to drop.

The Indian is hopeless and we have taught them very little.

The Jam Sahib was saying how badly they used his houses when a chief came to stay with him – wiping their betel-stained hands on silk curtains and spitting their blood-coloured chew everywhere. Misusing furniture and breaking everything and anything. He is building special houses for them. They ought to have a sanitary crusade and drop politics. It is all gas, hot air and squalor resulting.

There is an enormous amount of building going to be done all through India – specially under the Reform.[1] Is it our swan song? I only hope it may be a good tune well sung to our and India's dignity.

Whilst at Madras I received a telegram from Harcourt Butler asking me to build the Lucknow University and to state officially my terms.[2] That may prove a thrilling job as there is a river to deal with and a very understanding chief in Butler, full of human understanding and some Solomon wit.

I had many tender farewells at Madras and I have been allowed to spend £50 on buying books for the PWD architects. They have no books and this I am asking permission to do wherever I go – to buy books. Only those that Wren could have had access to but of what use is it to buy any book he did not know until we are able to do better than what he did? The tons of art publication might just as well go to the sea – save for record.

I reached Colombo on the 12th at about 7.30. and went direct to the Galle Face Hotel where a room with its own bathroom had been reserved for me. I was not met which was a little bit disconcerting, but I soon got in touch with people and my fair way was cleared from anxiety. Mr Duncum, secretary to the Chamber of Commerce, bear-led me and I saw Colombo and settled to my own satisfaction the site for the war monument[3] – and the popular vote being for a column of victory – its form.

1. The Government of India Act of 1919, which introduced a system of limited self-government in the provinces.

2. The designs were not executed.

3. Executed in 1921.

Instead of the usual angel I have suggested a brazier to burn petrol and make an occasion – a column of smoke by day and of fire by night. The Governor and the Chairman of Committee are in London where I shall see them but I achieved the agreement of the Committee in Colombo – the PWD whose chief is a charming Colonel (name forgotten!) The green of Colombo after the bare plains of North India gave a volte face feeling.

There is a fine church built by the R. Catholics with a monastery built during the Dutch occupation. Like at Cape Town the Dutch architecture is excellent in feeling and design – far better than any Britisher has achieved. Well placed and distinguished and without any of that innate and ignorant vulgarity in which the Britishers indulge.

The work suffers from indigenous labours but the mind behind is good. Baker, with all his mental unction, fails in this respect lamentably. Everything spoilt by some mental reservation which in practice produces bad, undigested design. In the old Dutch church the Dutchmen's faith in their own future is pathetic. The number of bare shields on tombs left to be filled by the generations yet to come and which never came.

Going through the native town – it was some great Hindu festival – the new year? but this I saw celebrated at Delhi or was it Bikanir? I came across a great decorated car dragged by natives (I don't know whether Cingalese or Tamils!) accompanied by a tornado of tom toms and crowds of very naked and very dark folk. I insisted on passing it and the police encouraged us. And then I saw what amazed me – a really beautiful – he was ascetic to look at – young man, covered with mud – or rather dust, garlanded with flowers and no clothes but a loin cloth writhing. He had just prostrated himself under this gaudy temple and its wheels had gone over him. Whilst we waited to get through the crowd he turned on his back and lay quiet. I don't know if he was killed – his eyes were closed and there was no evidence of injury. He was charming to look at. I cursed priestcraft and wondered why it was the Archbishop of Canterbury did not induce his flock to prostrate themselves under brewers' vans.

I got back to lunch when I received Barbie's telegram. 'Am engaged to Euan Wallace'.[1] How I long to know what you think

1. Euan Wallace (1892–1941), Conservative MP from 1922 and Minister of Transport 1934–41. He had been married before to Idina, daughter of Lady De La Warr, the 'Bolter' of Nancy Mitford's novels.

and how I longed to get into communication with you and to see you and Barbie. I telegraphed to Barbie with my heart full of love and emotion. Bless her I am so moved.

S.S. *Pilsna*   April 23.20.

I did a lot of work at Madras. Mrs Besant only returned on the day I left so I did not see her but saw Adyar across the river. It marches with Guindy – a place which is to become the Governor's House. The Government House in Madras to be used for government secretariat. The state rooms and the old Assembly Hall to remain intact for public functions. A new council chamber built, as pendant to the Assembly Hall, a war monument and a Victory Hall. But alas the English method of build-let-build makes impossible problems. Madras is intersected by waterways and rivers – none of which have been taken advantage of, and as the formation is one of sand ridges and boggy filled valleys they build on the ridges and leave to the future the difficulty of building on the mud flats.

In fact it is all just as short sighted and foolish as our wonderful system run by brass hatted educationalists alone can produce, who receive salaries and pensions too small for men, too much for purring opportunists.

And then they have a passion for domes and towers. 3 buildings are in prospect of which I saw the designs – all in a row, each a huge structure and each surmounted by 5 domes. Can you imagine St Paul's Cathedral with 5 domes and right and left of it buildings again with 5 domes and each separate building being distinguished with originality as though it was a virtue. And then there are the buildings already erected – possessing towers and domes, Eurasian in style, which can only produce that particular form of vulgarity in its architecture that the English occupation of India has for its monument.

13 Mansfield Street   Sept.17.20.

One thing – a very little thing – crossed me. Robert has gone off with my only pair of brown shoes. He shouldn't do it without saying. He is very callous about some things. I shall give him the shoes. I hope he won't hunger strike over them! A joke.

———

Homewood *Sept.18.20.*

I forgot to say about Robert taking your shoes! You mustn't be too serious and regard it as a sign of depravity! Barbie used to do just the same. It is very natural and really should be taken as a compliment. I felt immensely flattered at Barbie condescending to wear my clothes!

CHAPTER TEN

1920–1940

THE REMAINING LETTERS span the twenty years from 1920 to 1940. Though the flow of letters continues unabated, the quality is uneven, and there is 𝒔𝒖𝒎𝒆 [some] deterioration in Lutyens's handwriting. Even Lady Emily complained: 'with all my efforts I only master a word here and there!'

Lutyens visited India each winter from 1920 to 1931, when Viceroy's House was officially opened. But Lady Emily no longer stayed at home: during the 1920s she travelled the world in pursuit of spiritual grace and Krishnamurti, usually taking with her her two youngest children. Every summer after 1923 there was a gathering of the Order of the Star in the East, known as a Star Camp, at Ommen in Holland. In December 1921 Lady Emily accompanied her husband to India for the first time. He told her he was nervous lest she should 'suddenly think it right or comfortable to wear vegetable sandals or your hair undone'. She spent little time in New Delhi, and stayed mostly at the Theosophical Headquarters at Adyar, as she did on her four succeeding visits to India. In 1924 she took Betty and Mary to Australia, where Leadbeater had set up a teaching community in Sydney; in 1926 she and Mary were at Ojai, Krishna's home in California, for three months.

Then, in 1929, the merry-go-round came to a halt. Krishnamurti dissolved the Order of the Star in the East, rejected the role of Messiah and repudiated his followers, continuing as teacher of the world. Lady Emily was left lost and unhappy. She turned to her husband, who by now found the increasingly litigious and eccentric Lady Sackville nothing but a trial. 'He seemed', she wrote, 'to understand without words all that I was going through and welcomed me back without a single reproach or reminder of how much of our lives together I had wasted.'[1]

1. *Candles in the Sun*, p. 186.

Krishnamurti in 1926

As the children grow up they feature more in Lutyens's letters. Barbara, the only child who reacted strongly against her mother's way of life, achieved social success and, with her marriage to Euan Wallace, the conventional, well-ordered home she longed for. Robert, by contrast, eloped at the age of nineteen with Eva, a niece of Chaim Weizmann and seven years his senior – a marriage to which Lutyens was never reconciled. Robert wrote, painted and designed with equal facility; perhaps his greatest flair was for interior decoration, which he practised in the 1930s. Though without any formal training he joined his father as a partner in a few of his later buildings, notably Middleton Park, Oxfordshire (1938).

Ursula married Viscount Ridley in 1924. Elisabeth, the most Bohemian of the five, became a composer and enjoyed a *succès d'estime* as a pioneer of the twelve-tone scale. Mary became an author, first a novelist and later a biographer of note, best known for her works on the Pre-Raphaelites, Krishnamurti and her father.

The years between the wars found Lutyens as busy as ever. 'Only a few of us', recalled A. S. G. Butler, 'realised then that he worked much harder than anybody and that he rarely – if ever – thought of much except designing buildings.'[1] Though by now the most eminent of establishment architects, Lutyens was in some ways 'the greatest architect of the immediate past rather than the leader to the future'.[2] From Le Corbusier and the architects of the Modern Movement he was 'poles apart'. Nor was he at ease in the new world of post-war Britain: the age of the common man and the cocktail bar. Essentially an Edwardian, he was quite unable to project himself into the lives of the occupants of municipal housing schemes, office blocks or even luxurious penthouses. On the contrary, he was one of the generation for whom 'the twenties seemed that they might fulfil Edwardian promise of restored humanism. The end was no doubt coming, but till it came let us live, they said, as fully, as well, as handsomely as we can.'[3]

Something of this spirit pervades Lutyens's private work in the inter-war years. The Midland Bank, Poultry (1924–39), and Britannic House (1920–24) – 'that Edwardian cynosure, "a raging beauty"'[4] – are indeed masterpieces of classical design. So, too, is Gledstone Hall (1923), one of his last and grandest country houses. Yet there is something a little anachronistic about such a mansion in the 1920s: as Butler put it in 1950, Gledstone 'has as little to do with housing the people – our sole concern to-day – as a canvas by Titian has to do with distempering their ceilings'.[5]

The same can be said of Queen Mary's Dolls' House. The idea of presenting the Queen with a Dolls' House originated at a dinner-party given by Sir Herbert Morgan in 1920. With meticu-

1. *Architecture*, vol. i, p. 20.
2. Hussey, *Lutyens*, p. 377.
3. ibid., p. 469.
4. ibid.
5. *Architecture*, vol. i, p. 55.

Drawings for Queen Mary's Dolls' House

lous care and wit Lutyens made the designs and co-ordinated the sixty artists and one hundred and fifty craftsmen he persuaded to contribute. It was designed to boost the depressed trade of post-war Britain. Yet it was less an advertisement than, as A. C. Benson wrote in *The Book of the Dolls' House*, 'a memorial of the art and craft and manufacture of the time': more a museum in miniature than a blueprint for post-war life.

If at one level Lutyens's response to the harsh realities of his time was to re-create a vanishing world, at another, deeper, level he sought escape in pure aesthetics. It was in this latter vein that his most important works of these years were conceived: the Memorial to the Missing of the Somme at Thiepval (1927–32) and his unbuilt masterpiece, the design for Liverpool Cathedral. Both designs belong to what has been called his Elemental Mode, first evident at the Cenotaph: 'a type of design in which classical notation was gradually reduced or eliminated, retaining the elements and proportions, to which he added subtleties of entasis, visual compensation and curvature by means of a basically simple but complex geometry'.[1]

At Thiepval Lutyens was required to provide wall space for the names of the 73,357 men missing in the battles of the Somme between 1915 and 1918. His solution was a geometrical one, consisting of four solid blocks penetrated by a series of interlock-

1. Hussey, *Lutyens*, p. 462.

Sketch for the war monument at Thiepval

ing arches – the 'breathtaking' culmination of his work for the Imperial War Graves Commission.

The commission for Liverpool came about as a result of a meeting in 1929 at the Garrick Club with Richard Downey, the newly appointed Roman Catholic Archbishop of Liverpool. Downey aired his intention of building a cathedral, and soon afterwards invited Lutyens to Liverpool. 'I was surprised,' recalled Lutyens, 'and certainly as pleased, dare I say, as Punch':

> I went to Liverpool and arrived just before lunch. I was shown into a large dull-gloomed room, and waited, feeling nervous and rather shy, till in came His Grace – a red biretta on his head and a voluminous sash round his ample waist. . . . He held out a friendly hand. His pectoral Cross swung towards me, and the first words he said were 'Will you have a cocktail?'[1]

In the genial Dr Downey Lutyens found a client he could enjoy. And in the commission to build a cathedral he found an outlet for that mystical fusion of pure intellect with the spirit which he called 'aesthetic science'.

1. ibid., p. 527.

Lutyens's provisional design for Liverpool Cathedral was published in 1930; the final design – much modified – together with a model was exhibited at the Royal Academy in 1934. But, though the foundation stone was laid in 1933, by 1940 when work was suspended because of the war only the crypt had been built. After Downey's death in 1953 Lutyens's design was shelved on grounds of expense, and the circular erection by Frederick Gibberd – a disappointment on any reckoning – was built in its stead.

Lutyens's Cathedral is one of the finest buildings never built. The crowning achievement of his elemental classicism, it represents 'the latest and supreme attempt to embrace Rome, Byzantium, the Romanesque and the Renaissance in one triumphal and triumphant synthesis.'[1]

On board SS *Caledonia* [sailing to Bombay]   Dec.19.20.

I have been working very hard and the Captain has allowed me to occupy a position of splendid isolation on the bridge. But today and yesterday was so rough and it was all so uncomfortable he nobly gave me permission to work in the chart room. The windows had to be kept shut as the seas and their spray might get in – it was hot. But I got happy and unmindful of all difficulties when once I got my pencils into a zareeba wherein they could not roll.

I have been working on Gledstone Hall and the owner,[2] a pleasant cotton spinner, is on board so I have to work to keep his interest to a pitch higher than the toss of waves.

But Lord! how I sweated in that little red hot room at the top of the ship – up and down and oh! the slip slap on the windows and the big steering wheel moving mysteriously and mechanical whilst the engine bells ringing amidst all the hub and dub of a chart room. . . . Then my table was of glass to protect charts under it – not conducive to draughtsmanship.

1. Sir John Summerson, *Catalogue 1981*, p. 52.
2. Sir Amos Nelson (d. 1947). Gledstone, Yorkshire, was described in 1950 by Butler as 'a work of art worthy of being listed, one day, as a national monument' (*Architecture*, vol. i, p. 55). The garden was the last on which Lutyens collaborated with Gertrude Jekyll.

I have read the first, am now in the second vol. of Gibbon's *Decline and Fall*.

I always have and yet ever yet the hope of winning you back away from your cranks, to my eccentrics, or vice versa if you will. So you spin wonderful finest linen to cover my marvellously designed tables! and we purr not spar when together.

13 Mansfield Street   Aug.17.21.

I have had the first estimates for dolls' house furniture. 13 state portrait frames – £50, and have sent it to Mrs Marshall Field, and £30 for the cradle for the Prince of the Blood, which I have sent to H. Konig.[1] These are the first and the first attempt to land a fish so I await the replies with interest. The house itself goes on.

The Queen writes she is nervous as to how the dolls' house opens. She wants to be able to open it herself without calling servants! And asks questions about the hall door. Can't you see the Queen going hush hush to play with the dolls?[2]

The Wimbornes had a terrible squash at Ashby when the P[rince] of W[ales] was there so they are going to add lavishly in spite of taxes and hard times!

I sent a lot of pictures to Winston Churchill as to how to draw! I hope he will be amused![3]

1. 'The cradle was made of ivory and applewood with silver ornamentation.' The bills were sent to two of the 500 donors listed in *The Book of the Dolls' House*, ed. A. C. Benson and Lawrence Weaver (1924).
2. When Queen Mary eventually did play with the Dolls' House in 1924 she was puzzled by the pillowcases on the Queen's bed, which were embroidered 'M.G.' and 'G.M.' When she asked what they stood for, Lutyens replied: 'For "May George?" ma'am, and "George May!" '
3. In a letter to Ursula dated 14 August 1921, Lutyens wrote: 'I have been drawing a lot of pics for Winston Churchill to show him how to sketch and get

shapes a hat
this will turn into a boat
quite easy do you see?

and then my eggs   a horse

lovely lady sort of thing
against a well.

Delhi   Feb.20.22.

I showed the P of W[1] the model [of Viceroy's House]. All he said on sight of it through the periscope was 'Good God'. He spoke more to Baker in that he said Delhi should be stopped, money waste etc. He seemed nervous and bored, certainly self-conscious, but he has great attraction and is pleasant to look at. He hit a policeman on his legs with his cane who was shoving back a crowd of untidy masons. They, the masons, gleed at the rebuff to the hated policeman. I was sorry for the policeman too.

Delhi   March 4.22.

My own darling, I am so glad to hear that you are warm and happy. I am warm here and unhappy. There was a Delhi committee yesterday. Various questions came up – decoration etc. Baker's points of view always rattle me. The inclined way came up – the last point and we all went to the model room and cut the site. A lot of cross talk and Keeling announced it would cost 25 lacs – half as much nearly as Government House! 25 lacs is £166,650 about! Reading had written in July that he could not open the question again. But he has – it awaits his decision. £160,000 is a huge sum. It was £8000 in 1916. I cannot go on with Delhi if this is turned [down] now and this large sum involved. I must chuck it. My patience has been my undoing, and I can work if there is a fair prospect of a conversion to my view, my original plan and essential lines, but with this large estimate to repair it makes the question so serious that I have – if Reading is against me – to resign.

It will be a great relief getting away from Baker Rash. I shall speak to Montagu when I get back, or telegraph directly Reading decides – and the King – and then I shall have freedom to speak and make an explanation in the Press.

Baker played all his incidental music and put his little summer houses up against my incline. I have few years left and I must cut myself off [from] such a fiasco as this. Reading told me he would come out soon, but with Hailey on the Council I fear it will be useless, it all depends on the conviction Reading may have and the courage he has if his conviction is in my favour.

1. The Prince of Wales made a three-month tour of India in 1922.

Adyar[1]   March 9.22.

I was very much upset by your letter which arrived here this morning and sent you a telegram begging you not to take any action till you heard from me. I am frightfully sorry for your worry and disappointment but I think it would be absolutely fatal to your whole professional career if you resigned and on that point. It would be the biggest triumph of Baker's life and give every enemy a handle to blaspheme. You have made one big blunder and you must pay for it. Be a man and stand up to your own mistake. You are perfectly right to make your protest and do everything you can to get the matter altered but when once you are beaten take it like a man. Register your opinion and your protest in such a way that future generations will know and exonerate you from blame and then go ahead. There is something much bigger involved than only your own ideal of what is right for the job. You have a duty to India – a duty to the Indian Government and I think you would be doing a really wrong and mean thing to both if you resign now.

Now Montagu has gone, your chief friend and supporter, you must face a hand lost.[2] *Some day it will be recognised that you are right. Today, if you resign, you will have no support in India or England and it will simply be attributed to personal pique. Don't you see the Government dare not spend all that money now.*

[Lady Emily prevailed. Though the Government of India refused to reopen the question of the rise, Lutyens accepted his Bakerloo and saw Viceroy's House through to its completion in 1931.]

Hotel Castello, Trento, Italy[3]   Aug.26.24.

I do not give you much comfort or happiness so if at any time you feel it would make you happier to bring another woman into your life I shall never reproach you or feel you have wronged me. I so much want you to be happy.

1. Lady Emily was staying at the Theosophical Headquarters with Krishna and Mrs Besant, where she rejoiced in 'dining under the banyan tree seated on the ground with palm leaf plates' (letter from Lady Emily, 19 February 1922).
2. Montagu lost his seat in the election of 1922.
3. A beautiful old castle turned into a hotel where Lady Emily was staying with Betty, Mary, Krishna and Nitya.

---

13 Mansfield Street   Aug.29.24.

Another woman is doubtless alluring but how can I afford it?

Hotel Castello, Trento, Italy   *Sept.3.24.*

If Mansfield Street becomes too much of a white elephant let me take it over and run a community. This is only if we are in straits.
   If you can love another woman and be happy I shall only give you my blessing. You say you cannot afford it. Well, we must make every economy so that you can and we must think out how to do it.

13 Mansfield Street   Sept.8.24.

How can I take another woman? and give her a life with due protection etc. Oh Ems! You are impracticable. I know you mean sweetly and well and I appreciate your conscience which prompts your thought. All I do-or can do is to bless you and help you still your conscience but it is a rotten spoilt life and there let it rot! Your solution can only lead to a greater rot. Licence has a scourge at both ends.

Blagdon,[1] Northumberland   Sept.1.24.

I arrived here Saturday morning and found Ursy radiant and very happy, Matt engrossed in turning a little platinum box, useless no matter, on his lathe.
   I walked by the sea and rocks with Lady [Morrison] Bell[2] who was a Powerscourt, Irish, a regular Irishwoman, good fun but

   1. Lutyens was staying with Lord Ridley, who was engaged to Ursula. Built about 1730, Blagdon was altered by James Wyatt in 1778–91, added to by Bonomi *circa* 1830 and again in 1898; it was restored to its original shape by Ursula Ridley and Robert Lutyens in 1949. Gertrude Jekyll designed the quarry garden and a yew walk; Lutyens added a canal, a sunken tennis court and an ornamental pond at the end of the yew walk in 1937.
   2. Lilah Wingfield (b. 1888), daughter of 7th Viscount Powerscourt, married 1912 Sir Clive Morrison-Bell, Unionist MP 1910–31.

very cynical about love and marriage and boys and girls in particular. It made me feel I had not been firm enough about settlements. However, God wills and fate as faith, fulfils. Do you remember 'Yet as faith wills so fate fulfils?' Have I lost faith? since my fate is ill. Poor darling Emy and I sometimes see you –

Here come Ursy and Matt to talk house. Ursy sends you so much love . . .

I was disturbed and I forgot how it was I saw you, as something in a sea of misconceptions and a mirage of inconsequences, that sort of thing. Bless you.

Blagdon. The house is like a politician's thought materialised. Nothing fits and lots of bad ornament, misapplied at that. The endless gardens in different directions – half unfinished, the other half in process of destruction and nothing much kept up. It all wants reducing but that costs money. I have advised the children to do nothing. Wait and see. . . .

We have frightened Lady Ridley[1] (and amused her) by talking of towers and swimming bath.

The park is jolly and the views wide and dignified, but the trees are in a neglected state, it all wants some twenty hefty men as house, park and garden maids.

I have stayed here a day longer than I intended as we went over to Durham. I had never been to Durham so now I have seen it.

Oh the brutal mentality of the church – its pompous careless-ness in the preservation of these inherited buildings and the hideousness of all the squalid modernities of the surrounding towns and villages. There can be no healthy faith in the country and the fighting bishops become squabbling intellectinos.

Hotel Castello, Trento, Italy   *Sept.7.24.*

Such a dear letter from you from Blagdon. I knew you would hate the house and it is pretty dreadful, but to me there is such charm about the park, wide spaces and trees which compensate for everything.

1. Rosamund (Rosie) Guest (d. 1947), daughter of 1st Lord Wimborne, married 1899 the 2nd Viscount Ridley. She inherited little of the Guest money but much of their bossiness. She had plans drawn up to double the size of the house, building a replica of Blagdon linked to the original by an enormous gallery.

13 Mansfield Street   Sept.11.24.

I had a long talk with Rudyard Kipling. He said my great war stone, hating the word, was an inspiration and it looked well no matter where it was placed. The only mistake I had made was to have an inscription on it. Even my proposed 'Amen'. It wanted no inscription. It was Rudyard Kipling who made them put on 'Their names endureth for ever'[1] and even that was cut down from a longer proposition he had made. It was nice of him.

I also told him of my St Quentin monument[2] and he seemed pleased.

I teach all day.[3] Counting drawings and explaining what is wrong and why with them! Within my limitations a very practical school. It is the other 'teachers' who talk and upset work as Ruskin. He broke up years and years of effective teaching by his language and formulated ideas and thoughts as to how things should be. The practice awful. Somerset House on one side by a mediocre man[4] and the Natural History Museum on the Ruskin side by way of an example of a so-called great man – Waterhouse.[5]

13 Mansfield Street   April 7.25.

Next Saturday I go to America! returning May 2nd in time for the RA Banquet. My model for the monument in St Quentin has come out very well, it has gone to the RA. I am going to do the Embassy at Washington, a distinction. Dinner and lunch invitations come in by wire two a day from America so my time will be full. I rather dread it but it will be an experience.

Work goes on and I am busy.

I dined at the Other Club.[6] F.E.[7] and Winston were there. F.E.

1. 'Lutyens's forgetfulness on this "literary" point is typical' (Hussey, Lutyens, p. 389). 'Their name liveth for evermore' would be correct.

2. The scheme for a Memorial to the Missing at St Quentin was abandoned in 1927. The design was developed for the memorial at Thiepval.

3. Lutyens was Visitor of the Royal Academy Architecture School.

4. Sir William Chambers (1726–96) designed Somerset House (1776).

5. Alfred Waterhouse (1830–1905) designed the Natural History Museum in 1868.

6. The Other Club was a dining club founded by F. E. Smith and Winston Churchill in 1911 to bring together men of different views and vocations.

7. F. E. Smith (1872–1930), created Lord Birkenhead in 1919, was Secretary of State for India 1924–28. In 1930 Lutyens designed his altar tomb at Charlton, Northamptonshire.

and W. told me nothing and F.E. was in drink – not drunk somehow. Very witty but talked ceaselessly making a continuous speech and rather bad in form. The toast to the dead members since we met, by some odd chance got into a comic vein etc. Members left and we were all rather unhappy. Winston did his best to keep things straight. So the evening was a disappointment.

The *Daily Mail* gave me a lunch. The Dolls' House made £4970 at the Ideal Home Exhibition. The *Daily Mail* rounded up the figure to £5000 and then framed it in guineas – 5000 guineas.

On board S.S. "HOMERIC."   April 28.25.

Here I am returning! and it's all over.

We landed at the docks 3.30 Saturday afternoon. I was met by 3 or 4 architects – Corbett,[1] Hastings? Bolton? I have forgotten their names.

The reception was just a little formal and shy making and I broke the ice by saying to a very serious architect – walking through the dock buildings – 'Ah, so this is McKim's[2] great railway station!' He answered in all gravity, 'Oh no, these are the docks. You shall see the Pennsylvania later.' To which I retorted 'I think I have got your goat'. Roars of laughter and then it all went famous and chitter chat – quips, jibes and arms in arms, etc.

Next morning went off to Washington by a 10 o'clock train. I was early as usual so had a good look at McKim's great railway station [1902–11]. A colossal hall modelled on the baths of Caracalla – 150 feet high! Of no use. Great waiting rooms right and left and these led to another great iron roofed hall from which stairways went down to the trains underground. You are kept in the waiting rooms until a few minutes before the train is due to start and men bellow the information that echoes through the buildings. Anticipation of one's own train and the hollering of trains not the one one wants keep one on tenterhooks. Well the train came. We passed Pennsylvania, Baltimore and reached Washington about 3.30. The countryside is dreadfully untidy,

1. H. W. Corbett (1873–1954), influential skyscraper-designer and theorist.
2. C. F. McKim (1847–1909) of McKim, Mead & White.

little houses of wood stuck down anywhere. No gardens and all squalid and distressingly unhomely. The dogwood was in flower and cherry blossom out. But for a flowering tree here and there the country seemed a waste of tears.

I arrived at Washington. No one met me. I went [to] the Embassy in a taxi cab. Sir Esme[1] and Lady Isabella Howard were out. Lady Betty Feilding[2] was there. Jolly, young. She motored me rour̄ d the town and I saw everything and at 6 o'clock went and met Sir Esme and Lady Isabella at the station – another great pompous building built in the spirit of advertisement. Mighty fine as the spirit of religion rose the great cathedrals! The bulk of the buildings are in marble. The plan is not as good as Delhi or as fine. The buildings far better. The public patronage is alive whereas at Delhi it is nil. The Lincoln memorial is a great thing, placed too close to the Washington obelisk which again blocks everything, so big is it. They should have put it across the river, but then it would have been in Virginia which sentiment forbade!

A glorious thunder storm came on and the marble colonnade of huge dimensions and the ink black sky and vivid colouring of trees and red roofed buildings made an impressive spectacle.

We dined alone. Lady Isabella is a darling – more Italian than English – and Italian servants, quite charming and very good and all very much *en famille*. The eldest son, a boy of 21, very ill acute arthritis or something of the sort.[3] I sat with him some time and did all sorts of stunts with pencil and paper and he would come down to dinner and Lady I. was grateful to me, I think.

Lady Betty typed! my speech-to-come out for me for which I paid her 10 dollars. She is 19 so I could do it. I told her how greatly I objected to children, mine in particular, learning to type.

At 10 o'clock Monday Mr Brookes the architect,[4] came and he, Sir Esme and myself went to look at the site for the new Embassy. This, visiting a house just finished by Brookes, the Protestant Cathedral in process of construction and then the

---

1. Sir Esme Howard (1863–1939) married in 1898 (Maria) Isabella, daughter of Prince Giustiniani and 8th Earl of Newburgh. He was Ambassador in Washington 1924–30.

2. Lady Elizabeth Feilding (b. 1899), daughter of the 9th Earl of Denbigh, married in 1926 Eric Walker, MC.

3. Esme Howard (1903–26).

4. F. H. Brookes was the architect responsible for the execution of the drawings for the Washington Embassy sent out by Lutyens from London.

Roman Catholic Cathedral also in progress, occupied our morning. We got back just a little late for a 1.30 lunch. A few people were there but no one of consequence to my great adventure.

In the afternoon I went with Betty Feilding to Mount Vernon – the house of Washington. So charming overlooking a wide reach of the Potomac river, so pathetic and all so small. Colonel Dodge, the curator, took me over and let me into the rooms. An attic where Washington died, the best part of the house he kept for guests. It is very difficult to describe – a little manor house surrounded by smaller houses, butler's house, dairy, weaver's house, gardener's house, stables. Charming little box garden etc. etc. And down on the slope to the river Washington's tomb. It is a place of pilgrimage and was, Monday afternoon, packed with people.

We came back by Arlington – the great war cemetery of America or cemeteries. We got back in time for a late tea and then I went over the Embassy house – kitchens and chancelleries with Sir Esme. Then a dinner party and we had fun.

After dinner and all had gone I had a long talk into small hours with the Ambassador re the new Embassy etc.[1]

I left Washington early Tuesday – 8 o'clock – and arrived at New York 1.30.

Corbett, the architect, took me in charge. I went round offices etc. In the evening dined with Witney Warren in a super ornate flat. Eight of us. A dear old thing and found Mrs W.W. to be an old Parisian friend. We had lashings of food and drink and legged footmen etc. etc. Lor! the American architects are rich!

But it is a wonderful place. Alive, keen, friendly. Great achievement and alive only to greater achievement. The scale they can adopt is splendid – the skyscrapers growing from monstrosities to erections of real beauty and the general character of the work is

---

1. The Embassy, which was not built until 1927–28, is a combination of English Georgian and American vernacular, though 'the note is predominantly British – aristocratic but very robust' (Butler, *Architecture*, vol. ii, p. 46). On first entering the Embassy as Ambassador in 1940 Lord Halifax remarked: ' "This seems very familiar," and next morning, after passing a night which was a sharp reminder of the shortcomings of Lutyens as a domestic architect, he added: "It *is* very familiar" ' (Birkenhead, *Halifax* (1965), p. 475). Vita Sackville-West described staying there in 1933: 'McNed's Embassy here is lovely but the roof leaks and all the fires smoke. How delighted Grannyma [Lady Sackville] would be if I told her that!' (letter to her son Ben Nicolson, quoted in Victoria Glendinning, *Vita* (1983), p. 256).

of a very high standard indeed – far higher than anything on the continent or in England. They all are children with gigantic toys growing, I believe, to an equally gigantic manhood. But the place does want tidying up and pulling together.

Eerde, Holland[1]   July 17.26.

I am really troubled by your letter this morning and the thought of you in bed with a nurse and perhaps feeling wretched and lonely and I not there. Shall I come back? [He had an ulcer on the leg.]

13 Mansfield Street   July 17.26.

MacSack in spite of her heart and from her own bed flew to mine – me I mean – and brought George Plank[2] her guest with her. She lunched and dined, very good lunch and a very good dinner, and she brought caviar and Evian water. Bracken[3] came to dinner, talked 'Brackenly' and made a convert and I drank water whilst they all lapped up fermented grape and rye juices! Rosie [Ridley] lunches with me today and plays chess after.

MacSack in the Napoleon chair, I in bed, Plank in another chair all went to sleep after lunch. You would have laughed had you come in. Bracken brought me books as did MacSack so I have lots to read now.

The swelling has gone down and the shape almost normal. I lie in bed so

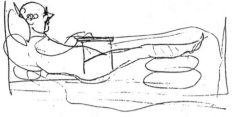

my leg on top of two pillows.

1. Castle Eerde, Ommen near Arnhem, which had been given by a rich Dutchman, became the European centre for the Order of the Star in the East.
2. George Plank, the American artist, for whom Lutyens built a cottage, Marvells, Five Ashes, Sussex in 1928.
3. Brendan Bracken (1901–58). 'Father did not like Bracken who often came to Mansfield Street and had the cheek to ruffle his hair' (Mary Lutyens, *Lutyens*, p. 230).

Government House, Gibraltar   Nov.28.26.

I left Guadalperal, lunched with Alba at the Liria Palace in Madrid and went off through the night to Algeciras.

A part of this house is a chapel, more rather a church, and I have been deeply ronged by the garrison at early service singing 'From Greenland's icy mountains'. All that Mother believed, felt and taught flooded back – the mysteries of the child's conception brain waved again. So I am feeling very sentimental and want you here with me.

But it is all beyond my reach – whether too high or too low – I only know it's a level I shall reach again.[1]

The books I ordered never arrived. I wonder why.

Another service has begun. The soldiers' band is playing a sentimental voluntary, bless them. The men sing again. Most disturbing. A hymn I know but can't name. How Nannie would love it. I want her second.

Did I tell you that Alba has given me a book to prove that Dante's *Divine Comedy* was all copied from the Koran and proves – or attempts to – the influence Mohammedanism had on the Christian outlook. 2000 years of goody goody and look around and there is little else but baddy baddy and the most successful seem but to crow on dunghills.

New Delhi   Dec.30.26.

Christmas night we all went to Belvedere[2] for dinner. There were 6 tables – 10 people at each table. Their Excellencies[3] were not announced – they just came in separately and you found them there! No ceremony at all, and after dinner Irwin danced with his

---

1. Sic. Ursula Ridley transcribed this sentence as '*never* reach', which is perhaps whàt Lutyens meant. Mary Lutyens also reads the sentence in this sense. Hussey made play of the sentence as it stands, interpreting it as a 'mystic premonition' of Liverpool Cathedral (*Lutyens*, p. 528).

2. Country residence of the Viceroy at Alipur, near Calcutta.

3. Edward Wood (1881–1959), 'a fox-hunting Yorkshire squire whose compassionate Christianity concealed a steely regard for law and order', was appointed Viceroy (at the suggestion of George V) and created Lord Irwin in 1925 (Rose, *George V*, p. 350). As Lord Halifax he served as Foreign Secretary 1938–40 and Ambassador in Washington 1940–46. He married in 1909 Lady Dorothy Onslow, daughter of the 4th Earl of Onslow.

Controller Colonel Muir! Also games, follow my leader and we all streamed through the kitchens and everywhere and the cooks were much astonished seeing the Viceroy coat off as childish as any one of us. Everyone said it was the best party they had ever seen.

Wimborne seems very happy and enjoys Raisina food![1] and gets up to breakfast, he will become a reformed character. He has brought no one with him which is a relief.

Ojai, California[2]   *Feb.4.27.*

I have learnt a great deal from being in this country. Labour conditions have driven people to do things for themselves and this has forced them to invent easy ways of running a house. It is so easy here to cook and clean – electric stoves, simple houses, bathrooms all white tiled, china handles – everything can be spotlessly clean with the minimum of labour. The fact of doing things for oneself and not always depending on servants gives one a sense of self respect. It will have to come in England also but it will be slow. It is really awful to me to think of Mansfield St and ten servants and I am trying to think how we could manage.

In a service flat of say 5 bedrooms – 3 sitting rooms (you and I,Betty, Mary, Nannie,) we should need no servants – cooking done below and a woman in to clean. Think it all over. Here, I clean, make beds, wash my clothes, get the breakfast – it is all so easy. Electric stove, electric coffee pot, electric toaster.

I am going to San Francisco at the end of this month to lecture.

13 Mansfield Street   July 16.27.

You ask me what I do. I am busy on a scheme for rebuilding Euston Station.[3] Don't talk about it or say anything, it is a 7,000,000 project if it comes off.

Then there is the Mercantile Marine monument of Tower Hill.[4] The graves folk have just passed my big monument at

1. No. 1 Raisina was Lutyens's own bungalow.
2. Lady Emily and Mary were staying in the Ojai Valley eighty miles from Los Angeles where Krishna had had a house since 1923.
3. This scheme was not executed.
4. Built in 1926–28 for the Imperial War Graves Commission.

Arras[1] with acclamation. I wait for Embassy Washington estimates. The Head Office, Midland Bank.[2] The completion of the AIO.[3] A house for Colonel Gaunt in Canada.[4] I wait instructions to go on with the Big Monument at Thiepval.

I am doing a jolly monument at Norwich.[5] I am interring Jack Horner at Mells and Mr Hackett at New York.[6] Delhi is ever with me. A house alteration for Falk.[7] Another reconstruction and garden for Hudson,[8] Sonning is being added to again.[9] A monument for Lord Cheylesmore.[10]

I have made sketches for the London University.[11] A big room for Joseph Duveen in New York.[11] My silver cups for St Paul's Cathedral[12] and a lot more. I must get up.

13 Mansfield Street   July 24.28.

I don't know what to say about more building in India. It is so far and the people – G[overnment] O[f] I[ndia] and Indians are so supine and the influences so political and anti real endeavour

---

1. Memorial to the Missing for the Royal Air Force and Royal Flying Corps, 1924–32.

2. Lutyens owed his connection with the Midland Bank to Reginald McKenna, who was Chairman 1919–43. He built four branches for the Bank. Like the others, the Head Office at Poultry (1924–39) was built in collaboration with other architects, in this case Gotch & Saunders of Kettering. Butler regarded it as 'Sir Edwin's most learned work' (*Architecture*, vol. iii, p. 27).

3. Britannic House (now Lutyens House), Finsbury Circus, for Anglo-Iranian Oil (1920–24). Like the Midland Bank buildings, this was a stone façade on a steel frame. Though it is 'one of the finest Neo-Roman offices to be built' (Gradidge, *Lutyens*, p. 160), the façade has little to do with what goes on inside the building.

4. At St Hilaire. Built in 1927.

5. War Memorial, 1927.

6. Monument to James K. Hackett in New York, 1927.

7. Stockton House, Wiltshire for O. T. (Foxy) Falk (d. 1972), discriminating collector and economist; according to his obituarist he 'played the gilt edge market as a virtuoso his violin'.

8. At Plumpton Place, Sussex.

9. Deanery Garden, Sonning.

10. Monument to the 3rd Lord Cheylesmore (1848–1925), Embankment Gardens, London.

11. The design for this was not executed.

12. Gold and silver communion plate at St Paul's as a monument to Lord Stevenson.

by ever changing and mixing purposes, that I should like to think it over and talk it over with you.

What was designed for Lucknow is of no use for another site and I want to revive in India a classical tradition such as the Greeks gave her and by which she so greatly profited. If I am thought of and coupled with Corbusier it means that admiration for one can only be tempered by affection. Corbusier and I are poles apart and any difficulty would raise a comparison with Corbusier and no doubt vice versa.[1]

The buildings are so badly kept up in India and all tradition of it seems lost in their only real interests – political fomentations.

They want me to build a capital in South America. This too means Spaniards, insurrections, riots and what not. I am very depressed. To hurry on Delhi at the last moment they have made the most terrible economies and omissions. Even the English are just callous and ignorant and in what I consider realities they only see a mock scenery and nothing deeper than an adjective.

The personal equation may be all right – I have direct access to the Viceroy – but a board! They were very difficult at Lucknow and they objected to tile roofs. I don't mind that but I do mind when they said it would look like Allahabad![2] and objected to costs as a building cost 15% of its cost in annual repair! That means rebuilding in every 7 years – worse than the Americans 30 years.

Your last letter, the one before this, you signed Your loving Mother! Was a husband ever so addressed, and what about the table of affinity?

1. Lutyens had reviewed the English translation of *Towards a New Architecture* by Le Corbusier in the *Observer*, 29 January 1928. 'M. le Corbusier's Theme is that architecture of our time should have the qualities of the machine,' he wrote. 'Architecture, certainly, must have geometric constituents, but lines and diagrams, in two dimensions, are not enough. Architecture is a three dimensioned art. To be a home, the house cannot be a machine. It must be passive, not active, bringing peace to the fluctuation of the human mind from generation to generation. For what charm can a home possess that can never bear a worn threshold, the charred hearth and the rubbed corner?'

2. Capital of the United Provinces, predominantly Gothic and Indo-Saracenic in style.

Garrick Club   Aug.20.28.

I went to Renishaw for Sunday. I found Lady Ida Sitwell much the same but more gaunt and even more unhappy looking. Sir George suave and smiling and fussy and keeping all his in strict control. Osbert, Sachie and Edith Sitwell were there – the latter more extraordinary than ever. Osbert as ever self possessed and growing more like his [great great] grandfather George IV[1] than ever. Sachie with his pretty wife.[2] Sachie is quick tempered and with selfish Papa and unhappy dipsotic Lady Ida it was like being on a volcano.

The great bare grey untidy house sinister. My bath was on a floor above me, the WC on a floor below and there was no po in my bedroom. Before dinner, after due refuge in the garden, I said to Sir George, As we are all *pee*'rs here may I have a po? So I got one with a laugh too.

Sunday morning a lady in the hall asked me was Lady Ida down. In all solemnity I pretended to misunderstand and brought her an eiderdown to her amazement!

This weekend I go to Manchester, Liverpool and Gledstone.

MacSack has taken up her own case,[3] being sick of lawyers. I must say – one or two I have seen – her letters are killing, brilliant in a vindictive way, but the satire and contempt she puts into them doesn't bode [well] for any peaceful settlement. I don't know whether to laugh or cry. If they could only laugh it would all be over.

Last Wednesday I went up to Norwich. I stayed with Colman – mustard. A very nice man with a wonderful collection of Cotman pictures, sketches, etc.[4] The Dean of Norwich and some odds and

1. Lord Albert Conyngham (1805–60), 1st Baron Londesborough and grandfather of Lady Ida Sitwell, was alleged to be the illegitimate son of George IV.
2. Georgia, daughter of Arthur Doble of Montreal.
3. A financial row with her daughter, Vita Sackville-West.
4. Russell Colman (1861–1946). He enlarged the collection of watercolours of the Norwich School started by his father, Jeremiah Colman (d. 1898); on his death he left the collection to the Castle Museum, Norwich.

ends and a big lunch next day in honour of Munnings[1] and the Norwich and East Anglian school of painters. Roger Fry[2] was asked and he came and had to second the vote to Munnings.

Now R.F. hates Munnings's painting and found it difficult so he told the Lord Mayor how he should control his city and quoted the Germans. There was a good deal of anger and 'Why did he speak?' and Roger Fry said 'Why was I asked?'

I have been to Jagger's[3] studio and Lord Burleigh[4] was there – to another sculptor naked – being model jumping at the Olympic Games. Gosh he is a beautiful boy. Jagger is doing the panels on the Jaipur column for me. The Indians that have seen it adore it.

New Delhi   Jan.17.29.

The super tax (£5000) on Delhi takes all my profits on Delhi for the eighteen years. It is hard. D—n Democracy!

Very busy over furnishings and the getting in in October. The big opening will be in '30–'31 after they have been in a year.

If the political situation improves they will have a big show – Hoheits – (Hardinge!) the Governors of all Dominions, etc.

Baker has collared the emblems of the Colonies for his babu court instead of my Great Place where they ought to be and H.E. agrees with me. But again I am too late as Baker has been to all the Governors etc. for their consent. I suppose if I did no real work and only wire pulled I could do the same. It is a bore this selfishness with no thought of the scheme as a whole.

The big dome is up to its springing.

We have a lot of English and French materials out here. They do make the Indian stuffs and materials look silly, but poor India is only politically ridden and not one ounce of brain power is used for material betterments.

Mustoe[5] has done extraordinarily well with the gardens. Last

---

1. Alfred Munnings (1878–1959), whose paintings exactly capture the spirit of equestrian society between the wars.

2. Roger Fry (1866–1934), critic and artist.

3. C. S. Jagger (1885–1934), who carved the elephants at the corners of Viceroy's Court.

4. As Lord Burleigh, the 6th Marquess of Exeter (1905–81) won the 400 metres hurdles in the 1928 Olympic Games.

5. W. R. Mustoe of the Horticultural Department.

winter they were a desert and a *débris* one at that. Now full of roses and beautiful roses. The tanks run and reflect and ripple and my rainbow in the deep fountain has come off – a vivid rainbow and children *can* find its start.

I do wish you were here but it will be better next year. It is very tiring going over the buildings. I went twice on Sunday and it deaded me! Now I go over bits every day.

They are very careless and the Indians are for ever damaging things and the messes they make! 'orrible!

Parker, the sanitary engineer, an Englishman, said this morning: 'It looks,' referring to Government House, 'very different from what I expected.' I said 'What did you expect?' He answered: 'I don't know.' This is after seventeen years working on the plans!

But I do think it is going to be a success and the Irwins seem very happy and long to get into it.

Jan.24.29.

Mail day comes across one's horizon like a comet! and here it is 6 o'clock and Lady Irwin just left the house. She comes out every other day and is very business-like and helpful and we settle a lot.

They all seem to like the house – wonderful! And the gardens are called by Indians 'God's own Heavens'. And no other house in India is like The Viceroy's House. The King has settled it to be so called.[1]

A Mr Roberts came out on Sunday – an amateur veterinary surgeon, snake catcher and with birds and beasts a sort of St Francis. He won't eat but one meal a day and lives with his birds and animals of all sorts – wolves, panthers, etc. on intimate terms.

He came out to tell me how to build nesting places and where, for birds of different sorts. Irwin says I may have mandarin ducks, paddy birds and other sorts in the gardens.

Lady Irwin is taking a lot of trouble over the furniture but after all these years and furniture for ever in view, they are only this year drying wood by an artificial method and using it at once without (what I believe to be essential) a year to dry in after the process has been given. The furniture, some of it, falls to pieces a

1. George V amended Irwin's suggestion of Viceroy's House to *The* Viceroy's House.

Shoosmith, Mustoe and Lutyens at New Delhi

The dome of Viceroy's House in construction

day or two after it is made. It is exasperating. The big dome is growing day by day.

The big glass chandeliers are going up and the house is beginning to get finished. But to get it all done by October, even the Viceroy's wing, I have very grave doubts. And the Indian never finishes anything and breaks 50% of what he temporarily fixes so that the amount of making good will be at least 25% of the work done and at a cost of another 25%. . . .

There is not near enough skilled supervision and no one seems to care so long as they can get to their clubs, gymnasiums, and whist and bridge drives, shooting, golfing, and play the part due and proper as befits their 'sahib' selves.

However one can but peg along but I get tired of having to make criticisms and praying the builders to have mercy on the job and look ahead a bit and be thorough.

Yesterday I went to look at the Bengali painters' work – three of them, that fat sleek creature that sang to us one day at the Sultan Singhs'[1] is one of them. One could draw a little bit, but they only know the most terrible patterns and those nerve wracking sodden gods and goddesses and to be mysterious and godlike you must draw everything wrong – foolishly methodless. Thank Very God of Very God that he wrought not our world on such lines and the old Indian work was, with all its, to us, weirdness, intellectually honest and thorough in its method. They will not draw from life. And then talk! the hind legs off a donkey and without their words – words soon forgotten – their pictures stand for all time as inexplicable nonsense. The saving grace is the manner in which they are painted won't last!

I am making a butterfly garden. The roses – wonderful, the mignonette perfumes the whole place. The fountains are not finished yet, so it is difficult to control the water and water levels in the canals and waterways, falls and cascades until one knows the amount of water the fountains give or need for effect and the resultant flow.

The big dome is going up and it is all beginning to look mighty fine and I do think it's a gentleman's house, though original in that it is built in India for India, Indian.

Mustoe comes to breakfast with me every morning, and so the

1. Hari Singh, Maharajah of Kashmir, for whom Lutyens designed a palace in Delhi in 1919 which was not executed.

days wag on. I takes just two hours to go over the Viceroy's House and then that's about half and as I do it nearly every day at least once I go to bed dog tired.

I have designed another nursery electrolier – hens, chickens and the falling egg, broken, spills its joke – the e. light![1] But this is a very lightsome mood, for the rest is solemn furniture, lamp-posts etc., fire dogs, fire irons, fenders and a host of stuff, panelling, mantelpieces etc. No two mantelpieces are alike and Lady Irwin likes them all. The big arch is growing[2] and begins to look upward and is fine and big.

New Delhi   Jan.31.29.

The cold spell is on us, there was ¼″ of ice and Mustoe was in tears, for acres of his plants have been killed by the frost. His car would not start and he could not get to the gardens before sunrise to pour cold water on them to prevent the ice thawing too quick and the Indian mullahs he found standing about doing nothing, shivering, instead of running about like lamplighters! However, he got eighty of them on the run, but he fears too late.

The Viceregal party have all gone off to Bikanir for one of those huge grouse killing parties for which entertainment he levies a tax on his people.

Blagdon, Northumberland   *Feb.6.29.*

I am very thankful I can be here with Ursy as these last weeks of waiting, for what at best is a painful ordeal, are very trying. And

1. There are replicas at Blagdon.
2. The All India War Memorial Arch was dedicated in 1931.

---

nowadays they make such a business of it, it becomes like an operation. Instead of remaining comfortably in one's own bed as I did they prepare a narrow single bed to look as like an operating table as possible and have a table full of boiled instruments, cotton wool, basins etc. till it gives one the jim jams.

We have embarked on Thackeray's Newcomes *and I think the baby[1] must be here before we finish it.*

New Delhi   Feb.7.29.

The Viceroy wants me to stay on a bit to get things settled – an awful bore, so I doubt if I get home before the end of March. But he is nice and appreciates the house more and more and he tells others so too.

Baker is out here. I saw him mouching about the Viceroy's House so I went up and showed him the gardens etc., but it was too dark to do more.

I want two mottoes – one for the Viceroy's state chair and the other on the Jaipur column. How would – 'A load of wisdom can but lift to God' do?

> 'Endow your thought with faith
> Your deed with courage
> Your life with sacrifice
> So all men may know the greatness of India.'[2]

I have written out a lot of such things and Mrs Shoosmith[3] has drawn the coverts of the Bible and combed the Psalms but nothing quite fits. 'In calamity faith, be in sorrow brave, in triumph humility.'

I do want to be back but I shall hate leaving the work for the finishing touches and the hands left are all thumbs and the wits of dough. Oh dear.

1. Nicholas Ridley, b. 17 February 1929.
2. The inscription on the Jaipur column, as condensed by Lord Irwin, reads:
   In thought faith
   In word wisdom
   In deed courage
   In life service
   So may India be great.
3. Majorie, wife of Arthur Shoosmith, Lutyens's resident architect in Delhi from 1920 to 1931.

I have had my nursery chandeliers made. They are most amusing. I started to paint them but very soon called in Mrs George[1] who has spent a week or more on them all day and they are delightful. A mystery man pulled out all the strings so now they are painted they can't be wired and another Indian smashed one all to pieces and it has to be made again and it will take another fortnight to complete and paint and then another week to paint in colour – three weeks lost. Just sheer slop and carelessness. It is exasperating.

I found a man with a pickaxe on his shoulder walking quickly through the house – right, left, right, left, bang, bang, bang. Corners of finished corridors being chipped off. They ought to be reduced to slavery and not given the rights of man at all and beaten like brute beasts and shot like man eaters. *There*.

I met at Bagpie's a Pandit Nehru[2] – Gandhi's friend and the most aggressive of the Swarajists. I liked the man – he has some wit. He lunches with me on Sunday and I am taking him over the Viceroy's House. He said if Gandhi was here he would certainly have brought him too.

He said Gandhi deplored the waste of money on architectural piles. I said it was all Indian work and much better to do than spin Kadda. That India where she once led in the fine arts is now deplorably behind times and peoples and the only live thing in India was half-baked statesmanship and agitation.

He said he had not thought of the buildings as an education to the Indian mason, craftsmen etc. I told him of our search for Indian materials that would wear etc. and the hopelessness of it. So I hope to get him interested.

He is a dear old man, drinks whisky, port, etc., mutton, everything. A black coat and jodhpurs on which I drew buttons so that he looked exactly like an English bishop. And that was all that he was fit for if he didn't help India in her material world.

---

1. Wife of the architect Walter George.
2. Pandit Motilal Nehru (1861–1931), Jawaharlal's father and Mrs Gandhi's grandfather. 'A politician of infinite subtlety and resource, supposedly more reasonable than many but inflexible as Gandhi himself in the pursuit of Swaraj.' Nevertheless his Gandhi cap was made by Scott of London (Birkenhead, *Halifax*, p. 220).

New Delhi   Xmas Day. 29.

The most tiring week I ever had since last mail – arranging furniture, seeing to things and driving men, hanging pictures. But Monday the 23rd came. The Viceroy arrived at 8 a.m. We had to get up at 7 in tail coats. It was raining which stopped in time but a thick white fog enveloped everything. At about 8 a very white sun peered through and made the world a ghost. We heard the booming of guns – some heard the bomb and it was not until after H.E.'s arrival that we heard his train had been bombed.[1] The bodyguard did soldierlike things, bugles blew and out of the fog H.E.'s car emerged.

The guard was inspected, then the city fathers presented an address to which H.E. replied. He then came up the stairway to the great portico where I was presented to him and others on the work. At a given signal the doors were opened – no key as there was no lock – and they, Lady Irwin and H.E. went into the house and we left them alone and for the first time in 17 years the house closed on me.

13 Mansfield Street   *Dec.26.29.*

MacSack sent very characteristic presents. To me smelling salts (bottle won't open!) and some Spanish jam. I wrote to Mr Bull [the butler] to find out what she would like and suggested a Pâté de Foie Gras. So she replies herself to say Bull is ill and she opens all his letters! and she would like a pâté better than anything as with diabetes she can eat so little! and Plank will be with her. She hears Mary is going to be married[2] and wishes to spend £50 on her as she did with Barbie and Ursy (Ursula says she gave her nothing as she had quarrelled with her!) or a bit of furniture worth that sum. I went off to Fortnum and Mason and got her a handsome Pâté and sent it by special messenger so I hope the present to Mary will mature!

1. The train bringing the Viceroy to New Delhi was almost derailed by a terrorist bomb.
2. Mary married Anthony Sewell in 1930.

Surrey   Sept.6.31.

*I love to think of your great building [Liverpool Cathedral] but I
do wish it had been model dwellings and not a church! If you had
been going to build a cathedral when we first married I should
have been thrilled, but now I could weep. Not that it will affect
you – your job is to make a glorious thing and you will. But it
saddens me that men should still be perpetuating superstition and
priest craft when I long to set them free from such things.*

In bed   Oct.4.31.

I was so glad of your loving, very loving letter and that you feel
better and frosty cobwebs revive you.[1]

Thursday afternoon I went up to Liverpool and found my
Archbishop[2] alone. Bishop Dobson is ill but better. I guess he will
get a move on up or out. He is a stupid old thing. We talked a
great deal. (A†B stands for Archbishop hereafter.) He was won
over to my wisdom by my saying a Cathedral was not a church to
worship *in*, it was a church to worship with.

A†B told me how he enjoyed bathing in Ireland, he apparently
is a great swimmer. He dived into the pellucid waters of the
Atlantic and came up vis à vis with a large seal. He was terrified,
thought it would bite his leg off. He dived to escape. He met the
seal again evidently in the same throes of escape. He got to shore,
safely and greatly relieved, to find a man who had got out his rifle
as he had seen a couple of seals. Of this couple he was one! I
should indeed have been bereaved had he been bagged!

Talking of my position in case of his death or translation he
tells me that my position as architect is in the annals of the
Vatican and they in Liverpool – a succeeding archbishop – would
find it very difficult if not practically impossible to move me. The
Pope would have to move. *El viva la Poppa!*

There was the great trouble in April prophesied by Miss Pride

---

1. She was at Castle Eerde, Holland.
2. Richard Downey (1881–1953), Roman Catholic Archbishop of Liverpool 1928–53. An Irishman, he was 5′4″ high and weighed 18 stone in 1932. By
1939 he had reduced his weight to 9 stone. He was buried in 1953 in a tomb
designed by Lutyens in the crypt of Liverpool Cathedral, after the largest
funeral Liverpool had ever seen.

with the English contractors – riots, stone throwing, and the – my – contractors had to go. There were great difficulties but the English contractor behaved with great consideration and magnanimity and Bishop Dobson approved a local man, Eaves. The A†B was away at the time as was I.

Now the A†B didn't want Eaves and to satisfy the Irish element he appointed an Irishman, Doyle, to act with Eaves. Eaves and Doyle naturally, perhaps, have started badly as in their complementary parts are to each uncomplementary. So it was I had to go up and we had a meeting. The A†B, Doyle and his son, his clerk of works, engineers as they call them, Eaves and his engineer.

Doyle is a very rich man and very generous and in any difficulty says 'Well I shall pay for it', a most comfortable man. Very big, coarse and inane to look at with a smile meant to win but creates fear. Eaves gentle, loquacious and everything a 'but' which riles the A†B. He objects to Eaves. He is not head of his firm and he does not want to be landed with a firm that builds busses and furnishes funerals, the A†B is very funny on the point, and at the meeting the great Doyle was very good, spoke little and to the point. I fear Eaves was a little unhappy but I left them in good fettle.

Friday was a *maigre* day to which I now conform. It is awkward being endowed with a large bit of beef when all else eat shrimps and turbot.

The A†B comes to London about 13th–15th when he will draw 'the first line'. The foundation of the Cathedral may be delayed. It is a question of economy.

Without you, darling, the Xwords have no attraction.

13 Mansfield Street   March 24.32.

Money came in not enough but with an overdraft I paid my surtax £5800. The cheque was telegraphed me from Montreal and I got it in time to satisfy the threat of the tax people. A great relief but I feel as thin as a moulted sparrow in a snowstorm. I have lost what might have been 2000 a year for ever and ever. RIP.

Warnings from Ireland not to spend money and just mark time

with my Irish scheme,[1] so – !

To alter a cottage not to cost more than £100 has come in, i.e. £6. £2 office, £1.10 tax. £1.10 me. Good and lively isn't it?

Only 4 letters this morning for help, so things may look up! The taxes I pay are taxed again as income so the bulk of my tax next year will be on the taxes I paid this year. Tax Vobiscum.

Am sending to the RA 5 drawings. 3 elevations. Section and plan of the Cath.[2] It is rum that our only source of moneys will be from a faith we neither hold or have and to that there is a ?

Surrey   *March 26.32.*

I was very glad to get a letter from you this morning. I don't know what you mean about Income Tax threat. Is it a joke or did you really imagine you were going to prison?

You must realise why you have got into such a bad position financially in spite of the enormous jobs you have had. First you have been badly advised – if you had become a Company it would have saved you thousands, but even now you hesitate about it. Thomas may be splendid over some things but he is not a business man. Francis Smith is old and not much use. Euan [Wallace] offered to help some years ago but it never came to anything.

The second thing is that you have not set aside the money for your income tax or put it on deposit in the bank where it would have been safe and handy at a reasonable rate of interest – but have given it to Cecil [Baring] to speculate with and so have had to sell out at a loss.[3] So for these two things you must blame yourself. Now what are we going to do?

We are not going to have two establishments. From every point of view it would be madness. Therefore we must leave Mansfield St – there is no alternative and go into a house we can run with two servants. And having decided to do this we must seriously set about getting a house. Thomas can take steps during April.

I am going to give all the household notice on April 1st. I think

1. The Irish National War Memorial in Phoenix Park, Dublin, 1930–40.
2. Now in the RIBA Drawings Collection.
3. Lady Emily perhaps did not make allowance for the slump.

you should consider doing the same to James[1] and in May send the car to Blagdon and save wages, garage, petrol, insurance etc. I shall stay away a lot in April – Ursy wants me – in May I am going abroad with Mary where I can live cheaply in Italy for a month. By June we ought to have a house fixed up and Mansfield St vacated. Do not pay any rates after June.

Darling I love you and we have so much to be thankful for – we have each other, we have our children and grandchildren. But do do take expert advice and do something instead of just groaning about it.

Lady Emily knits the first sleeve . . . Nanny Sleath knits the second.

13 Mansfield Street   May 9.32.

The alterations have begun,[2] and bangings in the morning wake me. I have a threatening of the old duodecimal tummy trouble so am resigned to hot water and Fripp's[3] magic pill. The cold is whorful.

1. The chauffeur, so named in order that Lutyens could say 'Home, James'. The car, a grey 'baby' Rolls Royce, had been a present from Lady Sackville in 1923; Lutyens repaid her for it by degrees.
2. Instead of leaving Mansfield Street, they altered it, moving the kitchen and dining-room to the first floor, enabling them to have fewer servants.
3. Sir Alfred Fripp (1865–1930), Surgeon in Ordinary to the King and the Duke of Connaught.

Lutyens and Ursula at Blagdon

A man from Johannesburg Art Gallery called. They want to complete my building there. All say it's the best modern building in SA! ... and won't let me alter the original plans but are worried about the picture lights. The man has been to all our galleries in London and none are so well lighted as mine! But the Johannesburg Corporation think that in London everything must be better. But it is fun getting a job in!

The other excitement today was Llewellyn President RA sent for me to give a message from the King – *this is private* and must not get about – he has told Llewellyn to arrange that my portrait

goes to Viceroy's House, and Llewellyn has recommended a bust.[1] Reid Dick will do it for love and then there will be the marble and the pedestal, which will probably come from the Leighton fund.

The King spent a long time at my Cath drawings, talked a great deal all complimentary.

A bord du Lamartine[2]   *Août* 20.32.

Here we are in sight of Greece and we arrive early tomorrow at Athens. The first day at Marseille we were rather miz and depressed.

Pompeii was the most tiring day I ever experienced. Clouds of dust, *chaleur énorme et marche marchont marchest toujours*, to yet another house precisely like the last, a ruin – a little bit of mosaic, another little bit of Pompeian paint – very bad for the most part. A touting common sort of common population, and then every other house had something that it was not possible for Ursy to see. Just pornographic dirt when exaggeration was the soul of wit.

Awful pen, and a delicious breeze blows my paper about and plays as 'twere a kitten.

A bord du Lamartine   *Août* 22.32.

Ursy remains my great and greatest solace, patient cheerful and translates the humantics with thoughtful humour. We are on our way to Constantinople and are nearing Gallipoli and the Dardanelles. Tomorrow we see St Sophia.

The Parthenon!

The most tragic spot I have ever visited, bare, barren, a

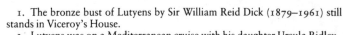

1. The bronze bust of Lutyens by Sir William Reid Dick (1879–1961) still stands in Viceroy's House.
2. Lutyens was on a Mediterranean cruise with his daughter Ursula Ridley.

Lutyens at the Parthenon

Waterloo of the waterless, tourist ridden and the Parthenon so knocked about as to become unpleasant, heart-breaking to see and the utter valuelessness of all human endeavour, that one could acclaim an Austin 7 full of belching motorists as the one permanent symbol we have left. 89 in the shade.

The Parthenon was there, all I knew it to be, was there, but oh so little of it left. No one silhouette was perfect. The restorations that are being attempted are woeful. It is a glorious remnant of what has never at its best [been] more than a unit, perfect in itself,[1] and its ruin is by its achievement the more disastrous to its being. It has no relation to its site, no dramatic sense such as the Romans had.

The site must have been chosen by extraneous causes. The settling of an eagle, a prophet's dream? I looked at it for long, and yet the more I looked the more depressed. The design is full of cunning and requires months of patient labour with accurate instruments to determine the method prompting its design. The podium and the cornice are on curves, the columns vary in length and the whole combination of vertical and horizontal lines runs,

1. Sic. Hussey has 'It is a glorious remnant of what has never, at its best, been a unit perfect in itself' (*Lutyens*, p. 539), which completely alters the sense.

labours conforming, to make the whole, one. Destroyed for its beauty by man, as God surely destroyed Pompeii for its bestiality and common labours.

The Erecthion, very disappointing and the Temple of the Wingless Victory, the same. The Temple to Theseus a box and little more. The evidence [of] an earthquake shock was amusing – the drums of the column being shifted this way and that way.

Two original Greek churches looked enticing but alas were shut. Near the Temple to Theseus was a small Turkish doorway in a ramshackle Turkish prison – well designed and interesting. I did not realise the Turks had any architects, but this doorway was well designed, well cut and refined.

As to craftsmanship the cutting of the marble at the Parthenon was superb, but the work is not so convincing when it comes to the bonding of the external angles of their 'cellas'.

We had a very welcome lunch at the Hôtel Grande Bretagne.

5 Eaton Gate   Oct.4.32.

I enclose Herbert's funeral service.[1] Aggie asked me to give it to you. It was very well done and the music exceptionally good. Crimson damask covered the coffin flanked by Italian candle-sticks, very Munsteady, but dignified with his stars and orders displayed thereon. The lesson Aggie chose remarkably befitting. It was all horribly moving.

Afterwards I saw Bumps[2], self-possessed and herself – very feeble she was in her bedroom with a delicious dark blue felt cap on her head. She was very happy with Bernard [Freyberg] who sees a good deal of her and asks her endless questions and waits for her deliberate answers in which she delights. She misses Herbert terribly as every day she had problems to set him on her daily affairs.

I noticed Bumps's hands had shrunk a great deal and had a slight shake, otherwise she looked well but very old, brown in the face as though sunburnt.

1. Lutyens designed the Jekyll family tomb in the churchyard of St John's Church, Busbridge, Surrey (1932).
2. This was their last meeting. Gertrude Jekyll died on 8 December 1932, and she was buried in the Jekyll tomb at Busbridge.

13 Mansfield Street   June 19.33.

I was miz when you went away, off! and left me with the
sorrowful and the grave. . . .

I looked and listened, they gave me their views, then I gave
mine. Antony[1] [used to] love the cross with 'sparks'. There was
the monument in the church and they thought a cross on the altar,
which is needed. The grave to be like a 'bed', four posts, on each
post a little figure and a larger figure in the middle being Queen of
the Air. I suggested the little figures would be stolen – with some
feeling of fear suggested in the church a cross hanging from the
arch that separates the Lytton Chapel and the Chancel.

We went in and talked no more about it until about 10.30
Sunday morning, when I started with pencil and paper. They
seemed very happy about it. Victor said 'Oh the comfort of
working with an artist' and all went well, when Pamela wept: I
wept too: I did say, rather brusquely 'How absurd this weeping
is'! . . .

The monument in the church will be a hanging cross with
sword and wings, and a sunburst round it being 29 stars (his age)
instead of a cross over the altar.

The grave outside, to be a slab of stone with flying sword and
wings, and then in an open stone frame Our Lady of the Skies.

In train from Chester   July 13.33.

At 5.30 I went to Art Schools at Kensington to judge, with others,
their work.

I had to do the architecture, very poor class of folk and perhaps
the more attractive for that. In my subject I took each student
some 10 in all separately and with my arm over his shoulder
talked to him and said what I thought etc. I did not realise at first

---

1. Antony Knebworth (1903–33) was killed in a flying accident. He was
commemorated by his father in the best-selling memoir, *Antony* (1935). The
memorials to him were erected in the Church of St Mary in the park of
Knebworth House, where Lutyens and Lady Emily were married. In 1942
Lutyens designed a memorial in the same church for Antony's younger brother
John Knebworth, killed in the war. Lutyens also designed Nanny Sleath's grave
in the same churchyard (1938). Aunt T had been buried there with a memorial
tablet by Lutyens in 1925.

that everyone could hear nor even that they were listening, so I was very easy and communicative about my work my difficulties etc. etc. and it was rather a success.

Got home at 12 and wondered who was in the house 2 gentlemen, I gathered that Betty was having a party, so hollared down the stairs – Betty! suddenly to realise it must be Krishnajee and luckily I woke no one up.[1] Had to catch the 8.30 so got up early and met Krishnajee in the bath room.

13 Mansfield Street   Aug.8.33.

I got back from Munstead this morning.

Went down to Eton with Winchelsea about a memorial there to his brother,[2] and then on from Eton to Munstead.

It is sad to see how the garden at Munstead W. has collapsed, but it can't be helped, no Bumps and no longer the 11 essential gardeners. Saw Timmy [Francis], read some 5 or 6 chapters of Bumps's life,[3] quite good but 'deadish' somehow.

I read Molly Carew's[4] book, very amusing, but a little bit shocking. Sex galore. I recognised myself as the old parent. Income tax, short with money. The man who travelled in a night train and did not remove his socks etc.

Grand Hotel, Forte dei Marmi, Viareggio   *Aug.11.33.*

I thought you would be rather shocked by Mary's book! But after all sex is the main theme of interest to young people now-a-days and it is after all the foundation of marriage about which she is writing. Did you also recognise me in the mother, who whenever

1. Betty and her husband Ian Glennie, whom she had married in 1933, were living in the basement at 13 Mansfield Street. Krishna stayed there whenever he came to London.

2. Denys Finch-Hatton (1887–1931) was killed in a flying accident in Kenya; his brother, the 14th Earl of Winchelsea, commissioned Lutyens to design a memorial bridge at Eton.

3. Francis Jekyll, *Gertrude Jekyll: A Memoir* (1934), with a foreword by Lutyens.

4. *Forthcoming Marriages*, Mary Lutyens's first novel, published in August 1933. She was staying in Italy with Lady Emily recovering from an illness.

her children are confiding in her is suddenly reminded of some-
thing entirely irrelevant and trivial!

In train, Rome to Paris   Oct.3.33.

Glorious, warm. The pilgrimage began.[1] 1st to St Peter's, and oh
dear, some 300 of the Liverpool folk processed to the Blessed
Sacrament chapel singing hymns and there were other pilgrim-
ages, French, German and what not processing around. We knelt
round the altar and sang 7 Pater Nosters, 3 Hail Marys the Creed
3 times and oh my poor knees and then on to the High Altar and
to the Lady Chapel, St Gregory's, processing and singing and
finishing up with God bless the Pope in which I joined heartily!
These manoeuvres they performed 3 times! but I slipped out, and
roamed about the great Church.

   The place was full of chant and song, these thousands of folk
singing different hymns in different languages, an effect not
unpleasant and reminiscent rather of a gigantic musical bee hive.

   Then to the hotel to lunch and soon after we went off to St
Paul's without the Walls, where the same performance took place
processing from altar to altar singing at the tops of our voices.
Here again I did one round religiously and then creeped, to join in
now and again, to ask a friendly priest some technical question as
to the religious or rubrical meaning of some inexplicable feature.

   I was taken through the crowd up the steps into the Papal
Palace.

   I was touched and told to kneel. I knelt – oh my poor knees.
Then two of the Papal Guard, and then the Pope in white with
two Monsignors in red. Then the Pope came down the line, there
were 6 of us, accompanied by Dr Downey.

   I said to [Monsignor] Adamson Must I kiss his ring – 'Yes you
must' so the Pope came and on my knees I kissed his ring.

   He talked to me in Italian. I had not an idea what he said. The
Archbishop told me afterwards, that he had seen and admired my
plans for the Liverpool Cathedral, glad the Lady Chapel was to
be built first, as the people in England seem to have forgotten the
existence of our Lady. The Archbishop was amused because the
only thing I could think of saying the which I did not know he

   1. Lutyens had gone to Rome to obtain the Pope's approval of his plans for
Liverpool, joining a pilgrimage led by Archbishop Downey.

saw, Thank you Sir – a pause – Thank you Sir . . . he then went on into the Audience Chamber, us following. I stood on the steps and the Pope occupied his throne, and spoke in Italian for some 25 to 30 minutes!

[Next day.] Did some sight seeing and at 1 o'c. I went to the British School. After lunch I heard all that Hubbard had to say. Very good looking, conceited through his own virility, gone off on the German Corbusier tack, bored with having to go through a course of measuring ancient buildings, to no useful purpose, as they have all been measured a 100 times before.

Two lady students a painter and a sculptress, both awful, Hubbard admiring them awfully, are collaborating on designing a Dominican Priory, all in the new nude school, grammarless and deeply adjectived.

I criticised fairly freely, but was fearful of driving the boy to extremes in rebellion and after I got him alone for a couple of hours. Now I shall have to report it all to the Commissioners at home. He had won the Prix de Rome – accepted the Prix de Rome and all it involved, and he was obliged to carry out the articles. At his age 22, discipline was invaluable and in after life he will get a lot of it and it is just as well to learn patience when young. I advised him to measure up some ancient building suitable for this purpose and then for his thesis take this building and translate it, whilst maintaining the proportions, to a modern building, and 'modern' decoration etc.[1]

It was dark when I got back to the hotel. Priests and bishops in and out of the hotel all day.

Saturday night I had my plans out. I had brought them out to be vetted. However all I had proposed was wonderful and perfect, and I seem to have known all and everything particular to the adoration of our Lady. This comes from having a wife I love . . .! so I know instinctively how to Hail Mary.

---

1. Pearce Hubbard (1910–65), architect. This advice seems to have sunk in; according to Lord Kinross, 'he had a talent for interpreting the old in a modern idiom' (*The Times*, 4 September 1965).

Palacio de Liria[1]   June 14.34.

Yesterday the house woke up about 12 o'c., the servants appeared tidy in Spanish black and it all came to as of old.

It was about 12 I saw Alba, in his office, very friendly and very much himself, hating the Republic. I went to the Prado in a yellow Rolls with the coronets as per usual. He has put them back. Eleven of his best pictures are in store, so the house has odd blanks.

In the afternoon, after a recognised siesta, that was 4, the secretary man with his wife, who was at school with Barbie and Robert at King Alfred's,[2] turned up. They took me to see the new university, new buildings a colossal lot of building all horrible modern jazz T squared mad stuff. It was started by King Alphonso. They gave him a present of £50,000 as a 25 years of reign present. It wasn't enough so he had a lottery which made £10,000,000! and lor! why don't we have lotteries? and then on about 30 miles out to the old university built 15–1600, a jolly old place and town very dilapidated but there.

Got back at ¼ before 8, and found Peñaranda waiting for me. This is a long story. Very much the same, as thin as ever but a little bit older, it must be near 10 years since I have seen him. It is very difficult.

Donna Carmen his wife leads a gay life and is not received by Alba or any one of his family, she is never asked or allowed in this house. Peñaranda comes to see his brother, but he won't eat here. He gets up at 4 o'c., dines at midnight, generally alone. I am dining with him tomorrow and as a concession to me we will dine at 10 o'c.!

He has had 21 estates taken from him – all the Montigo properties the Empress Eugénie left him. He owes a lot of money in England and France but he is not allowed to send any money out of the country and the little money he has abroad is in the hands of trustees to pay off those debts. He has one pony left and says he will not be able to afford to buy another, his boy (Timmy?) rides it.

He keeps Guadalperal going, but never goes himself. He has

1. Lutyens was in Madrid to lecture to the Spanish Institute of Architects.
2. The co-educational day school in Hampstead where Barbie and Robert were educated.

———

been there once to vote. The vote man, an old servant, asked him his name, qualifications? where he lived? etc. etc. not a word of recognition, though he was drawing wages from him. No one except the 3 civil guards knew him, and never left him or else he might have been shot.[1]

To give work he had a lot of planting done, having planted the fig trees they, the men who planted them, cut them down. They said he would have to plant them again! In the old days they, he and his people, lived almost as a family. All that good will and friendliness has gone.

He is very hopeful for a turn to the right.

At 9.30 we dined and Peñaranda went off and on his way looked in on Alba in bed! with bare toes sticking out of the sheets, on which he poised his slippers!

13 Mansfield Street   July 26.34.

I am glad I went down [to Tyringham][2] today. Father Phillips and 2 organ builders and a dear funny old man the master of music for the Cathedral Church in the Diocese of Liverpool were there. The organist played and the Priest sang, very well and they found it perfect for sound and quality etc. Full of praise both sound and form. Got back about 7.30 to find your letter.

Did I tell you of my visit to Lady Willingdon?[3] Luckily there were a lot of people there, so I kept everything on the chaff level. She tried, he too, to win me evidently by getting my bust done and put up as a pendant to one of Lord Hardinge. I mischievously suggested a niche I knew she has done away with, but oh no! high up in the open court. I told her I could not talk about the House. I

---

1. Peñaranda was shot in 1936.

2. Lutyens had designed the gardens and pavilions at Tyringham, Buckinghamshire for F. A. Konig, a Silesian banker with Theosophist leanings, in 1926. In the Temple of Music, a 'shrine of the humanist faith', where Lutyens loved to sit alone, the organ is in the crypt, beneath a brass grille in the floor (Hussey, *Lutyens*, p. 473). Lutyens devised a similar arrangement for Liverpool Cathedral.

3. Lady Willingdon combined bad manners with worse taste. She had a passion for mauve, and as Vicereine (1931–36) she covered every available surface in that colour – *mauve qui peut*. One of her worst crimes was to block the vista from Viceroy's House with a glass Olympic stadium dedicated to her and her husband.

was so distressed from what I had heard, and from American architects too, who may take the matter up. I told her that if she possessed the Parthenon she would add bay windows to it. She said she did not like the Parthenon, but I hope and trust that the irony of my remark may eat into her soul. She said she had spent very little Govt money, she got all she wanted from Bhopal[1] and other Princes. I have written to Irwin, because I believe the rule is that a gift given to the GOI by a prince is returned by the GOI [with] a present of equal value. She added, of course, the money was not given to me but to the House! I did not call her a Pimlico Poo which she ranks with in taste. She complained the house was called the Viceroy's House, not the Viceroy's Court for surely she held court there.

5 Eaton Gate   Sept.3.35.

I have *TO DAY* been up in the Air! I flew and have flown: fact. Gosh! how good to come home to earth, my own darling darling Emy I mean Earth. I know and appreciate your heavenly qualities, but you are mine in this my humbler sphere: for in Heaven God will claim you, and then I ask you? where shall I be? However I flew and am home again. God seldom gave me greater pleasure to be *au terre*.

Bressey[2] called with a car, and off we went to Croydon. Croydon proved to be a miniature railway station, empty and calm and apparently no passengers. We were weighed, with overcoat pipes tobacco etc. I weigh 14 stone. Bressey short, thin without pipes tobacco or overcoat weighed 12. So it was my spirits that were overweighting me. We went through ordinary official passages to emerge in a tar covered space with one or two flying machines standing about, looking as though they knew nothing – saw nothing – 'the devils'. We were given, by request, a two winged puppet with only 3 engines, a cabin to hold four, like

1. Hamidullah, Nawab of Bhopal (1894–1960), succeeded his mother (see p. 282) in 1926. A leading member of the Indian Chamber of Princes.
2. Sir Charles Bressey (1874–1951), Principal Technical Officer at the Ministry of Transport 1928–35. Lutyens was appointed consultant to him in 1935, and in 1938 they produced the Bressey–Lutyens Report on the Highway Development of Greater London. It was in connection with this work that the flight took place.

Four Queens in a Pack the Deuce to Play. It had long windows about 12 inches high 3ft wide. We had two officers, charming young men, apparently waiting for a spare daughter, but I had none to spare. One drove and the other to do the hollaring as from map to map. I soon let my map fall to the floor (it proved there was a floor).

We started off taxi-ing in a circular direction to get round on and then a roar began, which still goes on even after having given Robert lunch (this is put in to show I arrived back safely so you need have no anxiety as to the end of this story and can read on without undue anxiety: poor darling how you must be suffering) with a bump or tw ⌐ the roar ever increasing, we left our – my own world and went up – up – up – I held on tight, and didn't at all like the intermittent bumps, drops, the roar made conversation an uproar. We had only two wings, so as to get as big a viewscope down as was possible but the 2 side engines interrupted much and what interrupted more was the body of the flyboat.

A river is very difficult (unless something moves on the river with foam) to distinguish from a road or a railroad. We did not go over 1000 feet. The first thing I really recognised, but could not believe it quite so small, was Hampton Court. My bridge from the air looks ever so much better than any other. Why?! I know but shan't write it, but it was odd.

Hatfield, North Mymms.

The innumerable dwellings and developments you know at once whether a good architect or a bad had been at work. Very refreshing knowing one was looking at things from what one might call God's point of view.

London was covered with a pall of ink we did not go over it but round it.

It was striking the amount of green, the amount of garden space allowed to the average buildings and the countless number of tennis courts. The first batch of cows I thought were chickens! It was all very interesting, perplexing, and made the world a difficult place to keep tidy and soignée. The simplicity of Hampton Court and its childlike planning surprised me. The deliberate waywardness of all else was bewildering, the incoherent mass and undirected endeavour was the very last chapter of *Revelations*.

We taxied down with a roundabout turn or two, when the world canted and all world on end one side and all sky the other

Lutyens with the model of Liverpool Cathedral

brought one with a bump and a jolty run to safety i.e. terra firma and I was very glad, but this is my first experience.

Kildare Street Club, Dublin   March 25.36.

For days I have been miz – sleepless. I don't think I told you.

   The Liverpool Cath committee had been on their hind legs, and for a second time commanded me to push on with the Cathedral and leave out all granite, like asking you whilst knitting me a pair of woollen socks 'get on – omit all wool!' The Arch was perfectly furious squashed the committee and supported me so once again I breathed, and all is well.

———

I believe he gave them a great lecture on the necessity that I should be supported – that it was a cathedral, not any ordinary building that could be tampered with by a committee, in fact the Arch played trumps.

Everyone seems highly overjoyed at the monument [Irish National War Memorial] its pergola, fountains obelisks etc. I don't think there will be any difficulty in getting the extra £5000 we want, an extra entirely due to the nature of soil we discovered in building and levelling, a soil in which no plant would grow, a bad outlook for a garden!

5 Eaton Gate   Aug.10.36.

Met Oliver Lyttelton[1] at Wittersham, the two boys, the eldest [Antony] was at my Eton lecture! the other younger [Julian] at Summerfields, there was a Mr ? [Rev. Cyril Williams] headmaster I think of Summerfields, tall lank and solemn. D D [Lyttelton] was there too with whom I had long talks and a 15 year old daughter of Oliver's [Rosemary], with a halo of dark bushy red hair, very attractive.

The two days were passed in quiet and little more for me than house and garden talk. But last night after dinner their 'marvellous' gramophone began to play the Ballet (*Sylphides?*) – and I got up and danced you know my ballet? dancing, for an hour. I did all the parts, with various diversions, that of carrying D D on the palm of my hand was not successful nor was I able to carry Lady Moira with distinction however it was a huge success which was in itself embarrassing and today I am so stiff I can hardly move!

They wanted to bring the children down and see my exhibition but that I forbade. You will feel relief no doubt of not having been there.

1. Later 1st Viscount Chandos (1893–1972), son of Alfred Lyttelton for whom Lutyens had remodelled Wittersham in 1906. Married Moira, daughter of the 10th Duke of Leeds.

13 Mansfield Street   July 11.38.

I have had a bit of a rush and went off on Friday for the FABS'
[Foreign Architectural Book Society] outing. I enclose you the
itinerary.

Snowshill Manor and its owner Wade,[1] Lord of the Manor, a
most remarkable creature, short with a face like a death mask of
Henry Irving topped with a thick fuzz of grey black hair, cut like a
sponge! An old untouched manor house built down the side of a
steepish hill, not one touch of modern grace, spotlessly clean save
for the windows, thick leaded, small in deep reveals and then
mostly creeper covered. His bedroom is tiny, with a box bed, and
curtain, and to get to his bath he crosses in the open across a flat
between roofs. He owned it was not very comfortable when the
snow lay. He is a most admirable craftsman, carves and draws
beautifully and the whole house is a museum crammed, beautifully shown and arranged, of local countryside carts carriages,
clothes clocks ancient books uniforms hats batteries of kitchen
utensils china pottery leather and coopery. In a corner of the
garden a seaport – model. Ship houses barns, most beautifully
made, canal, docks and the great harbour, planted with dwarf
trees.

He loves toys, has never grown up he says. I am told his bravery
in the war was phenomenal. He must be an 'IT'. He has no
servants, lives alone, one woman in the garden and the garden at
every conceivable level and angle and another woman does the
house and keeps his enormous collection clean. The large amount
of brass work and other metals are as bright as the sun and amidst
all this collection in this ancient unrestored house 1500. He does
not go out, lest he buy something he can't afford. His mother was
a Bulwer and lived at Heydon [Norfolk]! so he is some sort of
cousin of yours! Ursy would adore it and would weep for him.
You would oh my it! and jump naked in the snow and dark!

Stanway Hall is a very disappointing place, the Wemysses were
away and the agent showed us round.

Postlip Hall a rather badly restored house. She is evidently well
off and Mitchell is her second husband. I guessed she was well off

1. Charles Wade (1883–1956) inherited a sugar fortune in the West Indies
and bought Snowshill in 1919. A follower of Baillie Scott, he restored the house
on Arts and Crafts lines, cramming it with his eccentric collection of objects. He
had designed several houses at Hampstead Garden Suburb.

Lutyens in the hall of 13 Mansfield Street

Lutyens in his favourite Napoleon chair

as she was so plain. Mitchell and she are horsy and hunt.[1] Simple smart folk. She is redeemed by her devotion to animals, birds and beasts etc. and I must say, when over looking the lake on fairly high ground and 100 yards or more away, she began calling Peter Peter, and amid the lake, beneath the water was a flash of black and white and a great fat penguin waddled up the bank, looking right and left, to her call. It is fed on herrings and only herrings and they are difficult to get. Whilst mating they eat nothing and if they don't get enough to start with to last over the result, they die. Flamingoes, cranes and other birds. A sumptuous tea and then whisky.

Delhi[2]   Nov.18.38.

Here am I in the air conditioned coupé on my way to Bombay, very well and very fit. This carriage is quiet, a little too cool, so I have put on my coat, and am as comfy as comfy can be.

I had H.E. for a quarter of an hour to myself last night and talked Delhi and then had H.E.R. for ten minutes as they were dining out. I told her that if she had not been a Queen I should like to kiss her. She at once put her arms round my neck and kissed me.

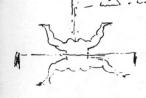

I went over and over the House and avenues and made a report, a great effort for me, but I think they will do everything and put the House back as I left it. I designed a fountain to commemorate Lady Willingdon's reign.[3] It had a great success but I had to do nearly a dozen of them for various members of the staff, Generals and members of the Government.

1. David and Clara Mitchell; her first husband was killed out hunting.
2. Lutyens visited India at the invitation of Lord Linlithgow (1887–1952), Willingdon's successor as Viceroy, to report on the restoration of Viceroy's House to its pre-Lady Willingdon state. He became dangerously ill with pneumonia and a thrombosis on the way.
3. Lutyens described a visit to the cinema the following year: 'Who *do* you think we sat next. I will keep the surprise for the turn over ... *turn over* Lord and Lady Willingdon with their offspring Nigs! I avoided sitting next to her! She was very gushing and wanted me to go and see her! She sat next Robert, she told him: Isn't it a pity that Lady [Linlithgow] so dislikes the Viceroy's House!' (to Lady Emily, 12 November 1939).

As usual all the ADCs and everyone are charming and no trouble so great but what it is joyfully taken. I saw a lot of old friends – Indian and English, and my time was very full. I had our old suite and had 3 tables in 3 separate rooms and each one got chock block with plans papers and writery.

I have been asked to write the whole history of the designing and building of Delhi right away from 1912. You will have to help me. It will begin with my first interview with Richmond Ritchie in 1911–12 and on to 1931, when I left the House I thought for good. I had not the nerve to say good bye to Irwin, just walked out into a blue world and I kissed a wall of the House. I have since rubbed the place very gently with my pocky hanky –!

Lady W. had begun to cut trees to make a soldiers' football ground – Linlithgow stopped as Viceroy-designate. She cut down about 80 blue gums. The gardens and trees had grown up enormously but the big trees have yet far to go. I went round all the trees with Mustoe, he was an angel coming from Jodhpur for 4 or 5 days. He was an enormous help as he had planted the trees and knew their names. I have got rid of the silly cypresses in the Indian Garden – they won't grow at Delhi – the Villa quite d'Este but in India detestable – joke! She had taken all the elephants off the main gate piers and put them about the garden – they have all gone back – and inside the house O MY, but of all this you will see my report.

Persotum is coming to meet me at Bombay, his grandson who was in my office of old is in the Viceroyal drawing office. I hear Persotum is very old and feeble, it will be an emotion seeing him again.

After 1930 Lutyens and Lady Emily spent more time together. 'In the last years of his life,' wrote Lady Emily, 'I like to think that we were closer to each other than we had ever been before.'[1]

---

1. Lady Emily Lutyens, *Candles in the Sun*, p. 186.

---

13 Mansfield Street   Feb.24.40.

My own sweet darling
        Monday, shall I see you? Dare I test the efficacy of prayer?
I'll chance it and pray.
    Shall I see you Monday Joy! or ~~Joy~~?
    No news in particular or ticular. Alba comes at 6, of this I shall
tell you on the prayerful Monday. You will be here (I pray) to
read my speech before delivery at Eton.
    I have come to the conclusion that all these war efforts start
wrong. They start by the talkatives, they appoint Presidents, Vice
Presidents, Chairmen and they all form Committees and they all
talk and they all get 5% at the most of what they set out for. And
then start 50 grim old faddists on an artist and destroy him and
his work with sermons.
    I say start small, with one or two men, achieve one small thing
and from that two and so on that it grow.
    Tonight I dine with Nicholson and then for a play – a fit of
coughing destroyed the last sentence.
    Bless you darling I love to think of you amidst spring snow
drops and daffodils.

                    I can see them springing.

                All love darling, Bless you
                        Nedi.

In the spring of 1943 his persistent cough was found to be cancer
of the lung, and he died the following winter at Mansfield Street,
surrounded by his drawings of Liverpool Cathedral. When she
reread the letters two months later Lady Emily found hers deeply
depressing, 'a revelation of such an *odious* person, so priggish
and tiresome, and Father so endlessly sweet and patient'. But
perhaps Ursula gave a truer picture of their marriage in her reply:

> he *did* love worship and adore you all his life. No whit less
> the day he died than the day he married you. It was much
> easier for him to love than for you, he had so big an
> occupation to absorb his time. In a way you were both
> romantics with very different backgrounds wanting a
> modus vivendi. . . .

———

INDEX

Houses built or altered by Lutyens in italics

Sketches reproduced by courtesy of the RIBA: 13, 31, 65, 75, 88, 156, 184, 203, 207, 249, 257, 337, 371, 394, 395.

Photographic acknowledgements
Centre of South Asian Studies, University of Cambridge, 327, 415; *Country Life*, 126; Imperial War Museum, 350; National Trust, 153, 204; Radio Times Hulton Picture Library, 437, 440; Surrey Record Office, 139